W9-CGQ-903

From Generation to Generation

From Generation to Generation

HOW TO TRACE YOUR JEWISH GENEALOGY AND FAMILY HISTORY

REVISED EDITION

Arthur Kurzweil

HarperCollins*Publishers*

HarperCollins books may be purchased for educational, business, or sales promotional use. For information, please write: Special Markets Department, HarperCollins Publishers, Inc., 10 East 53rd Street, New York, NY 10022.

FIRST EDITION

Library of Congress Cataloging-in-Publication Data
Kurzweil, Arthur.
From generation to generation: how to trace your Jewish genealogy and family history / Arthur Kurzweil.—Rev. ed.
p. cm.
Includes bibliographical references and index.
ISBN 0-06-270097-9
1. Jews—Genealogy—Handbooks, manuals, etc. 2. Kurzweil family. 3. Jews—Genealogy. I. Title.
CS21.K87 1994
929'.01'072—dc20 93-51262

94 95 96 97 98 ◆/HC 10 9 8 7 6 5 4 3 2 1

For Moshe

for Miriam

and for Malya

"The process of the soul's connection with the body—called the 'descent of the soul into matter'—is, from a certain perspective, the soul's profound tragedy. But the soul undertakes this terrible risk as a part of the need to descend in order to make the desired ascent to hither to unknown heights. . . . Indeed Creation itself, and the creation of man, is precisely such a risk, a descent for the sake of ascension."

RABBI ADIN STEINSALTZ, in
The Thirteen Petalled Rose

Contents

Acknowledgments xiii
Foreword by Elie Wiesel xvii
Introduction xix

1 *These Are the Generations: Climbing Up My Family Tree* 1

2 *How to Begin Your Search* 37
Introduction 37
Getting Started 38
Gathering Your History 43
Collecting Stories 43
Family Legends: Are They True? 44
Ten Common Family Myths—or Truths! 46
What Questions Should You Ask? 48
Oral History Questions and Topics 49
Tips on Interviewing Relatives 51
Observations on Those Who Don't Appreciate Genealogy 52
Following Leads Like a Detective 53
Taking Notes 53
Visiting Relatives and Others 55
Family Photographs 56
Writing Letters 57
Final Tips on How to Begin 58

3 *Checking the Records* 60
Prepare Yourself 60
Phone Books 61

Vital Records 62
Census Records 63
Census Records (State) 68
Tips on Dealing with Government Agencies 68
City Directories 69
Synagogue Records 69
The National Archives 70
What If You Were Adopted? 71
Canadian Research 73
Cardinal Rules When Dealing with Libraries, Archives and Other Institutions 74
Tips on Dealing with Librarians 75
Publishing Your Family History 76

4 *Jewish Genealogy: The Basic Sources* 78

Introduction: How Is Jewish Genealogy Different from All Other Genealogy? 78
Contemporary Books and Publications 81
Avotaynu: *The International Review of Jewish Genealogy* 82
Toledot: The Journal of Jewish Genealogy 111
The Encyclopedia of Jewish Genealogy 112
Encyclopedia Judaica 112
First American Jewish Families 113
Other Jewish Genealogical Publications 114
Textbooks 115
Rabbi Malcolm Stern's Basic Bibliography of Jewish Genealogy 117
Traditional Sources 121
Mohel Books 122
Ketubot 122
Rabbinic Descent 123
Approbations 125
Rabbinic Dynasties 127
Rabbinic Sources 128
Rabbinic Texts 131
Hebrew Subscription Lists 132

Yizkor Books 133
Bibliography of Eastern European Memorial (Yizkor) Books 136
Institutions that Collect Memorial Books 200
Archives, Libraries and Organizations 203
American Jewish Archives 203
American Jewish Historical Society 204
Jewish Historical Societies 205
The Central Archives for the History of the Jewish People 216
Jewish Genealogical Societies 217
YIVO Institute for Jewish Research 224
The Leo Baeck Institute 225
LDS Family History Library 226
Professional Genealogical Assistance 229
Committee of Professional Jewish Genealogists 229
Ten Commandments for Jewish Genealogists 237

5 *The Names in Your Family* 238

A Good Name Is Rather to Be Chosen than Great Riches 238
Patronymics 243
Place Names 244
Vocational Names 245
Descriptive Names 245
Names from Abbreviations 246
Matronymics 247
Some Examples 247
Personal Names 251
A Close Look at Your Name 252
For Whom Were You Named? 252
What If Your Name Was Changed? 253
Names Can Help You with Dates 255
Last Names from the Maternal Side 256
Hebrew, Yiddish and English Names 256
What Does Your Name Mean? 257
Some Thoughts About Jewish Names 258

6 *Holocaust Research: To Give Them Back Their Names* 260

Six Million Jewish People Is One Jewish Person—Six Million Times 260

Holocaust Research: The Search for Victims and Survivors 267

The International Tracing Service 267

Mauthausen Death Books 271

Yad Vashem 272

Memorial Books as Sources for Learning About Holocaust Victims 275

Locating Survivors 275

The Jewish Agency Search Bureau for Missing Relatives in Israel 280

Deportations from France During the Holocaust 281

Death Books 283

Holocaust Calendar of Polish Jewry 283

Pre-Holocaust European Phone Books 284

7 *Your Immigrant Ancestors* 287

Someone in Your Family Left Home 287

The United States 288

Canada 293

Israel 293

Who Were Your Immigrant Ancestors? 295

Tracing the Journey 300

How to Find the Ship that Brought Your Ancestors to America 300

How to Find the Steamship Passenger Lists with Your Ancestors on Them 302

How to Obtain Photographs of Your Ancestors' Steamships 305

Naturalization Records: An Important Genealogical Source 305

Sending for Family History Documents Is Legitimate 313

These Are the Generations 313

8 *The Old Country* 318

Walking the Streets of Your Shtetl 318

Discovering the Old Country 320

Memorbuchs 320

Beginning to Discover Your Ancestral Homes 321

Locating Landsmannschaften 322

Your Shtetl or Town During the Holocaust 323

The Blackbook 323

How to Locate Your Shtetl 324

Genealogical Sources in the Old Country: How to Do Research Long Distance 327

Visiting the Old Country 330

How to Plan Your Trip 336

Advice Before Traveling to Eastern Europe and the Former Soviet Union 339

9 *Jewish Cemeteries* 342

The History of Your Family Is Chiseled in Stone 342

Cemeteries as Family Bonds 345

A Walk Through a Jewish Cemetery 346

Visiting Jewish Cemeteries 348

Tombstones 348

Cemetery Plots 349

Tombstone Transcribing 349

How to Read a Jewish Tombstone 349

Tombstone Rubbings 352

Photographing Tombstones 352

Locating Cemeteries 353

Death Certificates 354

Wills 356

Obituaries 356

European Jewish Cemeteries 357

Appendix: A Family History Workbook 359

Bibliography 375

Index 377

Acknowledgments

Whatever merit results from this book, I eagerly share with all of those generous individuals who have helped me, knowingly and unknowingly. Any errors, misimpressions or negativity that may come from my work is my own responsibility and I will share it with no one.

Thanks are due to:

My editor, Rob Kaplan, new friend and teacher, who recognized the need for a fully updated book and inspired me to do it;

Jason Aronson, colleague and mentor;

Ed Rothfarb, Richard Carlow, and Robin Kahn Bauer, three friends from childhood, who shared the dedication page in the first edition, and who fully understand my desire to offer the new one to my children. Ed Rothfarb, gifted artist, has encouraged me to write since I was a little boy; Richard Carlow, whose special soul radiates with warmth and optimism, and who continues to be a life raft for me; Robin Kahn Bauer, a friend for over a quarter century, who always cares and lets me know she's there;

Dr. Lucjan Dobroszycki, who only shows me kindness, support, and respect. He is one of the men of greatness who have graced my life;

Danny Siegel, my first Talmud teacher, who grabbed me by my soul and raised me up;

Avery Corman, who has inspired me to write since I was a teenager and who encouraged me when I needed it most;

Alida Roochvarg, who noticed me when it seemed like nobody else did, and who gave a boost to my lifelong love affair with books;

Maurice Gottlieb, who respected my quest when many did not, and who reached back to the memories in his soul and offered them to me with his blessings;

Michele Zoltan, who always says yes when I ask for her help, and who helped open up a world to me that changed the course of my life;

Sam and Rose Kurzweil; who always fed me delicious food and memories at their table;

Hilda Kurzweil, who was thoughtful and generous to me and helped to launch my career as a public speaker;

Dr. Robert Sobel, brilliant professor and gifted writer, whose friendship and encouragement made a difference;

David Christman, Dean of New College at Hofstra University, who told me to stop writing short stories about my teenage fantasies and to write about Jewish tradition. His interest in my writing has always meant so much to me;

Zsuzsa Barta, my beautiful Hungarian cousin, whose friendship taught me that genealogy has to do with living relatives, not just ancestors;

Jozef Schlaf, my cousin from Warsaw, who took me into his home and was prepared to give me anything I wanted;

Steven W. Siegel, who cofounded *Toledot: The Journal of Jewish Genealogy* with me, and whose high standards and dedication have been inspiring to all of us who have worked with him. He has been my good friend since the day we met;

Zachary Baker, whose appreciation for Jewish genealogy has not only shown itself through his generosity to the users of the library he directs (YIVO), but also through his scholarly work in the field, including the bibliography of Memorial Books he was kind enough to let me include in this volume. Thank you, Zachary, for setting an example and for your friendship;

Dina Abramowicz, one of the great Jewish librarians, who treats all seekers with respect;

Julian Bach, who believed in this book and in its author, and who was a dream come true;

Bob Bender, the book's first editor, who is one of those gifted editors, taking manuscripts with potential and making them into books to be proud of;

Irving Adelman, and the reference department of the East Meadow Public Library, for teaching a young person that a library is the most exciting place in town;

Maris Engel, soul friend, confidant, and one of the few people I have ever met who I think is truly gifted and inspired, for her help on the first edition of this book, and for making this new edition happen. Without Maris and her efforts, this book simply would not exist. Her efforts went, as always, beyond my dreams and expectations, except to say that I have come to always expect breathtaking creativity and impeccable standards from Maris. Thank you, good friend, for sharing your gifts, including your divine spirit, with me;

Tuvia Frazer, for introducing me to a being of immense spiritual power, the Bobover Rebbe, and for caring about my soul. You have made my life much richer, and have made what seemed like an impossible bridge to cross into my accomplishment. For this, and much more, I offer my gratitude;

Gary Mokotoff, who agreed to let me draw upon material from *Avotaynu* for use in this book. Gary is one of the most important people in the world of Jewish genealogy. His journal and other publications, as well as his involvement in Jewish genealogical organizations have made a lasting impression. When the history of Jewish genealogical research is written, there will be more than a whole chapter written about Gary Mokotoff; and to Sallyann Amdur Sack, editor of *Avotaynu*, for her generosity and kindness to me; Sallyann, with Gary, are two of the great leaders in the field of Jewish genealogy;

Ira Scharff, whose efforts to help me find my roots have made a difference;

Rea Kurzweil, for the support you've given me, and for the descendants that we share;

My parents, Saul and Evelyn Kurzweil, for taking pride in my work, and for encouraging my pursuit of our family history. You have given me the resources and the room to soar, and you have cheered me on without fail;

Gary Eisenberg, coconspirator, there are no words for the kind of special friendship we have. I am in awe of how rare, deep, passionate, unfailing and constant it is;

Marion Cino, who often knows what I need before I do. Thanks for your support and wisdom;

Rabbi Malcolm Stern, for generosity offered without hesitation from the very beginning;

The staff of the New York Public Library, Jewish Division, for all of your help, patience and kindness;

Sesil Lissberger, for your friendship, guidance and the faith you have in me;

Rick Blum, who has watched my many journeys and always has shed light on them for me, with wisdom, humor and love;

The Coalition for the Advancement in Jewish Education (CAJE), for being the most inspiring Jewish organization in the world, and for asking me to be a small part of it;

Joseph K. Puglisi, inspirational and dedicated teacher, for making impressions on me that will last a lifetime;

Harold Wise, for his friendship and care, and for showing me just how profound genealogy can be;

Pamela Roth, for helping, of course, to prepare the manuscript for this book, but more importantly for all that we have shared;

Elie Wiesel, for his generosity to me. I knocked on your door when I was lost. You treated me like a welcomed guest, and whispered secrets to me that helped me to know my own soul;

Rabbi Adin Steinsaltz, my teacher, my rebbe, my spiritual father, my master.

Blessed are You, Lord our God, King of the Universe, Who keeps us alive, sustains us and has permitted us to reach this season.

ARTHUR KURZWEIL
JUNE, 1994

Foreword[1]

by Elie Wiesel

הסכמה

What is a name? A mask for some, a vantage point, a reminder for others. Sometimes it signifies danger, often support.

For Paul Valery, nothing is as alien to a human as his or her own name. Understandably so. Imposed from without, the name dominates the person and invades him or her, ultimately taking the person's place. So then why not rid oneself of it along the way?

In the Jewish Tradition, a name evokes a deeper and more respectful attitude. We are Semites because we are the descendants of *Shem*, which signifies: *name*. We call God, who has no name, "*Hashem*," the Name. In other words, our relationship with the name is of a mystical nature; it suggests an imperceptible, mysterious element. Its roots go deep into the unknown.

In the era of night a name was a source of danger and death. But at the time of the first exile, in Egypt, it brought salvation. The Talmud affirms: Because our ancestors did not change their name they knew deliverance.

In Jewish history a name has its own history and its own memory. It connects beings with their origins. To retrace its path is thus to embark on an adventure in which the destiny of a single word becomes one with that of a community; it is to undertake a passionate and enriching quest for all those who may live in your name.

Therein lies the value and the appeal of Arthur Kurzweil's beautiful and important book: It shows us that each name is a mysterious call transmitted from generation to generation in order to force themselves to question the meaning of their survival.

Let us listen to this call.

[1] This "Foreword" is actually a Haskamah. Since the fifteenth century, it has been a Jewish custom for an author to seek, from a great scholar or rabbi, a "Haskamah" or approbation, which approves or recommends the work to its readers. I have asked my teacher, Elie Wiesel, May his light shine, to continue this Jewish tradition. A. K.

Introduction

Like many authors who have written a how-to-book, I wrote *From Generation to Generation: How to Trace Your Jewish Genealogy and Family History* because nobody else had written it. When it first occurred to me to go to the library to see if anyone had written a guidebook on the subject, I found that there was hardly a mention of Jewish genealogy in any book anywhere. How-to guides on genealogy were mostly directed at individuals who had Revolutionary War ancestors—or wished that they had. However, no guidebook or advice was available for the Jewish person who was curious about his or her family history. While I was deeply involved, throughout the 1970s, in tracing my family history, I not only discovered sources that helped me, but also began to see that there were, in fact, many sources that were of specific value to the Jewish family historian. I discovered, to my great surprise, that the average Jewish family can trace their family history successfully. As I discovered more and more about my own family, I also began to write articles for newspapers and magazines on my research in particular, and the topic of Jewish genealogy in general. I also wrote a weekly column for New York's *Jewish Week* called "Tracing Your Jewish Roots." In that column I shared my discoveries with my readers, telling them how they could discover information about their ancestors.

The writing I did on the subject also led to invitations from Jewish organizations to speak on the subject. As I look back through my journals over the past years, I count over 600 lectures that I have delivered to Jewish groups on how and why to do Jewish genealogical research. From college campuses to Jewish Community Centers, from synagogues to Jewish Federations, invitations to speak on this subject have arrived in a steady flow ever since I first began to publicize my research successes.

During the late 1970s I wrote the first edition of *From Generation to Generation*. I was as shocked as anyone by its success. Both through my lecture engagements and the reputation of the book, I came to understand that there is a deep thirst among American Jews to discover their Jewish roots. The successful hardcover edition of the book was followed by an equally successful softcover edition, and with it came a burst of growth in interest in the subject.

From Generation to Generation, and the enormous amount of traveling and lecturing I did, was but one part of the fantastic growth of the field over the past fifteen years. When I first began my own research, for example, there was no such thing as a Jewish Genealogical Society. Today there are dozens of them throughout the U.S. and the world. I'm proud to say that some of those groups began as a result of my lecture appearances, but the growth of popularity of Jewish genealogy and the progress that has been made in the field is the result of the efforts of many people. As anyone who has been involved in Jewish genealogical research in recent years knows, some extremely gifted people have made huge contributions to our knowledge, and have helped considerably in the research of others.

The first edition of *From Generation to Generation* was published in 1980. It seems to have served many people well for many years, but it eventually suffered from simply not being able to keep up with the rapidly growing field. New sources and techniques were discovered, there were great changes in Eastern Europe and the former Soviet Union, addresses, fees and procedures for many government institutions changed, and much more.

One of the most significant changes over the past fifteen years has been the attitude toward Jewish genealogy by many of the scholarly institutions that are most important to the Jewish researcher. When I first began my own genealogy research, most of the Jewish libraries and archives I visited didn't know how to help me. I insisted that they had information that would help me. In many cases I showed them resources in their own collections that at first did not seem to be of value but later proved to be extremely important to Jewish genealogists. There is still a long way to go. However, Jewish genealogists have gained considerable respect over the past decade. Librarians have come to see, I think, that genealogy is a serious pursuit and that its result is often lifechanging. Librarians have seen how genealogical discoveries delight and transform the researcher, and they have discovered that the collections they maintain can make a difference in people's lives.

This volume is a completely revised and updated edition of *From Generation to Generation*. Every address and source has been verified. Corrections and new information (such as fees and form numbers) have been thoroughly researched, and the most significant new sources in the field have been added. As every seasoned genealogical researcher knows, every book in the field is out of date almost immediately. New discoveries are being made all the time, addresses and phone numbers keep changing, and whole new areas of research develop. This book is not an attempt to present the definitive guide to the field. No such guide is possible. Rather, *From Generation to Generation* is an attempt to help the reader get started with some successful genealogical discoveries.

One of the nicest compliments that I've received over the years has been from readers who tell me that they have read the book over and over and always find something new. This is not because they missed things the first time they read the book, but because of the nature of the genealogical process. The very source that is of no use to you today becomes the missing link to the information you will look for in the future. Like a big puzzle, it often happens that one little breakthrough opens up a whole new area. I have tried, in this new edition, to include all the useful sources that I think a researcher needs *to get started*. As the reader will see, there are many specialized books, journals and other sources with far greater detail about many important Jewish genealogical resources. This book hopes to serve as a starting point.

I have included anecdotes and facts that came as a result of my own personal research throughout the book, and particularly in the first chapter. I have been told by many readers that my personal story serves the book well, so despite some temptation to exclude this personal aspect, I have left this material in. My own personal research has continued over the years in a few ways I'd like to mention.

One area of growth is the deepening relationship I have developed with some previously unknown relatives, in particular my relatives in Eastern Europe. Through my genealogy research I discovered close relatives in Hungary and Poland, and these relationships have become among my most important and cherished possessions.

Another significant area of growth has been my discovery of the more religious branches of my family. Before I began my research I saw myself as a fairly well assimilated Jew, far more involved in American culture and Western thought than Jewish culture and religious thought. Perhaps the most surprising discovery I made in my research was that my great-great-great grandfather was a Chassidic rav in Europe, and that, although my branch may have drifted from that way of life, there were still branches of my family that lived and breathed Jewish tradition each and every moment of their lives. I have spent much of my genealogical research time over the past ten years getting to know these branches of my family and what their lives are all about. The religious communities in Brooklyn and Jerusalem include many of my relatives.

Getting to know them and their lives has had a profound effect on my life.

I didn't know it when I began my research, but I see now that my own search for information about my family history was really, at its core, a yearning for knowledge about my Jewish identity. Today, my family and I pursue a life filled with traditional Judaism. Study of Jewish texts is a regular activity for me and my household, Jewish celebration defines the rhythm of my life, my three children study at a yeshiva, and Jewish tradition transformed itself from a topic I wanted learn about to the foundation of my life.

When I am asked why I got interested in Jewish genealogy I often joke and say that I discovered that I had more in common with my dead ancestors than I did with my living relatives. . . and they are also far easier to get along with. In some ways I am not joking. The fact is that at a certain point in my life I was tired of hearing how my ancestors *died* as Jews and I wanted to know how they *lived* as Jews. As I discovered it, I also found out that I belong there. Slowly but surely over the years I have come to dress, eat, pray, study and generally live the way my relatives have lived for centuries. I am not tied to old customs for their own sake; rather I have discovered that the eternal ideas that have sustained our people for generations can still serve us well.

Genealogy is more than names and dates on a chart. It is more than sentimental stories about the good old (or bad old) days. It is not an effort to gain status by discovering illustrious ancestors. Nor is it an effort to build walls between people. For me genealogy is a spiritual pilgrimage. My generation comes after a terrible trauma for our people. A third of our family was murdered fifty years ago. Mass migration of Jews and the destruction of European Jewry cut most of us off from our identities. I was once told by a hostile relative, "Why be Jewish? Just be human." The trouble is that by just being human we become a part of the general culture that is far from "just human." My genealogical research served as a doorway for me. I entered the world of Jewish culture, Jewish thought, Jewish life, and I have come to see that Jewish ideas are profound, Jewish sages are nourishing for my soul, and that it is my obligation to fan the flame of Judaism by being an active part of it.

One specific mitzvah required of traditional Jews each day is to remember that we were slaves in Egypt. This mitzvah is not performed with a ritual object, nor is it an act that would cause someone to think you looked religious. Merely reflecting in your mind and hearing that we were slaves is, in itself, considered a spiritual act of great significance. It strikes me that this is strongly related to genealogy: The act of looking back on our heritage is a spiritual deed in itself. I am not saying that anyone who does Jewish genealogical research is going to become a religious, traditional Jew. Nevertheless, I do maintain that each person who is doing Jewish genealogical research, whether or not he or she acknowledges it, is responding to an inner yearning for a connection to our heritage.

Much of my genealogical research over the past several years has not been centered on library or archival research, nor has it focused on obtaining more documentation from government agencies in the U.S. or in the "old country." Rather, I have spent much time and effort cultivating relationships with previously unknown relatives. I have also focused on understanding Jewish thought, especially Jewish theology. I have discovered that our sages were profound and original thinkers whose slant on life and whose approaches to the riddles of existence are the most nourishing that I have thus far encountered. My friend Gary Eisenberg, an expert on the Jewish involvement in religious cults, will tell you that there is a disproportionate number of Jews in these groups. I believe that this is because these individuals are thirsty for spiritual nourishment and have not been able to find it in their local Jewish community. Many genealogists have had the same thirst, and have traveled centuries and continents, only to arrive home.

When I look at photographs of Jewish life in Eastern Europe before the Holocaust I often see bookshelves in the backgrounds. This observation led me to wonder just what those books were about. They were volumes of the Talmud and other classical Jewish texts. It was owing to my genealogical interest that I pushed myself to learn what was inside those books. What I found was the most subtle, most profound, most uplifting, most nourishing wisdom I had ever encountered. Genealogy is not just names and dates on a chart: It is a search for Meaning.

Genealogical research can be a painful activity. Family stories, like Jewish history, are often tragic. Recollections are often heartbreaking. But I firmly believe, based on my own experience and the experiences of countless others who have taken the time to pursue this research, that genealogy can be a life-changing activity. It is hard to explain from the outside, but when two genealogists meet there is a silent bond that exists because both people know that somewhere in between all the family interviews, and photographs, and forms, and documents, in between the books and journals, in between the last discovery and the next is some intangible yet very real sense that this pursuit is in some way a mission.

My most sincere and heartfelt prayers include my hope that this book will serve its readers—and the Jewish people—well. In recent generations our loved ones have been torn from us, but like a plant that has been cut back, we are now in the midst of a burst of growth and creativity that is revitalizing the Jewish people. Those of us who are involved with Jewish family history research will surely be seen, in generations to come, as vital links between past and future.

> I do not wish anything to happen in Jewish history without it happening to me.
>
> ELIE WIESEL
>
> Judaism is not just a matter of individual commitment. However personal one's involvement may be, Judaism always entails a linkup with past and future generations.
>
> RABBI ADIN STEINSALTZ

From Generation to Generation

1

These Are the Generations: Climbing Up My Family Tree

In the spring of 1970, I wandered into the Jewish Division of the New York Public Library for the first time in my life. The cross section of Jews who sat at the long tables in that room spread over many decades and many worlds. There were young Chassidic men leaning over rare rabbinic texts, and middle-aged Reform rabbis preparing for a future sermon. There were college women writing term papers on history, and scholars writing books on obscure topics.

Standing near the doorway, I looked around at the faces and the books they were reading and I wondered where I fit into this peculiar congregation of Jews. Some of them were reading Yiddish, a language barely known to me, and others were strict observers of the Law, a way of life I had not yet known. I was unlike them all, I concluded, and yet there I found myself, nonetheless, approaching the card catalog, looking for my own way, my own Jewishness.

As I walked toward the drawer of the library card catalog for a portion of the "D" titles and authors, I knew I was wasting my time. Why would this library—or any library—have information on the town of Dobromil, the town in which my father was born, the town I learned of as a child through the dozens of stories my father told me?

I have told many people that my father told me dozens of stories about the little shtetl in Galicia, the town of his birth, of his mother's and father's birth, of their marriage, and of their life "on the other side." Yet it is not true. I feel like there were dozens of stories, but there really were just a few, although these few had more power than any collection of wondrous tales that ever enchanted a child. There was the story of the day my father was brought to the shul by his mother to change his name. He was gravely ill, his father was in America saving money to send for his wife and three children. My father was dying. His mother carried him to the shul and renamed her son. He was born Saul; now he was Chaim—for "life." Surely the Angel of Death would be fooled.

And, of course, the Angel was fooled, and I thought of this as my father told the story to me whenever I asked him to recite the tale again. Vividly I imagined my father being carried by his mother. Vividly I imagined the Angel of Death searching for a little sick boy named Saul who was nowhere to be found. I knew, as my father told me the story with pure seriousness, that I was born because many years before the Angel of Death had been fooled.

Then there was the story of my grandmother's milk business in Dobromil. My grandfather was in New York, sending whatever money he could, but it was not enough. So my grandmother went into the milk business. She would go to the Christian peasants out in the fields and buy milk from them to bring back to the towns nearby and then resell it. My grandmother was a strong and healthy woman, but she could not carry all of the milk cans at once. So she would carry what she could as far as she could, and then she would return for the remaining cans. She would walk back to the point where she had left the first batch and then stop to rest. After this she would begin again, carrying what she could to the next point, and then returning for the remaining milk jugs. All by herself, she sold milk to the people in the nearby village.

This story, too, I imagined in minute detail. I walked, in my dreams, with my grandmother as she struggled with the heavy cans of milk. I stood with her as she poured the milk from the larger containers into the small jars and bottles of the people to whom she sold the raw milk. I asked to hear the story over and over, visualizing the field that we walked across together.

There may have been other stories, but just a few. Not nearly the dozens I thought I had been told. But I dreamed about the shtetl of Dobromil a lot, and, although I grew up in a suburban town in New York, I considered Dobromil home.

How can a young man, graduating college, raised in the most modern country in the world, near the city of New York, having (at that time) never stepped outside the borders of the U.S., consider a shtetl on the Russian-Polish border (which today hasn't a Jew in it), to be "home"? It was a question I had yet to solve, but I felt it nevertheless. Every time I sat and daydreamed about the little town, I felt warm and at home. Throughout my childhood my imagination ran wild with the few stories I was told, so by the time I had reached the card catalog of the library, I already had faces of townspeople, visions of dirt roads, corners of brittle shuls, and Shabbas candles on freshly laid tablecloths all crystal clear in my mind.

Expecting to find nothing as I flipped through the cards in the drawer in the library, I came across an item that startled me. The top of the card read Dobromil, and the description of the item indicated a book.

A book on Dobromil? Impossible, I thought. As clear as my dream of Dobromil was, as warm as my love for the town that was my father's for the eight years before he came to America, I didn't think Dobromil deserved a book. By its importance in my life it deserved much more, but how could such a small town take up the pages of a book, in the New York Public Library no less?

I filled out the form required for the librarian to retrieve the book as I sat at a table among the Chassidim and the scholars and the casual readers of the latest Jewish magazines. As I waited, I stared at faces around me. As I looked at the deep lines on the older faces, I wondered where these people were from, what they were reading, how they lived. Did they believe in God? Did they survive death camps? Who were they? What were their stories? As was a habit of mine, I began to create stories about the people around me. I invented histories for them. I gave men wives and women husbands. I gave them houses and apartments, pasts and tragedies. That man over there had been a widower for years. That one was a rabbi who hadn't "believed" in years, but who would never admit it to a soul. His face was plagued with guilt. The man across from me was a scholar with manuscripts in his desk, and was waiting for the world to discover his brilliance.

And then the book arrived.

I looked at the cover for a long moment, reading the words *Memorial Book—Dobromil* several times as I held the book and felt its weight of more than 500 pages. Flipping through the book I saw the Hebrew letters, English letters, and photographs pass quickly before my eyes. Several times I flipped the pages rapidly, almost not wanting to stop to examine the detail, mostly because I was too excited to look at one page while I wondered impatiently what was on the next.

Turning to the first page, a full-page photograph, I read the caption: "Main Street in Dobromil." There is no way for me to know how many minutes I sat staring at the picture. The photograph showed an unpaved road, several small buildings with slanted roofs, and a few people on the street. No one will believe that the picture was familiar to me, but in fact I had imagined it just this way.

Dobromil, Poland, ca. 1938, hometown of the author's father, grandparents and great-grandparents.

With this photograph, my dreams of years were confirmed. There *was* a Dobromil, it *did* have dirt roads, and little houses, and people who stood at the shul while the Angel of Death was being plotted against. As I came out of the trance that had me reliving each of the stories in all of the detail that I had filled in for years, I was able to begin to examine the book more closely. I continued to have a sense of disbelief, not fully realizing that in my hands was a book on a subject as profoundly important to me as this. A book on the shtetl of Dobromil was for me what a walk on the moon would be for a boy who grew up wanting to be an astronaut.

The book was in three languages: Hebrew, Yiddish, and English. Turning to the English section, I read the titles of the chapters including "Destruction of Dobromil," "Historic Dobromil," and "Personalities." One was called "Dobromiler Grandparents." My grandparents were Dobromiler grandparents, so I turned to the chapter to see what it said. It was a story written by a woman whose grandparents were from Dobromil. It was then that I looked at the front of the book to see when it was printed. The date was 1963. This confused me, because I could not understand how a book could be published so recently about a town that was such ancient history to me—regardless of the nature of my fantasies.

I decided to look through the book page by page, in order to examine the photographs scattered in plentiful quantities throughout. As I turned the pages I looked at the photos, glancing at the faces in each of the shots. It did not even cross my mind that I would see a face I would recognize. My father was just a boy when he left Dobromil and his father was a simple tinsmith. My father's mother was in the milk business, and the only other person whom I could think of at the time was my great-grandfather, the man whom I was named after, who also was a tinsmith. The possibility that they would be in this book was too remote to even consider.

It was for this reason that I was absolutely stunned when I saw a picture of Avrahum Abusch, my great-grandfather, as I looked at a group photo that took up an entire page.

Organization of businessmen in Dobromil, Poland, ca. 1925. Author's great-grandfather is in second row from bottom, fifth from left.

Had the man across from me not been engrossed in the Talmudic text in front of him, he would have seen me shake. As a person to whom the New York Public Library was the center of the modern world, I was overcome by the just-discovered fact that my great-grandfather had his picture in a book in that very place. A picture of my great-grandfather. I could say it over and over and it would still sound unbelievable to me.

I could sit still no longer. I ran to the librarian at the desk in the front of the room to share my discovery. To the best of my recollection, she took the matter quite casually. What was at the time the most exciting thing that had ever happened to me was taken in stride by the woman at the desk before me. I didn't understand why she couldn't appreciate the importance of my discovery. Part of me still doesn't. Because that discovery opened up the door to a search that has taken me many years and that, I am happy to say, offers no end in sight. The discovery of that photograph said one thing to me—one thing that changed my life: "You have a past," it said, "a past and a history, and you can discover it if you want."

The reason I recognized the photograph of my great-grandfather, Abusch, is because I had taken a great interest in him for years. Ever since I first heard the story of my father's name change from Saul to Chaim I wondered about my name as well. I was told that I was named after my great-grandfather, so I have always asked questions about him, collected pictures of him, and I became his imaginary friend. Actually, he became my imaginary conscience. For the longest time I envisioned him in heaven, watching me. This didn't upset me, nor did it frighten me, but I have to admit that there have been many times when I would base choices on what my great-grandfather in heaven would think. Even during the periods of my life when I rejected the notions of God, heaven, and anything supernatural, I still remained in a state of mind in which I would think about how my great-grandfather would feel if I did what I knew to be wrong. In those times, I did not believe that he was watching and judging, but rather that being named after him I had a responsibility to maintain his "good name." To this day I am convinced that this is a positive effect of learning about history and, in particular, family history. We have a responsibility to the past.

In the library, I took the book on Dobromil to the photocopy services and had a few pages duplicated. One was the picture of my great-grandfather. Another was the title page of the book. A third was a street map of the shtetl, Dobromil, complete with little squares representing houses, and Yiddish captions of many of the houses that I would have to get translated. I took the photocopies and went to visit my parents.

My father was amazed at the discovery I had made and was most excited by the map of the shtetl. Glancing at the map for no more than a few seconds, he unhesitatingly pointed to a spot on the map and said, "We lived here."

The spot he pointed to had a number, and we looked at the number guide to the map where my father read the Yiddish caption. It said, "The Glazier Ennis." We looked at each other and smiled. Ennis was my grandmother's maiden name and her family were glaziers. So, not

Ruchel Ennis, the author's maternal great-grandmother.

only did the book have a picture of my great-grandfather on my grandfather's side of the family, but it also had a map with the house of my grandmother's family.

How many times I had been in that house in my dreams. How many times I imagined eating at the table, playing outside, walking through the fields with my grandmother, helping her carry the milk cans back to the house. That house came to represent to me an entire world that I often longed for but knew I'd never find. It was a world that I knew had been destroyed; a world only my dreams could capture. I would never know if I was nearly correct in the way I imagined it. But now I had it on a map. Now I could place it at the exact point on earth where it still might be standing.

Where it still might be standing. This was another part of my daydreams. Often I wondered what happened to the house where my father grew up. Who lived there now? Who sat in the doorway that I have wanted to sit in? Years later I spoke to a man who went back to Dobromil shortly after the war. The town, which was once almost completely Jewish, was already occupied by the Ukrainians as if it had always been theirs. They lived in our houses, ate at our tables, and slept in our beds.

As my father and I looked at the map, he remembered more stories about his childhood and the town. I was delighted. I was also impressed by my father's memory. He had left Dobromil as a child of eight, and he had often been told by other family members that he could not remember much, probably because they themselves could not recall much, though they were older. But as my father looked at the map of the town where he spent the first eight years of his life, he proved them wrong time and again. He began to identify many places on the map with ease and finally turned to me and said, "See, I remember the place well."

I returned often to the New York Public Library Jewish Division to look at the Dobromil book. I was like a little child who asked for the same picture book from the librarian and sat with it, reliving the same fairy tale. It was not much different for me. I relived the fairy tale over and over again. Each time I returned to the book, I became more familiar with the faces in the photographs and they became my neighbors. The only section of the book I avoided with each visit was "The Destruction of Dobromil." I would not read it or look at those pictures. Not yet. I was not ready. I was still building the town. There was no way that I would let it be destroyed so quickly.

One day I decided to use the photocopy of the title page that I had made the first day I discovered the book. It included the names of a few men who had apparently put the book together. They were identified as the Book Committee. The organization of which they were a committee was the Dobromiler Society, which was a landsmannschaft. At that time I had no idea what a landsmannschaft was.

Landsmannschaften are organizations consisting of people from a town in Europe. In other words, people from Dobromil, and their families, joined together to form an organization when they arrived in America. (There are also landsmannschaften in Israel and other countries.) These organizations were homes away from home for new immigrants. People were able to associate with familiar faces, reminisce about the Old Country, and be of emotional and financial support to each other. Often the first thing a landsmannschaft did was to raise money to buy a burial plot for members.

The title page of the Dobromil book indicated that the Dobromiler Society was located in New York, so I deduced that the men on the Book Committee were also New Yorkers. I decided to call them.

I searched through the several New York City area phone books for the names and finally came across one that matched. They were all uncommon names that made my search easier. The man whose phone number I found was a Philip Frucht. I dialed his number and a man answered.

"Is this Philip Frucht?" I asked.

"Yes."

"Are you the man who helped to put the book on Dobromil together?"

"Yes. Who are you?"

"My name is Arthur Kurzweil," I answered. "You might have known my family. There was a picture of my great-grandfather in the book."

"What did you say your name was?" he asked.

"Kurzweil."

"I'm sorry," he said. "I knew most of the people in Dobromil, but this family I must not have known."

"But you must have known them. There was a picture in the book," I pleaded.

Again I repeated my name, but it did not help. It was then that an idea struck me. Though I knew my grandfather to be named Julius, his name in Yiddish—and therefore in Dobromil—was Yudl. I also knew that though my grandfather was a roofer in Brooklyn, he was a tinsmith in Dobromil. So I asked Mr. Frucht, "Did you know Yudl the tinsmith?"

Frucht's voice perked up. "Who are you to Yudl?" he demanded.

"I'm his grandson," I said.

The next thing I knew, Frucht was shouting into the next room to his wife, telling her that he was speaking to Yudl's grandson. He sounded as excited as I was.

"What did you say your name was?" he asked me again.

"Kurzweil," I said, pronouncing it the way I was always taught to say it. "Kerzwhile."

"You mean 'Koortzvile,'" Frucht pronounced it. "No wonder I didn't recognize it."

Inside myself, I was a bit ashamed. Though it was the way I was taught since childhood, it was not the way my grandparents said our name, or my great-grandparents, or their parents, or any of the people in Dobromil. I must have spoken my name incorrectly a hundred thousand times. I robbed it of its Jewishness and made it American.

It has been difficult to change that habit. Still, I am not as bad off as those people who do not even know the spelling of their name because of some episode that occurred at Ellis Island. I have come to believe that names are terribly important. I have already mentioned the significance of the knowledge that I had of being named for my great-grandfather Abusch. Actually, the importance of that went farther. Several times I have been told that I resembled Abusch, in personality as well as in looks—from old photographs of him. Psychologically, this had an impact, the same way that it would if I was told that I was a "bad boy." Children who are labeled "bad" often live up to the name. I too wanted to "live up" to the name of my great-grandfather. He was a kind man, I was told, so I wanted to be a kind man. He always had a good sense of humor, so I wanted to have a good sense of humor. He was religious yet modern, so I wanted to be religious yet modern. He was a role model that I took very seriously because of our shared name. How I would love to know whom *he* was named for!

Surnames are equally important. I could never understand how a person could change his or her last name. Of course, I know the history of it: it was often a survival tactic in response to anti-Semitism. But for me, changing one's name is like cutting off an arm. It is part of you. How can you bear to lose it?

After Mr. Frucht gave me a lesson in pronouncing my own name, I asked him if he knew my family. He did, indeed, and quite well. I learned many things from the conversation that followed, including the fact that my grandfather Yudl had once been a president of the Dobromiler Society himself. Frucht proceeded to tell me many stories about Dobromil and his relationship to my family, and finally suggested other people who would be able to fill me in on further details. After completing my talk with Mr. Frucht, I was elated and mystified. Perhaps it was the quality of Frucht's stories. He spoke about Dobromil as if it still existed as a shtetl. The affection he had for his town was inspiring, and it brought the town that much closer to me. But one of his comments made the biggest impact of all. After we spoke about Dobromil, the conversation turned to me. "What do you do?" he asked. I told him that I was a librarian, the head of a department, with a staff of people working with me. Mr. Frucht replied, "That's wonderful. It's always nice to hear about the success of a Dobromiler."

It was all that he needed to say to make my day, or perhaps my year! Here was a man, born and raised in Dobromil, calling me a Dobromiler, calling me a member of the shtetl. He didn't know that I had walked the streets of the shtetl in my dreams, that I had imagined the town to be mine for years, or that I had longed so often to go there. He didn't know that I had relived the stories told to me by my father so many times. Yet he called me a Dobromiler. My wish had been realized.

I have often wondered how many people would think all of this crazy. I still wonder. There is a touch of madness to this dreaming and feeling. Why in the year 1970 would a young man in his twenties, born and raised in New York suburbs, be elated at being called a member of a shtetl? What was the point? What did it mean? Who really cares? I have no answer for it, except to say that the more I learn about the shtetlach of my ancestors, the more at home I feel. It was in these places that my ancestors struggled to survive, and something within me drives my body and soul to visit the streets of my families' past. I visit them in photographs, in stories, in names, and in dreams. Mr. Frucht merely said out loud what I had been unable to say myself. I am a Dobromiler; I was born in New York but came out of a shtetl. In fact, as I reach farther and farther back in my past, I came out of Egypt as an Israelite. This is what the Passover Hagaddah says and it is true. My experience with Dobromil teaches me this.

I am a child of America, but I am a Dobromiler.

Malya Kurzweil, paternal grandmother of the author.

Finding the Dobromil book and speaking to Philip Frucht launched my casual interest about family history into an obsession. I often wonder when it really began. For a while I thought it was with the discovery of the Dobromil book, but something had to have brought me to the library. Then I thought it was the stories my father told me, but something made me ask to have them told over and over again. Most recently I have come to recall an incident that occurred early in my childhood. I was in my father's synagogue on Rosh Ha-shonah and I can recall sitting next to my father listening to the rabbi's sermon—which I did not understand. I must have been eight years old or so. But at one point in the sermon, the rabbi said that at this time of year God opens the book of life, a book with everyone's name in it, and decides who will live and who will die.

I remember wondering as the rabbi made that statement how God organized his book. Alphabetically, or by family? I imagined it to be by family, and to this day I visualize it in that way. In fact, I hope someday to be God's librarian for those books.

Obviously, my interest in family relationships had an early beginning, and more obviously as time went on, I saw it become, as I said, an obsession.

I began to contact people in my family on a random basis, taking trains and buses (and making phone calls to people too far away to visit) to gather information about the family. Each conversation led me to more people, and in very little time I had more than a hundred names of cousins and ancestors. I was particularly interested in talking to the oldest members of the family, asking them to reach back in their memories to the earliest people and stories they could recall. The family tree grew with amazing speed, and I was admittedly surprised by the cooperation I had gotten. Everyone was interested in telling me what he knew. I even received letters from people who had heard of my interest and had decided not to wait for me to get around to them. I found I had gathered names, dates, towns and stories about a huge number of people. The family, which I never knew to be that large, became enormous. Of course, many of the names I had gathered were of people who were no longer living, but the family was still quite large. One factor became very helpful to my research; there is a Kurzweil Family Circle that has been in existence for more than thirty-five years. Although the organization did not have any historical information to hand me, it did have a membership list as well as a cemetery plot. I visited the cemetery and sent questionnaires to the members of the Family Circle.

The questionnaires asked for information about each person's immediate family and his or her own ancestors. I included return envelopes and in a short period of time my mailbox was overflowing with filled-in questionnaires. I spread them all out on the floor and began to build a sizeable family tree stretching back several generations. I also received more names and addresses of people who were not members of the Kurzweil Family Circle and I wrote to them as well. Then I sent additional letters out to people asking for stories and I received more history about the family. In the course of my research I discovered a branch of the family who have lived in Israel for a few generations, branches of the family in cities around the U.S., and most surprising of all, I found the name of a cousin who still lives in Poland. At that time, he was just a name on a piece of paper, but today he is my cousin Joseph, with a wife Daniele and a daughter Anna. They live in Warsaw, and Joseph is the only member of the Kurzweil family who survived the war and still lives in Poland. He is a writer of Jewish history, which is surely a rare thing for anyone in Poland today. We write to each other regularly.

In time, I had accumulated a lot of information and was becoming quite familiar with the history of the family. My questions to older relatives surprised them. I asked them about things that they themselves hadn't thought about for decades. A crucial point came when I felt as if I was living in a different place at a different time. Again, my dreams at night took place far away in time and space. It was becoming unusual for me *not* to have a dream about some ancestor or other. I entered the world of my ancestors in my conscious and subconscious lives. At times I felt it unhealthy. Newspapers interested me less than historical accounts of Galicia that I borrowed from the library.

My picture collection grew as well, helping my dreams, undoubtedly, to create vivid images of the shtetl and the past. Some people loaned me photographs, others gave them to me. I also discovered a large box of pictures that my parents had filled with old photos of family members and street scenes. Eventually, I had just about exhausted every possible lead that I had on people who could contribute information about the family.

The process of meeting these people was wonderful. In effect, I was doing two things at once: building a family history and making new friends and acquaintances. Both were rewarding and priceless. It was fascinating to learn what paths my cousins' lives had taken. We all descended from the same people, but because of the different kinds of choices our closer ancestors made, we went in various directions. Remarkable was the physical resemblance between people who had never seen each other before. My cousin Joseph from Warsaw, for example, looks remarkably like my father.

When I completed the stage of my research that dealt with people I had known or was referred to, I began searching through phone books. Since Kurzweil is an uncommon name, it was a rather easy task—at least compared with a name such as Schwartz or Cohen. The New York Public Library has a collection of just about every available phone book in the world, so I spent hours combing them, looking for Kurzweils to call or write to. Again I was met with remarkable success. I came up with people who were definitely related to me but who knew nothing about my family. Several generations back, their ancestors and mine went in different directions, and sooner or later lost contact. Now, for the first time, cousins were getting to know one another. It was relatively easy for me to figure out if someone was a cousin. I had accumulated enough names and places to be able to discover the link in a rather short time. My family tree was organized well enough for me to have easy access to the material within it.

One phone call to an unknown Kurzweil met with an unusual series of circumstances. I called a man whose name was Arthur Kurzweil, just like me. I identified myself on the phone and told him what I was doing. He voiced disinterest and told me that he'd call me back if he became interested. I was upset by this, having experienced nothing like it in the months that I was pursuing my family history. But I decided, some weeks later, to call again and try my luck. I asked him politely what his grandparents' names were, and when he told me I immediately knew who he was. His grandparents came to America long before most Kurzweils and because of this they grew apart from the rest of the family, most of whom came to the U.S. rather late, historically. So it was obvious why we would not have known about him.

When he told me their names, I proceeded to tell him the names of some of his aunts and uncles.

"Your aunts and uncles must be Bessie, Morris, Pauline. . . "

"Who told you this?" he asked.

"And your parents must be Harry and. . . " I continued.

"Are we related?" he asked.

We certainly were, and I explained exactly what the relationship was. He still wasn't convinced. The phone conversation ended shortly after that, and there was still doubt in his voice. Later on, months later, he told me that he thought I was representing a business that does family-tree research for a fee.

His disbelief troubled me, as did his unwillingness to cooperate, since he could have been the link between me and many other people in his "missing" branch of the family. I wanted to make the family tree as complete as possible, and he was a source for quite a bit of information. Rather than give up, I decided to tackle the problem with even more energy than usual. It brought me to examining public records.

Until this point, I had very little experience with the use of public records. Actually, the only time I ever used them for my family-tree research was to get the death certificate of my great-grandfather, Abusch. Death certificates often provide the names of the deceased's parents, including the mother's maiden name. In this case, I was able to verify what I was already told by relatives as to my great-great-grandparents' first names, and I also learned the maiden name of Abusch's mother. This was important for two reasons. First, it added another major branch to my family tree. Second, it led me to the knowledge that my great-grandparents were first cousins.

So, I began to do research into this unknown branch of the family. I used census records that gave me information about household members in 1900. I sent for immigration records that provided still more information, and I went to the Surrogate's Court and looked up the wills of several people. It all added up to a lot of facts, though it was the difficult way of doing what could probably have been done in a conversation. But it was a fortunate thing also because in the process of looking for the items I was after, I discovered things about other branches of the family. In the end, I had a thick file of data on my entire family, provided by public documents in the U.S. This included the names of towns in Europe where people originated, dates of immigration, names of steamships taken to this country and even copies of the passenger lists of the ships. I have in my possession the passenger list of the ship that took my father and his brother, sister and mother to America in 1929. It is an important document to me, for obvious reasons.

Over the years, many people have asked me if I was related to Professor Baruch Kurzweil of Israel. Recently, Professor Kurzweil died. I had no idea if he and I were related, though I knew quite a bit about him, because of the fact that I am in the habit of looking for the name "Kurzweil" in just about every book I pick up. Since Baruch is perhaps the most famous Kurzweil in the world, his name has shown up often. Baruch Kurzweil was a leading literary critic in Israel. He was an Agnon expert and also was known for his critique of the work of Gershom Scholem. His criticism of Scholem made him quite a controversial figure (as did many other of his points of view) since Scholem is seen as almost untouchable when it comes to his field of research.

Although my knowledge of the work of Professor Kurzweil grew, I still did not have an answer to the question, Were we related? No one in my family, immediate or more distant, knew the answer, though many of us had been asked the very same question. Then one day I received a reply to one of the many letters I sent to Kurzweils around the world. I went through scores of U.S. and foreign telephone directories at the New York Public Library, and wrote to as many Kurzweils as I could find. Many people are in the habit of checking phone books for their last name whenever they are out of town; I do the same, and write to them. The letter I received on one particular day was from Israel. It was from an Amram Kurzweil, who began his letter with a warm message of support for what I was doing regardless (he said) of whether we were related or not. He then drew his family tree for me listing descendants as well as ancestors. At the top of his tree was the following sentence: "My grandfather's father (whose name I do not know) came from the town of Przemysl." It was the same town that I knew to be my great-great-grandfather's! As I examined the family tree further, I discovered the name Baruch Kurzweil.

This discovery had two pieces of significance to it. In the first place, it answered my question about Professor Kurzweil. Secondly, it taught me something about family history research. From all of my research on Baruch Kurzweil, I was led to believe that his family came from an altogether different part of Europe than my family. Items about Professor Kurzweil, provided in many different sources, included his biography and even some family background. Again, the region of his ancestry was given as a different part of Eastern Europe. Ordinarily, I would have drawn the conclusion that we were not related. The fact of the matter is that the accounts I read never went back far enough. But Amram Kurzweil, who is Professor Kurzweil's uncle, knew an earlier town of origin than any of the encyclopedic items I had found, and so I was able to discover that our families were from the same place originally. Of course, this still does not prove we are related, but if two Kurzweils come from the same town in Eastern Europe, it is likely we are.

Another letter from a Kurzweil in Israel brought more interesting results: One day I received a detailed piece of correspondence from a man named Dov Kurzweil. Although he was eager to exchange notes of the histories of our families, it was clear from his letter that we would not be able to establish any family links—at least not from what he knew. While Kurzweil is not a common name, however, it is not altogether rare in Europe, so it is quite possible that many Kurzweils are not related (though I must add that I am beginning to doubt that since I continue to discover more originally unknown cousins all the time). I wrote Dov back, thanking him for his letter, but adding that there appeared to be no relation.

Months later, a letter arrived from a man in California, also a Kurzweil. He responded to one of my many inquiries to Kurzweils around the country and the world. Again, as I read his letter it became clear that he was not related. His letter, however, was quite enthusiastic, and he indicated that he would love to hear from me and share information regardless of whether or not we were cousins. He said this because I told him in my letter that I had collected a mass of material on Kurzweil families around the world. One comment in his letter was odd. Near the end he wrote, "My father was an atheist, but I always assumed that we were Protestant."

As I reread his letter, I had the feeling that some of the details he provided were familiar. Though it was obvious that his family and mine were unrelated—at least for the past several generations—I was sure I knew some of what he had written. Then I remembered: The information he gave and the information given by the Kurzweil in Israel matched! They were not related to me, but they were related to each other. I wrote him back, explaining this to him, and adding that it appeared that his family was originally Jewish. I waited for a reply from him, sure that I would get one based on the enthusiasm he registered in his letter, but he never answered me.

After seven years of research on one of the many branches of my family, I realized that I had made a mistake: I had neglected all of the other branches. In large part, it was the fact that my last name is Kurzweil, which subconsciously made me think that I was more a Kurzweil than a Gottlieb, which is my mother's maiden name. For that matter, I was equally an Ennis, which is my father's mother's maiden name. I am also just as much a Klein, a Loventhal, a Rath, a Grünberger, and countless other names as well. The fact that we generally take the names of our father, added to the stronger family ties in my father's family, resulted in my becoming singularly obsessed with the Kurzweil family for, as I said, seven years.

There were some worthwhile results of this obsession, however. I would never have gotten as far as I did, had I spread myself thinly over a few families. On the other hand, the worst enemy of the genealogist is time, and I am yet to learn, I am sure, of people in other branches who have recently died and who would have told me much had I begun earlier. The results of my Kurzweil research are dramatic: I have a nearly complete genealogy of my great-great-great-grandparents and all of their descendants—nearly 500 of them. I have dozens of early photographs of the family, countless stories about individuals, and a wealth of information about the history of my ancestors. The one thing I did not forget to do is to obey a cardinal rule of family history research: *Share your findings*.

I deeply wanted to let everyone know what I had found. I wanted children in the family to be able to look at our family tree and see who their ancestors were. The family tree included seven generations, and it would be important for family members to be able to glance at the tree and see their ancestors as well as to understand how large the family was, and the paths they traveled. Another important part of my research, which I felt especially bound to share, was my Holocaust findings. More than 100 members of the Kurzweil family were killed in the Holocaust. I collected their names, their relationships to the rest of the family, their ages and, in many cases their specific fates. There are no graves for these cousins of mine; and no memorials. My family tree was their memorial. I wanted the family to know them and to remember them.

I decided to write a book. It would be a modest undertaking, privately printed as inexpensively as possible, which I would sell at cost to the family. It took me two years to finish the book, and it finally came to 140 pages, complete with all seven generations of the family, pages of photographs, history of the family, and an index so that anyone could easily find him- or her- self (or others) on the tree. The book was a labor of love and a grand success. Kurzweils from all over the world asked for copies. More than 100 books are on bookshelves in the homes of Kurzweils that I know. While I was putting the book together I became somewhat obsessed with it. I worked on it every spare moment at a frantic pace. I loved doing it, and the result is this: I now know that as long as those books exist, future generations of my family will know where they came from. They will know what tradition brought them to the point at which they are. They will know the names of the people who struggled to live and to bring up children. They will also know of those ancestors who were murdered by the Nazis. Most of all, they will know who they themselves are.

There is just one last chapter to the story of the Kurzweil family research. After I printed the family books, I helped to organize a party. To that party, which was a celebration of Chanukah, I invited everyone whom I had contacted during the years of my research. On the day of the party, more than 100 people came to celebrate. It was the largest gathering of Kurzweils—perhaps ever. Great-great-grandchildren of the same people saw each other for the first time. Friendships were made. Others were renewed (some people hadn't seen each other for forty years). It was everything that a family reunion should be. Most important, it provided us with the opportunity to understand firsthand what the Talmudic passage means when it says that if a human life is killed, it is as if a world has been killed, and if a human life is saved, it is as if a whole world has been saved. Each of us at that party were cousins, descended from the same two people. Had my great-great-great-grandparents not lived to marry and have children, none of us would have been there.

For seven years, as I said, I neglected the history of my mother's family. My mother, saint that she is, listened patiently to the unfolding story of my father's family, never expressing confusion over my apparent lack of interest in her history. In part, there was an obvious difference between families. My father was born in Europe and remembered a significant amount for an immigrant who arrived here at age eight; however, my mother was born in New York and knew almost nothing about her European background. She had never met her father's parents, and just met briefly with her mother's parents. She had very little to say when I asked her about the history of either side of her family.

In addition, her family was small. Whereas my father's family—both sides, in fact—had large Family Circles (family organizations with regular meetings, a cemetery plot and a history), my mother hardly knew more than her immediate family. On superficial view, her family seemed not to have had much of a history that could be discovered. There were no older members of the family in America alive to speak about the family. Generally, my mother could understand quite well why I did not pursue her family and its history.

One final factor was that my mother's family was significantly different from my father's in terms of Jewishness. My mother's father arrived in the U.S. by himself as a teenager and adapted to the American way of life rather quickly. Although he retained an internal sense of himself as a Jew, he was mostly assimilated. My mother's mother also arrived in this country at a young age, with her sister, and she too assimilated quickly. My mother, however, grew up in a different kind of home from my father's. His was the home of Orthodox immigrants. Hers was the home of assimilated Jews.

Zalman Leib Gottlieb, maternal grandfather of the author.

Helen Klein, the author's maternal grandmother.

Despite all of this, I had the desire to learn about my mother's family, and decided to begin. When I asked my mother who would be the best source, she instantly said that her cousin Maurice Gottlieb would be the person to see. Maurice, her first cousin, is an intelligent, quick-witted man who was born in Europe and who my mother thought would remember some things. Although he lived in New York, I decided to write to him. Many people find it easier to talk than to write, but I knew that Maurice had once wanted to be a writer. I always try to get people to write about their history. Their letters become documents to save forever.

Maurice wrote back a lovely letter detailing what he knew about the family and its history. He named the towns in Europe where the family originated, and the people who made up the family tree. He mentioned some occupations and a few other details. The most surprising item was that his grandfather—who was my great-grandfather—was a rabbi. I was shocked. Could it be that my grandfather, the assimilated American, was the son of a rabbi? On closer reading, I understood that although the man was a rabbi, he worked, at times, as a slaughterer (a shochet), and that he did not function in the way that I know rabbis to function. He had smichah (was "ordained"), but did not have a congregation. It was fairly common for a man to have smichah. Nevertheless, it was startling to learn that this branch of my family was so religious.

I telephoned my mother and asked her if she knew that her own grandfather was a rabbi. She admitted that she recalled that her father told her this, but that she never believed him. It just didn't seem likely.

Also in the letter from Maurice was the fact that the family name was not Gottlieb, but was changed from the original name of Rosenvasser. This interested my mother. Imagine spending your life thinking that your name is your own, only to find out that it was originally something else—Rosenvasser in fact!

Weeks passed and I did little more to pursue the history of my mother's father's family. The discovery that the family name was Rosenvasser and not Gottlieb became something of a family joke. My father began to call my mother Miss Rosenvasser, and I too made reference to the name on many occasions—perhaps to the point of being obnoxious. I checked the name "Rosenvasser" in several Jewish encyclopedias but found nothing. I looked through a few New York phone books and found the name spelled two different ways: Rosenvasser and Rosenwasser. Despite this, I did not call these people or write to them. What would I say: "My family name used to be Rosenvasser and I wonder if we are related"? I did do this in my Kurzweil research, but it was when I had more to offer. Usually when I call or get a call from someone named Kurzweil, I immediately know how the person is related after he tells me the name of his grandparents. But I had far too little to go on to begin to make telephone inquiries in this case. In addition, the news that our name was Rosenvasser was still too recent a discovery for me to fully believe it.

After a while it happened that my grandparents (my mother's parents) moved out of their apartment, which they had lived in for several decades, and went to live with my parents. My grandparents were in their mid-eighties and my grandfather had been held up at gunpoint. Their move was an opportunity for me to find things in their apartment that might give me additional leads concerning their family history. Both of my grandparents had denied for years that they had any photographs, letters, or anything that would help me in my search. They both told me their parents' names and that was all. They claimed that there was nothing else to know.

I was far from convinced. It is impossible to save nothing of family interest during a lifetime of more than eighty years. When my mother and I went to their apartment on Dyckman Street in upper Manhattan to put things in boxes and pack up the place, my belief was confirmed. Not only was it untrue that my grandparents had saved nothing, but the drawers, closets and hidden compartments of their apartment were a virtual museum of family history. I found a huge box of photographs, some dating back to the early 1900s in Europe. I found a large bundle of letters received by both of my grandparents from their families in Europe who stayed and were killed in the Holocaust. I found nearly every birthday card that my grandmother had ever received. I found scraps of paper with the names and birthdates of all of my grandmother's brothers and sisters, some of whom I would never have discovered had it not been for these papers. I found receipts for tickets on cross-Atlantic steamships. I found copies of letters of inquiry regarding Holocaust victims in my family. I found tefillin of my grandfather and members of his family. I found old, valueless European money saved from Europe. And finally, I found two framed pictures, each containing the images of married couples, one my grandmother's parents and the other my grandfather's parents.

Morton Klein and Hannah Grunberger, maternal great-grandparents of the author. Presov, Czechoslovakia.

I showed the photos to my mother immediately. "Of course," she said, "I haven't seen them for years. Those are my grandparents."

Asher Yeshaya Gottlieb and Blima Ruth, maternal great-grandparents of the author.

The contrast between the two couples was, as they say, like night and day. My grandmother's parents appeared to be a fairly modern, well-dressed, cosmopolitan couple. Her father was wearing a three-piece suit, cufflinks on the shirt, a ring on his finger, and pince-nez glasses. His wife wore a fancy dress, her hair appeared to be styled, and she wore a large brooch on her dress. They posed for the picture standing against each other, and the photo was taken indoors, a flowing curtain appearing in the background.

I describe the picture in detail to contrast it with my grandfather's parents. His mother wore a peasant dress and a kerchief around her head. No hair was visible. His father wore a long black coat from neck to foot and a broad-brimmed hat. He had a long white beard and side-curls of a few inches. They posed for the picture outside, an old fence in the background. They were both sitting down, at least a foot apart.

I was fascinated by the contrast between these two couples whose children married each other several thousand miles away from where these photographs were taken, but my attention quickly was drawn to my grandfather's parents, who were obviously Chassidic. His father was the rabbi, the shochet! I could not take my eyes off the photograph. I stood staring into my great-grandfather's eyes, which stared back at me. I looked at his side-curls, his long coat, his hands folded gently on his lap and I wondered who this man was. I was his great-grandson, and yet the distance between us, not only in miles and years, but in ways of life, was startling. My own great-grandfather was a Chassid. If not for this photograph I might have never known.

It was shocking that I had never been told about this. It was always my belief that my father's family was the religious side of the family, but here before me was the photograph of just a few generations ago, of my great-grandfather, a Chassidic man. The progression of history began to come clear. My grandfather, as a teenager, left Europe and his family and traveled to America, land of opportunity. He cut his side-curls, said goodbye to his rural Chassidic community, and went in search of a "better" life. Upon arrival in America he discovered a different world and rapidly became a part of it. I have to admit that I was always troubled by this. My Jewish involvement has, over the years, become more and more traditional and it has been largely an uphill battle for me. I was not raised in a very traditional home, and this was partly because of my family history: My mother's parents were not traditional and this affected my upbringing. Had my grandparents been, I too might have had a different kind of life. But this feeling was dramatically resolved when I brought the newly discovered photograph of my great-grandparents to their son—my grandfather. I also showed my grandfather another photograph I had found of him as a young man. In it, he was dressed in a modern suit with spats, a stylish hat and was holding a cane!

My grandfather was excited by the sight of both pictures. He repeated over and over that those were his parents, and also enjoyed seeing this picture of himself as a young man. He then told me that the picture of him was taken in Europe. I was confused because I knew that he came to America as a teenager and this was a later picture. He told me that he went back to visit his parents twenty years after he had left them. It was an incredible thing to imagine. Here was a picture of a fully Americanized man, the son of a Chassid, returning to see his parents and family. One could just imagine the scene when he arrived in town looking the way he did as compared to the way his father looked. And I was right! My grandfather told me that his own father was upset by how his son had changed. His father wanted him to stay there and not to return to America, the country that made him leave the old ways. My grandfather refused, of course, and returned to America. The rest of the story is obvious: Had my grandfather stayed and returned to the religious ways of his family, he would have shared their fate—the Death Camps. Yet he returned, continued to assimilate, and I, his grandson, was born years later. *And today, I connect once again with the tradition of my great-grandfather, through my family history research.*

I remembered that the letter from my mother's cousin, Maurice, who had originally written to me telling me about the family and what towns we had come from, also contained his regret that he could not find a picture of his grandparents. Now that I found one, I wanted to call him and share with him what I had found. I arranged to visit with him and show him the photograph. I also hoped to get more information from him. I suspected that he knew much more than he wrote in his letter. When I arrived at his home, it quickly became apparent that Maurice knew quite a bit about the family history. He identified many photographs for me, told me stories about members of the family and taught me a lot. But one item, which he mentioned to me in passing, was the clue that became the key to centuries of family history. Maurice told me that as a child he was scolded for playing a childhood prank. The way in which he was scolded was memorable, because he was told, "That's no way to behave, especially since you are an 'ainicle' of the Stropkover Rebbe." At the time I did not know that the term "ainicle," although it generally means "grandson," actually means "descendant" in that context. In any case, my genealogical ears perked up and I knew that I had hit upon a major find.

That night was somewhat sleepless for me. I couldn't wait to go to the library the next day and find out about "the Stropkover Rebbe." If my mother's first cousin was his descendant, then I was too, and it would be an important and meaningful discovery for me. The following morning I went to YIVO—The Institute for Jewish Research in Manhattan—and began to search for anything I could find about the Stropkover Rebbe.

YIVO, the finest archives and library of Eastern European Jewish material in the world, had a book with biographical material on Chassidic Rebbes, with an index by town. It was just what I needed. I looked up Stropkov and found that there were several rebbes who were known to have been connected with the town of Stropkov at one time or another. I struggled with each entry written in Hebrew and one by one I rejected each as possible ancestors. When I finally got to the last entry I was startled to see the name of Chaim Joseph Gottlieb. My mother's name was Gottlieb. He must be my ancestor! I was terribly excited for about one minute, until I remembered that Maurice wrote me that the name of our family was not originally Gottlieb but Rosenvasser. Suddenly, I was afraid that this was not my ancestor at all, but that we had simply taken his name because of his reputation as a rebbe. I knew that people named children after their teachers, and perhaps this was a similar case.

Still, there was something within me that said that he was my direct ancestor. I had a feeling about it, and knew that eventually I would understand how the name Rosenvasser came into the picture. It seemed likely that Chaim Joseph Gottlieb was an ancestor since the names matched and since it also confirmed the story by Maurice about being scolded as a child. Another possibility was that the name Rosenvasser was the original name and that it predated the rebbe.

What I found myself doing from that point on was breaking just about every genealogical rule in the book, especially the following two: Never make claims that you aren't sure of, and, Do research from the known to the unknown. You start with what you know and you see how far back you can go, step by step. You should go backward, one generation at a time. This rule is to discourage people from picking out a famous individual from history and trying to make a connection. It has been shown often enough that people who set out to prove that they descend from an illustrious figure do it—regardless of how accurate their findings are. In other words, it is not respectable genealogy research to pick King David and then try to establish descent from him. Except for the fact that I had some good clues to go on, I was doing just that. It is not advisable methodology.

The other rule that I broke was telling everybody I knew that I was a descendent of the Stropkover Rebbe, Chaim Joseph Gottlieb. At the time it was just circumstantial evidence, but it was such an exciting possibility to be a descendant of a Chassidic Rebbe that I couldn't help it. The only good part about it was that it pressured me to get to work immediately and to find out the truth.

The short biography of the rebbe that I found included the fact that he wrote a book called *Teev Gitten v'Kiddushin*. YIVO did not have the book, but the New York Public Library Jewish Division did, so I went to examine it. I was amazed to see that the book contained a brief genealogy including the names of the rebbe's grandfather (which would take me back to the 1600s!), and the rebbe's sons, one of whom was named Usher. My great-grandfather was named Usher, and for a minute I thought I had solved the whole problem, until I realized that the dates were wrong. There would have to be at least one generation between the rebbe's sons and my great-grandfather. I still hadn't established a link. It occurred to me that my great-grandfather, Usher, might have been named after the rebbe's son Usher, but it was still speculation.

After examining the rebbe's book in the library, I wondered if there were any disciples of his alive and in New York. I discussed the question with a librarian in the Jewish Division, and when she noticed that the "approbation" (seal of approval) for the book was written by Chaim Halberstamm, the Sanzer Rebbe, who was a contemporary of Chaim Joseph Gottlieb and whose descendants live in New York, she suggested that I contact them. I made a few phone calls, but no one seemed able to help me. A few days later a Jewish newspaper in New York, *The Jewish Week,* called me for an interview. I was going to be interviewed on radio station WEVD the following week to talk about some of my genealogy research, and the newspaper wanted to make a feature story out of it. In the interview I mentioned my belief that I was a descendant of the Stropkover Rebbe, well aware of the fact that it was still speculation. The newspaper ran the story, and it was the best thing that could have happened at the time.

In response to the article, I began to get phone calls from people who also claimed descent from the rebbe. The first call, in fact, was from someone whose name sounded familiar. I recalled that my mother's cousin, Maurice, had suggested I call him for more information about the family. I never did, although I did file his name and number away for future use. It is significant that I mention this because although it is true that my interview with the newspaper offered me an opportunity that few people get, it is equally true that had I followed the advice of my mother's cousin, I would have discovered the same thing. It is important to track down the most obscure leads because they might very well bring you to a pot of genealogical gold.

The man told me that he too was a descendant of the Stropkover Rebbe, and we proceeded to compare notes. Within a few minutes the man realized that he knew who I was and that we were definitely related. He knew my mother and her brother and her parents from years ago. When I asked him how we were related he said, "We're cousins," but he knew little more than that. It was an answer I had learned to expect. So many times in my research I had encountered people who were sure we were related, but knew nothing more than that. Although he wasn't able to provide any more information about our relationship, just the fact that he felt we were related and that he also knew he was a descendant of the Stropkover Rebbe, permitted me to be more at ease about my claim of descent. But, of course, I was not satisfied and wouldn't be until I was able to document my relationship to Chaim Joseph Gottlieb with names and dates and carefully spell out each generation between us.

What the man on the phone was able to do, however, was to give me the name of another man who might be able to help. His last name was also Gottlieb and he was a cantor. I called him and I was spared the need to make introductions since he had heard me on the radio the night before. He asked me to hold the wire and came back a minute later with a copy of the rebbe's book, although it was a more recent edition. It was a reprint of the original with an added preface that was a biography of the rebbe! On the phone I told the man everything I knew about my family, including all the names I knew, but he was unable to match me up with the genealogical information provided in the biography. I was disappointed but not discouraged. A final piece of information that he told me was that the man who wrote the biography lived in Brooklyn. He gave me the man's phone number.

The biographer's name was Rabbi Israel, and when I called him he was nice enough to suggest that we meet to pursue the question. He also told me where I could get a copy of his book. The next morning I went to Williamsburg to purchase the book from the source suggested by Rabbi Israel.

It was the first time I had ever gone to Williamsburg. I have been a New Yorker all my life, however, I was always a bit afraid to go there. I had heard too many stories about the Chassidim in Williamsburg who do not like outsiders. I felt hostile toward them, wondering why they thought they had the right to look down upon other Jews who were not like them. But my experience that first time was just the opposite. I found the people on the street and in the shops to be quite friendly and I realized that I had only heard the sensational stories. I liked everyone I met.

When I arrived at the address given to me by Rabbi Israel, a young girl answered the door and asked me to wait a minute. She returned soon afterward and brought me down the street to a grocery store and a young man who appeared to be her brother. They spoke in Yiddish for a few seconds, after which she left. The young man, who appeared to be about my age, was dressed in traditional Chassidic street clothes with an apron for working. He brought me down the block to a storage room.

It was there that the books were kept. He looked for a clear copy, brushed off the dust, and sold it to me. Together we walked back to his store. Before we said goodbye I asked him why it was that he had these books to sell. He told me that his father printed them. I asked him why his father printed them. He answered me by saying that he was "an ainicle of the Stropkover Rebbe." He used the very same words that my mother's cousin Maurice had used when I first began this journey.

It then dawned on me that I was standing in Chassidic Williamsburg with a young man, a Satmar Chassid I later found out, who was a cousin of mine. He and I both were descendants of the same Chassidic Rebbe (assuming my belief was correct). To be honest, I must admit that I did not tell him I was also a descendant of the rebbe. I was afraid that he would wonder why I was obviously not Chassidic. In some ways, I wondered myself—though I knew. Yet it was startling to see how strange fate is. There we were, both of us the same age, both of us stemming from the same family tree, and yet we were in two different worlds. His line took him to Williamsburg, and mine took me elsewhere. It was confusing and fascinating.

It was then that I remembered from one of the many conversations I had had, that there was a Gottlieb's restaurant in Brooklyn and that the owners of this restaurant were descendants of the same rebbe. I located the address and decided to go there for lunch. The owner of the restaurant wasn't there, but his son-in-law was, and we had a conversation, briefly, about the rebbe. Yes, he said, it was true that they were from that family and the owner would be back the next day. I was disappointed, but I was also excited by my new possession—the book by the rebbe and the biography within it. I called Rabbi Israel, the biographer, and made an appointment for Sunday, just a few days away.

Those next few days were a blur to me. I was so preoccupied by the whole experience that I couldn't think about anything else. I simply counted the hours until I could see Rabbi Israel, who would surely be able to link my branch of the family with the rebbe. Finally, Sunday came and I went to Rabbi Israel's home. The rabbi was a pleasant and kind gentleman who made me feel quite at home. He asked me if we could speak in Yiddish and I was sorry to have to tell him that I could not. He took me down to his basement where his library was and we discussed my family. Again I repeated everything I knew, but nothing seemed to match. Again the name Usher was the same, but the dates were obviously wrong. I felt I had reached a dead end. It appeared that with all of the circumstantial evidence I had gathered, it was nothing more than that. If the rabbi who wrote the biography of the rebbe could not help me, then who could? I began to feel I was wrong from the beginning: I shouldn't have made any claims, even to myself, without knowing for sure. Now it seemed as if there was nothing more to do but go back to thinking that my mother's family was a small one, that they may have known the rebbe's family in Europe and may have even taken his name, but other than that there was no relationship. I would have to be satisfied with the truth, and with a genealogy that went back no further than my great-grandfather.

I looked dejectedly at Rabbi Israel, but continued a general conversation about my research. He, too, had the hobby of genealogy, and he showed me some of the material he had collected on Chassidic families. Since he was showing his collection, I decided to show him what I had brought with me. I gathered whatever I had concerning the Gottlieb family and showed him pictures and other documents. One piece of paper in particular interested him. It was a piece of stationery, with a letterhead that read, "Bistritz and Vicinity Aid Society." It also had my grandfather's name on it listed as financial secretary. I had found the stationery in my grandparents' apartment.

Rabbi Israel looked at it and told me that there was a man in the neighborhood who was from Bistritz. He was known as the Bistritzer Rebbe. Rabbi Israel suggested that he might be able to help me. Handing me his phone, Rabbi Israel looked up the rebbe's phone number and told me to call him. Thinking back on that morning, I'm glad I was forced into it. I doubt very much that I'd have the courage to call a rebbe by myself. It's just not something that I'm accustomed to doing. When I dialed the number from Rabbi Israel's home, a man answered the phone. He asked me if I could speak Hungarian and I said no. I asked him if he could speak English and he said "A little." I told him that I was a grandson of Zalman Lieb Gottlieb from Bistritz, and I asked him if he might have known him. He told me that he knew Pinchas Gottlieb. Pinchas was a brother of my grandfather and I was excited to hear that I was speaking to a man, a rebbe, who knew a great-uncle of mine. I also knew that Pinchas had been killed in the Holocaust.

The rebbe asked me to come to his address which was just a few blocks from where Rabbi Israel lived. I quickly left Rabbi Israel after thanking him for his help. I was disappointed by what had happened, but I was distracted by my imminent visit with a rebbe.

When I arrived at the address, I was surprised to be at a synagogue. I expected an apartment or a house, but there I was standing at the steps of a synagogue with a sign in Yiddish announcing it to be the Bistritzer synagogue. The rebbe came to the door and asked me to come in.

At that moment, what I entered was not just another synagogue run by another rabbi, but a different world from the one I had known. The shul was a room, a square room, crowded by benches and long tables, books spread upon them. The room was dimly lit, tallisim hung in several spots around the place, and I stood there for a few moments taking it all in. It was unlike anything I had ever seen, except in photographs of shtiebles in Europe. And then I knew that I was in a shtieble, just like the ones my ancestors prayed in, and the fact that this one was in Brooklyn and that my ancestors were in Europe made no difference once the door was closed. The rebbe was an elderly man, bearded of course, and slightly bent from age. Yet he was very quick and his eyes were bright. His face was serious, but friendliness came through. He asked me to sit down, and I did, at one of the long benches in front of one of the long tables. The rebbe said he would be back in a moment. I examined the room from every angle, imagining the activity that must occur each day at prayer times and each Shabbas. What was then a silent room must burst with religious energy, the same kind that my great-grandfather, with his long coat, wide-rimmed hat and beard with side-curls must have had just three generations ago. I was truly in another world and was delighted by this opportunity.

The rebbe returned and we spoke briefly about my family. He knew my grandfather's brother, and also knew he had been killed in a Death Camp. He told me they had studied together. After he had run out of things to tell me, in his broken English, about my family in Europe, I decided to tell him the story of my search for a connection with Chaim Joseph Gottlieb, the Stropkover Rebbe. I told him every detail, like a fool, as if he cared. But he listened with intense interest, asking questions along the way. I concluded by saying that Rabbi Israel had been unable to help me, and I wondered if he remembered whether my family descended from the rebbe.

One of the most intriguing aspects of this whole encounter was the seriousness with which he took what I was saying. He communicated to me, by his questions and his comments, that what I was doing was very important. He never explained why, but continued to indicate this to me. I, on the other hand, wondered if I was taking up too much of his time by talking to him about what I thought must be dead ends. He never once seemed impatient, however; on the contrary, he seemed eager to spend as much time as I wanted in discussing the matter.

One of the additional pieces of information I had discovered along the way was that my great-grandfather's father was named Shlomo. I knew this from the inside cover of my grandfather's Bible where many years ago he wrote brief genealogies of his mother and father. Rabbi Israel was unable to use this additional name for my purposes, but the rebbe seemed interested. He looked through the biography of the Stropkover Rebbe that Rabbi Israel had written, and while flipping through the pages he kept repeating "Usher ben Shlomo, Usher ben Shlomo, Usher ben Shlomo." The rebbe just repeated those names, the names of my great-grandfather and his father, over and over to himself as he looked through the biography. It was obvious that he was looking for the names, but I was sure he would not find them there. A few times while he was examining and reading the biography, a phone in a back room rang. The rebbe was so involved in the biography that it was not until the fifth or sixth ring that he stood up and walked to the back to answer it. Each time the phone rang, the rebbe took too much time to answer it and it stopped before he got there. When he returned to look through the biography again, he seemed happy that he didn't have to talk on the phone so that he could get back to his reading.

In the meantime I just sat there, watching the rebbe continue to read the book and repeat the names, "Usher ben Shlomo, Usher ben Shlomo." I sat there staring and looking around the room. My imagination was active during those minutes, wondering what it was like when the room was filled with praying Chassids. Suddenly, the rebbe spotted something on a page. He brought it to the window, since the light in the room was rather poor. He then came back and sat down and said, "Shlomo was the son of the rebbe."

I didn't know what to do. I knew that he was wrong since Rabbi Israel told me each of the names of the rebbe's sons. But I was not comfortable telling this rebbe that he was incorrect. Somehow it just didn't seem right to contradict a rebbe. I decided to say, "Really?" in a confused and somewhat doubting voice.

He looked again and said, "No, no, no, no, no." He shook his head in apparent disappointment in himself and sat in silence for a few minutes staring at the book. He then looked up and told me that where he was from it was a custom to take a mother's last name rather than a father's. In fact, he said, this was so in almost 50 percent of the cases in his community in Europe. Then he said, "The rebbe Gottlieb had a daughter Gittel. Her husband was Shlomo Zalke." He paused and then said in a deep, confident tone, as if he were making a proclamation, "This is your Shlomo. You come from them and take her last name. This is my opinion."

His remarks sounded final, and he ushered me to the door. There was something unreal about the whole thing, especially the way it

Hand-written genealogy found in the front cover of the author's grandfather's Bible.

ended, but the rebbe seemed absolutely convinced that his opinion was right. When I left, I looked at the biography and reread where it said that the rebbe's son-in-law was named Shlomo Zalke, not just Shlomo. For some reason, the name Zalke sounded familiar. I rushed home and looked again at the genealogy written by my grandfather in his Bible. There it was. He did not just write the name Shlomo, but Shlomo Zalke! I had forgotten about this! It was now obvious. And it was obvious that I was, in fact, a descendant of the Stropkover Rebbe. Everything matched: the names, the dates and even the story about the name not originally being Gottlieb. We had taken the name of the rebbe's daughter rather than his son-in-law. I had finally found the link.

The rebbe in Brooklyn was able to solve the entire issue for me. The fact that my great-great-grandfather, Shlomo Zalke, took the name of his wife, Gittel Gottlieb, explains the fact that Maurice was told the name was not originally Gottlieb. I couldn't wait to call my mother and share the news with her. When I did she was delighted to hear all of my stories. My father, whose family I had researched for seven years, stood by with a smile on his face, as I detailed the generations of my mother's family back farther than I was ever able to get with the Kurzweil family.

There is a postscript to this story that I must add, though it is not nearly complete. In fact, the very day before I wrote this I discovered additional information that brings my family history to even earlier beginnings. In response to the article in the newspaper, *The Jewish Week,* which ran the story about my research, I received a letter from a delightful young woman whose husband is a descendant of the Stropkover Rebbe. This makes us cousins, of course. Her name is Michele Zoltan, and we have established a nice friendship based on our mutual interest in the history of this family. Michele offered to translate the biography of the Stropkover Rebbe for me from the Hebrew. The first chapter was extraordinary.

The chapter speaks about the rebbe and his lineage and indicates that his mother was a descendant of Rabbi Isaiah Horowitz, a renowned rabbi of the 1500s and early 1600s. After doing a little bit of checking, I was able to trace Rabbi Horowitz's family back several generations to the 1400s. In other words, I am a descendant of Rabbi Isaiah Horowitz (known as "the Holy Shela'h"), and consequently I am a descendant of his ancestors as well.

My discovery that I am a member of this rabbinic family and a direct descendant of the Holy Shela'h was one of the most eye opening moments in my entire search. The Shela'h, by the way, claimed to be a descendant of King David, thereby making me a direct descendant of King David as well. Whenever I think of this, my reaction is a mixture of pride as well as responsibility for me to try to live up to such a special past.

I also discovered that there is a Yeshiva in Jerusalem named after Chaim Joseph Gottlieb, the Stropkover Rebbe, and that it is run by some of his other descendants. I was fortunate enough to schedule a trip to Israel in order to visit the Yeshiva and its leaders. I cautiously walked into the Yeshiva's modest building in the Mea Shearim section of Jerusalem, and, as I walked through the threshold, I entered a new world—or perhaps I should say, an old world. There were lines of tables and benches with adult students sitting before open volumes studying the wisdom of sages. It looked like film footage from an era that had gone by, but I quickly learned that this scene is not unusual at all. It was just that I descended from a branch of my family that left the traditional Jewish way of life, so it is not surprising that it was foreign to me. I didn't know it at the time but my discovery of being descended from the Stropkover Rebbe and my visit to this Yeshiva was another step in my personal quest to find my place within Jewish religious tradition.

I also discovered that a group in Borough Park, Brooklyn, also descendants of the Stropkover Rebbe, meet once a year on the occasion of the anniversary of the death of the Stropkover Rebbe. The gathering is both a fund-raiser for the Jerusalem Yeshiva as well as an opportunity for the descendants of the Stropkover Rebbe to come together in order to renew family ties. I have attended this event each year for the past several years and have gotten to know a branch of my family that just a short time ago I didn't even know existed. These cousins, many of them Chassidim and many devoted to a strict Jewish way of life, have opened their hearts and lives to me in a most generous way. At one of the annual gatherings, they even honored me. It was heartwarming to know that they recognized the long journey that I have been taking.

From the tiny, assimilated family of my mother, I am now able to document descent back through some of the most illustrious rabbis of the past several centuries to the 1500s. And I do not intend to stop here.

After having celebrated at some length the discoveries that I have made about my ancestors, I feel compelled to remind all of us that the Talmud warns: "A learned bastard takes precedence over an ignorant High Priest." In other words, illustrious ancestors are meaningless if we, ourselves, are not learned and worthy on our own. The crucial question that arises when genealogical discoveries are made is this: "What do we do with the knowledge of who our ancestors were?"

I find that learning about my family history draws me farther and farther into Jewish Tradition. The more I learn about my ancestors, the more I learn about Jewish history and therefore, Jewish learning. The more facts I have about the lives of my ancestors, the more I learn to respect them and feel grateful to them for their decisions. It matters little, on one level, whether they were religious or not. I respect them for surviving as Jews and for being able to live and raise children, who eventually raised me. I learn much about courage when I understand what it was like to make the decision to journey to America. I continue to learn about faith and belief as I discover the obstacles set before my ancestors in Jewish history.

A special kind of awe comes over me when I learn about an ancestor of mine such as Isaiah Horowitz, who lived around 1600. Here was a man whose life and works are still known today for their greatness. The energy and power that this man had can be described by comparing it to ripples in water: A small force pushed into a body of water will create small ripples that will last a few seconds. The more powerful the force, the greater the ripples and the longer the duration of the vibrations. Such a powerful force was this direct ancestor of mine. There is no question in my mind that he was largely responsible for the religiosity of his descendants. As I examine those descendants I can see how devoted they were to learning and Torah, and, like strong ripples in water, he was one of the forces behind them. So powerful were the vibrations he sent that they reached me in the 1970s. His message traveled a great distance, not only in space but also in time. His influence has spread for nearly 400 years.

I certainly do not claim to lead a life on a par with his, but I am influenced by him. Just the fact that I am able to document my descent from him indicates how powerful an influence he has been. As I make this kind of discovery about an ancestor, I am forced (delightedly so) to encounter his life and teachings and to learn from them. This is the purpose of family history within the Jewish Tradition. It is not to make boastful claims about ancestors. It is not to take credit for the achievements of others, nor is it to take responsibility for the actions of others. But it is to continue to receive a message, first given at Mount Sinai, and still transmitted today. The message of Sinai is handed down through generations, and, as a famous Midrash says, the Torah is given at Sinai every moment if we will only listen for it and hear it. I do not claim to accept every letter of its message, but I do try to receive the message nonetheless. My family history helps me to connect with that event, and with the history of the Jewish people. In this way, I celebrate my ancestors and the lives they led.

2

How to Begin Your Search

INTRODUCTION

The most current event in Jewish history is happening right this moment—with you. Surely there are things happening now that will be remembered in the future, although your life and mine will be forgotten. In a real sense, you are a part of Jewish history. In the twenty-first century, Jews will look back and see you and your life as Jewish history in much the same way that we look back on the lives of our grandparents and great-grandparents as fitting into a special chapter of history.

It is in this spirit that Jewish genealogy ought to be first approached: You are a part of Jewish history and you must explore the rest of Jewish history by beginning at home with yourself. Jewish genealogy begins at home. Throughout this book we will discuss the many documents, books, photographs and other material that will help to make your family history a rich one. Before we can go any further, however, we have to start now, with this very moment.

So, we begin with a simple enough question, whose answer is actually the key to the entire pursuit of genealogy. The question is: How did you get to where you are this very minute? By this, I do not mean how did you travel to the spot on which you are sitting or standing, but rather what were the circumstances under which you arrived where you are?

Another way to approach this question is by describing a game we often play. Have you ever thought to yourself, "If I never met you, I would never have met. . . " Or, "If it weren't for my meeting you by chance, then this and that would not have happened to me." For example, had I not skipped a grade in elementary school most of my friends would not be my friends today, and my life would have been very different!

Every action we take sets off a chain reaction of events that affects the future. I am sure we can all think of dozens of things that would or would not have happened if it were not for something else.

So it is with genealogy and family history.

One of my grandmothers came to America with her older sister when they were fifteen and seventeen, respectively. In other words, two young girls, all by themselves, set off for America in a steamship seventy-two years ago! Had they not been on that boat, I probably would never have existed.

This is a perfect illustration of our "game." Decisions made by our ancestors had significant (if not vital) effects on our lives.

Mathematically speaking, each of us had 1,024 direct ancestors in just the last ten generations. This is not aunts, uncles, or cousins. Just *direct* ancestors (parents, grandparents, great-grandparents, etc.). Again, in just ten generations, we've had 1,024 direct ancestors. We each have two parents, four grandparents, eight great-grandparents, sixteen great-great-grandparents, and so on. If we imagine any *one* of those people—let's say one of our several great-great-great-great-grandmothers—and imagine that she was killed as a child in a pogrom, we would not be here today. If any one of those 1,024 direct ancestors had been killed as a child before being able to marry and have children, we would not be here. Likewise, out of the 512 married couples in the last ten generations in our families, if one person had decided to marry someone else instead, we would not be here.

This illustrates how clearly the decisions and fate of our ancestors affected each of us. Even more dramatic perhaps is the fact that if any one of your ancestors had converted or married outside of Judaism, you might not bc here as a Jew reading this book on Jewish genealogy.

Therefore, we begin our journey into our family history with ourselves and we repeat the question: How did you get to where you are this very minute?

To answer this question, you have to begin to explore the recent history of your family. Actually, you have to ask the same question of your parents: How did *they* get to where they were all their lives? And of course, to answer that question, you must ask the question of *their* parents, and so on.

Getting Started

1) *Where do I start? I've always wanted to trace my family but I don't know how to begin.*

The Kurzweil Family Circle, a Cousins Club in New York.

Since everyone has a different family, there is no perfect system for every family historian. There is no chart for all families to use by filling in the blanks, since we each have different-sized families. There is no step-by-step order to your research, since each of us will find different problems and successes when climbing our family trees.

There is a place where each of us can begin, however, and that is with ourselves. Get a big loose-leaf notebook to use exclusively for your family history. Begin by writing down everything you know. Your name. Your parents' names. Their parents (your grandparents). Aunts, uncles, cousins. Dates of birth, marriage, death. Places. In other words, take inventory of what you already know. If you know a lot—great! If not, that is why you are beginning your family history research.

2) *But how do I keep track of what I write down? Is there a system or format that I should use?*
Some people have devised elaborate coding and filing systems to keep track of their family history notes. Others have made simple and useful systems that serve the same purpose. In the "workbook" appendix of this book, you will find some simple forms and charts you can use to keep track of the information you compile. Don't worry too much about your system. Just

make sure you *write down everything*. Don't rely on your memory for anything. If something is written down you will find it. If not, you might lose it forever. Write clearly; inability to read one's own handwriting is a common problem among researchers.

3) *After I write down everything I know, where do I go from there? Do I just trace one branch of my family or do I trace all branches at once?*
When you are just beginning, your first priority is talking to relatives. Your first priority among the relatives is the oldest of them. Therefore, you ought to begin by phoning, visiting, or writing the oldest living relatives on *all* branches of your family. Otherwise, you might get very involved with one branch of your family while other branches, quite frankly, are dying off! I would bet that there is not one genealogist who has been able to avoid saying, "If only I had spoken to him a long time ago."
After you have spoken to your oldest relatives on all sides of the family, you can zero in on one branch. Remember: The books, archives and libraries will wait. The people will not.

4) *Do you mean to say that I must research all branches of my family? What if I am just interested in one particular branch?*
Of course, you can do what you like. But consider two things. First, that although you are just interested in one branch today, your interest may broaden in the future. By then, it may be too late to interview important family members. Second, keep in mind that if you don't become the family historian, chances are that nobody will. You have the opportunity to capture and save your family story. Don't let it disappear.

5) *What's next? After I have interviewed all of my relatives, where do I go from there? I'm anxious to trace back as far as I can and most of my relatives don't remember too far back. Aren't there books or vital records that I can check to trace back through the generations?*
One of the two great misconceptions held by beginning family historians is that they can quickly go to a reference book and find out all about their family. Of course, the other great misconception is that no records exist and that tracing Jewish families is impossible. Both notions are wrong. There are plenty of excellent and effective sources (as you will learn by reading this book), but if you are just beginning, you are not ready for them

yet. Be patient. You do not discover your family history overnight. Like any other hobby—stamp-collecting, for example—you slowly build on your collection. Watching it grow and then suddenly, months later, seeing that you have really built something to be proud of is what it is all about.

6) *That still doesn't answer the question. What's next?*
Again, there is no system for everyone. This book is not a simple step-by-step guide. I would suggest that you read through the book and see the *possibilities.* Learn what sources exist. This will give you a better idea what information you *need.* Tracing your genealogy and family history is always a detective process. Your new discoveries will be based on information you already know. One fact will lead to another and another. By reading through this book, you will get a good idea of what you need to know in order to discover new information. In fact, it would be a good idea to read over the entire book even before talking to your oldest relatives. In this way you will learn what kinds of questions to ask and what kinds of information you ought to be looking for.

7) *Do you mean to say that from this point on, I'm on my own? Isn't there a checklist of things to do? I feel lost.*
Research isn't easy, but don't be afraid of it. Just get involved. Decide what you'd like to know (with this book helping you to crystalize those ideas) and go after it.

If you really want a next step, I will at least share with you the mistake of *most* beginners: Most of us *never* interview enough relatives! We are so eager to "begin the research and the discoveries" that we fail to understand that it is the *people* in your family who can offer you the most information.

So, your next step, after contacting your oldest living relatives, is to contact other relatives. *The best leads, the best information and the best stories I have gathered for my family history have come from relatives.* Although I have discovered a great deal in record books and libraries, none of that would have been possible without information provided by people.

If you *ever* wonder what to do next, ask yourself: Whom have I not yet interviewed?

8) *Isn't it true that Jews cannot trace their family histories because of name changes and the destruction of records?*

Not at all! In my own case, I've traced back to the 1500s on one side of my family, and the late 1700s on another. In the latter case, I have traced 500 descendants of my great-great-great-grandparents to places all over the world. On another branch of my family, I have located copies of my great-grandparents' marriage record in Hungary from the mid-1800s that includes information about my great-great-grandparents. I have also located information on 103 members of one branch of my family—all 103 of whom were killed in the Holocaust.

Jews *can* trace their genealogies and family histories, and that is what this book is all about. By the way, genealogy has been a part of our tradition ever since the first chapters of Genesis.

9) *Is there any special equipment needed for all of this?*
There will be more detailed discussions of this throughout the book, but I will mention briefly some standard items that will come in handy throughout your search.

A cassette tape recorder. When you interview family members, tape them. How I would love to have a recording of my great-grandfather—but I can't. What I *can* do is provide the same kind of thing for my descendants.

File folders, paper, notebook, etc. Be generous with these items. The better your note keeping and record keeping are, the better off you'll be when you need to record or find something.

Envelopes, stationery, postage stamps. Family history depends heavily upon writing letters. Keep a supply of these things at all times so that mailing letters and other requests for information does not get held up because you haven't had a chance to go to the post office.

10) *Should I aim for any specific goal in my family history? Should I try to go back as far as possible or to find as many living relatives as I can? Where does it end?*
Don't worry about it ending; you're just beginning. As far as your "goal" is concerned, that's up to you. You might want to specialize in one subject—let's say, "What happened to your family during the Holocaust." Or you might want to go as far back as you can on one branch. Tracing your genealogy and family history is open-ended. People often ask me if I have finished my research. No, I haven't. I have been researching my family history for many years and I have no intention of stop-

ping. It hasn't been full time. It's like any other hobby: Sometimes I work on the family history like a madman for a week or two. Other times I neglect it for a few months. The only difference between it and other hobbies I have had is that this one has affected me in profound ways. I feel a great sense of connection with my family and with Jewish history. And I feel a responsibility to that history to continue as a link on an ancient chain of Jewish Tradition.

On the other hand, I could have stopped at any point with the knowledge that I had gathered a lot of material about the history of my family and that it was now saved from disappearing. It was now a part of the history of my family that would not be forgotten.

As you enter your family history, you will find that it will take you in many directions. You will develop your own special interest within it as you proceed. If you want to trace back as far as you can, go in that direction. If you want to trace living members of your family, do that. If you have other interests within your family history, pursue them.

The most important advice is this: Begin now. Don't wait until tomorrow.

GATHERING YOUR HISTORY

Collecting Stories

Your family tree is only the bare framework of your family history. Without the stories, legends, tales and episodes of your cousins and ancestors, all you will have is a dry collection of names and dates.

When you interview or correspond with relatives and others, encourage them to tell stories, and be sure to record these stories either by writing them down or by taping them. A cassette tape recorder is one of the finest tools a family historian can have. In future years, when your descendants listen to the family history you have recorded, they will have the priceless experience of hearing the voices you have heard, and they will be able to listen, firsthand, to the same tales which you received from the many people with whom you have spoken. Imagine what it would be like for you to be able to hear stories told by your great-grandparents. By recording stories yourself, you will be able to offer this precious gift to future generations of your family.

Cassette tape recorders are small enough and silent enough to be

Bar Mitzvah photo of Saul Kurzweil, the author's father.

inconspicuous. They rarely inhibit the person whom you are recording. Nonetheless, it is important that you tell people when you are recording them, for ethical reasons. In addition, you can purchase, for a few dollars, an attachment for your telephone so that you can record phone conversations. But again, you must tell people what you are doing.

> The stories I most like to tell are the ones I heard from my grandfather.
>
> ELIE WIESEL, *A JEW TODAY*

FAMILY LEGENDS: ARE THEY TRUE?

I once had a conversation with Elie Wiesel about my family history research. At one point in our exchange, he said to me, "Are you getting stories?"

I told him I was.

"Are you writing them down?" he asked.

"Yes, I'm writing them all down."

"Very good," Wiesel said. "This is very important. You should collect as many stories as you can. Write them down. Save them. You should have a file. Label the folders by name and save the stories. This is very important."

I was well aware of Elie Wiesel's interest in stories, but I was also taken by the personal concern that he expressed and the detail with which he explained a file system for me to use. In fact, I was maintaining just the kind of file system he had suggested.

After a pause, I said, "Of course, I don't think that all of the stories I've been told are true."

"What does it matter if they are true?" Wiesel replied.

I mention this conversation with Elie Wiesel because a discussion regarding the "truth" behind family legends is an important one. Genealogists who are serious about their work have tried to be strict for a long time in accepting only that which can be documented and verified. This is a reaction to the many people who have made false claims about who their ancestors were and what they did. I, too, want to underline the notion that claiming things that are false is the worst family history "sin" possible. On the other hand, there is something to say for recording and even investigating family tales that have dubious origins.

The rule of thumb I use is this: I record everything. Even the wildest stories (and I've heard some good ones!) are saved. The stories become an important part of the family history—not as fact, but as legend. I am careful to record not only the tale, but its source. Even if it's not true that my great-great-grandfather once offered a plate of food to a hungry man who happened to be Franz Josef, who in turn made my great-great-grandfather his personal guard, I still think it's important that the story has survived and has come down to me.

Don't perpetuate a fraud, but don't rob your family history of its richness by being "scientific." A tale that is not "true" in fact, can be quite "true" in its message. In the case of my great-great-grandfather, the story says that he offered food to a stranger and did not know he was the emperor. He also did not think he would be rewarded for his act of charity. It's a good lesson.

> R. Joshua ben Levi said: He who teaches his grandson Torah, the Writ regards him as though he had received it direct from Mount Sinai.
>
> TALMUD, KIDDUSHIN, 30A

Ten Common Family Myths—or Truths!

During the past several years, I have had the great opportunity to speak on the subjects of Jewish family history and genealogy to more than 600 groups. In addition, I have received letters from hundreds of readers of my articles on the same subjects. I am constantly hearing family stories from people who have heard the same tales from their relatives. These people are often quite eager to share their stories with me and believe wholeheartedly that their stories are true.

After hearing scores of stories by so many different people, I began to realize that many of the same legends kept popping up. Over and over again I would hear variations of the same stories. Here are the bare outlines of the ten tales I have heard most often:

1) *"We descend from the Baal Shem Tov."*
The Baal Shem Tov, founder of Chassidism, is the subject of a great number of legends, and family legends are included. He is claimed as an ancestor by large numbers of people, and is in competition with the next two individuals as "The Most-Often-Claimed Jewish Ancestor."

2) *"We descend from the Vilna Gaon."*
The Vilna Gaon, one of history's great Talmudists, was an eighteenth-century Lithuanian luminary.

3) *"We descend from King David."*
Jewish Tradition states that the Messiah will spring from the House of David, so to descend from King David is to open the possibility that the Messiah will come from your family. In fact, a lengthy genealogy in the New Testament attempts to document this connection between King David and Jesus.

4) *"We are related to the Rothschild family."*
I do not know whether it is to claim heir to the fortune, or simply to say that once they brushed shoulders with the richest Jewish family in modern history, but a huge number of people seem to claim this relationship.

5) *"My ancestors were rabbis."*
It's very possible, but often I have the sense that someone remembers an old man with a long beard and therefore assumes he must have been a rabbi.

6) *"There is a fortune of money buried under our house in Eastern Europe."*

If I were to add up the amount of money each of the tellers of this tale has claimed is in a box below his or her old home, it would be greater than the contents of Fort Knox.

7) *"My family left Spain during the Inquisition."*
For me, this is a fascinating story. Certainly many of us do indeed descend from Jews who left Spain centuries ago. But there is little documentation of individual families who left or were expelled. This means that either many families are adopting these stories as their own, or that the story has in fact been handed down from generation to generation since that time. Of course, either reason could be true for different people!

8) *"My ancestors were horse thieves."*
Frequently this is said as a joke. Often people will speculate and say, "If I trace my family, I'm sure we'll find horse thieves," as if to say, "the truth will finally come out!" The fascinating thing is that this claim is also made in dead seriousness by so many people.

9) *"Everything in our town was destroyed in the Holocaust. Not a house or person was left. Nothing was saved."*
I am often deeply moved when people say this, not because it is true, but because they believe it. I am certainly not disputing the fact that these people have these awful events in their memories. But I have visited many towns in Eastern Europe that were at one time Jewish towns. The vast majority of the Jewish populations of these towns as well as the buildings were destroyed, but the towns were not—in many cases—as completely obliterated as people say. I have found Jewish cemeteries in places where people report they were leveled. I have found surviving Jews in places where people say every last Jew was killed.

My point is not to lessen the damage done or to belittle the person who tells this, but rather to point out the psychological as well as physical effect of the Holocaust. I also mention this to encourage the researcher *not* to give up his or her research simply because something like this is reported.

10) *"My family knew Emperor Franz Josef I personally."*
Franz Josef I of Hapsburg who lived from 1830 to 1916 is a great folk-hero to the Jews in recent years. Friendly to the Jews of his empire, he became a popular figure among the Jewish

> population. Often he would be spoken of by Jews as "the Emperor, may his majesty be exalted." It was not uncommon to find a picture of Franz Josef on the wall in the homes of Jews. He was a friend to the Jews, at least when compared with almost every other European leader in history, and it is probably for this reason that so many Jewish families claim they knew him personally. My family, too, has a Franz Josef story as part of its history.

Each of these ten stories got to be true in some cases. Some of us *do* descend from King David, the Baal Shem Tov, or the Vilna Gaon. Some of us *do* come from Spain originally. Some of us *are* related to the Rothschilds. Many of us *do* have rabbis in our past. Some of us *must* have been horse thieves.

It is striking how often these claims are made, however. The purpose of discussing these stories is not to say that if you have a similar story in your family you should automatically dismiss it. On the contrary, record the story, remember it, and even pass it along to the next generation. It is my belief that there is a germ of truth in each story. It is our job to learn the stories, enjoy them and perhaps speculate as to how or why the story originated.

> The study of history will never become obsolete, and a knowledge of one's grandfathers is an excellent introduction to history.
>
> MAURICE SAMUEL

What Questions Should You Ask?

When you interview a relative or any other individual for your family history research, it is important that you prepare yourself in advance for the meeting. Effective oral history cannot occur if you just ask questions off the top of your head with little or no thought about what you want to know, what is important to ask, and what are the best ways of asking.

You will want to be thorough, but it is my own personal opinion that you should strike a balance between your own specific interests and more general topics. In other words, try to cover a broad range of areas but don't avoid focusing on the areas of greatest interest to you. In my own case, I have little interest in politics but a large interest in religion. I try to ask questions concerning politics when it is relevant, but my interviews with relatives have a decided slant toward the religious. I am most interested in the religious thoughts, activities and evolution of my family.

The following questions should serve as a guide to your oral history interviews. Do not simply go down the lists of questions and ask them one by one. Rather, pick the questions that interest you, and use them to begin a conversation. Rely on the questions and on your notes to get started, but know when to put them aside in order to engage in a free-flowing dialogue. If you simply go down the lists asking questions, the oral history will be dull and stiff. Each of these questions has the potential to begin a long, in-depth discussion about the topic at hand.

ORAL HISTORY QUESTIONS AND TOPICS

European Roots

1) What towns did your family come from in Europe? Where were those towns located?
2) Who were the immigrants to America? Did you come here, or was it your parents, grandparents, etc.?
3) Do you know the specific reasons for your family coming to America?
4) If you came to America, who came with you?
5) Describe the trip.
6) Did you experience anti-Semitism in Europe?
7) In what port did your ship dock? Do you know the name of the ship and the date it arrived?
8) What was life in Europe like? What are some of your early childhood memories?
9) Did your family live in one town in Europe, or did various branches of the family live in different places? Did your own family move from one place to another?
10) Who was the first person in the entire family to come to America?
11) What contact continued with the Old Country? Did you receive letters from relatives who remained in Europe? Were those letters saved?

Personal and Family Life

1) What were your parents' names? Your mother's maiden name?
2) Where were they from?
3) How many brothers and sisters do you have? What are their names? What was the order of their birth?

4) Did they marry? Have children? What are their names?
5) What are their occupations? What was your father's occupation?
6) Did your mother work?
7) What do you remember about your grandparents? Do you know their names, including maiden names? Where were they from? What were their occupations?
8) Do you remember your great-grandparents? Their names and anything about them?
9) Where were they from?
10) Whom were you named after? What do you know about that person?
11) What is your spouse's name? Your children's names?
12) Where did your family live in the U.S.? Did they live elsewhere?
13) What memories are especially vivid from your childhood?
14) Do you remember your first job and how old you were?
15) What were the living conditions in your home as a child?

Religious Life

1) Was your family religious?
2) In Europe, were they Orthodox or Chassidic?
3) If they were Chassidic, did they follow any particular rebbe?
4) Did the religious life in your family change when you came to America—or over the years?
5) Was there any resistance to coming to America on the part of anyone in your family for religious reasons?
6) Did your family belong to a synagogue in America?
7) Is there a family cemetery plot? Where is it? Who bought or organized it?
8) Do you remember your childhood during holidays such as Passover or the High Holidays? Others?
9) Is there a family Bible?
10) Did you have a Bar/Bas Mitzvah?
11) Do you remember the shul in Europe? What was it like?

Artifacts

1) Do you have your ketubah (marriage document)?
2) Is there a family photo album?
3) Do you have old photographs?
4) Are there any family heirlooms that have been passed down

from generation to generation? Do you know through whom they have been passed down?

5) Do you have any old candlesticks, kiddish cups, or tefillin? (Do not give the impression that you want them—just that you'd like to *see* them.)
6) Do you have your passport? Your parents' passports?
7) Do you have your citizenship papers? Your "first papers"?
8) Do you have your birth certificate?
9) Do you have any old letters written by family members?
10) Are there any recipes that have been in the family for a long time?
11) Are there any other old family history items, such as diaries, Bibles, books, etc.?
12) Is there a written genealogy in the family?
13) Do you know anyone else in the family who would have old family documents?

> Tell ye your children of it, and let your children tell their children, and their children another generation.
>
> JOEL 1:3

Tips on Interviewing Relatives

1) Try to interview people twice, on consecutive days if at all possible. The reason for this is simple: After the first interview, the person being interviewed will go to bed and dream about things that he or she had not thought of in years. The interview the next day will be great!
2) Don't ask yes or no questions. Phrase your questions so that they will inspire stories and anecdotes.
3) Sometimes relatives don't want to be interviewed. One way to inspire them is to have them present while you are interviewing someone else. The "silent" one will often add his or her two cents. Another effective idea is to show your interview subject a document or photograph of him or herself. This will often open up an otherwise shy or noncooperative relative.
4) Old photographs inspire great conversations. Sit with relatives and ask them to tell you about the people and places in your old photographs.
5) Tell the people who you are interviewing that you will report

your genealogical discoveries to them. This promise (keep it!) is usually an effective incentive.

6) Prepare your interview. Don't think that you can ad-lib a good interview. Quality interviews come as the result of careful thought and planning.
7) Tape all your interviews. Even telephone conversations can be taped.
8) If you don't tape your interviews, make sure to type your notes as soon as possible. Too many genealogists have scribbled so fast that they can't read their own notes.
9) Interviewing relatives, especially those you don't know, takes courage. Be proud of yourself for pursuing your genealogy. Remember that your research has the potential for changing a person's life. When a young person in your family needs to know about his or her place in the world, his or her ancestors, your research will be beneficial.

> Grandparents, ever a source of family lore, may also be living examples to be emulated. If one's grandparents are no longer accessible, it may still be possible to trace one's Jewish roots back to earlier generations. Such a search amounts to an acceptance, not merely a reluctant acknowledgement, of the pluralism and diversity in Jewish tradition. Even in Ezekiel's messianic vision, there are separate gates to the Temple for each of the twelve tribes.
>
> ADIN STEINSALTZ

Observations on Those Who Don't Appreciate Genealogy

1) Some people think genealogy is a waste of time. They have a right to their opinion.
2) Don't get discouraged by the people who think "you have your head in the past," or "you're wasting your time." When people say that to me, I try to use it to remind myself not to be judgmental of others.
3) Frequently I see that people have a misimpression about genealogy. They think that it is names and dates on a chart. It's our responsibility to show people that genealogy is far more. Don't bore people with long stories about the family; instead, infect them with your enthusiasm.

Following Leads Like a Detective

Family history is not a simple matter. You will not be able to find out everything you want to know from any one book, relative, library, archive or photograph. Like a detective, you will have to listen carefully for "leads" that will help you to discover more and more. When you interview a second cousin of your mother who suggests that "Aunt Bertha could tell you more," you must get in touch with Aunt Bertha. If someone mentions, in passing, that a branch of the family once lived in Omaha, Nebraska, you should check it out. If a family legend says that an ancestor of yours was in the Civil War, do the research to find out if it's true.

In my own particular case, one tiny clue, mentioned once, was able to send me on the road to trace my family back to the 1500s! In another case, a small lead helped me to discover my cousin and his family who survived the Holocaust and still live in Warsaw. I can tell countless stories of dramatic family history discoveries that I have made due simply to the fact that I investigated the most obscure clues I heard. In almost every case, the effort paid off.

> Our past is not behind us, it is in our very being.
>
> Ben-Gurion, "Call of the Spirit"

Taking Notes

An important part of your family history research will be taking notes. If you are in a library checking out a book source, or in an archive examining public records, or visiting a relative for oral history, note taking will be vital. Many amateur researchers make the dangerous mistake of thinking that they will remember what they have been told during an interview or what they have seen in a book. Caution: You will forget! If you are like most people, you will, very shortly into your research, begin to get sources and places confused.

It is much like the vacation you have taken. After a while you begin to forget where you saw what. When you return home and tell your friends about your trip, you are unsure if it was Rome or Florence where you ate at that fabulous restaurant.

Take notes. Good note taking is a skill that develops over a time, so it is generally best to write down as much as possible. It is also advisable to type your notes after a session of note taking. Type your notes as soon as possible to avoid being unable to read your own handwriting (which so often happens!). Also, if you type your notes the same day you have take them, they will be fresh in your mind and you will be accurate.

Many people feel that note taking is a waste of time, but if you plan to do a good job on your family history it is essential, which you will discover yourself after very little time as a researcher.

Often the question arises, "How do I keep track of my information? Should I set up a file system? An index card file? How do I make sense out of all my little notes and papers?" These are difficult questions to answer. I can suggest two approaches. The first is to invent a system that works for you. Don't worry about whether it's "right" or the best system. If it works for you, it is the best system. My second suggestion—and this is only for those of you who cannot or would not invent your own system—is to go to the library and consult the many "how-to" genealogy books that explain some simple and some elaborate systems for keeping records. Also, ask your librarian if your library has some privately published family histories and genealogies (most libraries do, having received them as gifts). These will help you set up a system of your own based on the experiences of others.

There are many books on the market that offer charts and forms you can fill in to keep track of your family's history. Although I have yet to see a book I am perfectly happy with, almost all of them are useful. I suggest you consult or buy one and adapt it to your own interests and to your own family. For example, many books have charts that ask for "date of baptism." This clearly does not apply to the Jewish researcher. On the other hand, the general format of these "fill-in" books can help a great deal when you try to put your gathered information into some order.

> I, Ahimaaz, the son of Paltiel ben Samuel ben Hananel ben Amittai, sought God's aid and guidance in order to find the lineage of my family and He bountifully granted my request. I concentrated my mind and soul upon this work; I put the family documents and traditions in order, and I narrated the story in rhymed form. I began with the earliest tradition during the time of the destruction of Jerusalem and of the Temple by the Romans; then I traced it through the settlement of the exiles in the city of Oria in Italy (where I am now living) and the arrival of my ancestors in Capua; and finally, I have concluded with my own generation. I have written it all in this book for the use of future generations.
>
> AHIMAAZ BEN PALTIEL, JEWISH POET, BORN IN 1017

Visiting Relatives and Others

One of the most rewarding yet time-consuming aspects of family history research is visiting people. Yet, however much time is required, the investment invariably pays off.

Do not expect or desire that all your information will come to you. Often people do not write letters, or do not write them well. In addition, a story told by a relative will almost always be better in person than on a page. Think of yourself: If you had to write a story on paper, you would probably not embellish it the way you would if you had the opportunity to tell it aloud.

Family history also is not simply the collection of names, dates and stories. The process of meeting new people, sharing discoveries and experiences and making new friends is a fringe benefit (if not a reason in itself) of your family history project.

Another fascinating phenomenon has happened to me many times. I will establish a correspondence with a relative and will acquire a lot of new information. On occasion I will call the person and will receive even more family history over the phone. Then the information source will "run dry," but I will visit the same person who had no more to tell me and discover that there is much more to hear and see. Photographs will be found, old passports and documents will appear, additional stories will be remembered and I will regret not having visited sooner.

It is a particular mitzvah to visit an elderly person. So often I have been given the opportunity to bring a little bit of joy into someone's life by visiting with a person who was delighted to share information with me. One strong suggestion concerning the visiting of older relatives in particular: Don't just visit once and forget about them. An occasional phone call, a note, or even additional visits are important. Otherwise you have just "used" them. After you have made an acquaintance or have reestablished a family relationship, it is incumbent upon you to take responsibility for it. It takes very little effort to call and say hello, or write a short letter to someone who has shared a part of his or her life with you.

> A people's memory is history; and as a man without a memory, so a people without a history cannot grow wiser, better.
>
> I. L. Peretz

Family Photographs

You must ask of each person whom you interview for your family history to show you his or her old photographs. Family photographs are an important and exciting part of your family history pursuit, and it is a special experience to be able to see pictures of your ancestors, of your ancestors' siblings, and of Holocaust victims whose photographs may exist.

As I visit people and see their photographs, I know that I want to have copies of many of them. Yet, I am certainly not going to ask for them (old photographs are among people's most precious possessions), and I even hesitate to borrow them. In the first place, I do not want to risk losing them, and second, it becomes quite expensive to have them reproduced. There is a solution to that problem, however. It is relatively easy to duplicate them yourself.

All you need are a 35mm camera and a close-up lens that can be bought relatively inexpensively at most camera shops. In other words, if you already have the camera, your investment will be minimal. You will break even after duplicating just a few photographs when you compare this process to the usual lab fees.

When you visit people who have old photographs, bring your camera and the lenses. If you use a close-up lens, all you have to do is set the photograph down on a table, make sure that there is enough light, and take a photograph of the photograph. It is necessary to use a tripod to make sure the camera does not move. The cost of tripods varies.

You can build a collection of old photographs for a small investment with this process and you also will have negatives of the photographs that can be made into prints for pennies. You can then make prints for people who might like copies of some photographs from your collection. Often I have photographs of people that other family members would love to have. Copies of photographs make nice gifts, and act as incentives for them to share more with you.

This is only one way to duplicate photographs. With a little time and patience it works quite well. However, there are other ways to do the same thing. I suggest you visit a good camera shop and ask about equipment available to make copies of your old family photographs. Depending upon how many photos you have to duplicate, how involved in this process you want to get and how much money you are willing to spend, there are several options open to you. It is also worth mentioning here that as photocopy machines get better and better, photocopying becomes a more effective way to copy photographs.

> Jews who get a certain spiritual tonic from the reflection that they are somehow related to the creators of the Bible and to its ethical values forget that the relationship was passed on to them by the men who begot their fathers. Who were these men? Under what circumstances did they nurture the relationship for transmission? What tone and color had their lives? What purpose did they conceive themselves to be serving in their obstinate fidelity to the relationship? What hopes had they for themselves—and for their grandchildren?
>
> MAURICE SAMUEL, *THE WORLD OF SHOLOM ALEICHEM*

WRITING LETTERS

Although it is almost always better to visit relatives when searching for family history, distance forces us to write letters at times. In addition, family historians use the mail to make inquiries to strangers who might be related or who might be of help. There are several "rules" or guidelines to follow when writing for family history information:

1) Try to avoid using a form letter, even if you are writing to many people for the same kind of information. You will get better results with personal letters.
2) Explain clearly at the beginning of your letter what you are doing and why. Many people are suspicious when it comes to talking about "family matters," especially since there are some companies that try to make money by offering to research your family tree. I have never had a problem with people suspecting my motives, but I think this is the result of my making them clear from the beginning.
3) Identify yourself in the letters. The more you say about yourself, the more other people will offer about themselves. Tell them about your family history, both to inspire them to do the same and to help them to trust you.
4) Promise that you'll write them again and that you will share your discoveries with them—and then keep your promise!
5) Do not ask too many questions in one letter. A letter filled with questions is not apt to get a response.
6) You might want to try a questionnaire, but keep it simple and short. It is more effective to ask a little with each letter than to try to "get everything" at once. Also, you do not want to "use"

people. You want to establish friendships. The longer the relationship, the more rewarding it will be—both personally and informationally.

7) Always enclose a self-addressed stamped envelope. This is for the convenience of your respondent. Although you should not expect everyone to answer every letter, a self-addressed stamped envelope will increase your rate of return. You cannot send such an envelope outside the U.S., but you may want to send an addressed envelope and International Reply Coupons, which can be purchased at your local post office. These coupons can be redeemed in other countries for stamps, and this will serve the same purpose as sending stamps.
8) Finally, be warm, friendly and polite in your letters. Do not insist that people send you information. Writing letters is an opportunity to be pleasant and to brighten someone's day (or more). Take that opportunity and use it!

Final Tips on How to Begin

1) Start now, not tomorrow. Every family historian has, at one time or another, wished that he or she began earlier.
2) Write down what you know. Anywhere. It doesn't have to be input into a fancy database or inscribed with elegant calligraphy in a fancy book. Just scribble down what you know: names, dates, towns. Genealogists go, as they say, "from the known to the unknown." Writing down what you know about your family history makes what you need to find out much clearer.
3) Get your tape recorder in order, buy fresh batteries, or buy a new one. A cassette tape recorder is inexpensive and is an essential tool for the family historian.
4) Identify your oldest relatives. That means: make phone calls, write letters, do what you can to locate the oldest relatives. It may be a second cousin who nobody has been in touch with for years. Be the one to get in touch. The oldest relatives need to be interviewed, visited, pestered. They have old photographs, old letters, old documents. Make your oldest relatives your best friends.
5) Don't let anyone discourage you. There will be people who will think you are wasting your time by doing genealogy; there are people who will think you are nosey; there are people who will not be willing to talk with you; there are people who will not

answer your letter; there are librarians who will not want to be "bothered"; there are archivists who will try to make you think they own the material in the archives that pay their salaries; there are librarians who will not think that genealogy is important enough for them; there are siblings who will be puzzled by you; cousins who will think you are a fanatic. Don't let anything discourage you. Genealogy is a holy pursuit. For those who believe, no explanation is necessary; for those who don't believe, no explanation is possible.

3

Checking the Records

PREPARE YOURSELF

Prepare yourself to enter the world of libraries, archives and governmental agencies. Keep in mind that your journey can be an endless one. This is good news and bad news. The good news is that the resources available are considerable, and growing all the time. You can *never* investigate all the possibilities in one lifetime. The bad news is that libraries, archives and governmental agencies are not always easy to work with.

Sometimes they are. Sometimes a library is well staffed, well funded, well organized and a dream come true.

Sometimes an archivist is also a sensitive person who not only cares about "the collection" but also about people.

Sometimes the human being who opens up your letter at some bureaucracy you had to be in touch with is interested in helping and who, perhaps, has a supervisor who cares about such things.

All too often, the opposite is true.

Nevertheless, prepare yourself for some astounding discoveries, amazing breakthroughs and lots of information that is available to you about your family and its history. There will be forms to fill out, directions to follow, lines to get on, fees to pay and patience to learn, but the results will be worthwhile.

People often say to me, "There's nobody left to talk with about the family history." I have two responses. My first response is that I don't believe it. I don't believe you have tracked down every possible living source. There is some distant cousin somewhere to be found. My second response is that libraries, archives and governmental agencies throughout the world have information about my family. And yours.

Prepare yourself.

> Blessed is he that remembers what is forgotten!
>
> S. Y. AGNON

PHONE BOOKS

Contemporary phone books can be of help when searching for missing or new relatives. Although it is almost impossible to use a telephone book when looking for new relatives named Cohen or Levine, you might find it productive if your name is less common.

I have looked up the name Kurzweil in hundreds of phone books and have contacted many of the people whose names I have found. In a great number of cases, I have discovered relatives who did not know we were related—nor did I know about them until I made the contact. Often it was just a matter of asking a few questions to determine where on the family tree a newly discovered branch of the family belonged. Over the past several years I have discovered "lost" branches of my family in Israel, across the U.S. and in Poland.

Many large public libraries have good collections of telephone books. The New York Public Library Research Library, for example, has nearly every available telephone book in the world! Also, many foreign telephone books have English editions.

When contacting a stranger, either by phone or through the mail, it is important that you identify yourself and explain what you are doing. You want to inspire trust. Tell the person about yourself, something of what you have already researched, and promise to share your results (and do it!). I have sometimes found it difficult to call a stranger and to begin a conversation about family history, but it has almost always been rewarding.

You should surely check the Israeli phone books if you have an uncommon last name. There is an English language edition, and you might discover a branch of your family that settled there either before the Holocaust, or even afterward.

I never thought that I had relatives living in Israel until I looked up the name "Kurzweil" in the Israeli phone books. I wrote to several people, and when they wrote back, the information about their parents, grandparents and towns in Europe where they came from matched with my family tree.

Several years ago I was eager to locate a cousin of my father who survived the Holocaust and was reported to have stayed in Poland. I did not know his address, nor did I know where he had been for the past thirty years. But I went to the Polish phone book of 1974 and found his name, address and telephone number. I wrote to him, and a few weeks later I received a letter in return. It was, indeed, my cousin, whom nobody had been in touch with for years! We have since written to each other every few weeks, and we have become quite close. I have visited him in Poland and I helped sponsor a trip for him to visit my family in New York. His daughter also visited us in New York; as one can imagine, the trip to America, for her, was extraordinary. I have no doubt that it changed her life. All because I looked up his name in the Polish phone book. (See Chapter 6 for more on pre-Holocaust telephone books.)

Vital Records

Birth, death, marriage and divorce records in the U.S. can be quite helpful, but it would be impossible to generalize as to what information each provides. This varies both from place to place as well as from year to year. Costs for these documents also vary, and you can never be sure of the current price either; I've seen prices fluctuate from one month to the next.

The best guide to these records can be found in the U.S. Department of Health and Human Services booklet *Where to Write for Vital Records*, available from the U.S. Government Printing Office, Washington, D.C. 20402, or from their branch offices around the country (check locally).

This booklet costs $2.25 as of this writing, and provides information on each state regarding the procedure required to obtain copies of birth, death, marriage and divorce documents.

The information on these documents is not standard and therefore will vary from place to place in the U.S. as well as from year to year in the same location, but a few interesting examples of what I have found would be useful in illustrating the value of these American sources.

Often a person will say to me, "My great-grandmother came to the U.S. many years ago. She is no longer alive, nor is anyone else in her generation who can answer some questions. I cannot even find out the names of her parents." My immediate response is, "Have you obtained her death certificate?" More often than not, a death certificate asked (and still asks) the name of the parents of the deceased. Although there might be no one alive today who knows the answer to that question, chances are someone *did* know at the time of her death.

One of my great-grandfathers came to America and died here. I wanted to know his parents' names, so I sent for his death certificate. When it arrived, I learned his father's name and his mother's name. Most important, I learned the maiden name of his mother! When death certificates ask for the names of the parents of the deceased, they will usually include a request for the maiden name of the mother. So, when my great-grandfather's death certificate arrived, another branch of my family began to appear.

Interestingly, his mother's maiden name was the same as his wife's maiden name. So my first thought was that there must have been a mistake: How can his wife and his mother have the same last name? Unless, of course, they were related! I asked around in the family and was told that my great-grandparents were first cousins.

Marriage records are also of great value, since these records will ask the names of the bride's parents and the groom's parents.

There is one additional thing to keep in mind when searching for these records. Often you will send to the appropriate agency for copies of these records and they will reply that they do not have them. A number of possibilities exist. It may be an error on the part of the clerk who made the search. Or it may be your error—perhaps your grandmother died somewhere other than where you think. Or possibly the record was lost. In any of these cases, do not give up. Try other alternatives. For example, if you cannot locate your grandmother's death certificate but are anxious to find her parents' names, try to locate the death certificate of one of her brothers or sisters. The same thing goes for marriage records: Try to find records of siblings. In other words, you must be a detective. You must think of every possibility and every alternative. It isn't always easy, but it's almost always worthwhile.

> Be fruitful and multiply, and replenish the earth.
>
> GENESIS 1:28

CENSUS RECORDS

The federal government has taken a census of the country's population every ten years since 1790. Census records can all be consulted for family history research, although some have restrictions on them. The only census that is not available is the 1890 Federal Census, which was destroyed (except for small portions) in a fire.

The census records can be of enormous assistance to you when you are researching your family history. The information will be valuable on its own, and it will give you clues to seek additional facts. You will also be able to search the census records for people with your last name in an effort to locate new or unknown relatives. By reviewing the kinds of information to be found in the records, you can see how helpful they can be.

There are many differences among these census records from decade to decade. For example, the records of 1790–1840 list only the head of the household by name, whereas the later records list the names of each member of the household. You will have no choice, obviously, but to accept the difference among the records.

Each federal census from 1790 through 1920 is available on an unrestricted basis to researchers. Although you can do your own research from the census records up to 1920, someone will have to do it for you for the records compiled since then.

Write to:

U.S. Dept. of Commerce
Bureau of the Census
P.O. Box 1545
Jeffersonville, IN 47131

and ask for form BC-600 (Application for Search of Census Records), if you want information from census records for 1930 to the present.

If your research takes you back before 1850 in the U.S., you will be pleased to know that most of the censuses from 1790 to 1850 have been indexed and these indexes are in book form. The 1850 index in particular will be very useful for those German-Jewish families that arrived at the beginning of the major German-Jewish wave of immigration to America. Many of the National Archives branches have these indexes, as do major genealogical libraries.

The National Archives in Washington, D.C., and the Regional Archives Branches of the National Archives have all of the Federal Census records from 1790 to 1920 on microfilm.

It is always best to do the research by yourself, because you cannot be sure that anyone else has been thorough. Once I searched a federal census for a few hours until I found a part of my family in the records. I was sure they were listed (at least I believed they were) and it wasn't until I checked several alternate spellings of the name that I found it.

Someone else probably would have given up after a few minutes—and rightfully so.

Census records before 1900 are filed geographically, so you must know the address of the individual or family in order to find the records. Often the use of a city directory (see page 68) is of help in this case. For the 1880 and 1900 censuses, there is a name index. This index is not alphabetical, however, but is filed by what is known as the Soundex System. In this system, the names are filed by "sound"—the phonetic sound to be exact. This is of great help since it avoids most problems of misspellings or alternate spellings.

Many local libraries have different parts of the federal census, and it would be worthwhile to check the nearest large public library to see what it might have. In addition, as we mentioned before, there are branches of the National Archives around the country. The following is a list of those branches:

The Regional Archives of the National Archives and Areas Served

NEW ENGLAND REGION:

380 Trapelo Rd
Waltham, MA 02154
617-647-8100

Connecticut, Maine, Massachusetts, New Hampshire, Rhode Island and Vermont

NORTHEAST REGION:

201 Varick St
New York, NY 10014
212-337-1300

New Jersey, New York, Puerto Rico, and the Virgin Islands

MID-ATLANTIC REGION:

Ninth and Market Sts, Room 1350
Philadelphia, PA 19107
215-597-3000

Delaware, Pennsylvania, Maryland, Virginia and West Virginia

SOUTHEAST REGION:

1557 St. Joseph Ave
East Point, GA 30344
404-763-7477

Alabama, Georgia, Florida, Kentucky, Mississippi, North Carolina, South Carolina and Tennessee

GREAT LAKES REGION:
7358 South Pulaski Rd
Chicago, IL 60629
312-581-7816
Illinois, Indiana, Michigan, Minnesota, Ohio and Wisconsin

CENTRAL PLAINS REGION:
2312 East Bannister Rd
Kansas City, MO 64131
816-926-6272
Iowa, Kansas, Missouri and Nebraska

SOUTHWEST REGION:
501 West Felix St
P.O. Box 6216
Fort Worth, TX 76115
817-334-5525
Arkansas, Louisiana, New Mexico, Oklahoma and Texas

ROCKY MOUNTAIN REGION:
Building 48
Denver Federal Ct
P.O. Box 25307
Denver, CO 80225
303-236-0817
Colorado, Montana, North Dakota, South Dakota, Utah and Wyoming

PACIFIC SOUTHWEST REGION:
24000 Avila Rd
P.O. Box 6719
Laguna Niguel, CA 92607
714-643-4241
Arizona; the southern California counties of Imperial, Inyo, Kern, Los Angeles, Orange, Riverside, San Bernardino, San Diego, San Luis Obispo, Santa Barbara and Ventura; and Nevada's Clark County

PACIFIC SIERRA REGION:
1000 Commodore Dr
San Bruno, CA 94066
415-876-9009
Northern California, Hawaii, Nevada except Clark County and the Pacific Ocean area

PACIFIC NORTHWEST REGION:

6125 Sand Point Way, NE
Seattle, WA 98115
206-526-6507

Idaho, Oregon and Washington

ALASKA REGION:

654 West Third Ave
Anchorage, AK 99501
907-271-2441

Alaska

You should also send to the National Archives for their package of information on genealogical records. This material is free. A letter to one of the branches listed here or to the National Archives, Washington, D.C. 20408, asking for this information is all you need.

A final note must be mentioned regarding the accuracy of the census records, as well as all public records: You cannot be sure that anything is 100 percent accurate. There is always room for human error, and if you find two conflicting pieces of information, you must use your own judgment as to what is true.

The U.S. Department of Commerce, Bureau of the Census, has issued a booklet called "Age Search Information," which is an invaluable sourcebook for every family historian. Don't be misled by the title; this publication is far more than a guide to getting birth information.

In simple yet detailed form, it explains how to get census records, citizenship records and military records, and gives information sources for local birth, marriage and death records. The booklet also discusses resources at the Library of Congress, the Daughters of the American Revolution, the Mormon Church, state census records and adoption records. There is also a section on "missing persons."

The publication provides the addresses of the state agencies that can give you birth and death records. It also gives the addresses of the National Archives branches throughout the country as well as dozens of other addresses to write to for genealogical information.

This booklet is a must for every family historian. The current price is $1.75, and it can be obtained from

Superintendent of Documents
U.S. Government Printing Office
Washington, D.C. 20402

Send for this publication. It is well worth the investment.

Census Records (State)

In addition to the federal census, states have also taken censuses, often during years when the federal government did not. Check to see whether the states you are interested in have census records. You might inquire at your public library, state libraries and genealogy libraries of local historical societies for this information.

To give one example, there was a 1905, 1915 and 1925 census for New York. 1915 and 1925 are available at the State Archives, Albany, New York 12230. All three are available from the respective county clerks throughout New York State.

> A clan and a family resemble a heap of stones: one stone taken out of it and the whole totters.
>
> Genesis Rabbah

Tips on Dealing with Government Agencies

1) Many people think that the government will find their genealogical questions inappropriate. Not true. Genealogy is a business for many governmental agencies. If they have information you want, and they can provide you with it, they will. And they'll charge a fee for it. So don't hesitate.
2) Don't think that you have no right to the information you are requesting. Although there are certainly lots of restrictions on access to information, there is also lots of information available. The Freedom of Information Act is only one of many pieces of legislation that protects "the right to know" in the U.S.
3) Don't take no for an answer. When you ask for a document from a government agency, it is often by filling out a form and mailing it in. You wait days, weeks or months, and then you get a reply. Sometimes you hit pay dirt; sometimes they say "we can't find it." Don't believe them. I have heard many stories and have had my own experience back this up: What one clerk will not find, the next clerk will. (Does this mean that when you get a "no" answer you should repeat your efforts? It's up to you.)
4) Don't be intimidated by the forms you have to fill out. Do the best you can. If you didn't do it right, they'll tell you (usually with another form letter). Some of the forms are pretty scary. Just go line-by-line and you'll probably get it right.

City Directories

A city directory looks very much like a phone book and serves much the same purpose—which is to identify people by name and address. City directories have been published in hundreds of cities and towns, large and small, since the 1800s. Some cities still publish these directories, although New York City stopped in the 1930s. If a city of interest to you has ever published city directories, a collection of them is probably in the public library of that city.

Of what use is a directory? Suppose you know that your great-great-grandfather came to New York City in the 1880s but you know little more about him. If you check the directories of New York City for that time period, you might find him listed. The listing might include his occupation (it usually does), and sometimes the directories even include a wife's name in parentheses next to the listed name. You will also learn his address. If you begin to check the directories by year for this period, you can determine what year he is first listed and what year he stops being listed. These are clues to the year he arrived in the city (and perhaps the country) as well as when he died (although he simply might have moved).

A city directory can also be useful in connection with census research. For most census records you must know the address of the person. Since phone books are relatively recent publications, a city directory is an excellent source of old addresses.

> No father should give his son the name of a wicked man.
>
> RASHI

Synagogue Records

There is no systematic way of searching out synagogue records nor is there any guarantee that they exist for the particular location or time period that you want. Nevertheless, you should keep in mind that synagogues have generally kept records of different kinds, and it might be worth your while, if you know which U.S. synagogues your ancestors joined, to investigate the possibility that the synagogue still exists, or that the records do.

Synagogues kept various kinds of records; it varies from place to place. Often birth, marriage and death records were kept as well as membership records. Inquire whether or not the synagogue still exists.

If it does not, a local investigation might turn up the location of the synagogue's records.

According to the late Rabbi Malcolm H. Stern, genealogist for the American Jewish Archives, synagogues have been known to keep four types of records:

1) Minute books of congregational meetings (which Rabbi Stern says have often been lost);
2) Account books that contained lists of membership (many of which have also been lost);
3) Congregational histories and communal histories, which are often privately published and are available from the synagogues themselves as well as from large Jewish libraries;
4) Vital records, which include birth and circumcision records, Bar Mitzvah records, marriage records and death records.

Availability of all of these records varies from synagogue to synagogue and at this point there is no general accounting of these records.

Both the American Jewish Archives and the American Jewish Historical Society have collections of synagogue records. Their addresses can be found elsewhere in this book. It would be worthwhile to write to both of these organizations in an attempt to locate old U.S. synagogue records.

If an old synagogue to which your family belonged is still functioning, writing or visiting might prove worthwhile. Be aware, however, that the average synagogue is not staffed to search through records. They might be very hesitant to do a search for you—or even to let you search the records. There is no rule of thumb or formula for success here.

> Every man has three names: one his father and mother gave him, one others call him, and one he acquires himself.
>
> ECCLESIASTES R., 7:1–3

THE NATIONAL ARCHIVES

Although we discuss the National Archives (Washington, D.C. 20408) in various other parts of this book, it would be useful to mention it here in a general context. The National Archives has millions of records in its collections. Among those of particular genealogical interest are:

Census schedules 1790 to 1920
Passenger arrival lists
U.S. military records:
- Revolutionary War
- War of 1812
- Indian wars and related wars
- Mexican War
- Civil War
- Spanish-American War
- Philippine Insurrection
- Burial records of soldiers
- Veterans' benefits records
- Pension records

Land records
Passport applications

A complete description of these and other records can be found in the "Guide to Genealogical Research in the National Archives," available from the U.S. Government Printing Office, Washington, D.C. 20402, or from their local offices. The current price is $25.00 for the softcover edition. You can also send to the National Archives itself for their "free pamphlets concerning genealogical records."

The records of the National Archives can prove invaluable, particularly if your family has been in the U.S. for several generations.

What If You Were Adopted?

The subject of an adopted child's search for his or her natural parents is a controversial one. Complex feelings exist on the part of all those concerned: the adopted child, the adoptive parents, the natural parents, and the people who keep the records.

A full discussion of the issue would not be possible or appropriate here. However, the subject of an adopted child's search for natural parents and the subject of genealogy have an obvious relationship. It is certainly an issue that must be continuously explored rather than avoided or feared. An observation of mine may be appropriate here: *Each and every* time I have lectured on the subject of Jewish genealogy to children or teenagers a question is raised by someone in the audience regarding this issue. The question is usually a simple one: "How can someone who is adopted trace their family?" I have lectured to dozens of young groups and the question never fails to be raised, sometimes in front of the whole group and sometimes privately afterward by a young person who is struggling with this problem.

My response is always the same. I begin by noting that it is an important and deeply personal issue. I then add that the decision to search for one's natural parents is a serious one and that much thought must go into the decision in order to be considerate to everyone involved. I then mention that there are organizations that help in the process of searching for one's natural parents (as well as aid in the emotional issues that spring from this). My concluding comment directed at the young questioner, who most probably is an adopted child considering such a search, is this: Jewish genealogy and family history offer a special and unique opportunity for someone who is adopted. If you were adopted I would strongly suggest that you research the family history of your adoptive parents. Just as they adopted you as their child, you can adopt their history as your own history. This is one powerful way for you to tie the link even more strongly between you and your parents—people who have loved you very much.

If you are an adopted child, there is an organization that can help you in your search for your natural parents—if you decide to make that search. It is:

ALMA
850 Seventh Ave
New York, NY 10033
212-581-1568

ALMA (Adoptees' Liberty Movement Association) publishes a newsletter and a handbook (for members) called *Handbook for the Search*.

An excellent book exploring the entire subject of adopted children searching for their natural parents is *Lost & Found: The Adoption Experience* by Betty Jean Lifton, HarperCollins Publishing, New York, 1988. This book is worthwhile reading for all individuals involved in "the adoption experience." Also included in the book is a long list of "Adoptee Search Groups" around the country. This is the best and most moving book on this difficult subject that I have seen.

> To honor parents is more important even than to honor God.
>
> SIMEON B. YOHAI, TALMUD J, PEAH, 1.1

Canadian Research

The first step in beginning research on Canadian genealogy and family history is to obtain a booklet called *Tracing Your Ancestors in Canada*. It is available from the National Archives of Canada, 395 Wellington Street, Ottawa, Ontario K1A 0N3. This guide will give you an overview of Canadian sources and will describe what Canada has available to the researcher. In many cases the kinds of resources that I have described for the U.S. are also available—in different format, years and so on—in Canada.

For example, Canada has census records; birth, marriage and death records; land records; military records; immigration records (including some passengers lists); and naturalization (citizenship) records.

In many cases there are sources in Canada equivalent to those in the U.S., particularly passenger arrival records. There are three types of landing records maintained by the Canadian Government: records of arrival in Canada prior to 1900; records of arrival from 1900 to 1921; and records from 1921 to the present.

Arrival records prior to 1900. Records of ship arrivals at Quebec City from 1865 and Halifax from 1881 are kept by the Archives branch in Ottawa. You must know the name of the passenger, year and month of arrival and the port into which the immigrant came. Send your inquiries to:

Archives Branch
National Archives of Canada
395 Wellington St
Ottawa, Ontario, K1A 0N3

Arrivals from 1900 to 1921. Passenger lists (manifests) have been maintained for this period, but are on microfilm in chronological order. There is no index, which means that you must have fairly precise information concerning any individual in order to locate his or her records. Write to the address above for further information on how to obtain these records.

Arrivals from 1921. These records are the easiest of the three to obtain since they are filed alphabetically. If you have the correct spelling as it was upon arrival, the records can usually be located. Of course if you can provide additional information it will be that much easier for the Archives staff to be of help. Again, the Archives branch mentioned above should be contacted for more information.

Although this is not an exhaustive list of Jewish sources in Canada, it is a good beginning. Do not think that these places will be able to do research for you, or that they will all know exactly where to send you for your research, but they have the most experience with genealogical inquiries and are good places to start.

Important Canadian Resources

Lawrence Tapper, *Archival Sources for the Study of Canadian Jewry*, National Archives of Canada, 395 Wellington Street, Ottawa, K1A ON3, Canada. (free)

Janine Roy, *Tracing Your Ancestors in Canada* (rev. 1991), National Archives of Canada, 395 Wellington Street, Ottawa, K1A ON3, Canada. (free)

Arthur Kurzweil and Miriam Weiner, *The Encyclopedia of Jewish Genealogy*, Vol. I (Northvale, New Jersey: Jason Aronson, 1991).

> Why did God create one man, Adam, rather than creating the whole human race together? It was to show that if anyone causes a single soul to perish, it is as though he caused a whole world to perish; and if anyone saves a single soul, it is as if he had saved a whole world.
>
> MISHNAH, SANHEDRIN 4:5

CARDINAL RULES WHEN DEALING WITH LIBRARIES, ARCHIVES AND OTHER INSTITUTIONS

Throughout this book you will learn about libraries, archives and other institutions that will be of interest when pursuing your Jewish family history. The following are basic principles to keep in mind when making contact with them.

- Most historical institutions are understaffed and the employees are overworked and underpaid. Be friendly and polite when making your inquiry, and be appreciative when receiving your answer.
- *Do not* expect the staff members of historical institutions to do research for you (unless they have a system whereby they charge by the hour for such a service). Librarians and archivists can and should help you to locate material, but just so that *you* can then do the research. They can be of general assistance in

helping you to find material on your subject, but they cannot read the material with you or for you.

- Much of the material of use to you in Jewish research is *not* in English. Staff members of Jewish historical institutions *cannot* translate for you. Translation is very time-consuming. Bring someone along who can translate for you.
- The questions you are about to ask a librarian might be brand-new for you but have probably been asked a thousand times by a thousand others. Be patient with the librarian who is not patient with you. On the other hand, keep in mind that the staff of the library is there for you. Don't dominate their time, but use their skills. Most of all, appreciate their help.
- When you write to an institution for information, always include a self-addressed stamped envelope. Not only is it the correct thing to do, but also, since most people do not do this, you will be appreciated by the receiver.
- Most important, be prepared with an intelligent question. Of course, there is no such thing as a stupid question; it is stupid only if you do not ask. But librarians are always being confronted by people who have not done their own homework and think that the librarian should do it for them. For example, *do not* enter a Jewish library with an interest in researching your family history if you have yet to interview your family for basic information. The more information you can bring with you, the better the librarian will be able to assist you.
- Specifically relating to family history and genealogy, avoid questions such as "I'm doing research on my family from Russia named Schwartz. Can you help me?" If all you know is that your family is from Russia and their name was Schwartz, you have not done your homework.
- Finally, most Jewish institutions offer their resources for free, but that does not mean that you are without a responsibility to that institution. Consider joining the organization if membership is offered. If not, a donation would be nice.

Tips on Dealing with Librarians

1) Most librarians are human. Some are saints. Others, impossible. (I have a Masters in Library Science so I claim some right

to make these generalizations.) I've met some librarians who were creative, enthusiastic and wonderful. I've met others who should switch careers. Again, most librarians are human, just like you and me.

2) Don't ask a librarian a question without doing a little homework. If you give the impression that you know what you are doing, it helps the librarian to be responsive. If you haven't even done the smallest amount of preparation, the librarian will have less respect for you or will take you less seriously. Some people don't even formulate their questions until they walk up to a librarian. Don't do this. Be prepared.
3) Most libraries have several librarians. Try to figure out who is who. If you find a nice one, try to go back to that same person before settling on another one. Some librarians like genealogists; others don't. Keep alert to this.
4) Don't tell the librarian your whole family history. As fascinating as your family is to you, others often could not care less. Just get to the point with your questions.
5) If you don't think a librarian is serving you well, I suggest that you complain to the administration of the library. Just make sure you have a good case.

Publishing Your Family History

There will probably come a time when you will want to publish your research findings for the benefit of the other members of your family who want a copy of what you have discovered. Hundreds of Jewish family histories have been privately printed and range from several typed pages that have been photocopied and stapled to hardcover books of several hundred pages.

There are many things to consider when thinking about printing your family history. All considerations must include the price of production of course. If you have only a few pages of information, you can easily type them and get them offset rather cheaply. If you want to reproduce photographs, you can have them offset too. The more ambitious you are, the more it will cost. If you want to have a small book printed, the cost could be considerable. A conversation with a good printer can answer most of your questions.

I would suggest that you go to a large public library or any of the major Jewish libraries I have discussed in this book (especially YIVO and the Leo Baeck Institute). They will have many samples of Jewish family histories for you to examine, from inexpensive products to fancy volumes. Not only can you get an idea of what to aim for with your own project, but you can also see the various formats designed to record the information you have gathered. Don't decide against publishing a family history just because you cannot produce a fancy one. Even the most modest family history will become a cherished item for your family members.

> Rav Judah has said in the name of Rav: Ezra did not leave Babylon to go up to Eretz Yisrael until he had written his own genealogy.
>
> BABA BATHRA, 15A

4

Jewish Genealogy: The Basic Sources

INTRODUCTION: HOW IS JEWISH GENEALOGY DIFFERENT FROM ALL OTHER GENEALOGY?

Genealogy has always been an important topic within Jewish tradition. We find genealogy in the very first chapters in the Bible itself, and genealogy can be seen as playing a part in the lives of Jews from ancient times to the present.

In the Bible we see many aspects of genealogy. One of the Torah portions read in the synagogue is even called Toledot, the Hebrew word for genealogy. In Genesis, Chapter 10, one can find the "Table of Nations," appearing to constitute the basic foundations of the human family tree.

This chapter is to be found directly after the story of the Flood. The chapter lists, in detail, the descendants of the three sons of Noah. Each of the descendants represents not only an individual but also the founder of a future nation, hence the term "Table of Nations." What this succeeds in doing is to explain the sources of nearly every nation known to the region whose story is told throughout the Bible. As the many books of the Bible unfold and nations, tribes and individuals appear, most of them find their source back in Chapter 10 of Genesis.

As you can see from the genealogical chart, the following list of names appears as descendants of the three sons of Noah. Based on early beliefs as well as recent Biblical scholarship, the list indicates which groups and countries each name represents:

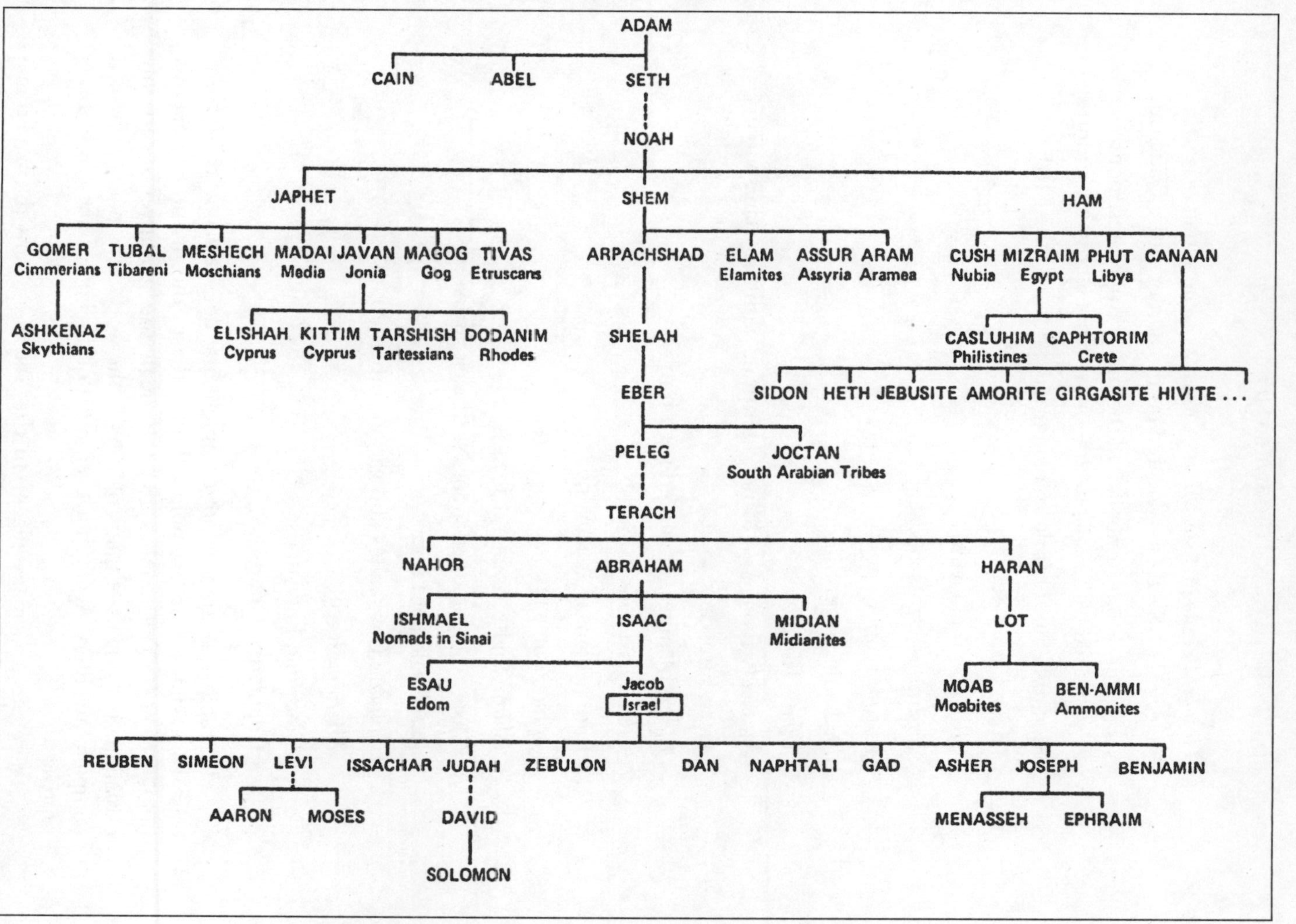

Biblical genealogy including the Table of Nations.

Gomer: People of Asia Minor known as Cimmerians

Magog: The Scythians, located on the border of the Caucasus

Ashkenaz: From Armenia and the upper Euphrates (not to be confused with Ashkenazim—Jews from Germanic countries)

Madai: People of Indo-Iranian origin known as the Medes

Javan: From Greece

Elishah: From Cyprus

Tarshitth: Tartessians

Kittim: From Cyprus

Dodanim: From Rhodes

Tubal: Tibareni

Meshech: From Asia Minor, identified with Assyrian sources

Tiras: Etruscans

Elam: Elamites, identified with Iran

Ashur: Assyrians

Lud: Lydians of Asia Minor

Aram: Arameans

Joktan: South Arabian tribes

Cush: Ancient kingdom of Northeast Africa

Put: Region of Libya

Canaan: Canaanites and various other groups

Mizraim: Egypt

Casluhim: Philistines

Caphtorim: Crete

The Table of Nations is not complete, nor does it claim to be. Genesis 10:5 states, for example, "From these the maritime nations branched out." This implies that although the narrative is certainly explaining the origins of many nations of the world, it is not supplying a complete inventory. Again, however, most of the known ancient world is represented.

There are also many places in the Talmud where the traditional Jewish interest in the subject of genealogy can be found. For example, the three groups of Jews, known individually as Kohen, Levi and Yisroel, are of concern in the Talmud, and we continue these designations to this day. It is refreshing, by the way, to find the rabbis of the Talmud teach, "A learned bastard takes precedence over an uneducated high priest." (Hor. 3:8)

There are many sources and research methods unique to Jewish genealogy. For example:

- Jewish names are traditionally two-generation names. My Hebrew name is Avraham Abba ben (son of) Chaim Shaul (my father).
- In Europe, Jewish records were kept separately from others.
- Most Jewish last names are distinctively Jewish.
- The Holocaust, only 50 years ago, profoundly affected most Jewish families in the world. Ironically, extensive Nazi and Holocaust records are also mostly of Jewish families.
- There are unique Jewish documents, such as Ketubot (marriage contracts), mohel books, Memorial (Yizkor) Books and haskamot (approbations).
- Rabbis usually maintained an extensive family tree, known as a "yichus brief."

Until now in this book, I have discussed sources of interest to genealogists from all family backgrounds. I will begin now to describe the extensive, highly useful sources of specific interest to the Jewish genealogist.

> The search for roots, even in the simplest genealogical sense, is likely to be a meaningful experience on both the personal and religious levels.
>
> ADIN STEINSALTZ

CONTEMPORARY BOOKS AND PUBLICATIONS

The Jewish genealogist's bookshelf can fill up quite rapidly. Family historians are interested not only in names and dates but in background information: What was life like in the towns where my great great grandparents came from? How did they get to those towns? Where did they live before? The books and publications that offer pieces of the picture add up quickly. You could fill up your mailbox with newsletters and journals, and fill your shelves with books when the genealogy bug bites.

There are, however, a handful of sources that I think are essentials, either to own, or to have access to. Don't underestimate their value.

AVOTAYNU: THE INTERNATIONAL REVIEW OF JEWISH GENEALOGY

The single most significant development in the field of Jewish genealogy over the past decade has been the appearance of *Avotaynu*. *Avotaynu* is both a quarterly publication to which one subscribes (*Avotaynu: The International Review of Jewish Genealogy*), as well as a publisher of books, monographs and microforms. Its founders, Gary Mokotoff and Sallyann Amdur Sack, are important trailblazers; their work has had an impact on all of us who are involved with Jewish genealogy.

Avotaynu (it means "our ancestors"), the publication, is essential for all Jewish genealogists. You *must* subscribe to it. Back issues are also available. *Avotaynu* is so important that I have reproduced a complete index of all of the back issues for the first eight volumes. This index alone illustrates the huge amount of information now available to Jewish family historians.

Avotaynu's book publishing program is getting off to a wonderful start. Look carefully at all of the resources available from *Avotaynu*, and keep your eye on them in the future. *Avotaynu* has become *the* cutting edge in the genealogy world.

Avotaynu, Inc.
P.O. Box 900
Teaneck, NJ 07066

Index to the First Eight Volumes of Avotaynu

Below is an index to articles that have appeared in the first eight volumes (1985–1992) of *Avotaynu*. Only major articles are shown. Not shown is the U.S. Update column, which is a digest of articles that appeared in publications of the Jewish Genealogical Societies. The articles in Volume III, Number 4 and many in Volumes IV–VIII, Number 4, were human interest features and, therefore, are not part of the index. Each entry shows a description of the article followed by the Volume/Number/Page. Back issues can be purchased for $7 ($8 outside U.S. and Canada) from *Avotaynu*; the complete set of 29 issues is $158. Note: Most earlier back issues are available in photocopy version only.

Algeria

Brochures on colonization of Algeria VIII/3/51
Civil records of Algeria and Morocco VI/1/29
Algerian Jews VIII/3/52
Jewish community in the Touat Oases VII/4/60

Argentina

Argentina, the Other Golden Land V/2/16
Book Review: *Jewish Immigration to Argentina* VII/2/34
History of the Jews of Argentina II/3/21
Sources of Vital Statistic Records III/3/18

Australia

Australian Jewish Historical Society I/1/11
Demography of Australian Jews in 1986 census IV/2/24
First governor Arthur Phillip's Jewish origins VII/1/24
History of the Jews of Australia I/1/03
Jewish genealogical societies founded VII/4/58
Activities of Australian JGS VIII/4/53
Migration of Belgian Holocaust survivors III/1/21
Origin of Australian Jewry VI/2/19
Comments on "Origin of Australian Jewry" article VI/3/21

Belarus (also see USSR/Russia—General)

Byelorussian archival holdings VI/3/10
Minsk archives will research for $1,000 VII/3/46
Inquiries made at Minsk archives VI/3/39
Location of Vitebsk records VII/2/39

Belgium

Accounting of Belgian Jews after Holocaust IV/2/17
Antwerp as haven for Jews after Spanish Inquisition VII/2/23
Antwerp as a transit point from Eastern Europe to U.S. I/2/08
Antwerp between the Wars III/2/20
Families who have lived in one place for generations V/1/15
Holocaust survivors of Belgium II/1/23
Status of Jewish genealogy in Belgium I/1/11
The Jews of Antwerp II/2/14

Marranos of Antwerp VIII/2/36
New Belgian books on the Holocaust VI/2/25
Jews Who Contributed to the Belgian State Since Its Independence VI/3/20

Book Reviews

Address book for Germanic Genealogy VIII/3/62
Ancestry's Red Book VIII/3/63
Archival Sources for Canadian Jewry IV/2/25
The Archives VIII/2/54
Australian genealogy books in print III/3/31
A Biographical Dictionary of Canadian Jewry, 1909–1914 VIII/4/61
Bukharian Jews VIII/4/62
Dictionary of Surnames—some comments VI/2/26
Do People Grow on Family Trees? VIII/3/62
Edge of the Diaspora VI/4/57
Encyclopedia of Jewish Genealogy VII/1/34
Family Diseases: Are You At Risk? V/3/34
First American Jewish Families VIII/2/53
Following the Paper Trail: A Multilingual Translation Guide VIII/3/63
Gedenkbuch VII/3/36
Genealogica Hebraica: Jews of Portugal and Gibraltar VI/4/58
Genealogical Resources in the New York Metropolitan Area V/1/29
The Genealogist's Address Book VIII/4/62
Guide to Jewish Italy VIII/1/55
Handbook for Archival Research in the USSR V/4/10
In Search of Your European Roots II/1/32
Jewish Community of Frankfurt V/3/34
Jewish Genealogy Beginner's Guide VII/4/66
Jewish Immigration to Argentina VII/2/34
Jewish Personal Names: Their Origin, Derivation and Diminutive Forms VIII/3/61
Comments on *Jewish Personal Names* review VIII/4/66
The Jews in Poland and Russia—Biographical Essay III/1/38
Jews of Posen in 1834 and 1835 IV/2/26
Jews of Toronto: A History to 1937 III/2/32
From King David to Baron David VI/2/23
The Library VI/4/58
The Library of Congress VI/3/32

Lithuanian Jewish Communities VII/3/36
The Lord's Jews VIII/2/52
Resources for Jewish Genealogy in the New York area II/2/28
Russia Gathers Her Jews IV/3/17
The Sephardic Journey: 1492–1992 VIII/3/63
State Census Records VIII/4/62
The Source I/1/16
Their Father's House VI/3/33
The Unbroken Chain VI/1/37
Where Once We Walked VII/1/33

BRAZIL

Additional books by Egon and Frieda Wolff VII/3/28
Books on Jewish tombstone inscriptions in Brazilian cemeteries IV/3/19
Crypto Jews in the State of Pará VI/1/29
Dicionario Biografico—1500–1808 V/3/23
Dicionario Biografico—Volume 4 VII/4/58
Famous Jewish Brazilian families VI/4/50
History of the Jews of Brazil IV/3/19
Jews, Judaizers and their slaves VII/1/20
Sources of genealogical records VI/3/20
Memorial to two Jews buried in Vassouras VIII/4/53

CANADA

Book planned: *Archival Sources for the Study of Canadian Jewry* III/2/34
Book Review: *Archival Sources for Canadian Jewry* IV/2/25
Book Review: *Jews of Toronto: A History to 1937* III/2/32
Cemeteries in Quebec and Maritime Provinces computerized VIII/3/50
1901 Federal census to be available soon VIII/4/54
Dun & Bradstreet records V/1/15
History of emigration from France IV/1/20
Jewish Public Library of Montreal II/2/14
Jewish genealogical resources in Canada VIII/4/27
Immigration records at Archives of the Canadian Jewish Congress II/3/12
Inventorying Jewish cemeteries VI/3/20
Jewish genealogical research in Canada IV/3/4

Jews of Toronto	I/2/09
Jews of Toronto	V/3/24
Jewish archives of Toronto	VIII/3/50
JIAS inventories at Canadian Jewish Congress	III/2/16
JIAS records—Toronto	II/3/15
Some Montreal Jewish holdings	VIII/3/50
Plan to document cemeteries of Ontario	VII/2/24
Planned compilations	VI/4/51
Record books of Park Memorial Chapel	VII/4/58
Sources for early Jewish-Canadian history	VII/2/23
Toronto's Roseland Cemetery burials documented	VII/4/58
United Restitution Organization (URO)	V/3/24
United Restitution Organization finding aid available	VI/1/25
Work of Jewish Genealogical Society in Montreal	I/1/12

CARIBBEAN

A visit to St. Eustatius	II/2/31
Jews in the Islands of the French West Indies	V/4/13

CYPRUS

Documenting Cypriot Jews	V/2/26

CZECHOSLOVAKIA

Austro-Hungarian military records available	VI/1/41
History of record keeping in Bohemia	VII/3/22
Complete catalogue of records for the Jewish communities of Bohemia and Moravia, excluding that of Prague	VII/3/20
Genealogical research in Czechoslovakia: an update	VI/3/8
Important address for Czechoslovakian research	V/4/05
Jewish genealogical research in Czechoslovakia	IV/1/03
Jewish genealogical research in Slovakia	VII/1/8
News for Czechoslovakia	VI/1/41

DENMARK

The origins and history of Danish Jewry	VIII/1/35

ENGLAND

An American perspective on London research	II/3/17
Availability of papers given at International Seminar	IV/1/20

Bevis Marks Records Part 4 VII/2/25
Bibliography used at family history workshop II/2/16
Book available about Jews arriving in Birmingham 1933–1945 IV/3/20
Status of Chief Rabbi's records VI/2/26
More on status of Chief Rabbi's records VI/3/20
Describes status of Chief Rabbi's records VI/3/38
Describes resources available from Court of the Chief Rabbi VIII/2/58
Guide to British Census Records II/2/21
Census of 1891 released VIII/2/36
Research using the 1891 census VIII/2/42
History of preservation of documents in Office of the Chief Rabbi of UK VII/1/17
How to obtain vital statistic records from the United Kingdom II/1/23
Hyamson and Colyer-Fergusson collections VII/1/15
Comment on Hyamson and Colyer-Fergusson collection article VII/2/25
Locates Hyamson and Colyer-Fergusson collections VII/3/46
More on the Colyer-Fergusson collection VIII/2/28
Immigration records in London II/3/16
Jewish cemeteries in London II/3/23
Jewish Genealogical Society of Great Britain founded VIII/2/36
First meeting of JGS of Great Britain VIII/3/50
Jewish yearbook of 1896 I/2/09
Jews of Birmingham, work of the Jewish Historical Society I/1/13
Resources at Jews College VIII/3/50
Listing of London Jewish cemeteries available V/2/17
London International Seminar—Sources of British Records III/3/04
Older London burial records and sites VII/3/24
Maritime museum wants oral histories and records V/1/15
Conference on Jewish Patterns of Migrations planned in England for June 1993 VIII/4/65
Organizational division of British Jewry VII/2/24
Pamphlets about Jewish communities in Britain I/1/12
Poor Jews Temporary Shelter registers (1896–1914) VII/4/58
Proceedings of Second International Seminar available V/2/17

Recent acquisitions at the Museum of the Jewish East End	III/2/20
The value of wills to the genealogist	III/1/20

Ethiopia

Jewish Life in Ethiopia and Kenya	V/2/13

Europe—General

Book Review: *In Search of Your European Roots*	II/1/32
In pursuit of Zionist ancestors	VII/1/13
Survey of Jewish sites in Europe planned	VII/2/14
Synagogue art research in Europe	VII/2/11

France

How to trace your Alsatian roots	I/2/28
Colloquium of the JHS of Alsace-Lorraine	VI/3/23
An index to the 1784 census of the Jews of Alsace	VIII/3/21
Books of genealogical significance	VIII/4/54
Census of Jews of Besancon	VII/1/27
Sources in Bordeaux-Bayonne area	IV/3/20
Dictionary of Bordelais Jewry	IV/3/20
Name adoptions from Colmar	VII/4/59
Family genealogies, California Jews	III/1/24
Jews of Fontainebleau, Arles and Denmark	V/1/16
Books on fate of French Jews during Holocaust	IV/3/18
How to trace your French roots—regional analysis	IV/1/22
Microfilms about Jews of Lorraine at LDS Library	VIII/4/55
Luneville, book to be published	V/2/27
Jews of Lyon	VII/1/27
Jews of Marseille	VII/4/60
Holdings of Municipal Archives in Marseille	VIII/2/37
Jews in Metz before 1792	II/3/25
Jews of Metz	II/2/16
My ancestors from Metz	IV/2/22
Marriage contracts of Moselle	V/4/23
Sources for Jewish genealogy in Moselle region	IV/1/21
Jews of Nice	VI/1/30
Jews of Paris—a bibliographic history	II/2/18
Jewish sections and cemeteries in Paris during 19th century	II/3/24
Judeo-Portuguese communities in southwest France	VIII/1/28

Parisian libraries holding genealogical material VI/1/30
Departmental archive at Seine-et-Marne III/2/22
Municipal archives in Strasbourg III/2/23
Jews of Sultz in the 17th century IV/2/21
Papal Jews, Jews of North Africa, Metz II/1/26
Sources from Provence-Cote d'Azur VII/3/29
Sources in Paris, Jews of Metz I/2/11
List of surnames adopted in 1808 VIII/3/51

GALICIA

A research trip to Galicia II/3/19
About Galicia II/3/18
Demographic records of Galicia, 1772–1919 VIII/2/7
Location of Western Galicia vital statistic records VII/2/14
More on location of Galician records VII/3/43
Sources of information about Galicia V/3/22
The Kollel Galicia Archive (in Jerusalem) VII/3/23
Vital statistic records for eastern Galicia now in Warsaw archives VIII/2/11
Work continues on *Encyclopedia of Galician Rabbis and Scholars* VIII/4/65

GENERAL

Archival publications (List of Jewish Archives worldwide) I/1/07
Avotaynu to publish gazetteer of Eastern Europe V/3/38
Avotaynu travel file planned II/3/34
Pioneer praises publication (*Avotaynu*) VIII/4/66
Biography of Jewish Genealogy VII/1/22
Cemeteries: information source about the living V/4/22
Comments on *Avotaynu* articles (family and place names) V/1/03
Computers and Genealogy VI/1/11
Computer bulletin boards as a tool for the exchange of data VIII/2/33
A proposed standard in genealogical software systems for identifying Jewish persons with no surnames VIII/1/40
A proposed standard for identifying Jewish months in genealogical data bases VIII/3/64
Suggests alternate codes for Jewish months VIII/4/64

Comments on naming convention VIII/2/56
Concludes a generation equals 24 years VII/3/45
Disputes King-for-a-day legend VI/3/38
Improvements made to Family Finder VI/3/37
Using an independent research service: costly results VIII/4/49
Using an independent research service: FAST works VIII/4/50
Gazetteer of Eastern Europe nearing completion VI/4/13
Genealogical networking VI/4/16
Genealogical research by mail II/1/17
Genealogy software: Relativity VII/3/38
Genealogy software: Personal Dorot VII/3/39
Genealogy and Electronic Bulletin Boards VI/1/13
Holocaust works V/4/21
Is it really luck? V/2/15
Jewish Genealogical Family Finder used to try to save a life VI/1/14Supp
Jewish Genealogical Family Finder marks tenth anniversary VIII/1/42
Plans for Jewish Genealogical People Finder VII/3/3
Jewish Genealogical People Finder acquires 50,000 entries VIII/1/50
JGPF adds new capabilities VIII/3/59
Jewish genealogical societies worldwide VII/1/31
Jewish Soundex-A revised format II/1/19
Jewish Travel Guide 1991 VII/3/47
Landslayt groups as a complement to Jewish genealogical societies VI/4/14
Microfiche now available through *Avotaynu* VII/4/57
No one can do my research as I can! VI/3/6
Our 1,048,576 ancestors IV/1/37
Proposal for a Jewish Soundex code I/1/05
Proposed Standard Numbering System for Individuals, Generations and Charts in Jewish Genealogy VI/3/3
More books on Rabbinic research VII/4/67
Sources for study of the urban Jewish immigrant experience VII/4/55
Suggestions if planning to visit European Jewish cemeteries II/2/20
Tracing Jewish ancestors—a pioneer looks back V/3/03
UN War Crimes Files are genealogical source V/4/23

WOWW wins awards VIII/2/59
WOWW is wow! VIII/3/66

GERMANY

Additional German resources given VIII/2/55
Adoption of family names in Prussia (1804) I/2/23
Availability of German maps circa 1888 IV/2/17
Availability of German-Jewish Records V/2/12
U.S. National Archives material on Jews from Bavaria and Bremen VII/3/16
Book Review: *Jewish Community of Frankfurt* V/3/34
Book Review: *Jews of Posen in 1834 and 1835* IV/2/26
Books and periodicals from Germany VIII/3/35
Mormons have microfilmed 1938 German-Jewish census VIII/3/65
Comparing most common German-Jewish surnames with their American counterparts VIII/1/30
Condition of German Jewish cemeteries V/1/34
East German Jewish archive to open by 1994 V/3/38
East German genealogical records VIII/1/32
More Jewish holdings in East German archives VIII/2/13
German cemeteries documented VI/2/39
German-Jewish Records in the Mormon library VI/3/4
Hamburg records aid genealogists VI/2/30
Lesser known records in the Hamburg State Archives VII/3/6
History of personal records of Jews in Germany VII/2/9
Translating Judeo-German VIII/3/28
Jewish genealogical research in the German Democratic Republic VI/2/6
More on condition of German Jewish cemeteries V/2/26
Gedenkbuch, list of 130,000 German Jews persecuted by Nazis III/1/24
Provides *Gedenkbuch* information VII/3/46
German-Jewish periodicals: a genealogical resource V/3/20
German-Jewish Records at the Genealogical Society of Utah III/1/03
Jewish records in East Germany VI/1/3
Jews of Baden-Württemberg VII/1/28
Jews of Blomberg V/4/15
Jews of Gleiwitz III/3/21

Jewish records held in Leipzig Archives VII/4/28
Jewish Community Office in Leipzig has many valuable records VIII/1/34
Leipzig office has 1936 census (of Jews) VIII/2/55
Plea to index Weissensee Cemetery VI/1/29
Twenty miles of Prussia archives VIII/1/33
The Sephardim of the Altona Cemetery VIII/1/14
Wedding records in Berlin 1723–1813 IV/2/21

GREECE

Bibliography of Greek Jewry VIII/2/40
Greek Jewry VIII/4/56

HOLLAND

Jews of Aalten VII/3/30
Jewish community of Alkmaar VII/2/27
Jewish community of Amersfoort VII/2/26
Amersfoort circumcision register VIII/2/39
Amsterdam sources for Jewish genealogical research VI/3/24
Amsterdam—Jerusalem of the West VII/4/17
Books available from Dutch Jewish genealogical society VII/3/29
Documenting the cemetery of Scheveningseweg VI/1/30
Dutch publications of genealogical interest VI/3/24
List of Jews of Friesland in 1749 VII/4/61
Genealogical research in the Netherlands V/2/18
Genealogical sources at the Institute for Dutch Jewry in Jerusalem VI/1/31
Jews of Gennep VII/3/30
Emigration lists of Holland-American Line VIII/4/57
Given name changes in Dutch documents VI/2/27
Jewish holdings in Municipal Archives of The Hague VII/3/29
Jewish archival holdings V/1/16
Jewish Historical Museum publishes booklet on Dutch-Jewish history IV/2/20
List of marriages of Portuguese-Jewish community in Amsterdam 1650–1911 IV/3/21
Marriage index 1550–1811 planned V/3/25
Marriages in Mokum reviewed VIII/2/38
Origin of Dutch surnames III/2/30
Record keeping in Holland from 1811 V/2/17

Records of the Jews of Rotterdam VII/4/60
Sources of information in Holland III/3/22
Sources of information in Holland IV/1/23

HUNGARY

Books on Hungarian Jews planned VIII/2/15
Hungarian-Jewish records at the Genealogical Society of Utah IV/1/11
A report on selected Hungarian Jewish cemeteries VIII/3/37
Hungarian group publishes deportation list VII/3/44
Group to document all Hungarian Holocaust victims VIII/1/37
Jewish records in Hungarian archives III/2/13
Plans to document holdings of Hungarian Jewish Archives VI/3/25
Questions Yiddish name for Hungarian towns V/2/27
Professional genealogist in Hungary VIII/2/40
Recommendation for genealogical research firm VIII/4/56
Searching your Hungarian roots III/3/17
Some problems of genealogical research in Hungary VII/3/17
Yiddish names for Hungarian towns IV/3/23

IRAQ

Sources of information V/1/35

IRELAND

LDS Family History Library has Irish-Jewish records VII/3/47

ISRAEL

A Genealogical Trip—Sources of Information III/3/14
Avotaynu contributes WOWW database to Yad Vashem VIII/2/15
Beit Maramaros VII/2/15
Beth Hatefutsoth opens genealogy center I/2/03
Montefiore census of Jews of Palestine in 1839 III/3/22
The 19th-century Montefiore censuses VIII/2/25
Census of 1939 to be indexed VI/2/27
Central Archives for History of Jewish People publishes Polish holdings IV/3/22
Dorot Genealogy Center makes three major announcements IV/3/14
Dorot genealogy center seeks 1,000,000 names IV/2/15

Dorot Center founder gives position paper V/3/13
Dorot Center—a major disappointment VII/2/3
Dorot Center success story VII/4/61
Encyclopedia of Galician Rabbis project needs financial help VI/1/42
Genealogical items at Jewish National and University Library I/2/12
Genealogical sources at the Institute for Dutch Jewry in Jerusalem VI/1/31
Guide to resources in Israel: an update VII/2/4
Central Archives for the History of the Jewish People V/1/18
Operation of Hall of Names (at Yad Vashem) VII/3/43
Israel trip yields additional (genealogical) finds VI/1/9
The Kollel Galicia Archive VII/3/23
Lauds efforts of Batya Untershatz VI/4/62
Translator for Nefus registers found VIII/2/57
Censuses from the Ottoman Empire VII/2/27
More resources in Israel VII/2/6
Two sources for research on British Palestine VIII/3/35
Pinkasim Hakehilot (Encyclopedia of European communities) II/1/26
Recent acquisitions of various Israeli archives II/2/19
Their Father's House: Studies and Sources in Family History VI/3/26
Tombstone inscriptions of cemetery at Mount of Olives I/1/13

ITALY

Guide to Jewish Italy VIII/1/55
Jewish genealogical research in Italy VIII/1/20

LITHUANIA

Association of Lithuanian Jews in Israel III/1/24
Book on Lithuanian Jewish communities delayed VI/1/41
Book on Lithuanian Jewish communities to be published VI/4/62
Dvinsk, genealogy and post-Holocaust questions VIII/4/6
A genealogical trip to Lithuania: the host's perspective VII/1/3
How to plan a family trip to Lithuania VIII/2/12
Jewish Vital Statistic Records in Lithuanian Archives VI/4/4
Letter from Jewish Community of Kaunas V/4/21
Marijampole society VI/3/39

Lithuania reluctant to allow microfilming of Jewish documents VIII/4/3
Numerous photographic essays of Jewish Lithuania planned VIII/2/57
Explains 1795 Revision List VIII/3/66
A trip to Skoudas, Kavarskas and Ukmerge VIII/4/9
Vital records of Lithuanian Jewry found VI/2/3
Missing YIVO records may be found V/2/26

MOROCCO

An analysis of Moroccan-Jewish surnames II/2/10
Books about Spanish Jews of Morocco VII/2/26
Civil records of Algeria and Morocco VI/1/29
Jewish surnames III/2/23
Sources of information VIII/2/37

NEW ZEALAND

Alexander Turnbull Library VIII/2/41
Book on Auckland Jewry VII/1/28
First workshop on genealogy III/2/24
History of Jews of New Zealand I/2/13
Not Strictly Kosher—Pioneer Jews in New Zealand V/3/26
Tracing relatives in New Zealand II/2/20

NORTH AFRICA

Matrimonial register of Tunis V/4/13
North African Jewry V/3/25

POLAND

Breakthrough in access to Polish-Jewish records IV/1/10
Caricatures in Polish vital statistic records VI/1/16
Survey of Jewish cemeteries yields results VIII/4/17
Doing research in the Polish State Archives IV/3/21
A genealogical tour through Poland VI/3/16
Index to Polish-Jewish records at Genealogical Society of Utah II/1/05
Jewish genealogical research in Poland V/2/08
Jewish Historical Institute in Poland V/2/07

Jewish records at the Genealogical Society of Utah II/1/03
Jewish researcher in Poland VI/3/39
Jews in Poland today VI/4/63
List of former Jewish residents of Lodz V/4/15
Polish maps available in the U.S. VIII/1/58
Origin of Russian-Jewish surnames III/2/03
Polish trip for Jewish genealogists planned VI/1/41
Professional genealogists in Poland V/4/04
Program Judaica to document Jewish history VI/3/19
Sephardic migrations into Poland VI/2/14
A 1992 research trip to Poland VIII/4/12
Trip to Poznan: The Poland that was not V/3/16
Update on project to microfilm Jewish records in Poland IV/3/12
Using Prussian Gazetteers to locate Jewish religious and civil records in Poznan VI/2/12
Weiner discusses developments in Poland and Ukraine VIII/3/64

Portugal

Bigamy among 18th century Jews, the Jews of Gibraltar III/1/25
Wants to restore (Lisbon) Portuguese cemetery VIII/4/67
Census of Jews of Gibraltar VII/1/27
Genealogia Hebraica, Portugal e Gibraltar IV/1/24
Volume II of *Genealogia Hebraica* available VII/2/29
Volume III of *Genealogia Hebraica* available VII/3/30
Four volumes of *Genealogia Hebraica* now available VIII/2/42
History of Jews after the Inquisition II/3/27
Historical notes about Jews of Portugal VIII/3/52
Jews of modern day Portugal I/1/14
Marranos living in Portugal I/2/14
Portuguese marranos VIII/3/52

Rabbinic Genealogy

Are all Ashkenazim descended from Rashi? VI/1/28
Ashkenazic Rabbinic Families III/3/07
Baal Shem Tov project II/2/03
Chabad-Lubavitch literature as a genealogical source VIII/3/40
Expands on Chabad article VIII/4/66
Can we prove descent from King David? VIII/3/29
Rashi's descent from King David VIII/3/31
Question origin of surname Katz VII/3/28

A seventeenth-century Luria manuscript VII/2/19
Questions Luria documentation VII/3/28
Comments on Rosenstein's Luria lineage VII/3/47
Historicity of the Rashi Descent VI/1/28
Descendants of Rashi: Opinion 1 IV/2/07
Descendants of Rashi: Opinion 2 IV/2/09
Descendants of Rashi V/1/Sp.Sup
Descent of Rashi: A review VI/2/35
Response to Jacobi's Rashi article VI/2/36
From the seed of Rashi VIII/3/32
Rosenstein responds to critics VIII/1/57

ROMANIA

Romanian holdings in the Diaspora Research Institute VI/2/13
Selected sources on Romania at the Central Archives of the Jewish People VI/1/15
Iasi Jewish records missing VII/3/45
Says Romanian records exist VIII/3/64
Origins of the Jews of Romania and their history up to the Basic Rules of 1831–32 VIII/2/19
Jewish genealogical society founded VII/3/30
Genealogical records (in Romania) have been destroyed VIII/2/42
Political situation in country VIII/4/57
Romanian records in LDS Family History Library VII/3/44

SCOTLAND

Books on Scottish Jewish history V/1/19
Books on Scottish Jewish genealogy VII/3/31
Research using the 1891 census VIII/2/43
Cemetery burials in major Scottish cities VII/4/62
Passage to America through Scotland V/4/07
Scottish-Jewish Archive Centre IV/2/23
Scottish Jewish records V/4/15
Search for my namesake—Scottish style IV/1/18

SEPHARDIC JEWRY—GENERAL

Additional resources for Sephardic genealogy VIII/2/59
Biography of Sephardic Jews and the Holocaust VII/2/17
The Marrano Diaspora VIII/1/9

The Ottoman Empire and Jewish genealogy VIII/1/17
Ottoman Empire resources VIII/1/18
Sephardic Jewry; recommended readings VI/4/52
Sources for researching my Sephardic ancestors VII/1/18
Resources for Sephardic genealogy VIII/3/48
Spanish Inquisition in Americas VII/1/19

SOUTH AFRICA

Addresses of government archives and Jewish organizations VIII/2/44
Augments South African resources VIII/4/67
Jewish community of South Africa—an outline II/2/13
Assistance in locating South African relatives VI/2/28
Why so many South African Jews are Litvaks V/1/19
Mormon resources in South Africa VIII/2/44

SOUTH AMERICA—GENERAL

Travelers guide to South America VII/2/39

SURINAM

Jews of exotic Surinam and their history VIII/2/16

SPAIN

Book: *History of the Jews of Aragon* IV/3/20

SWITZERLAND

Jews of Berne VIII/2/45
Family names found in various locations IV/1/24
Family trees deposited in Zurich VII/4/63
History of Jews of Switzerland II/1/26
Towns of Hagenthal and Hegenheim VIII/4/57
Jews in the Fribourg Territory VI/2/28
Public records offices in Europe V/1/21
Cemetery in Zwingen VIII/4/57

SYRIA

Genealogies of 30 families from Aleppo documented VII/4/61
Spanish-Jewish "nobility" of Aleppo, Syria VII/2/17

TURKEY (ALSO SEE "SEPHARDIC JEWRY")

Turkish-Jewish cemeteries of the Ottoman period VIII/3/45

UNITED STATES

Addresses and publications of United States societies II/2/27
AJGS plans to assist Russians looking for American relatives VIII/1/58
AJGS to maintain list of European researchers VIII/2/6
AJHS acquires early printed American Judaica V/4/06
American Jewish Yearbook: A genealogical resource IV/3/16
Balch Institute to publish Russian Arrivals 1880–87 VIII/3/56
Book planned: *Encyclopedia of Jewish Genealogy* III/2/34
Book Review: *Genealogical Resources in the New York Metropolitan Area* V/1/29
Book Review: *Encyclopedia of Jewish Genealogy* VII/1/34
Encyclopedia of Jewish Genealogy to make debut VI/3/37
HIAS offices, continued III/2/18
HIAS—Baltimore II/3/11
HIAS—Boston II/3/10
HIAS—Philadelphia II/3/06
HIAS—New York II/3/03
HIAS—Hebrew Immigrant Aid Society II/3/02
History of the US-USSR Archival Exchange Program VIII/1/3
Holocaust material at the American Jewish Archives V/4/08
INS success story V/4/22
Jewish Genealogical Family Finder now available on 11 bulletin boards VII/2/16
Klau Library and the American Jewish Archives VIII/2/30
Leo Baeck Institute resources await seminar attendees VIII/1/39
Lesser known resources at the U.S. National Archives IV/1/07
Library of Congress catalogues genealogies VIII/4/64
List of Jewish Genealogical Societies throughout the world III/1/33
Map resources at the U.S. Library of Congress VII/4/43
Expands on Library of Congress map article VIII/1/58
Mokotoff appointed to FGS Board of Directors VI/2/39
Mrs. Jaffe finds her relatives I/2/26
National Archives branches acquire additional microfilms V/1/22
New microfilms available from U.S. National Archives VIII/1/36

Naturalization and Visa records at U.S. Immigration and Naturalization Service V/1/12
Greater access to U.S. Naturalization records VIII/1/41
A network of people finders IV/2/11
Planning continues for Polish-Jewish archives at University of Connecticut V/3/15
Plans for Summer Seminar on Jewish Genealogy IV/2/33
Portrait of my grandfather II/3/04
Public access to U.S. Naturalization index sought VI/1/6
Recent acquisitions at YIVO Institute III/2/29
Report on Seventh Summer Seminar on Jewish Genealogy IV/3/03
Report on plans for Eighth Summer Seminar on Jewish Genealogy V/1/11
Russian consular records to be indexed I/2/04
Corrections to microfilming of Russian Consular Records completed VIII/1/57
The elusive Russian Consular Records VIII/3/13
More on Sean Ferguson legend VI/1/42
SAGAS update VII/2/38
Search publishes research guides to many cities III/2/26
Search publishes resource guides V/2/24
Seeking descendants of the Baal Shem Tov V/4/22
Social Security Death Index new genealogical resource VIII/1/42
Eleventh Summer Seminar to be New York Experience VII/4/16
Third International Seminar: An Update VII/1/7
Texas company offers computerized tracing services VII/4/65
USSR/US archival exchange takes initial step IV/2/15
Miriam Weiner wins columnist award VI/2/39

Ukraine (also see USSR/Russia—General)

Surname list of Berdichev available VI/1/43
Crimean Jewish names V/1/05
Eastern Galician records available from Polish archives V/2/26
Important address for (Ukrainian) research V/4/05
Kiev Library has wealth of uncatalogued Judaica VIII/4/47
Newly available materials on Jews/Jewish history in Lviv VIII/3/12
Yiddish Meidan: an agricultural colony in Ukraine VIII/3/17
Resources for Ukrainian genealogical research V/2/04
Ukraine: Resources for research VI/2/8
Records of Jews in the Vinnitsa Oblast Archives VIII/3/10

Weiner discusses developments in Poland and Ukraine VIII/3/64

USSR/Russia/—General (also see "Belarus" and "Ukraine")

Are we descendants of Khazarian Jews? II/2/05
A cemetery in (Irkutsk) Siberia VI/4/50
Book Review: *Handbook for Archival Research in the USSR* V/4/10
Bukharan Adventure VI/4/15
Commentary on RAGAS agreement VII/2/4
International conference on genealogy held in Russia VIII/4/35
RAGAS creates computer link between Washington and Moscow VIII/3/67
Experiences on a trip to the former Soviet Union VII/1/6
Genealogical inquiries to Soviet Union VI/3/39
Genealogical service inaugurated for Russia, Belarus and Ukraine VII/2/3
Report on a Jewish genealogical seminar in Moscow VIII/3/8
Some glimpses of studying Jewish genealogy in Russia VIII/4/31
History of the US-USSR Archival Exchange Program VIII/1/3
Joint Distribution Committee records in Russia VIII/4/64
Survey of Judaica in former Soviet Union planned VIII/4/65
A note on accessing Russian Voter Lists VIII/3/67
Records of Russian magnates as a genealogical resource VIII/4/37
Mutriken records V/1/34
More Russian genealogical resources found in the U.S.Library of Congress VIII/1/7
New strategies necessary for Soviet inquiries VI/1/6
Origin of Russian-Jewish surnames III/2/03
Jewish patronymic and metronymic surnames in Russia VII/4/3
Russian business directories as aids in genealogical research IV/2/03
Russian business directories VI/4/23
Russian business directories—an update VII/3/13
Russian government to allow genealogical inquiries IV/3/02
Russian sources in Western libraries VI/4/20
My Russian Research VII/4/29
Soviet success stories VI/1/8
Soviet trip (by archivists) delayed VI/3/21
Jewish surnames in the Russian Empire VIII/3/3
U.S.-Soviet accord include plans for genealogical exchange V/2/03
U.S. genealogical team visits Soviet archives VI/2/3

U.S./USSR Genealogical Exchange Advisory Board holds meeting V/4/03
Vital statistics in Czarist Russia V/3/06
Records of Jews in the Vinnitsa Oblast Archives VIII/3/10
Vladmir Tarasov answers VI/2/5
Writing to Russia for genealogical information VII/3/4

Avotaynu *Family Finder*

The Family Finder section of *Avotaynu* gives readers the opportunity to place notices about areas of their research. *Avotaynu* accepts these entries at $10 for the first 25 words and 25 cents for each additional word. Name, address and telephone number are free. Here is the Family Finder section of *Avotaynu*'s Spring 1993 issue.

Arthur Aronoff, 4907 Redford Road, Bethesda, Maryland 20816, (301) 951-9655. Seeking data about the family of Leib **Aranovich** (Louis **Aronoff**, in New York after 1915) from Kraslava, Latvia, and Anna **Neihaus Aronoff**, from vicinity of Vilna (in New York after 1920).

Ralph N. Baer, 1250 Fourth Street, SW, Apt. 707, Washington, D.C. 20024 (202) 554-2483. Looking for descendants of Max **Baer** (born 1896 Malsch Landkreis Karlsruhe) and wife Nelly, apparently lived in Dayton or Akron; children: Sophie, Richard and Helen. Also descendants of Walter **Cahn** (born 1895 Düsseldorf) and wife Gertrud **Bamberger**. Children Hans and Wolfgang apparently lived on Long Island, New York.

Mrs. W. I. Bellany, 42 Barton Road, Lancaster, LA1 4ER, U.K. Seeking information on **Mark Scheinman**, son of Samuel Joseph **Scheinman** and Ada **Davigdor Scheinman**, Mark's wife, Bertha **Calmenson,** daughter of R. Jesse **Calmenson**, also Charles **Yaffe** and wife Pauline—lived Chicago? All emigrated to U.S. in the 19th century—place of origin unknown. So far all I have are myths; would love some facts.

Rick Bercuvitz, 28 Broadlake Road, Colchester, Vermont 05446, (802) 864-4192. Seeking descendants of: **Sack** family originally from Salant, Lithuania. Daughter Amalia (b.c. 1860) married Baron **Taub**, lived in Kursk. **Fratkin** family from Passaic, New Jersey, previously from Priluki, Poltava, Ukraine. **Wilensky** or **Nariv** families from New York, originally **Narivlansky** from Borossna or Priluki, Poltava, Ukraine. Hyman or Malke **Singer** (Originally **Klausnik** from Salant or Kovno,

Lithuania, b.c. 1850) daughter from New York, Tillie **Levine**; son from Pittsburgh, Felix **Singer** (d. before 1966). Bernard **Fried** (b.c. 1855) (2nd wife Brocha) from Philadelphia, children include Sam, Dr. Morris, Katie and Jenny (married a pharmacist). Son of Julius or Joseph **Seigler** (or **Sigler**) by 2nd wife. Julius is buried in Escondido or Santa Barbara, California (died c. 1932). Descendants of Lester **Hurwitz** or Evelyn (nee Hurwitz) from Buffalo; Morris, Sam or Harry **Altman** from Rome, Syracuse or Buffalo, New York (originally from Luthuania). **Grushlawsky** from Telz or Salant, Lithuania. Descendants of Isadore **Mann** from Boston, Massachusetts or Portland, Maine.

Julien Berman, 2350 Montevallo Road #1510, Birmingham, Alabama 35223, (205) 871-9034. Seeking information on family of Label **Hazon Bergman**, wife Zelda **Weinberg**, and his two sisters; born around 1825, Kaunas, Lithuania; died 1913 Grinkeshik or Ragola, Kaunas, Lithuania.

Julien Berman, 2350 Montevallo Road #1510, Birmingham, Alabama 35223, (205) 871-9034. Searching for family of Isaac **Weinberg**, born around 1849, Kaunas, Lithuania; died Atlanta, Georgia, around 1920s. Sisters: Zelda, Bessie, Gussie. Brothers: Nathan and Hyman from Ragola, Kaunas, Lithuania or Grinkeshik.

Julien Berman, 2350 Montevallo Road #1510, Birmingham, Alabama 35223, (205) 871-9034. Seeking information on family of Zahara **Millerkofsky** (**Millkofsky**) and wife Shayna **Neharna Lippman**; born 1840. Children: Avram Velvul, Sarah, Hanah Rifka, Marya, Yankal, Kreva, Vilnaguberniya, Lithuania.

Roberta Wagner Berman, 1265 Pearl Street, La Jolla, California 92037. Searching the world for **Chameides**. My great-great-grandfather Chameides was a rabbi in Zaleszczyki, Galicia (mid-to-late 1800s), as was his son Israel (died ca. 1900).

Joseph Chadajo, 15 Margery Road, Brockton, Massachusetts 02402; (508) 588-3285. Seeking information about the **Xadaio** family of Thessaloniki, Greece, and (**H**)**Olender** family of Wloclawek, Poland. Also English genealogy of Saadia-ben-Yosuf (Saadia the Gaon).

Sylvan M. Dubow, 5563 Chillum Place NE, Washington, DC 20011. Descendants of residents of Kovarsk, Anikat, Vilna, Vilkomir,

Lithuania, surnamed **Dubovsky** (**Dubow**) who settled in Chicago, Illinois. Please furnish immigration, birth, marriage and death information.

Arlene B. Edwards, 1001 Highlight Drive, West Covina, California 91791, (818) 915-5354, FAX (818) 966-2744. Seeking families of Jacob and Leon Goodman (was Guttman) born Bucharest, Romania, mid-1800s. Emigrated to New York City or suburbs. Two of eight children born to Shimon Mayer and Chana Sara Guttman. Siblings: Solomon, Samuel, Rose, Sophie, Polly, baby Lizzie. Many of family emigrated to Montreal!

Alan Feigenbaum, 1261 55th Street, Brooklyn, New York, 11219, (718) 633-0494. Seeking information on **Feigenbaum, Silber** and **Schiff** families. My ancestors with these names lived in or near Schendashov, Galicia, Poland, in 1800s.

Karen Lee Fielding, 7073 Bridges Road, Cincinnati, Ohio 45230. Seeking any information on the family of Johanne and Johannes **Finkler** (**Finck\Finklestein\Finkle\Fink\Finke**). He was born ca. 1840, Prussia; she 1856, Prussia. In Cincinnati, Ohio, for 1880 census with following children: Nathan, 1869; Helen, 1856; Catherine, 1866; Henry, 1867; Charles, 1876; and my great-grandfather, John, born October 5, 1874 in Cincinnati, Ohio. All but John and Martin moved west to Indiana, then California (Hollywood).

Morris Gordon, Box 5850, Baltimore, Maryland 21208, (410) 486-1809. Searching for **Grondowsky/Grandowsky** from Bialystock, Grodno or Lomza, Poland. **Cherkassky** from Zlatopol or Kamenka, Ukraine.

David C. Grossack, 62 Central Avenue, Hull, Massachusetts 02045, (617) 925-5253. Seeking information from families who can trace their history to Sabbatian Frankist and Doenmeh movements.

Shoshana Hantman, 410 Benedict Avenue #5D, Tarrytown, New York 10591, (914) 332-4632. Looking for relatives of Shaye **Kagan/Cohen**, d. 1916 in Kiev-Teteev, Ukraine, whose daughter was Rebecca **Cohen Wishnoff**, d. 1929 in Camden, New Jersey. Also seeking Hyman/Herman **Wishnoff**, d. 1950s in Philadelphia area, whose brothers were Harry and Abraham **Wishnoff**. Also: links to brothers David, Benjamin and Aaron **Hantman**, b. in late 1800s in Yekaterinoslav-Dnepropetrovsk, Ukraine; and Jennie (**Zloteh**) **Shedrinsky**, daughter of Izik **Shedrinsky** of Kievguberniya. Finally, links to Israel **Gershon Geller**, who married Mary **Aptaker**, b. Ukraine. Or any information about Yekaterinoslav-Dnepropetrovsk.

Martin Isserlis, 32 Dexter Drive N., Basking Ridge, New Jersey 07920, (908) 953-0440. Seeking ancestors and relatives of **Isserlis** (or **Isserles**) family from Galicia (Lvov, Tarnopol, Zborov, Kozova areas). Also from Belarus (Bobruisk), Odessa, Leningrad, Bukovina (Itskany) and Lithuania (Kovno, Kelem, Shavli). Also seeking information on **Labiner** family from Tarnopol or Zborov, relatives of **Charlap** (or **Charlik**) family who were descended from **Brandeis** family. Also seeking descendants of Jossel **Rothstein** from Galicia (Kozova).

Lenore Kramer, 90 Birch Lane, Woodmere, New York 11598, (516) 374-1347. Searching **Weinman(n)**, Komarom, Hungary. Brothers: David (Josephine [**Pepi**] **Weinberger**), Bernath (**Kadi Weinman[n]**), Bedrich/Fritz (Johanna **Schlesinger**); sister: Julia (Samuel **Chaskes**). David, Bernath, Kadi, Julia to America. Bedrich's children: Kadi, Rose, Helen (Oskar **Vadasz**), Isidore, Marushka. Philadelphia branch of **Chaskes** includes Fannie, Ernestine, Morris.

Lenore Kramer, 90 Birch Lane, Woodmere, New York 11598, (516) 374-1347. Searching Rivka Chaya **Samulovits**, born Varano (?), Hungary, and Ignatz/Isaac **Jacobovits** married 1840–1850, Kiraly **Helmctz**, Hungary, now Kralovsky-Chlumec, Slovakia. Children: Yetta (Bernath **Lefkowitz**), Mary (Henry **Josephowitz**), Sadie (Max **Pollak**), Rosie (Charlie **Goldstein**), Aaron (Regina **Geller**), David (Katie **Freireich**). **Samulovits** changed to **Samuels**, **Samlowe**, etc. **Jacobovits** changed to **Jacobs**, **Jacoby**, etc. May be related to **Glucksman**, in lamp business, 1920–1940. Cousins in Brooklyn, 1920–1945, named **Schmalheiser**.

Lenore Kramer, 90 Birch Lane, Woodmere, New York 11598, (516) 374-1347. Searching **Goldberger**, born Tasnad/Szilagy-Cseh, Carpathian Mts., Hungary/Romania. Moshe married ca. 1850. Son Adolph married Esther **Bohm**. Daughters: Olga, Gizi, Erizi, others. Son Ezekiel, Chicago, married Natalya **Grunwald**, second wife; daughters: Rose and Serena. Son Samuel married Amelia **Bohm**. Amelia's sisters married **Rose**, **Deutsch**, **Purgess** (**Purjesz**), **Weinberger**, **Bohm**. Samuel's children: Alex, Charles, Morris, Ferenc (Frank), Helen, Blanche.

Lenore Kramer, 90 Birch Lane, Woodmere, New York 11598, (516) 374-1347. Searching Jakob **Geller** and Rose **Simonovitz**, married ca.

1857, Palocsa, Hungary, now Plavec, Slovakia. Children: Nathan (Rosa Lif/p/kowitz), Adolph (Bertha **Folkmann**), Herman (Annie **Senft**), Leah/Ella (Israel **Hochhauser**), Sali (Herman **Kandel**), Regina (Aaron **Jacobowitz**). All sons and Regina came to America. Jacob's brother had daughter, Margaret **Galos**.

Janice Lawrenz, P.O. Box 2221, Gosford, NSW, 2250, Australia. Seeking information on **Freidman/Friedman** families from Rossane? Poland/Russia, and descendants Biber, California and others. Also Solomon **Freidman/Friedman** who lived in California. He married Ethel **Levy** in Sydney 1899, had a daughter Rita, born Brisbane. Migrated to California. Also **Macnovitch** Warsaw, Poland.

Janice Lawrenz, P.O. Box 2221, Gosford, NSW, 2250, Australia. Seeking information and descendants on Hyman Mandel **Freidman/ Friedman**. He married Rachel Hilda **Levy** in Perth 1896, had 2 boys and girl: David Adolphus (born Sydney), Benjamin (born Sydney), Cecelia (birth unknown). Migrated to USA. Hyman returned alone to Perth (died in Perth 1947). **Biber** families also.

Janice Lawrenz, P.O. Box 2221, Gosford, NSW, 2250, Australia. Seeking information and descendants on Majer **Czerniak** (changed to **Cohen**) married Bajla Ruchla (Rachel) **Esnener** in Kolo, Poland. Migrated first to England, then to the U.S. Had 4 children: Lewis, Kitty, Hannah, Janie.

Betty A. **Lechter**, 14-H Nob Hill, Roseland, New Jersey 07068, (201) 228-7278. Seeking relatives of Charles and Esther **Wolfson** (cousins, same surname) possibly from Kiev around 1882; Chicago 1889–93; NYC 1894–1913; East Orange, New Jersey, 1913–22 (after Charles' death). Members Orach Chaim, NYC. Chicago births: Mina, Etta, Rose, Louis. NYC births: Jeanette, William, Carolyn, Hannah, Pauline, Morris. Charles' mother: Rachel **Resnick**. Esther's parents: Rebecca, Aaron; grandparents: Lazarus **Golden**, Mordecai **Wolfson**, Paie **Edelstein**; brother: Nathan. Charles was peddler, then jeweler in NYC. Possible family in Galveston, Texas; Westchester County, New York.

Robinn Magid, 221 Colgate Avenue, Kensington, California 94708, (510) 524-2297. Seeking descendants of Oscar **Kur** (**Glick**?) in Johannesburg; Jacob **Belkin** in Montreal; Isaak **Belokrinitsky** (**Belkin**?) in Toronto; Louis **Bell** in Philadelphia; and **Brody** family in Springfield,

Massachusetts. I'm researching pre-1826 Lublin Civil Records. Know a shortcut? (No Surnames!). Seeking from Lublin: **Cygielman**, **Tenenbaum**, **Szulfryd**, **Frydliber**, **Herszberg**, **Klawier**, **Mehltopf**, **Fernand**, **Rozenryb**, **Rotbar**.

Leonard Markowitz, 1279 June Road, Huntingdon Valley, Pennsylvania 19006, (215) 947-7374. Researching: Yakov **Zolotnicky** (**Solotnitsky**) and Chanah **Habian**, Priluki, Ukraine (1900); Schmuel Yakov **Morgenstern** and Malke **Oliner**, Luzna/Gorlice, Austria (1860); Herman (Chaim) **Markowitz**, Auschwitz/Bytom Galicia (1870); Helena (**Chaiah**) **Poltowska**, Czestochowa, Poland (1870); Abram **Rosenberg** and Sarah **Horowitz** (**Pozner**), Kovno, Lithuania (1867).

Joel Nathan, P.O. Box 335, Doncaster, Victoria 3108, Australia, (3) 852 0277. Seeking information on the families of Charles, David, Abraham and Rebecca **Cohen** whose parents, Hersch and Rachel **Cohen**, arrived in Philadelphia in 1903.

Louis Pinkett, 76A Peregrine Drive, Voorhees, New Jersey 08043, (609) 751-1524. Seeking information on Israel **Pinkett** and/or Disha **Pinkett**, died in New York City 1926–1928. Also Sadie **Lipshitz**, married to Louis **Pinkett**, son of Israel and Disha approx. 1902–1908.

Carol Rombro Rider, 2707 Moores Valley Drive, Baltimore, Maryland 21209, (410) 484-8159. Researching **Rombro** anywhere, especially near Vilna or Tulchin, Ukraine. **Moskovici/Moskowitz**, **Blum/Bloom**, **Lebovici/Lebowitz** from Drenceni or Husi, Romania. **Abramowitz**, **Joseph**(s) from Bratslav, Ukraine.

Carol Rombro Rider, 2707 Moores Valley Drive, Baltimore, Maryland 21209, (410) 484-8159. Researching **Kushner/Kusnir** from Dinovitz, Ukraine or Argentina. **Weiner** from Smorgon, Lithuania or Vilna. **Simmons** (all spellings) from Vilna. Also need to hear from anyone who has researched Mexican records (Catholic).

Books Available from Avotaynu

Where Once We Walked

By Gary Mokotoff and Sallyann Amdur Sack

Named "Outstanding Reference Book of the Year" (1991) by the Association of Jewish Librarians. Named Finalist, Holocaust Category (1991) by the Jewish Book Council. This book documents more than

21,000 towns in Central and Eastern Europe where Jews lived before the Holocaust. It pinpoints each town's location, providing the exact latitude and longitude and its direction and distance from the closest major city. Also included are Jewish population figures from before the Holocaust. It doesn't end there! For readers who want more information about the Jewish history of the towns, included are citations for as many as 40 books that reference each town. An additional 15,000 alternate names include Yiddish names, names under former political regimes and just plain synonyms.

Cost: $69.50 plus $4.50 shipping and handling

A Dictionary of Jewish Surnames From the Russian Empire

By Alexander Beide

What does my last name mean? Where did it come from? When did we acquire it? Why did we acquire it? Russian-born mathematician, Dr. Alexander Beider, spent six years researching the answers to these questions in Moscow, St. Petersburg and Paris. The result is a 752-page compilation of 50,000 Jewish surnames from the Russian Pale of Settlement (excluding the Kingdom of Poland). For each name, Dr. Beider describes the precise geographic distribution within the Russian Empire at the start of the twentieth century. The meaning of every name is explained. Spelling variants are given. This book is the only systematic, scientific work of its type; broader in scope than anything of its kind ever before attempted. This book is the definitive statement on the subject.

Cost: $75.00 plus $4.50 shipping and handling

Jewish Personal Names: Their Origin, Derivation and Diminutive Forms

By Rabbi Shmuel Gorr

The late Rabbi Shmuel Gorr (1931–1988) was not only a scholar, but, in the true rabbinic tradition, he was also a teacher. This work reflects this philosophy. The structure of the book is unique. The names are not organized alphabetically, but by root name. All variants of the root name are shown together, with footnotes explaining how these variants were derived. Family names originating from personal names also are presented. Thus, the reader is educated as well as informed. Publication of this valuable book serves as a fitting memorial to Rabbi Gorr's many contributions to Jewish genealogy. 124 pages.

Cost: $15 plus $2.50 shipping and handling

A Biographical Dictionary of Canadian Jewry 1909–1914

BY LAWRENCE F. TAPPER

Taken from the pages of *The Canadian Jewish Times*, the only Anglo-Jewish newspaper in Canada at that time, are the familial and social relationships of Canadian Jewry, including their links to American and British relatives, their births, bar mitzvahs, marriages and deaths, as well as information concerning their communal and synagogue activities. This reference work indexes data by event and by geographic area. Each topic lists surnames in alphabetical order and directs the researcher to the appropriate page where date of publication, volume and issue number for each entry can be found. Researchers can then examine the original newspaper issue from which the entry was taken. Never before has a single document included such a wealth of factual data about this period of Canadian Jewish history.

Cost: $35.00 plus $3.50 shipping and handling

Send check or money order to *Avotaynu*, Inc., P.O. Box 900, Teaneck, NJ 07666

Or pay by Visa or MasterCard by calling 1-800-866-1525

Microfiche Now Available from Avotaynu

Now you can purchase for your personal use, key indexes invaluable in advancing your genealogical research. These are being made available on microfiche because of its low cost. Microfiche readers are available at most libraries in your area.

1) **Jewish Genealogical Family Finder**. Database of ancestral towns and surnames being researched by some 2,000 Jewish genealogists throughout the world. Indexed by town name and surname. 27,000 entries. *1 fiche—$5.00*
2) **Jewish Vital Statistics Records in Slovakian Archives**. Index to birth, marriage and death records located in archives of Slovakia. *1 fiche—$10.00*
3) **Index to the 1784 Census of the Jews of Alsace**. Documents some 20,000 Jews who were enumerated in this census. In four sequences: by surname; by given name; by town; for married women, by maiden name. *1 fiche—$10.00*
4) **1993 Version of the Jewish Genealogical People Finder**. The 1993 version has 200,000 entries! Database of individuals who appear on family trees of Jewish genealogists. *14 fiche—$21.00*

5) **Jews Living in Canadian Maritime Provinces—1901.** Gleaned from 1901 census. *1 fiche—$5.00*

6) **Jewish Genealogical Consolidated Surname Index.** Recently updated! List of more than 100,000 unique surnames showing in which of 10 different databases each appears. Databases are Jewish Genealogical Family Finder, Jewish Genealogical People Finder, Russian Consular Records, *Palestine Gazette*, Emergency Passports, *Memorial to Jews Deported from France*, *First American Jewish Families*, U.S. State Department Records, Refusniks and *Gedenkbuch*. Indexed using the Daitch-Mokotoff Soundex System. *4 fiche—$6.00*

7) **Index to Russian Consular Records.** List of over 70,000 persons who transacted business with the Russian Czarist consulates in the U.S. from about 1849–1926. *7 fiche—$10.50*

8) **Publications of the Jewish Genealogical Societies—1977–1990.** A set of most of the newsletters and publications of Jewish-American genealogy published between 1977 and 1990. *24 fiche—$36.00*

9) **Index to Department of State Records Found in U.S. National Archives.** Five indexes: Index of Jewish applicants for emergency U.S. passports 1915–1924; Index to registration of U.S. citizens—Jerusalem, 1914–1918; Index to Jewish names in protection of interests of U.S. citizens in Romania, Germany and Poland; Index to Jewish names in protection of interests of U.S. citizens in Russia; Index to Jewish names in protection of interests of U.S. citizens in Austria-Hungary. *7 fiche—$10.50*

10) **Galician Towns and Administrative Districts.** List of 6000 Galician towns and the administrative districts to which they belong. *2 fiche—$3.00*

11) **Gazetteer of Central and Eastern Europe.** Consolidated listing of Board on Geographic names for 350,000 place names in Austria, Bulgaria, Byelorussia, Czechoslovakia, Estonia, Germany, Hungary, Latvia, Lithuania, Moldavia, Poland, Romania, Ukraine and Yugoslavia. Two sequences: alphabetic shows place name, country code, latitude and longitude. Daitch-Mokotoff Soundex sequence shows town name and country code. *15 fiche—$22.50*

12) **Black Book of Localities Whose Jewish Population Was Exterminated by the Nazis.** Alphabetical list (independent of country) of 32,000 communities in Eastern Europe where Jews lived prior to the Holocaust. *2 fiche—$3.00*

13) **Palestine Gazette**. List of over 28,000 persons, mostly Jews, who legally changed their names while living in Palestine during the British Mandate from 1921–1948. Indexed by original surname and new surname. Combined surname index using the Daitch-Mokotoff Soundex System. *6 fiche—$9.00*
14) **Index to Memorial to the Jews Deported From France.** Alphabetic list of 50,000 surnames that appear in *Memorial to Jews Deported From France*. Shows surname and convoy number. *1 fiche—$1.50*
15) **Index to Burials in Two Jewish Cemeteries in Washington, D.C.** Cemeteries are Washington Hebrew Congregation Cemetery and Adas Israel Cemetery. *2 fiche—$3.00*

TOLEDOT: THE JOURNAL OF JEWISH GENEALOGY

In the winter of 1977, Steven W. Siegel and I got together to found *Toledot: The Journal of Jewish Genealogy*. I remember the first time I met Steve: Here was a person who was obviously very articulate, extremely capable and an absolute mensch. After discovering that we both had a passion for Jewish genealogy, we also discovered that we both saw the need for a publication devoted to the subject. We were coming across new sources, new information and new search strategies all the time, and we wanted to share them with others. *Toledot* became a forum for those of us who wanted to build a network of Jewish family historians for the purpose of helping each other.

We published *Toledot* as a quarterly for several years, sometimes missing a quarter, sometimes offering a double issue, but always pleasing its readers. We included "how-to" articles, bibliographies, articles about surnames and much more. One very popular and useful series was our catalog of the towns in Poland, Hungary and Germany for which the Mormons have Jewish records.

After we stopped publishing, we continued to make back issues available; but now much of the contents of back issues of *Toledot* are out of date. Nevertheless, it would be worthwhile to find a library that owns the back issues. Or contact *Avotaynu*; they offer the back issues on microfiche. You never know what you might find. And while we're on the subject of *Avotaynu*, I'd strongly urge you to subscribe. It is truly an essential publication for Jewish genealogists.

Looking back on the time we spent publishing *Toledot* makes me proud. Steve Siegel and I were publishing what, at the time, was the only periodical in the world specializing in Jewish genealogy. Today there are several such publications; and even a superficial scanning of them reveals, to the person familiar with *Toledot*, that *Toledot* had a great influence on them.

THE ENCYCLOPEDIA OF JEWISH GENEALOGY

If the book you are now reading is Jewish Genealogy 101, *The Encyclopedia of Jewish Genealogy* is Jewish Genealogy 102. There is a need for the dissemination of useful information that is being discovered all the time by those of us who are actively pursuing our family history. When I first began my search, there was hardly a reference to the notion of "Jewish genealogy." There was British genealogy, Irish genealogy, Polish genealogy—there was a whole library of material available to non-Jews.

But over the past dozen years, Jewish genealogy has become a well-known phenomenon. It is taught in Jewish religious schools (see *My Generations: A Course in Jewish Family History*, page 115); there are seminars; organizations; travel tours; periodicals; books; and more—all directly related to Jewish genealogy. *The Encyclopedia of Jewish Genealogy* is an effort to bring useful information to the serious researcher.

One highlight of Volume I of *The Encyclopedia* is its catalog of towns whose Jewish records have been microfilmed by the Mormon Church (see page 226).

Another extremely useful section of *The Encyclopedia of Jewish Genealogy* is its state-by-state presentations of the Jewish genealogical resources that are available in the U.S. Included is a thorough description of how the Mormon Church can be useful in your research.

I would say that there are three essentials for the Jewish genealogist: the book you are reading, *The Encyclopedia of Jewish Genealogy*, and a subscription to *Avotaynu* (see page 82).

The Encyclopedia of Jewish Genealogy, edited by Arthur Kurzweil and Miriam Weiner (Jason Aronson Publishers, Northvale, NJ 07647). To order copies, call 1-800-782-0015.

ENCYCLOPEDIA JUDAICA

I call recall the moment, over twenty years ago, when I first discovered the remarkable *Encyclopedia Judaica* (known among Jewish librarians and others as the "EJ"). Sixteen volumes in length, with a beautiful binding, attractive endpapers, and articles on just about every topic you can imagine, the EJ is a gold mine of information.

Most synagogues have an EJ, as do most public libraries with medium size collections. It is also available for purchase, and I highly recommend it. It will provide your home with a lifelong resource of Jewish knowledge.

The EJ has a volume that is the index for the other fifteen volumes. This is the key to using this magnificent set of books.

Some of the things you can find in the EJ are:

1) Towns: Do you know the names of the towns in your family history? You'll be pleased at how many of these towns have brief histories in the EJ.
2) Your last name: It might not be as remote as you think to locate someone with your last name through the EJ. If your name is unusual, give it a try.
3) Background Information: The EJ provides material on just about every Jewish topic. As you learn details about your family history, the EJ will answer lots of questions.
4) Hasidic Dynasties: The EJ has many family trees in it, especially of hasidic families.
5) There are lots of useful maps in the EJ. Look up countries of interest as well as obsolete geographic areas (like Galicia).
6) I often just take a volume of the EJ and browse. It provides a rich Jewish education for its readers.

First American Jewish Families

I have yet to meet a man as generous as Rabbi Malcolm H. Stern. I was proud to call Rabbi Stern a friend. It was Rabbi Stern who I first turned to for help when I began my Jewish genealogical research.

It was in the early 1970s, and when I went to the card catalog of a large university library (seeking information on "Jewish Genealogy") the only reference to the subject was a book, called *Americans of Jewish Descent*, written by Rabbi Malcolm H. Stern. I arranged to see the book through interlibrary loan, and when it arrived I was impressed and also disappointed. I was impressed because Rabbi Stern's book was an attempt to document the family trees of every Jew in the U.S. before the year 1840. In 1840 there were about 10,000 Jews in the U.S., and Rabbi Stern (with the support and talents of his wife) wanted to trace each of their families and their descendants. The book was huge and, as I said, most impressive.

I was disappointed because I knew that the contents of the book had little to do with my ancestors who arrived in America in the next century!

Nevertheless, I wrote to Rabbi Stern, asking for advice, and he promply wrote back with suggestions and encouragement. I have since learned that over the years countless Jewish family historians have received support—in many ways—from the remarkable Rabbi Stern.

When Steve Siegel and I launched *Toledot: The Journal of Jewish Genealogy*, we began our efforts at the dining room table in Rabbi Stern's home. He allowed us to search through all of his correspondence (I think he saved everything) to compile a mailing list of potential subscribers. The result was quite beneficial to us.

Over the years, Rabbi Stern became an important force in the world of genealogy, Jewish and general. He assumed leadership positions in national organizations, was highly regarded by genealogists and archivists worldwide, and his contributions to the development of the field of Jewish genealogy is incalculable.

A revised and updated edition of Rabbi Stern's study of Jews and their descendants in the U.S.—and newly retitled: *First American Jewish Families, 1654–1988*—was published in 1991 and is distributed by Genealogical Publishing Co., Inc., 1001 North Calvert Street, Baltimore, MD 21202.

Other Jewish Genealogical Publications

Although *Avotaynu* is the finest periodical of its kind, there are other newsletters and publications that specifically deal with Jewish genealogy. No list would be definitive since new developments are happening all the time. Several of the local Jewish Genealogical Societies publish newsletters, most notably the Los Angeles Jewish Genealogical Society, the Jewish Genealogical Society of Cleveland, and the Jewish Genealogical Society of New York. Other publications include:

Stammbaum: The Newsletter of German-Jewish Genealogical Research

1601 Cougar Ct
Winter Springs, FL 32708

ROM-SIG NEWS: Jewish Genealogical Special Interest Group for Romania

c/o Paul Pascal
184 Strathearn Rd

Toronto, Ontario M6C 1S4
Canada

Also of interest is:

L'Dor V'Dor
The Catalog for the Jewish Genealogist
203 Commack Rd, Suite 138
Commack, NY 11725
(516) 462-1191

Founded and run by Naomi Bard Feller, L'Dor V'Dor is a mail order company that specializes in publications of interest to Jewish family historians. L'Dor V'Dor stocks most of the important publications that are in print and mentioned in this book.

TEXTBOOKS

During the past 15 years, I have lectured to hundreds of Jewish groups around the U.S. on the subject of Jewish genealogy. Slowly but surely, the message that genealogy can be an effective teaching tool has been heard by Jewish educators. This is reflected in the fact that more and more children attending Jewish Afternoon, Sunday, and Day schools are coming home with homework assignments having to do with family history. Teachers know that genealogy can be exciting and informative—and fun! I can think of no better way to influence a young person's sense of responsibility for the future of the Jewish people than to show the child that he or she is the result of many past generations. When a young person sees himself or herself as a link on a chain of history, that chain grows longer and stronger.

There are two publications that can be extremely useful when working with children who want to pursue Jewish family history. *My Generations: A Course in Jewish Family History* has been used in hundreds of synagogue schools as part of the religious school curriculum. Published by Behrman House, 235 Watchung Avenue, West Orange, NJ 07052, it is essentially a "fill-in-the blanks" book in which I show the young reader how I was able to gather lots of information from my family by simply talking to relatives. I then provide spaces for the young person to record the results of his or her own family history information-gathering.

My Generations: A Course in Jewish Family History also has a teacher's guide available, written by the gifted Jewish educator, Dr. Alan A. Kay. Ideal for classroom use, Dr. Kay's guide provides teachers with

The wedding photo of Avraham Abusch Kurzweil and Hinda Ruchel Lowenthal, paternal great-grandparents of the author.

project ideas, lesson plans, duplicating-machine masters and lots of tips on how to successfully use Jewish genealogy in the classroom.

I suppose I have a bias, since I am the author of *My Generations: A Course in Jewish Family History*, but I am happy to report that teachers find it quite a lively topic. It's not just another subject; it can change lives. I have also heard that some synagogues use the book for intergenerational projects. One synagogue on Long Island has an annual "Grandparents' Shabbat" where grandparents and their grandchildren come together in the synagogue for activities. One of the activities is using *My Generations.*

Another publication for educational purposes is *The Chain That Stretches from Sinai: Creating a Family Tree*. This handsome booklet, published by The Living Memorial-The Hebrew Academy of Cleveland and Torah Umesorah is called "A Student/Parent Learning Project" and is also designed for use by children as a way to inspire interest in Jewish family history and genealogy. Copies can be obtained from:

The Living Memorial
1860 South Taylor Rd
Cleveland Heights, OH 44118

Rabbi Malcolm Stern's Basic Bibliography of Jewish Genealogy

Compiling a bibliography on Jewish genealogy is a courageous act. There are so many sources, large and small, that no one bibliography could possibly contain all of the sources. What is important to one genealogist may be of no use to the next. The late Rabbi Malcolm Stern compiled an annotated bibliography in an attempt to cover what he sees as the basic sources, both printed material as well as institutions. Although many of Rabbi Stern's recommendations repeat items throughout this book I think it is useful to present it here nonetheless.

Bibliography of Jewish Genealogy

Compiled and Annotated by Rabbi Malcolm H. Stern, FASG

Manuals and Sourcebooks

Baxter, Angus. *In Search of Your European Roots: A Complete Guide to Tracing Your Ancestors in Every Country in Europe.* (Baltimore: Genealogical Publishing Co., Inc., 1985, 289 pp.) A country-by-country description of resources [now outdated for Eastern Europe]. Includes a chapter on Jewish sources in Europe and Israel.

Cohen, Chester G. *Shtetl Finder Gazetteer.* (Bowie, MD: Heritage Books, Inc., 1989, 145 pp.) Paperback. Locates with varied spelling many of the Jewish communities of Eastern Europe, identifying by name some prominent citizens of each. [cf. Mokotoff-Sack, below]

Eakle, Arlene and Johni Cerny, eds. *The Source: A Guidebook of American Genealogy.* (Salt Lake City: Ancestry, Ltd., 1984, 786 pp.) Chapters indicate where to find every type of record in the U.S. Lists LDS microfilms of vital records for Jewish communities in Germany, Poland and Hungary (updated in *Avotaynu*. See Periodicals).

Eichholz, Alice, ed., *Ancestry's Red Book: American State, County & Town Sources.* Revised ed. (Salt Lake City: Ancestry, c1992). A state-by-state listing of genealogical resources, supplementing *The Source.*

Gedenkbuch, compiled by the Bundesarchiv, Koblenz, and the International Tracing Service, Arolsen, Germany, with the cooperation of Yad Vashem, Jerusalem. (Koblenz, 1987, 2v.) Lists 128,000 Jewish victims of Nazis in Germany, 1933–45, citing last place of residence, birth date, death date, and circumstances of death, where known.

Guzik, Estelle M., ed. *Genealogical Resources in the New York Metropolitan Area.* (New York: Jewish Genealogical Society, Inc., 1989, 404 pp.) Detailed guide to every agency between Albany, New York, and Trenton, New Jersey, that could provide data of use to Jewish genealogical research, including many specific records, hours of opening, public transportation, finding aids, fees and restrictions. Appendices include: bibliography and locations of yizkor books, vital record application forms, soundex codes, available foreign telephone directories, U.S. city directories, newspapers and Jewish cemeteries. Indexes.

Kurzweil, Arthur. *From Generation to Generation: How to Trace Your Jewish Genealogy and Family History.* (New York: HarperCollins, 1994, 384 pp.) A very personal approach to each step; updated and completely revised.

Kurzweil, Arthur and Miriam Weiner, eds. *The Encyclopedia of Jewish Genealogy.* (Northvale, NJ: Jason Aronson, Inc., 1991). Vol. I: Sources in the United States and Canada. An up-to-date finding aid to sources of Jewish genealogical information.

Mokotoff, Gary and Sallyann Amdur Sack. *Where Once We Walked: A Guide to the Jewish Communities Destroyed in the Holocaust.* (Teaneck, NJ: Avotaynu, 1991). A gazetteer of 21,000 Central and Eastern European localities, arranged alphabetically and phonetically under the Daitch-Mokotoff Soundex System, so that various spellings can be found readily.

Rottenberg, Dan. *Finding Our Fathers: A Guidebook to Jewish Genealogy.* (Baltimore: Genealogical Publishing Co., Inc., 1986, xiv + 401 pp.) Paperback reprint of 1977 ed. The pioneer "how-to" with a list of every Jewish surname appearing in a variety of sources.

Sack, Sallyann Amdur. *A Guide to Jewish Genealogical Research in Israel.* (Baltimore: Genealogical Publishing Co., Inc., 1987, xiv + 110 pp.) Detailed guide to the accessibility and holdings of each agency. Appendices include: yizkor books and landsmannschaften listed at Yad Vashem Library; list of towns represented at 1981 World Gathering of Holocaust Survivors.

Sack, Sallyann Amdur and Suzan Wynne. *Russian Consular Records Index and Guide.* (New York: Garland Publishing Co., 1987). An index to names in the 250,000 case files from former Czarist Consular offices in the U.S., 1860–1924, on microfilm at the U.S. National Archives.

Zubatsky, David S. and Irwin M. Berent. *Jewish Genealogy: A Sourcebook of Family Histories and Genealogies.* (New York and London: Garland Publishing Co., 1984, 422 pp.) Finding aid to published and manuscript genealogies in many Jewish archives and libraries. Arranged by surname.

Zubatsky, David S. *Jewish Genealogy,* vol.#2.

Periodicals

Avotaynu: The International Review of Jewish Genealogy. 1985–#. Sallyann Amdur Sack and Gary Mokotoff, eds. Quarterly. (P.O. Box 1134, Teaneck, NJ 07666). Articles and data of general Jewish genealogical interest written by an international group of authors.

Family Finder, compiled by Gary Mokotoff. Updated quarterly and distributed to each society affiliated with the international Association of Jewish Genealogical Societies. A computerized printout of more than 9000 ancestral surnames and 7000 place names being researched by members of Jewish Genealogical Societies. Arranged alphabetically by surname and by town.

Mitteilungen der Gesellschaft fuer juedische Familienforschung, 1924–1939. Arthur Czellitzer, ed. Fifty issues, published by a pre-Holocaust Berlin genealogical society. Contains lectures, vital records and queries. Available at some research libraries and archives.

Search: The Quarterly Journal of the Jewish Genealogical Society of Illinois. 1980– . Alan M. Spencer, ed. (c/o Janette Woods, 4823 N. Lawndale, Chicago, IL 60625). Articles of varied interest, including resources for researching Jewish genealogy in individual U.S. cities.

Toledot: The Journal of Jewish Genealogy, 1977–1980. Steven W. Siegel and Arthur Kurzweil, eds. (some back issues available c/o P.O. Box 6398, New York, NY 10128). Articles on methodology, vital records, queries and book reviews.

Research Archives and Libraries

Note: These sources do not have staff to research for you, but will let you know if they have books or manuscripts on specific topics. In any genealogical query, always enclose a self-addressed, stamped envelope.

American Jewish Archives, 3101 Clifton Avenue, Cincinnati, OH 45220 (on the campus of Hebrew Union College). Specializes in data on Jews in the Western Hemisphere. Many genealogies, vital records, biographies, organizational and congregational records and newspaper indexes. Finding aids: Clasper, James W. and M. Carolyn Dellenbach. *Guide to the Holdings of the American Jewish Archives.* (Cincinnati: 1979, 211 pp.) See also: Zubatsky and Berent (above).

American Jewish Historical Society, 2 Thornton Road, Waltham, MA 02154 (on campus of Brandeis University). All areas of American Jewish history, including organizational and institutional records, as well as family documents. Finding aids: Union Catalog of Manuscripts; handout on genealogical holdings.

LDS Family History Library, 35 North West Temple, Salt Lake City, UT 84150. The world's most complete and technologically current genealogical library; open to all. Books and microfilms include Jewish records from many countries, notable Poland, Germany and Hungary. Microfilms may be obtained on interlibrary loan at local Mormon libraries. Computerized and microfiche catalogs available at branch libraries. Finding aid: Cerni, Johni and Wendy Elliott, eds. *The Library: A Guide to the LDS Family History Library.* (Salt Lake City: Ancestry, Ltd. c1988). Separate chapters are devoted to records for each region of the U.S. and countries abroad.

Leo Baeck Institute, 129 East 73rd Street, New York, NY 10021. Library and archive of surviving records of Jews from German-speaking lands. Finding aid: Union Catalog of Manuscripts.

Library of Congress. Jefferson (main) Building, housing Genealogy and Local History, Independence Avenue between 1st and 2nd Streets, SW, Washington, D.C.; connected underground with Adams and Madison Buildings. Contains every book submitted for U.S. copyright, city directories, maps, gazetteers, Hebraic Division. Finding aid: Neagles, James C. *The Library of Congress: A Guide to Genealogical and Historical Research.* (Salt Lake City: Ancestry, 1990, xii + 381 pp.)

National Archives and Records Administration, 8th and Pennsylvania Avenue, NW, Washington, D.C. 20408. Research room has federal censuses 1790–1910 (1920 will be available in 1992), passenger arrival indexes, eighteenth and nineteenth century military records, some naturalizations, land records. Regional branches have microfilm copies and regional records. Finding aids: *Guide to Genealogical Research in the National Archives.* (Washington, D.C.: 1982, 304 pp.; Szucs, Loretto Dennis and Sandra Hargreaves Luebking, *The Archives: A Guide to the National Archives Field Branches.* (Salt Lake City: Ancestry, Ltd., c1988, vxii + 340 pp.)

New York Public Library. Fifth Avenue and 42nd Street, New York, NY 10018. Jewish, Map, Microfilm and Local History and Genealogy Divisions contain useful materials. Finding aid: Guzik, *Genealogical Resources in the New York Metropolitan Area.* (above)

Yivo Institute for Jewish Research, 1048 Fifth Avenue, New York, NY 10028. Library and archive of data from Yiddish-speaking lands. Finding aid: Guzik, *Genealogical Resources in the New York Metropolitan Area.* (above)

Collected Genealogies

Rosenstein, Neil. *The Unbroken Chain: Biographical Sketches and Genealogy of Illustrious Jewish Families from the 15th–20th Century.* 2 vol. (The Computer Center for Jewish Genealogy, 654 Westfield Avenue, Elizabeth, NJ 07208, 1990 2v.) [An enlarged revision of the 1977 ed.] Includes descendants of the Katzenellenbogen family—Hassidic and other rabbis, Mendelssohn, Martin Buber, Karl Marx, Helena Rubinstein. Index of surnames only.

Sackheim, George I. *Scattered Seeds.* 2 vol. (R. Sackheim Publishing Co., 9151 Crawford Ave., Skokie, IL 60076.) Chronicles 13,000 descendants of Rabbi Israel, one of the two martyrs of Rozanoi (Ruzhany), Byelorussia—executed after a blood libel of 1659. Indexed.

Stern, Malcolm H. *First American Jewish Families.* (Ottenheimer Publishers, Inc., 300 Reisterstown Road, Baltimore, MD 21208, 1991, 441 pp.) Reprint of 1978 edition with added update section. Contains genealogies of all available Jewish families settled in America prior to 1840, traced where possible to the present. 50,000 name index.

TRADITIONAL SOURCES

There are some genealogical sources that are unique to Jews. Some, like the Mohel book (the record book traditionally kept by those who performed the ritual circumcisions in Jewish communities) reflect special aspects of Jewish traditional life. Others, like yizkor books (memorial volumes published in memory of communities that were destroyed during the Holocaust) reflect what the late Jewish historian Lucy Dawidowicz called "the war against the Jews."

These traditional sources can often become the doors to the soul of the Jewish genealogical pilgrimage:

Mohel Books

The Mohel book is another Jewish phenomenon that helps us to view Jewish history through individuals. A Mohel book is a record book kept by the Mohel, or circumciser, listing each boy whom he circumcised. These books, many of which still exist from old communities, are an intriguing and unique record of Jewish male births in communities.

Finding a Mohel book for a particular community, and then finding a reference to someone in your family is a long shot, but it would be worth checking by more ambitious family researchers. The Leo Baeck Institute, 129 East 73rd Street, New York, NY 10021 has a collection of Mohel books of German origin. The Central Archives for the History of the Jewish People in Jerusalem also has Mohel books for scattered communities around the world.

Ketubot

The ketubah, or marriage document, is still another custom in Jewish history that underlines the individuals who are a part of it. Very often ketubot will be handed down from generation to generation within a family. Ketubot record the names of the individuals being married and often include other family names as well. In the seventeenth and eighteenth centuries illuminated ketubot were popular, making the documents attractive as works of art.

Although the possibility is remote that you will be able to find a Torah curtain or ritual object, a Mohel book or a ketubah from a few hundred years ago with reference to your family, I have mentioned them for two reasons. The first is to present these customs to you in an attempt to illustrate how Jewish ritual can be seen from family perspectives. The second reason is more important. I would like to see a revitalization of these customs on the same personal level they once attained. In other words, it would be important for us to think in terms of personalizing ritual objects. If you can, donate a Torah curtain to your shul with an inscription in reference to a loved one. Or donate another type of ritual object. An alternative is to engrave the ritual objects you use at home. The pair of candlesticks you use on Shabbas would have increased meaning if they were not only inscribed, but also passed down to children with names on them. Perhaps the names of your ancestors.

You could do this for any number of items: a kiddush cup, a seder plate, a Chanukah menorah, a talis bag. To engrave or inscribe a brief family tree on any of these items would do wonders in helping to insure that they will be used and respected in future generations. Again, we can imagine that the power of names is dramatic. Although a kiddush cup used each Shabbas becomes special in its own right, how much more special does it become when it contains the names of beloved ancestors. And if your children know stories about the names engraved on the cup, how much more meaningful will the use of the cup be. There is always the problem that the object will get more respect than the act of the ritual itself. This is something we always have to be wary of, but, done in the right spirit, the personalizing of Jewish ritual objects can help to pass Jewish Tradition from generation to generation through the use of the names of ancestors inscribed on them.

The same idea can be used in connection with a Mohel book. It is rare today not only for there to be Mohel books, but also for there to be a Mohel performing a bris. Again, I would suggest that this ritual be returned to its proper place—in a Jewish setting—and a way to "underline" this would be to reinstitute the use of Mohel books. Appropriate birth rituals exist for males and females. When the rituals are performed, the names of the children should be inscribed in a record book in order to record the birth in a Jewish setting and not simply a secular setting, that of the birth certificate. Presently, when we seek proof of birth, we go to a secular agency, usually a Bureau of Vital Statistics. This is an example of one more phase of life being taken over by the secular. In order for us to be "rooted" in our Jewish lives, I think it is necessary to revitalize the use of the Mohel book and an equivalent for girls, in order to have a birth recorded within the Jewish community.

Finally, the ketubah is a document that is widely used but that is often not given the attention it should receive. The use of the ketubah stretches back hundreds of years. For centuries, Jewish marriages in your family for centuries usually used a ketubah. Again, although you will not have much luck in locating old ketubot in your family, you should inquire as to whether any were saved. Finally, when you are married, you should take care to find an attractive ketubah, fill it in with accurate genealogical information (perhaps even adding as many generations as you know) and use the ketubah as a record of family interest. The ketubah will stay in your family as an important document for your descendants to view.

There are opportunities in many aspects of our lives not only to make them Jewish, but also to inject a sense of family and generations in them. If you are getting married, try to locate a yarmulke that was used at some other important occasion in your family. If you lay tefillin, try to locate an ancestor's pair. Express an interest in your family to use those Jewish objects that have been used before. You may not be able to reach back to the Middle Ages, but in symbol (and so in your soul) you will be a part of our long tradition, which does indeed go back for centuries.

Rabbinic Descent

It is not impossible to trace your family back into the early centuries of this millennium. This depends, however, upon the possibility of finding a link between a branch of your family and a rabbinic or well-known family. Although you may have doubts as to this being possible, I need only refer you to my own story in the first chapter to illustrate the point that a most unsuspecting family might descend from illustrious rabbinic lineage.

Among the English, old genealogies are most often available for royal families. In the case of the Jews, our royal families have been those of the rabbis. It is the genealogies of the rabbis throughout the centuries, which in hundreds of cases still exist in great detail, and which go back to the Middle Ages.

Again, the point should be stressed that the possibility that you descend, in at least one branch, from a rabbinic family, is not that remote. The mathematics of it explain it best. In the Kurzweil family, I have traced all of the descendants of my great-great-great-grandparents. They lived in the beginning of the 1800s. In all, their descendants number close to 500 people. In other words, from two people in 1800 have come 500 people. It is easy to see that with each additional generation the number will increase greatly. Or we look at it from the other direction: If each of us counts the number of direct ancestors we have up to our great-great-great-grandparents, we each count 62 people. One more generation and we each have 126 direct ancestors. One more generation and we have 254 direct ancestors. In other words, each of us has 254 direct ancestors and we are not even past the 1700s for many of us. Either way we look at it, from the past forward, or from the present backward, we can come up with a large number of relatives. It is not a farfetched possibility to think that in just one of those cases, an ancestor of ours was either a rabbi or someone who married a rabbi.

Of course, it is not our goal to try to find a rabbi in our family tree. But if we *happen* to find such a case, it is much easier to trace our own families, generation to generation, back through the centuries. Again, the warning must be stated: *Do not* try to pick a rabbi and prove descent. This is nonkosher genealogy! But if a family tradition says that you were a descendant of someone who might be more well-known than the average person, it would be worthwhile to follow up that clue.

Why is it easy to trace the families of rabbis? There are a few reasons, one of which is known as "yichus." "Yichus" is the Biblical word meaning "genealogy," but the term, in more common usage, has come to mean "family background." It was the custom for many centuries (and still is among some) to try to arrange marriages between one's children and a learned family, or a family with a fine reputation as scholars. To marry into a family with this kind of reputation is to marry a family with yichus. Although at the root of this custom there is the recognition of the importance of scholarship and reputation, the dangers are obvious: There is the development of social classes based on the achievements of others, as well as the attempt to marry for self-serving motives.

The result of this custom has been for families to go to the trouble of documenting their lineage to prove illustrious descent. Although the accuracy of these documents, many of which are in the possession of families, is generally reliable, many families went to great lengths to try to document their descent back to King David, which was traditionally the finest lineage a person could have.

There is a fine line between claiming something you do not deserve based on the achievements of your ancestors, and recognizing the influence of your ancestors and their achievements upon you. This distinction must be made when discussing another source of early rabbinic genealogies. It was often the custom, among rabbis and their families, to make it known that they were the descendants of earlier rabbis of fine repute. Although this would certainly have some effect upon the way they were treated by the community, it is safe to say that a rabbi who did not earn his own reputation did not achieve great heights. So, although a rabbi had to stand on his own, it was nevertheless the custom to make it known that he was a descendant of someone of high esteem, if this was the case. Very often in a document written about a rabbi, or more often in a book written by a rabbi, an introduction will be written that will include the highly respectable lineage of the author. Since many works by rabbis were published posthumously, there were many opportunities to include introductions containing praises for the author. These introductions, usually written by the children or disciples of the rabbi, included biographies of the author. These biographies will often include genealogical information.

APPROBATIONS

Another part of these published works are "approbations." An approbation is a "seal of approval" that was written by a rabbi who either knew the author or had read the manuscript and recommended it as a document of worth. Although the approbations were supposed to serve almost as a "book review," they often contained a great deal of information about the author. It is not unusual for an approbation to give additional genealogical and biographical information about the author. Very often an approbation of one book will lead the reader to a second book where the reader will discover a marriage in the rabbi's family to another famous rabbinic family, which further extends the genealogy.

Let us assume, for example, that you are able to document descent from a rabbi who lived in the nineteenth century. It is not unlikely that he wrote a book, or wrote a manuscript that was later published as a book. The book would certainly have his name on it, and this alone would take you back at least one more generation since Jewish names include the name of the person's father. It is likely that the book contains one or more approbations (often there are several). A reading of the approbations might enable you to find biographical remarks about the rabbi/author, tracing his descent from another rabbi in an earlier generation. In this way, multigenerational genealogies can be created by combining the information found within rabbinic approbations.

A brilliant example of the use of approbations and other similar sources is a book titled *The Unbroken Chain* by Dr. Neil Rosenstein (CIS Publishers, New Jersey). In this two-volume work, Rosenstein has

הסכמת

הרב הגאון האמיתי מופת הדור רשכבה"ג בוצינא קדישא חסידא ופרישא ע"ה פ"ה קדוש יאמר לו מוה' חיים האלבערשטאם יצ"ו נ"י אב"ד דק"ק צאנז יע"א

הנה יד שלוחה אלי מהני תרי אחי הרבני המופלא מוהר"ר מנשה נ"י. והרבני המופלא מוהר"ר אפרים נ"י בניו לאותו צדיק המנוח הרב המאוה"ג בו"ק חו"פ מוה' חיים יוסף זלה"ה שהי' אב"ד בק"ק סטראפקוב, והלך למנוחות וקמו בניו הנ"ל ונתעודדו לעשות נחת רוח לאביהם הצדיק ז"ל שיהי' שפתותיו דובבות ולהוציא לאור חיבור יקר אשר פעל ועשה אביהם המנוח ז"ל וידיו הי' רב לו בטיב גיטין וקידושין. ובקשו ממני הסכמה על החיבור הזה ונראיתי לדבריהם ואף ידי תכון עמהם להוציא לאור חיבור יקר הנ"ל. ומצוה גדולה להיות בעזרתם. והמסייע להם יתברך בכל טוב הה דברי המדבר לכבוד התורה ולומדי'.

יום ד' ע"ו מרחשון ברכות לראש צדיק לפ"ק.

פה צאנז. הק' חיים האלברשטאם

Approbation by Rabbi Chaim Halberstam for a book by the author's ancestor, Rabbi Chaim Josef Gottleib. This approbation, like most, includes genealogical information.

pieced together genealogical information included in approbations and additional biographical sources and has created a genealogy extending from the fifteenth century to the present. The remarkable part of this piece of research and scholarship is its presentation of the dramatic way in which the generations since the family's beginnings in the fifteenth century have gone their separate ways. In this huge work, Rosenstein has been able to trace hundreds of contemporary families back through the centuries. Although his book is quite large, Rosenstein admits that it is not nearly complete, which indicates that many more contemporary families stem from the same lineage. It must also be remembered that Rosenstein's work is one small part of Jewish family history and that there is room for the same kind of work to be done among the vast number of other families in Jewish history.

There is an important precedent being set by Rosenstein. Although the author himself is a descendant of the original family, his research goes far beyond the documentation of his own lineage. Rosenstein has constructed an enormous Jewish genealogy that includes hundreds of other branches. If more of this kind of research would be done, it would be easier for contemporary families to make connections with families of earlier centuries. It is absurd for any of us to pick a family in the sixteenth century and hope that if we research the genealogy we will make a connection with our own; however, it is not a farfetched idea to do the kind of general Jewish genealogical research Rosenstein has done in an effort to help countless numbers of people to trace their family history.

> God created Adam rather than creating the whole human race together for the sake of peace among mankind, so that no one could say, "My ancestor was greater than your ancestor."
>
> MISHNAH, SANHEDRIN 4:5
>
> If a man casts aspersions upon other people's descent—for instance, if he alleges that certain families and individuals are of blemished descent and refers to them as being bastards—suspicion is justified that he himself may be a bastard.
>
> MAIMONIDES, *MISHNEH TORAH*

Rabbinic Dynasties

It is not redundant but, rather, important to stress once again the dangers of going ancestor hunting. It is *not* acceptable to assume that since your last name is the same as that of a famous rabbinic family (or anyone else for that matter) that you are related.

On the other hand, if you do trace descent, *accurately,* from a rabbinic family, you will probably be able to accumulate a great deal of information. Many rabbinic genealogies have been documented, and a thorough check at the major Jewish libraries is suggested to locate such material.

The Index volume of *Encyclopedia Judaica* contains genealogical charts for the major Chassidic dynasties from the founder of Chassidism, the Baal Shem Tov, to the present (pp. 160–167).

> If three consecutive generations are scholars, the Torah will not depart from that line.
>
> JOHANAN B. NAPPAHA, TALMUD: BABA METZIA, 85A

Rabbinic Sources

Often people assume that an ancestor was a rabbi simply because they were told by a relative who remembers somebody with a long beard. Long beards have been known to grow on people who were not rabbis.

On the other hand, if you were told that your great-great-grandfather was a rabbi, there is no reason to immediately assume that it is impossible. However, even if it is true, it doesn't mean that the rabbi was famous or even that he worked as a rabbi. A traditional ordination or "smichah" was given to many people who simply graduated from a rabbinic course of study. They may have gone on to become merchants or innkeepers.

Most often, when a tradition that claims a rabbi in its past is passed to you, the claim is a specific one. For example, "We descend from the Dobno Maggid" or "We descend from the Stropkover Rebbe." When you are searching for information about a certain rabbi, you need to know some clue that you can pursue. Generally, this is either a name or a place. If you know the rabbi's name, you will have to use the following biographical directories by looking for the rabbi's name. If you know the name of the town, then you will have to do town history research.

The following are the best rabbinic biographical sources. Keep in mind that not every rabbi will appear in them. The local rabbi of a small Polish town might or might not be listed. If not, there is still the strong possibility that he will show up in a history of the town.

1) *Otzar Harabanim; Rabbis' Encyclopedia,* by Rabbi Nathan Zvi Friedman, Bnei-Brak, Israel. This volume is a biographical directory of 20,000 rabbis from 970 to 1970. There is a name index, a town index, a book index, and cross references to the rabbis' fathers, fathers-in-law, sons and students, if any of them were also rabbis. The book is a fantastic piece of scholarship. Many Jewish bookstores carry this volume. It is written in Hebrew.
2) *HaChasidut* by Yitzchok Alfasi. This book devotes itself exclu-

sively to Chassidic rabbis, from the Baal Shem Tov, founder of Chassidism, to the present. The book was published in 1977. The volume includes a name and town index, but the name index is a bit difficult to work with since it is by first name. This might seem impractical, but in fact it is the best way to index a book in which many of the individuals simply do not have last names. The book is organized by Chassidic dynasty, giving the reader a good idea who the teachers and students of the rabbis were. The book is also well illustrated with photographs and drawings of many of the rabbis. Facsimiles of the rabbis' signatures are also reproduced when available. This book also is in Hebrew.

3) *Ohole-Schem* by Scholom N. Gottlieb, published in Pinsk, 1912. This was a directory, with addresses, of rabbis throughout the world in 1912. It is written in various languages, but the names of the rabbis are almost always in roman alphabet. The YIVO Institute for Jewish Research has a copy of this book and of all the other rabbinic biographies mentioned here.
4) *Bet Eked Sepharim; Bibliographical Lexicon* by Ch. B. Friedberg, published by Baruch Friedberg, MA Bar-Juda, 49, Sheinkin St. Tel Aviv, 1951. This four-volume work is a massive bibliography of rabbinic literature from 1474 to 1950. If a rabbi wrote a book, it is likely to appear here. The set of books includes an index of rabbis.
5) *Meorei Galicia; Encyclopedia of Galician Rabbis and Scholars, Vols. 1–4,* by Rabbi Meir Wunder, Institute for Commemoration of Galician Jewry (Vol. 4 was published in 1990). Four volumes have been published so far. The fifth and final volume will cover the last two letters of the Hebrew alphabet, Shin through Tav. This important series of books is written in Hebrew but the author plans "ultimately" to translate all the volumes into English.
6) *Atlas Eytz Chayim* by Raphael Halperin, Department of Surveys, Tel Aviv, 1978. Through a series of 70 chronological, genealogical and synchronical maps, tables, diagrams and graphic illustrations, the author has documented brief biographical information on more than two thousand rabbis and scholars from 940 to 1492. The unique aspect of this book is the way the author has shown the relationships between the individuals mentioned. The diagrams, charts and illustrations indicate teacher-student, father-son and colleague relationships. Included with the book is a huge folded poster literally mapping in time the lives of 2,091 individ-

uals in Jewish history. This entire volume is an important addition to the field of rabbinic genealogy.

Although all of these books are in Hebrew, even a knowledge of the Hebrew alphabet will allow you to use the indexes in search of names of individuals and towns. If and when you find something of interest, someone with a knowledge of Hebrew can help you.

If these books are not available in local libraries, once again you must do your best to locate them. YIVO Institute for Jewish Research has all of these books, as does the Jewish Theological Seminary Library. Many good Jewish bookstores carry some of them. If not, they may be able to order them for you. As a last resort, you can purchase them for yourself through Shefa Press (see index).

> Lineage is not just a matter of empty self-congratulation. All lineage, and not just that of nobility, carries with it a certain responsibility. A great person discovered among one's ancestors is not just a cause for bragging but something that must be related to and learned from.
>
> ADIN STEINSALTZ

There are other ways to track down information on rabbis. As noted, *Encyclopedia Judaica* is always a source to check; Memorial Books for specific towns are also fine sources.

There has yet to be a definitive volume on the subject of rabbinic genealogy, but over the years a few people have shown impressive results regarding their own investigation into the subject. I have had the pleasure, over the years, of becoming familiar with the work of:

1) Dr. Neil Rosenstein. Dr. Rosenstein is a surgeon who lives with his family in Elizabeth, New Jersey. His contribution to the field of Jewish genealogy has been most impressive. His several publications are all superb, and it is important to note that the beginning of the Jewish Genealogy Society phenomenon started at his initiative, with the founding of the first Jewish Genealogical Society.

Dr. Rosenstein's most important publication is:

The Unbroken Chain: Biographical Sketches and the Genealogy of Illustrious Jewish Families from the 15th–20th Century (CIS Publishers, 180 Park Avenue, Lakewood, NJ 08701). Make sure to get the second edition. The original publication was one volume; an updated and much expanded two-volume edition was subsequently published.

2) David Einsidler. A dedicated Jewish genealogist and an extra special soul, David Einsidler has earned a reputation as an expert on the subject of rabbinic genealogy. He has been published in various places. Check back issues of *Avotaynu* as well as the newsletter of the Jewish Genealogical Society of Los Angeles.

> A man must not rely on the virtues of his ancestors: if he does not do good in this world, he cannot fall back on the merit of his fathers, for in the time to come no man will eat off his fathers' works, but only of his own.
>
> MIDRASH PSALMS, 146:3

RABBINIC TEXTS

If you have located an ancestor who may have written a Jewish text, there are several libraries that should be checked to see if those books are available. They are:

YIVO Institute for Jewish Research
1048 Fifth Avenue
New York, NY 10028

Jewish Theological Seminary Library
3080 Broadway
New York, NY 10027

Mendel Gottesman Library of Judaica and Hebraica and Archives
Yeshiva University Library
Amsterdam Avenue and 185th Street
New York, NY 10033

Klau Library
Hebrew Union College
Cincinnati, OH 45220

The New York Public Library
Jewish Division
Room 84
42nd Street and Fifth Avenue
New York, NY 10018

There may be a large university library near you with a good Judaica collection. It would be worthwhile to check there as well.

> God prefers your deeds to your ancestor's virtues.
>
> MIDRASH, GENESIS RABBAH, 74

HEBREW SUBSCRIPTION LISTS

In the past (and sometimes even today), Jewish scholars who wanted their books published would do it themselves. They or their representatives would go from town to town trying to sell "subscriptions" to a forthcoming book. The potential reader would pay in advance to support the publication of the volume. In return, the author of the book would usually publish the subscriber's name in the book—for two reasons. First, as an incentive to subscribe. After all, if your name was to appear in a scholarly Jewish text you might be more apt to invest. Second, in order for the "publisher" to know who ultimately gets the book, a list of towns and names must be produced for distribution purposes.

The result of all this is that within thousands of rabbinic and scholarly books that have survived until today we can find lengthy lists of towns and individuals in those towns. The persons listed are the ones who subscribed, prepublication, to the book.

The late Berl Kagan put together a magnificent book on the subject. The remarkable task that Kagan set for himself and that he completed is the indexing, by town, of thousands of subscription lists in Jewish books.

Hebrew Subscription Lists, with an Index to 8767 Jewish Communities in Europe and North Africa (the Library of the Jewish Theological Seminary of America and KTAV Publishing House, Inc., New York, 1975) is the result of Berl Kagan's efforts.

What Kagan has done is to go through the thousands of books published during the last few hundred years that had subscription lists in them. Every time a town name appeared, he noted the name of the town, the name of the book, and the number of people who subscribed to the book. In other words, for you to use Kagan's book genealogically, you would look up the name of a town in your family history. Under the listing of that town you would find the titles of Jewish books and a number following the title. The number would indicate how many people in that town subscribed to that book.

Once you discover that a particular book was subscribed to by certain people in your town, you can go to the original book (to be found at the Jewish Theological Seminary library or in other good Jewish libraries) and examine the subscription list. What you just might find is a name familiar to you.

What would such a discovery mean? Well, if you found an ancestor of yours on a subscription list in an old Jewish text, you would now know nothing more—but nothing less—than that your ancestor helped to support this particular book in which his name appears. It would not offer you any great new discovery of an unknown ancestor, but it would tell you something somewhat significant about that individual.

By the way, the whole process of checking Kagan's book and then checking each old text is a very long one. This step of your research should be saved for a time when you have just about reached dead ends with everything else. But it is a fascinating and educational process.

> The ancestors of the arrogant never stood at Mount Sinai.
>
> TALMUD: NASHIM, 20A
>
> If a man's relative is rich, he claims kinship; if poor, he disowns him.
>
> D'VARIM RABBAH 2

YIZKOR BOOKS

One of the best sources for learning about Jewish communities are Memorial Books. These volumes, also known as Yizkor Books, are books of several hundred pages which tell the story of the Jewish community of one town (or a town and surrounding villages). The Memorial Books have been published and continue to be published by landsmannschaften or individuals. Members of landsmannschaften, because of their affection for their old community as well as their admirable historical sense, have published these books as a tribute to their old homes and the people who were murdered during the Holocaust.

Several hundred Memorial Books corresponding to the same number of villages, shtetlach and cities have been published. Often the tiniest village will have a large book devoted to its history, reflecting the devotion of the survivors. Most of the Memorial Books have been published since the Holocaust, though many books of a similar nature were published before the current era. Books were often written and published to describe tragic events in the lives of communities, and to memorialize the victims of those events. Many books can be found in response to pogroms, for example.

The post-World War II Memorial Books usually take the same or similar format. There are historical articles about the location, photographs, maps, illustrations and names of Holocaust victims. Often advertisements can also be found in the books; in these cases, space was sold to survivors in order to raise publication money. These advertisements are in themselves good sources for information about individuals. The ads often contain photographs as well.

The Memorial Books are usually been written by many people. The landsmannschaften gather articles on different aspects of life in the location, and these are collected for the book. Although the major emphasis of the Memorial Books is the fate of the town during the Holocaust, the books also contain some of the finest historical material about the towns. It is for this reason that Memorial Books are a good general source, regardless of when a family left a town. Even if your family left the town of Skala in 1901, the Skala Memorial Book would be of interest.

Although the Jewish communities of Eastern Europe have been the largest producers of Memorial Books, Jewish communities in Western Europe, especially Germany, have produced many as well. However, a general difference between most of the German works and the Eastern European Memorial Books is that the German books are usually the effort of one person, whereas the Eastern European books are collective works.

One of the drawbacks to the use of Memorial Books for many people is that they are written primarily in Hebrew and Yiddish, although many books have English sections that consist of translations of some of the Yiddish or Hebrew, in most cases. However, this should not stop you from examining these books. Certainly, people can be found who can translate the material. In addition, the photographs contained within the books are wonderful to experience. Often, of course, the photographs are hardly "wonderful," however, for they will be of Holocaust atrocities that took place in the locations discussed in the books.

Another feature of a majority of these books is a name index which is of great assistance when doing family history. The indexes are never complete, though, and should not be relied upon as the only thing to check for family history.

Memorial Books can be used in a variety of ways. The most obvious is to read them to find material on members of your family. This is *not* unlikely, particularly since in the case of smaller communities the chances of your being related to many people in the town, through marriage if nothing else, are great. But in addition to personal family research, Memorial Books can provide other information. We have already mentioned the value of the photographs, which are often the greatest source of information on particular towns that exists. Memorial Books also often discuss religious life in the towns, and frequently focus in on the rabbis or Masters who taught in the towns. The influence of a rabbi on his following was often (and continues to be for many) the most profound in a person's life. There is little question but that knowledge about an ancestor's rabbi or rebbe is knowledge about an ancestor.

Many of the Memorial Books have street maps of the towns as well. These maps range from the most general views to house-to-house detail. Often you can, with the aid of a relative who was from the town, locate the exact place where your family's home stood. These maps can also give you a vivid idea of the size of the town of your ancestral home.

In the same way that you can "enter" the life of an historic figure by reading his or her biography, you can enter the towns of your ancestors by reading the biographies of the towns themselves. Memorial Books are exactly that: biographies of towns that no longer exist, but that at one time were known as home to your ancestors.

As I mentioned at the beginning of this book, a spark that fired my interest in family history was the day I discovered a picture of my great-grandfather, a tinsmith in the tiny shtetl of Dobromil, Poland, in a Memorial Book. I've told the story of that discovery many times, and have often invited people to look for Memorial Books for the towns of their ancestry and attempt to do the same.

One day I was showing a student of mine the wonderful book collection in the New York Public Library Jewish Division, which is the place I originally found my great-grandfather's picture. When we entered the room I asked my student to tell me the names of the towns where her ancestors were from. She looked at me knowingly, and said, "It's not going to happen to me. Don't be funny."

I insisted that we look anyway, and we found several photographs of members of her family, as well as an essay written by her grandfather!

I could tell many other true stories just like this one. The moral: Look for Memorial Books of your towns!

Bibliography of Eastern European Memorial (Yizkor) Books

Compiled by Zachary M. Baker, August 1993

This is a revised version of the "Bibliography of Eastern European Memorial Books," compiled by Zachary M. Baker, that was published in the Jewish Genealogical Society's *Genealogical Resources in the New York Metropolitan Area* (New York, 1989, edited by Estelle M. Guzik). This also updates the *Bibliography of Eastern European Memorial (Yizkor) Books,* compiled by Zachary M. Baker, that was issued as a separate publication by the Jewish Genealogical Society (New York, 1992, edited by Steven W. Siegel).

This bibliography is arranged in three sections: General Reference Works, Countries and Regions, Localities. The last two sections are arranged alphabetically by place name.

Official forms of place names are given, with an indication in parentheses of the countries to which the localities belonged before World War I: (AH) Austria-Hungary, (R) Russian Empire. (The bibliography in the 1983 edition of *From a Ruined Garden* indicates the country to which the locality belonged between the two world wars.)

Book titles are given in transliteration from the Hebrew or Yiddish originals. Place names that appear within book titles are, however, not systematically transliterated but are instead given in their official forms. English titles are supplied in brackets after the Hebrew or Yiddish titles. An asterisk (*) after an English title indicates that the translated title was supplied in the work itself. Otherwise the titles have been translated by the compiler.

The languages in which the book is written are noted at the end of each citation as follows: (H) Hebrew, (Y) Yiddish, (E) English, (F) French, (G) German, (Hu) Hungarian, (J) Judezmo, (P) Polish, (R) Russian, (Ro) Romanian, (S) Spanish, (SC) Serbo-Croatian.

The following cross-references are used:

A) A "see" reference sends the reader from an alternate spelling of a place name to the official form.
B) A "see under" reference sends the reader from the name of a locality discussed in a special chapter of a book on another locality to the full citation for the latter book.
C) A "see also" reference sends the reader to other books that include chapters on a locality.

General Reference Works

Arim ve-imahot be-yisrael; matsevet kodesh le-kehilot yisrael she-nehrevu bi-yedei aritsim u-tmeim be-milhemet ha-olam ha-aharona [Towns and mother cities in Israel; memorial of the Jewish communities which perished. . .]. Ed.: Y. L. Fishman (Maimon). Jerusalem, The Rav Kuk Institute (H)

vol. 1, 1947. 371 p., ports.

vol. 2, 1948. 354 p., ports.

vol. 3, *Warsaw.* [By] D. Flinker. 1948. 308 p., ports.

vol. 4, 1950. 313 p., ports.

vol. 5, *Stanislawow.* Eds.: D. Sadan, M. Gelerter. 1952. Ports., music.

vol. 6, *Brody.* [By] N. Gelber. 1956. 347 p., ports., map.

vol. 7, *Bratislava (Pressburg).* [By] Sh. Weingarten-Hakohen. 1960. 184 p., ports.

Pinkas ha-kehilot; entsiklopediya shel ha-yishuvim le-min hivasdam ve-ad le-aher shoat milhemet ha-olam ha-sheniya [Pinkas hakehillot: encyclopedia of Jewish communities*]. Jerusalem, Yad Vashem Martyrs' and Heroes' Remembrance Authority, 1969– .

Romania. vol. 1: Eds.: Theodore Lavi, Aviva Broshni. 1969. 224, 552 p., illus. (H)

vol. 2: Eds.: Jan Ancel, Theodore Lavi. 1980. 5, 568 p., illus., maps (H)

Germany. vol. 1: *Bavaria.* Ed.: Baruch Zvi Ophir. 1972. 12, 683, 40 p., illus. (H,E)

vol. 2: *Württemberg, Hohenzollern, Baden.* Ed.: Joseph Walk. 1986. 12, 549 p., illus., maps, ports. (H)

vol. 3: *Hesse, Hesse-Nassau, Frankfort.* Ed.: Henry Wassermann. 1992. 12, 725 p., illus., maps. (H)

Hungary. Ed.: Theodore Lavi. 1975. 8, 557 p., illus. (H)

Poland. vol. 1: *The communities of Lodz and its region.* Eds.: Danuta Dabrowska, Abraham Wein. 1976. 15, 285, 15 p., illus. (H,E)

vol. 2: *Eastern Galicia.* Eds.: Danuta Dabrowska, Abraham Wein, Aharon Weiss. 1980. 31, 563 p., illus., maps (H,E)

vol. 3: *Western Galicia and Silesia.* 1984. 23, 392 p., illus., maps (H)

vol. 4: Warsaw and its region. 1989. 24, 482 p., illus., maps (H)

vol. 5: Volhynia and Polesie. Ed.: Shmuel Spector. 1990. 9, 341 p., illus., maps (H)

The Netherlands. Authors: Joseph Michman, Hartog Beem, Dan Michman. 1985. 10, 434 p., illus., maps, ports. (H)

Latvia and Estonia. Ed.: Dov Levin. 1988. 11, 396 p., illus., maps, ports. (H)

Yugoslavia. Ed.: Zvi Loker. 1988. 382 p., illus., maps, ports. (H)

Countries and Regions

Bessarabia (R). *Al admat Bessarabia; divrei mehkar, zikhronot, reshimot, teudot ve-divrei safrut le-kviat ha-dmut shel yahaduta* [Upon the land of Bessarabia; studies, memoirs, articles, documents and essays depicting its image]. Ed: K. A. Bertini. Tel Aviv, United Assoc. of Former Residents of Bessarabia, 1959. 2 vols.: 266, 213 p., ports. (H)

Bessarabia (R). *Bessarabia ha-yehudit be-ma'aroteha; ben shtei milhamot ha- olam 1914-1940* [The Jews in Bessarabia; between the world wars 1914—-1940*]. [By] David Vinitzky. Jerusalem-Tel Aviv, The Zionist Library, Gvilei Bessarabia, 1973. 2 vols.: 719 p., illus. (H)

Bessarabia (R). *Pirkei Bessarabia; measef le-avara shel yahadut Bessarabia* [Chapters from the history of Bessarabian Jewry]. Eds.: L. Kupferstein, Y. Koren. Tel Aviv, "Netiv," 1952. 140 p., ports. (H)

Bessarabia (R). *Yahadut Bessarabia* [The Jewry of Bessarabia]. Eds.: K.A. Bertini *et al.* Jerusalem, The Encyclopaedia of the Jewish Diaspora, 1971. 986 columns, ports., maps (H)

Bulgaria. *Yahadut Bulgaria* [Bulgaria*]. Eds.: A. Romano *et al.* Jerusalem, The Encyclopaedia of the Jewish Diaspora, 1967. 1018 columns, ports., maps, facsims. (H)

Carpatho-Ruthenia (AH) see Karpatalja

Crimea (R). *Yahadut Krim me-kadmuta ve-ad ha-shoa* [The Jews of Crimea from their beginnings until the Holocaust]. Ed.: Yehezkel Keren. Jerusalem, Reuben Mass, 1981. 337 p., illus. (H)

Galicia (AH). *Gedenkbukh Galicia* [Memorial book of Galicia]. Ed.: N. Zucker. Buenos Aires, "Zychronot" Publ., 1964. 334 p., ports., facsims. (Y)

Galicia (AH). *Pinkes Galicia* [Memorial book of Galicia]. Ed.: N. Zucker. Buenos Aires, Former Residents of Galicia in Argentina, 1945. 638 p., ports. (Y)

Galicia (AH). *Sefer Galitsye gedenk bukh* [Anales de Galitzia (Sefer Galitzia)*]. Ed.: Yosef Okrutny. Buenos Aires, Farlag "Galitsye" baym Tsentral Farband fun Galitsyaner Yidn in Buenos-Ayres, 1968. 408 p., illus., ports., facsims. (Y; introd.:S)

Greece. *In memoriam; hommage aux victimes juives des Nazis en Grèce,* 2nd ed. Ed.: Michael Molho. Thessalonique, Communauté Israélite de Thessalonique, 1973. 469 p., illus. (F)

[Greek ed., 1974: 502 p.]

Karpatalja (region) (AH). *Karpatorus* [Karpatorus*]. Ed.: Y. Erez. Jerusalem, The Encyclopaedia of the Jewish Diaspora, 1959. 590 columns, ports., facsims. (H)

Karpatalja (region) (AH). *Sefer shefer harere kedem; golat Karpatorus-Marmarosh be-tiferet u-ve-hurbanah* [The beauty of the mountains of yore; the Karpatorus-Marmarosh exile. . .]. [By] Shlomo Rosman. Brooklyn, Zichron Kedoshim, 1991. 528 p., illus., maps, ports. (H)

Karpatalja (region) (AH). *Sefer zikhron kedoshim le-yehudei Karpatorus-Marmarosh* [Memorial book of the martyrs of Karpatorus-Marmarosh]. [By] Sh. Rosman. Rehovot, 1969. 643 p., ports. (Y)

Latvia. *The Jews in Latvia.* Eds.: M. Bobe *et al.* Tel Aviv, Association of Latvian and Estonian Jews in Israel, 1971. 384 p., illus. (E)

Latvia. *Yahadut Latvia; sefer zikaron* [The Jews of Latvia; a memorial book]. Eds.: B. Eliyav, M. Bobe, A. Kramer. Tel Aviv, Former Residents of Latvia and Estonia in Israel, 1953. 458 p., ports., map (H)

Latvia. *Yidn in Letland* [Latvian Jewry*]. Ed.: Mendel Bobe. Tel Aviv, Reshafim, 1972. 368 p., illus. (Y)

Lithuania. *Bleter fun yidish Lite* [Lithuanian Jews; a memorial book*]. Ed.: Jacob Rabinovitch. Tel Aviv, Hamenora, 1974. 289 p., illus. (Y,H,E)

Lithuania. *Lite* [Lithuania], vol. 1. Eds.: M. Sudarsky, U. Katzenelenbogen, J. Kissin. New York, Jewish-Lithuanian Cultural Society, 1951. 2070 columns, viii p., ports., maps, facsims. (Y); [Lithuania], vol. 2. Ed.: Ch. Leikowicz. Tel Aviv, I. L. Peretz, 1965. 894 columns, ports., facsims. (Y)

Lithuania. *Lithuanian Jewish Communities.* [Edited by] Nancy Schoenburg, Stuart Schoenburg. New York, Garland Publishing, 1991. xi, 502 p., maps. Translated from vol. 3 of *Yahadut Lita* (1967). (E)

Lithuania. *Yahadut Lita* [Lithuanian Jewry*], vol. 1. Eds.: N. Goren, L. Garfinkel *et al.* Tel Aviv, Am-Hasefer, 1959. 648 p., ports., maps, facsims., music (H); vol. 2, 1972 (H); vol. 3. Eds.: R. Hasman, D. Lipec *et al.* Tel Aviv, Association for Mutual Help of Former Residents of Lithuania in Israel, 1967. 396 p., ports., maps (H); vol. 4: The Holocaust, 1941–1945. Ed.: Leib Garfunkel. Tel Aviv, 1984 (H)

Lithuania. *Yidishe shtet, shtetlekh un dorfishe yishuvim in Lite: biz 1918: historish-biografishe skitses* [Jewish cities, towns and villages in Lithuania*]. [By] Berl Kagan. New York, B. Kohen, 1991. ix, 791, v p. (Y)

Maramures (region) (AH). *Sefer Marmarosh; mea ve-shishim kehilot kedoshot be- yishuvan u-ve-hurbanan* [The Marmaros book; in memory of a hundred and sixty Jewish communities*]. Eds.: S. Y. Gross, Y. Yosef Cohen. Tel Aviv, Beit Marmaros, 1983. 58, 436, 151 p., illus., map, ports. (H,Y,E)

Maramures (region) (AH) see also under Karpatalja

Poland. *Megilat Polin* [The scroll of Poland]. Part 5: Holocaust, vol. I. Jerusalem, Society of Religious Jews from Poland, 1961. 351 p., ports., facsims. (H,Y)

Polesie (R). *Kuntres "Ve-ad dor ve-dor emunato"...* [His faith extends from generation to generation; description of Jewish life that existed in Eastern European communities before the Holocaust*]. Jerusalem, The Memorial Committee for Kedoshei Polesie and Volin [1987/88]. 118 p., illus., maps, ports. (H; introd.:E)

Salaj (region) (AH). *Sefer yehude Salaj-Szilagy: toldotehem, kehilotehem,* *mishpehotehem. . .* [Memorial-book of Salaj-Szilagy Jewry*]. Ed.: Giladi David. Tel-Aviv: Council of Szilagy Jews in Israel, 1989. 338, 414 p., illus., map, ports., facsims. (H,Hu,E)

Transcarpathian Ruthenia (AH) see Karpatalja

Transylvania (AH). *Toldot ha-kehilot be-Transylvania; perakim mi-sevalot ha- yehudim ve-nitsane ha-gevura bi-tekufat ha-shoa be-Hungaria* [History of the communities of Transylvania]. [By] Yehuda Shvartz. Hadera, Ha-Aguda Yad le-Kehilot Transylvania [1976]. 293 p., illus. (H)

Ukraine (R). *Shtet un shtetlekh in Ukraine un in andere teyln fun Rusland; Forshungen in yidisher geshikhte un yidishn lebnsshteyger* [Cities and towns in the history of the Jews in Russia and the Ukraine*]. By M. Osherowitch. New York, The M. Osherowitch Jubillee [sic] Committee, 1948. 2 vols. (305, 306 p.) (Y)

Ukraine (R). *Yidn in Ukraine* [Jews in the Ukraine*]. Eds.: M. Osherowitch, J. Lestschinsky *et al.* New York, Association for the Commemoration of the Ukrainian Jews, 1961-1967. 2 vols. (342 p.), ports., maps, facsims. (Y)

Zaglebie (AH). *Pinkes Zaglembye; memorial book.* Ed.: J. Rapoport. Melbourne, Zaglembie Society and Zaglembie Committee in Melbourne; Tel Aviv, Hamenorah, 1972. 82, 613 p., illus. (Y,E)

Zakarpatskaya Oblast (AH) see Karpatalja

LOCALITIES

Akkerman (R). *Akkerman ve-ayarot ha-mehoz; sefer edut ve-zikaron* [Akkerman and the towns of its district; memorial book]. Chairman of the editorial board: Nisan Amitai Stambul. Tel Aviv, Society of Emigrants from Akkerman and Vicinity, 1983. 511 p., illus., map (H)

Aleksandria (R). *Pinkas ha-kehila Aleksandria (Wolyn); sefer yizkor* [Memorial book of the community of Aleksandria (Wolyn)]. Comp.: Shmuel Yizreeli; ed.: Natan Livneh. Tel Aviv, Aleksandria Society, 1972. 314 p., illus. (H)

Aleksandrow (R). *Aleksander* [Aleksandrow, near Lodz]. Ed.: N. Blumenthal. Tel Aviv, Association of Former Residents of Aleksandrow in Israel, 1968. 391 p., ports., facsims. (H,Y)

Alt Lesle (R) see Wloclawek

Amdur (R) see Indura

Amshinov (Mszczonow) (R) see under Zyrardow

Andrychow (AH) see Wadowice

Annopol (R). *Rachov-Annopol; pirkei edut ve-zikaron* [Rachov-Annopol; testimony and remembrance*]. Ed.: Shmuel Nitzan. Israel, Rachov/Annopol and Surrounding Region Society, 1978. 80, 544 p., illus. (H,Y,E)

Antopol (R). *Antopol (Antepolie); sefer yizkor* [Antopol (Antepolie) yizkor book*]. Ed.: Benzion H. Ayalon. Tel Aviv, Antopol Societies in Israel and America, 1972. 11, 754, 170 p., illus. (H,Y,E)

Antopol (R). *Antopol (5400–5702); mi-toldoteha shel kehila ahat be-Polesie*

[Antopol, 1648–1942; from the history of one Jewish community in Polesie]. Ed.: Yosef. Tel Aviv, 5727 [1966/67]. 164 p., illus. (H)

Apt (R) see Opatow

Augustow (R). *Sefer yizkor le-kehilat Augustow ve-ha-seviva* [Memorial book of the community of Augustow and vicinity]. Ed.: J. Alexandroni. Tel Aviv, Association of Former Residents of Augustow and Vicinity, 1966. 549 p., ports. (H,Y)

Auschwitz (AH) see Oswiecim

Babi Yar (R). *Yisker-bukh fun di umgekumene yidn in Babi-Yar* [The Babi Yar book of remembrance*]. Eds.: Yoseph Vinokurov, Shimon Kipnis, Nora Levin. Philadelphia, Publishing House of Peace, 1982. 202, 82 p., illus., ports. (Y,R,E)

Bacau (Romania). *Kehilat Bacau; historiyah yehudit mefoeret* [The community of Bacau]. [By] Meir Eibeshits; [Ed.]: Y. Voladi-Vardi. Tel Aviv, Hasofrim, 1990. 240 p., illus., ports. (H)

Baia Mare (AH) see Nagybanya

Baklerove (Bakalarzewo) (R) see under Suwalki

Baligrod (AH) see under Lesko

Balin (R) see under Kamenets-Podolskiy

Balmazujvaros (AH) see under Debrecen

Banffy-Hunyad (AH) see under Huedin

Baranovka (R) see Novograd-Volynskiy

Baranow (AH). *Sefer yizkor Baranow* [A memorial to the Jewish community of Baranow*]. Ed.: N. Blumenthal. Jerusalem, Yad Vashem, 1964. xvi, 236 p., ports., tabs., facsims. (H,Y,E)

Baranowicze (R). *Baranovits; sefer zikaron* [Baranovits, memorial book]. Tel Aviv, Association of Former Residents of Baranovits in Israel, 1953. vi, 668 p., ports., map, facsims. (H,Y)

Baranowicze (R). *Baranovitsh in umkum un vidershtand* [Baranowich in martyrdom and resistance*]. Ed.: Joseph Foxman. New York, Baranowicher Farband of America, 1964. vol. 1: 5, 107 p. (Y)

Barylow (AH) see under Radziechow

Baytsh (AH) see Biecz

Beclean (Betlen) (AH) see under Des

Bedzin (R). *Pinkas Bendin* [Pinkas Bendin; a memorial to the Jewish community of Bendin*]. Ed.: A. Sh. Stein. Tel Aviv, Association of Former Residents of Bedzin in Israel, 1959. 431 p., ports. (H,Y)

Bedzin (R) see also under Piotrkow Trybunalski

Belchatow (R). *Belchatow yisker-bukh* [Belchatow memorial book]. Buenos Aires, Association of Polish Jews in Argentine, 1951. 511 p., ports., map (Y)

Belgorod-Dnestrovski (R) see Akkerman

Beligrod (AH) see under Lesko

Belz (AH). *Belz; sefer zikaron* [Belz memorial book]. Ed.: Yosef Rubin. Tel Aviv, Belz Societies in Israel and America, 1974. 559 p., illus. (H,Y)

Bendery (R). *Kehilat Bendery; sefer zikaron* [Yizkor book of our birthplace Bendery*]. Ed.: M. Tamari. Tel Aviv, Bendery Societies in Israel and the U. S., 1975. 446, 42 p., illus. (H,Y,E)

Bendin (R) see Bedzin

Beresteczko (R). *Hayeta ayara. . . sefer zikaron le-kehilat Beresteczko ve-ha- seviva* [There was a town. . . memorial book of Beresteczko. . . and vicinity]. Ed.: M. Singer. Haifa, Association of Former Residents of Beresteczko in Israel, 1961. 555 p., ports., map, facsims. (H,Y)

Bereza-Kartuska (R) see under Pruzana

Berezno (R). *Mayn shtetele Berezne* [My town Berezne]. [By] G. Bigil. Tel Aviv, Berezner Society in Israel, 1954. 182 p., ports., map (H,Y)

Berezo (AH) see under Postyen

Bershad (R). *Be-tsel ayara* [Bershad*]. [By] Nahman Huberman. Jerusalem, The Encyclopaedia of the Jewish Diaspora, 1956. 247 p., port. (H)

Berzhan (AH) see Brzezany

Beszterce (AH) see Bistrita

Betlen (AH) see under Des

Biala Podlaska (R). *Podlyashe in natsi-klem; notitsn fun khurbn* [Podlasie en las garras del nazismo*]. [By] M. I. Faignboim [Feigenbaum]. Buenos Aires, Committee of Friends, 1953. 241 p., illus. (Y)

Biala Podlaska (R). *Sefer Biala Podlaska* [Book of Biala Podlaska]. Ed.: M. J. Feigenbaum. Tel Aviv, Kupat Gmilut Hesed of the Community of Biala Podlaska, 1961. 501 p., ports., facsims. (H,Y)

Biala Rawska (R). *Sefer yizkor le-kedoshei Biala Rawska* [Memorial book to the martyrs of Biala Rawska]. Eds.: Eliyahu Freudenreich, Arye Yaakobovits. Tel Aviv, Biala Rawska Societies in Israel and the Diaspora, 1972. 255 p., illus. (H,Y)

Bialobrzegi (R). *Sefer zikaron le-kehilat Bialobrzeg* [Memorial book of the Byalovzig community*]. Ed.: David Avraham Mandelboim. Tel Aviv, Council of the Town of Bialobrzeg, 1991. 396 p., illus., maps, ports. (H)

Bialystok (R). *Bialystok; bilder album. . .* [Bialystok; photo album. . . *]. Ed.: D. Sohn. New York, Bialystoker Album Committee, 1951. 386 p. (Y,E)

Bialystok (R). *Der Bialystoker yisker-bukh* [The Bialystoker memorial book*]. Ed.: I. Shmulewitz. New York, Bialystoker Center, 1982. xi, 396, 205, x p., ports., illus. (Y,E)

Bialystok (R). *Pinkes Bialystok; grunt-materyaln tsu der geshikhte fun di yidn in Bialystok biz nokh der ershter velt-milkhome* [Pinkos Bialystok (the chronicle of Bialystok); basic material for the history of the Jews in Bialystok until the period after the First World War*]. Ed.: Yudl Mark. New York, Bialystok Jewish Historical Association, 1949—-1950. 2 vols. (Y)

Biecz (AH). *Sefer zikaron le-kedoshei ayaratenu Biecz* [Memorial book of the martyrs of Biecz]. Ed.: P. Wagshal. Ramat Gan, Association of Former Residents of Biecz and Vicinity in Israel, 1960. 243 p., ports. (H,Y)

Bielica (R). *Pinkas Bielica* [Book of Belitzah-Bielica*]. Ed.: L. Losh. Tel Aviv, Former Residents of Bielica in Israel and the USA, 1968. 511 p., ports., map, facsims. (H,Y,E)

Bielitz-Biala (AH) see Bielsko-Biala

Bielsk-Podlaski (R). *Bielsk-Podlaski; sefer yizkor. . .* [Bielsk-Podliask; book in the holy memory of the Bielsk-Podliask Jews*]. Ed.: H. Rabin. Tel Aviv, Bielsk Societies in Israel and the United States, 1975. 554, 44 p., illus. (H,Y,E)

Bielsko-Biala (AH). *Bielitz-Biala (Bielsko-Biala); pirkei avar* [chapters from the past]. [By] Elijahu Miron. Israel, 1973. 182 p., illus. (H,G)

Biezun (R). *Sefer ha-zikaron le-kedoshei Biezun* [Memorial book of the martyrs of Biezun]. Tel Aviv, Former Residents of Biezun, 1956. 186 p., ports. (H,Y)

Bikovsk (Bukowsko) (AH) see under Sanok

Bilgoraj (R). *Bilgoraj yisker-bukh* [Bilgoraj memorial book]. [By] Moshe Teitlboym. Jerusalem, 1955. 243 p., illus. (Y)

Bilgoraj (R). *Khurbn Bilgoraj* [Destruction of Bilgoraj]. Ed.: A. Kronenberg. Tel Aviv, 1956. x, 365 p., ports. (Y)

Bisk (AH) see Busk

Bistrita (AH). *Bistrits; "ir ve-em be-yisrael. . .* [Bistrits; mother city in Israel]. [By] Nata Aryeh Gafni (Vaynshtok). [Israel], Association of Former Residents of Bistrits-Nasod, [1990?]. 157 p., illus., ports. (H)

Bitolj (Turkey) see Monastir

Bitshutsh (AH) see Buczacz

Bivolari (Romania). *Ayaratenu Bivolari* [Our town Bivolari]. Eds.: Moscu Abramovici *et al.* Haifa, Bivolari Immigrants Organization in Israel, 1981. 160, 37 p., illus. (H,Ro,E)

Bledow (R) see under Mogielnica

Bobrka (AH). *Le-zekher kehilat Bobrka u-benoteha* [Boiberke memorial book*]. Ed.: Sh. Kallay. Jerusalem, Association of Former Residents of Bobrka and Vicinity, 1964. 218, 38 p., ports., facsims. (H,Y,E)

Bobruisk (R). *Bobruisk; sefer zikaron le-kehilat Bobruisk u-benoteha* [Memorial book of the community of Bobruisk and its surroundings]. Ed.: Y. Slutski. Tel Aviv, Former Residents of Bobruisk in Israel and the USA, 1967. 2 vols.: 871 p., ports., map, facsims. (H,Y)

Boiberik (AH) see Bobrka

Bolechow (AH). *Sefer ha-zikaron le-kedoshei Bolechow* [Memorial book of the martyrs of Bolechow]. Ed.: Y. Eshel. Association of Former Residents of Bolechow in Israel, 1957. 352 p., ports. (H,Y)

Bolimow (R) see under Lowicz

Boremel (R) see under Beresteczko

Borsa (AH). *Sefer zikaron Borsha, o: ayarat-ahavim be-yarketei ha-karpatim* [Memorial book of Borsha, or: The beloved village by the foot of the Carpat[h]ians*]. Written and edited by Gedaliahu Stein. Kiryat Motzkin, 1985. 655 p., illus., maps, ports. (H)

Borszczow (AH). *Sefer Borszczow* [The book of Borstchoff*]. Ed.: N. Blumenthal. Tel Aviv, Association of Former Residents of Borszczow in Israel, 1960. 341 p., ports., facsims. (H,Y)

Boryslaw (AH) see under Drohobycz

Bransk (R). *Braynsk; sefer ha-zikaron* [Brainsk; book of memories*]. [By] A. Trus and J. Cohen. New York, Brainsker Relief Committee of New York, 1948. 440 p., ports., facsims. (Y)

Bratislava (Pozsony) (AH) see under *Arim ve-imahot,* vol. 7

Braslaw (R). *Emesh shoa; yad le-kehilot/gevidmet di kehiles Braslaw. . .* [Darkness and desolation; in memory of the communities of Braslaw, Dubene, Jaisi, Jod, Kislowszczizna, Okmienic, Opsa, Plusy, Rimszan, Slobodka, Zamosz, Zaracz*]. Eds.: Machnes Ariel, Klinov Rina. [Israel], Association of Braslaw and Surroundings in Israel and America; Ghetto Fighters' House and Hakibbutz Hameuchad Publishing House, 1986. 636 p., illus., maps, ports. (H,Y,E)

Bratislava (Pozsony) (AH) see under *Arim ve-imahot,* vol. 7

Braynsk (R) see Bransk

Brest Litovsk (R) see Brzesc nad Bugiem

Breziv (AH) see Brzozow

Brezova nad Bradlom (Berezo) (AH) see under Postyen

Briceni (R) see Brichany

Brichany (R). *Britshan; Britsheni ha-yehudit be-mahatsit ha-mea ha-aharona* [Brichany; its Jewry in the first half of our century]. Eds.: Y. Amizur *et al.* Tel Aviv, Former Residents of Brichany, 1964. 296 p., ports., map (H)

Brichevo (R). *Pinkas Brichevo* [Memorial book of Brichevo]. Ed.: K. A. Bertini. Tel Aviv, Former Residents of Brichevo (Bessarabia) in Israel, 1970. 531 p., ports., map, facsims. (H,Y)

Briegel (AH) see Brzesko

Brisk (R) see Brzesc nad Bugiem

Brisk Kuyavsk (Brzesc Kujawski) (R) see under Wloclawek

Brody (AH) see under *Arim ve-imahot,* vol. 6

Broslev (R) see Bratslav

Broszniow (AH) see under Rozniatow

Brzesc Kujawski (R) see under Wloclawek

Brzesc nad Bugiem (R). *Brisk de-Lita* [Brest Lit.(owsk) Volume*]. Ed.: E. Steinman. Jerusalem, The Encyclopaedia of the Jewish Diaspora, 1954-1955. 2 vols., ports., map (H,Y)

Brzesko (AH). *Sefer yizkor shel kehilat Briegel-Brzesko ve-ha-seviva* [Memorial book of Briegel-Brzesko and vicinity]. Eds.: Hayim Teller, Liber Brenner (Yiddish). Ramat-Gan, 1980. 267 p., illus. (H,Y)

Brzezany (AH). *Brzezany, Narajow ve-ha-seviva; toldot kehilot she-nehrevu* [Brzezany memorial book*]. Ed.: Menachem Katz. Haifa, Brzezany-Narajow Societies in Israel and the United States, 1978. 28, 473 p., illus. (H,Y,E)

Brzeziny (R). *Bzhezhin yisker-bukh* [Brzeziny memorial book*]. Eds.: A. Alperin, N. Summer. New York, Brzeziner Book Committee, 1961. 288 p., ports. (Y)

Brzeznica (R) see under Radomsko

Brzozow (AH). *Sefer zikaron kehilat Breziv (Brzozow)* [A memorial to the Brzozow community*]. Ed.: Avraham Levite. [Israel], The Survivors of Brzozow, 1984. 348, [16], 195 p., illus., maps, ports. (H,Y,E)

Buchach (AH) see Buczacz

Buczacz (AH). *Sefer Buczacz; matsevet zikaron le-kehila kedosha* [Book of Buczacz; in memory of a martyred community]. Ed.: I. Kahan. Tel Aviv, Am Oved, 1956. 302 p., ports., facsims. (H)

Budapest (AH) see under *Arim ve-imahot,* vol. 1

Budzanow (AH). *Sefer Budzanow* [Book of Budzanow*]. Ed.: J. Siegelman. Haifa, Former Residents of Budzanow in Israel, 1968. 319 p., ports., maps, facsims. (H,Y,E)

Bukaczowce (AH) see under Rohatyn

Bukowsko (AH) see under Sanok

Bursztyn (AH). *Sefer Bursztyn* [Book of Bursztyn]. Ed.: S. Kanc. Jerusalem, The Encyclopaedia of the Jewish Diaspora, 1960. 426 columns, ports., facsims. (H,Y)

Busk (AH). *Sefer Busk; le-zekher ha-kehila she-harva* [Busk; in memory of our community*]. Ed.: A. Shayari. Haifa, Busker Organization in Israel, 1965. 293 p., ports., facsims. (H,Y,E,P)

Byalovzig (R) see Bialobrzegi

Bychawa (R). *Bychawa; sefer zikaron* [Bychawa; a memorial to the Jewish community of Bychawa Lubelska*]. Ed.: J. Adini. Bychawa Organization in Israel, 1968. 636 p., ports., map, facsims. (H,Y)

Byten (R). *Pinkas Byten* [Memorial book of Byten]. Ed.: D. Abramowich, M. W. Bernstein. Buenos Aires, Former Residents of Byten in Argentina, 1954. 605 p., map, facsims. (Y)

Cakovec (AH). *Megilat ha-shoa shel kehilat kodesh Cakovec* [Holocaust scroll of the holy community of Cakovec]. [By] Moshe Etz-Hayyim (Tibor Grunwald). Tel Aviv, 1977. 182, 12 p., illus. (H,SC)

Calarasi (R) see Kalarash

Capresti (R) see Kapreshty

Cernauti (Czernowitz) (AH) see under *Arim ve-imahot,* vol. 4

Cetatea-Alba (R) see Akkerman

Charsznica (R) see under Miechow

Chelm (R). *Sefer ha-zikaron le-kehilat Chelm; 40 shana le-hurbana* [Yizkor book in memory of Chelm*]. Ed.: Sh. Kanc. Tel Aviv, Chelm Society in Israel and the U.S., [1980/81]. 828 columns, illus. (H,Y)

Chelm (R). *Yisker-bukh Chelm* [Commemoration book Chelm*]. Ed.: M.

Bakalczuk-Felin. Johannesburg, Former Residents of Chelm, 1954. 731 p., ports., facsims. (Y)

Chernovtsy (Czernowitz) (AH) see under *Arim ve-imahot,* vol. 4

Chervonoarmeisk (R) see Radziwillow

Chmielnik (R). *Pinkas Chmielnik* [Memorial book of Chmielnik]. Tel Aviv, Former Residents of Chmielnik in Israel, 1960. 1299 columns, ports., facsims. (H,Y)

Chodecz (R) see under Wloclawek

Cholojow (AH) see under Radziechow

Chorostkow (AH). *Sefer Chorostkow* [Chorostkow book*]. Ed.: D. Shtokfish. Tel Aviv, Committee of Former Residents of Chorostkow in Israel, 1968. 418 p., ports., facsims. (H,Y)

Chorzele (R). *Sefer zikaron le-kehilat Chorzel* [Memorial book of the community of Chorzel]. Ed.: L. Losh. Tel Aviv, Association of Former Residents of Chorzele in Israel, 1967. 272 p., ports., facsims. (H,Y)

Chrzanow (AH). *Sefer Chrzanow* [The book of Chrzanow]. [By] Mordechai Bochner. Regensburg, 1948. xiii, 377 p. (Y)

Chrzanow (AH). *Sefer Chrzanow; lebn un umkum fun a yidish shtetl* [Chrzanow; the life and destruction of a Jewish shtetl*]. [By] Mordechai Bochner; translated by Jonathan Boyarin. Roslyn Harbor, NY, Solomon Gross, 1989. xiii, 320, 168 p., illus., ports., map (Y,E)

Ciechanow (R). *Yisker-bukh fun der Tshekhanover yidisher kehile; sefer yizkor le-kehilat Ciechanow* [Memorial book of the community of Ciechanow]. Ed.: A. W. Yassni. Tel Aviv, Former Residents of Ciechanow in Israel and in the Diaspora, 1962. 535 p., ports. (H,Y)

Ciechanowiec (R). *Ciechanowiec; mehoz Bialystok, sefer edut ve-zikaron* [Ciechanoviec-Bialystok district; memorial and records*]. Ed.: E. Leoni. Tel Aviv, The Ciechanovitzer Immigrant Assoc. in Israel and the USA, 1964. 936, 78 p., ports., facsims. (H,Y,E)

Ciechocinek (R) see under Wloclawek

Cieszanow (AH). *Sefer zikaron le-kehila kedosha Cieszanow* [Memorial book of the martyred community Cieszanow]. Ed.: D. Ravid. Tel Aviv, Former Residents of Cieszanow in Israel, 1970. 331 p., ports. (H,Y)

Cluj (AH) see Kolozsvar

Cmielow (R) see under Ostrowiec

Cracow (AH) see Krakow

Csaktornya (AH) see Cakovec

Csenger (AH). *Sefer yizkor le-kedoshei Csenger, Porcsalma ve-ha-seviva* [Memorial book of the martyrs of Csenger, Porcsalma and vicinity]. [By] Sh. Friedmann. Tel Aviv, 1966. 108, 60 p., ports., facsims. (H,Hu)

Czarny Dunajec (AH) see under Nowy Targ

Czerbin (R) see under Ostroleka

Czernowitz (AH) see under *Arim ve-imahot,* vol. 4

Czestochowa (R). *Churban Czenstochow—The destruction of Czenstokov— Khurbn Tshenstokhov.* [By] Benjamin Orenstein. [Western Germany], Central Farwaltung fun der Czenstochower Landsmanszaft in der Amerikaner Zone in Dajczland, 1948. 463 p., illus., ports. (Y in Latin characters)

Czestochowa (R). *Sefer Tshenstokhov* [Memorial book of Czestochow]. Ed.: M. Schutzman. Jerusalem, The Encyclopaedia of the Jewish Diaspora, 1967–1968. 2 vols., ports. (H,Y)

Czestochowa (R). *Tshenstokhover landsmanshaft in Montreal* [Czenstochover landsmanschaft in Montreal*]. Ed.: B. Orenstein. Montreal, The Czenstochover Society in Montreal, 1966. 349, [28] p., ports. (Y)

Czestochowa (R). *Tshenstokhov; nayer tsugob-material tsum bukh "Tshenstokhover yidn"* [Czenstochov; a new supplement to the book "Czenstochover Yidn"*]. Ed.: S. D. Singer. New York, United Relief Committee in New York, 1958. 336, iv p., ports. (Y)

Czestochowa (R). *Tshenstokhover yidn* [The Jews of Czestochowa]. Ed.: R. Mahler. New York, United Czestochower Relief Committee and Ladies Auxiliary, 1947. cxliv, 404 p., ports., facsims. (Y)

Czortkow (AH). *Sefer yizkor le-huntsahat kedoshei kehilat Czortkow* [Memorial book of Czortkow*]. Ed.: Y. Austri-Dunn. Tel Aviv, Haifa, Former Residents of Czortkow in Israel, 1967. 435, 36 p., ports., map, facsims. (H,Y,E)

Czyzewo (R). *Sefer zikaron Czyzewo* [Memorial book Tshijewo*]. Ed.: Sh. Kanc. Tel Aviv, Former Residents of Czyzewo in Israel and the USA, 1961. 1206 columns, ports., facsims. (H,Y)

Dabrowa Gornicza (R). *Sefer kehilat yehudei Dabrowa Gornicza ve-hurbana* [Memorial book of Dombrawa Gornitza]. Eds.: N. Gelbart *et al.* Tel Aviv, Former Residents of Dombrowa Gornitza, 1971. 696 p., ports., facsims. (H,Y)

Dabrowica (R). *Sefer Dombrovitsa* [Book of Dabrowica]. Ed.: L. Losh. Tel Aviv, Association of Former Residents of Dabrowica in Israel, 1964. 928 p., ports., maps, facsims. (H,Y)

Dabrowica (R) see also under Polesie (region)

Daugavpils (R). *Dvinsk; the rise and decline of a town.* [By] Yudel Flior; translated from the Yiddish by Bernard Sachs. Johannesburg, Dial Press, [1965?]. 188 p. (E)

Daugavpils (R). *Le-zekher kehilat Dvinsk* [In memory of the community of Dvinsk]. Haifa, [1975]. 63 p., illus. (H)

Daugieliszki (R) see under Swieciany

David Horodok (R) see Dawidgrodek

Dawidgrodek (R). *David Horodoker memorial book - Memorial book of David-Horodok.* Translated from the Yiddish and part of the Hebrew original [by] Norman Helman. Oak Park, MI, David Horodoker Women's Organization, [1981]. 129 p., map. (E)

Dawidgrodek (R). *Sefer zikaron Dawidgrodek* [Memorial book of David-grodek]. Eds.: Y. Idan *et al.* Tel Aviv, Former Residents of Dawidgrodek in Israel, [195–]. 487 p., ports. (H,Y)

Dawidgrodek (R) see also under Polesie (region)

Debica (AH). *Sefer Dembits* [Book of Debica]. Ed.: D. Leibl. Tel Aviv, Association of Former Residents of Debica, 1960. 204 p., ports. (H,Y)

Deblin (R). *Sefer Deblin-Modrzyc* [Demblin-Modrzyc book*]. Ed.: D. Shtokfish. Tel Aviv, Association of Former Residents of Demblin-Modrzyc, 1969. 694 p., ports., facsims. (H,Y)

Debrecen (AH). *Mea shana le-yehudei Debrecen; le-zekher kedoshei ha-kehila ve-yishuvei ha-seviva* [Hundred years of Debrecen Jewry; in memory of the martyrs of Debrecen and vicinity]. [By] M. E. Gonda. Tel Aviv, Committee for Commemoration of the Debrecen Jewry, 1970. 264, 409 p., ports., facsims. (H,Hu)

Dej (AH) see Des

Delatycze (R) see under Lubcza

Dembits (AH) see Debica

Demblin (R) see Deblin

Derecske (AH). *Sefer zikaron le-yehudei Derecske ve-geliloteha* [Emlékkönyv Derecske és vidéke zsidósága* — Memorial book to the Jews of Derecske and its environs]. [By] Arje Moskovits. Tel Aviv, Society of Derecske Emigrants in Israel, 1984. 186, [93], 185 p., illus., facsims., ports. (H,Hu)

Derecske (AH) see also under Debrecen

Dereczyn (R). *Sefer Dereczyn* [Deretchin memorial book*]. Tel Aviv, Deretchiners Societies in Israel and USA, [196–]. 494 p., ports., facsims. (H,Y)

Derewno (R) see under Rubiezewicze; Stolpce

Des (AH). *Des. . . , Bethlen, Magyarlapos, Retteg, Nagyilonda és kornyeke* [. . . and vicinity]. Ed.: Z. Singer. Tel Aviv, Former Residents of Des, [197–]. 2 vols. (683 p.), ports., facsims. (Hu)

Devenishki (R) see Dziewieniszki

Dibetsk (Dubiecko) (AH) see under Dynow (*Khurbn Dynow*)

Dieveniskes (R) see Dziewieniszki

Dinov (AH) see Dynow

Disna (R) see Dzisna

Divenishok (R) see Dziewieniszki

Dmytrow (AH) see under Radziechow

Dnepropetrovsk (R) see Yekaterinoslav

Dobromil (AH). *Sefer zikaron le-zekher Dobromil* [Memorial book Dobromil*]. Ed.: M. Gelbart. Tel Aviv, The Dobromiler Society in New York and the Dobromiler Organization in Israel, 1964. 389, 138 p., ports., facsims. (H,Y,E)

Dobryn (R) see under Wloclawek

Dobrzyn (R). *Ayarati; sefer zikaron le-ayarot Dobrzyn-Golub* [My town; in memory of the communities Dobrzyn-Gollob*]. Ed.: M. Harpaz. [Tel Aviv], Association of Former Residents of Dobrzyn-Golub, 1969. 459, 29 p., ports., facsims. (H,Y,E)

Dobrzyn (R). *Yisker bletlekh* [Our village*]. [By] Shmuel Russak. Tel Aviv, 1972. 6, 90 p., illus. (Y,E)

Dokszyce (R). *Book in memory of Dokshitz-Parafianow. . . .* Ed.: David Stockfish; [excerpts] translated by Yariv Eldar. Israel, Organization of Dokshitz-Parafianow Veterans in Israel and the Diaspora, 1990. 116 p. (E)

Dokszyce (R). *Sefer yizkor Dokszyce-Parafianow* [Dokszyc-Parafianow book*]. Ed.: D. Shtokfish. Tel Aviv, Assoc. of Former Residents of Dokszyce-Parafianow in Israel, 1970. 350 p., ports., facsims. (H,Y)

Dolhinow (R). *Esh tamid-yizkor le-Dolhinow; sefer zikaron le-kehilat Dolhinow ve-ha-seviva* [Eternal flame; in memory of Dolhinow]. Eds.: Josef Chrust, Matityahu Bar-Razon. Tel Aviv, Society of Dolhinow Emigrants in Israel, [1984 or 1985]. 718 p., illus., maps, ports. (H,Y,E)

Dombrava Gornitsha (R) see Dabrowa Gornicza

Dombrovitsa (R) see Dabrowica

Drodzyn (R) see under Stolin

Drohiczyn nad Bugiem (R). *Sefer Drohiczyn* [Drohiczyn book]. Ed.: D. Shtokfish. Tel Aviv, 1969. 576, 67 p., illus. (H,Y,E)

Drohiczyn Poleski (R). *Drohiczyn; finf hundert yor yidish lebn* [Memorial book Drohichyn*]. Ed.: D. B. Warshawsky. Chicago, Book-Committee Drohichyn, 1958. viii, 424 p., ports., map, facsims. (Y)

Drohobycz (AH). *Sefer zikaron le-Drohobycz, Boryslaw ve-ha-seviva* [Memorial to the Jews of Drohobycz, Boryslaw and surroundings*]. Ed.: N. M. Gelber. Tel Aviv, Assoc. of Former Residents of Drohobycz, Boryslaw and Surroundings, 1959. 224 p., ports. (H,Y)

Droshkopol (R) see Druzkopol

Druja (R). *Sefer Druja ve-kehilot Miory, Drujsk, ve-Leonpol* [The book of Druya and the communities of Miory, Druysk and Leonpol*]. Ed.: Mordekhai Neishtat. Tel Aviv, Druja and Surrounding Region Society, 1973. 255 p., illus. (H,Y)

Druja (R) see also under Glebokie

Drujsk (R) see under Druja (*Sefer Druja*)

Druzkopol (R). *Ayaratenu Druzkopol* [Our town Droshkopol]. Eds.: Y. Shiloni *et al.* [Haifa], Former Residents of Droshkopol in Israel, 1957. 108 p., ports. (H), mimeo.

Druzkopol (R). *Di geshikhte fun mayn shtetele Druzkopol* [The story of my "stetele Droshkopol"*]. [By] A. Boxer (Ben-Arjeh). Ed.: S. Eisenberg. Haifa, 1962. 108 p., ports (Y), mimeo.

Dubene (Dubinowo) (R) see under Braslaw

Dubiecko (AH) see under Dynow (*Khurbn Dynow*)

Dubno (R). *Dubno; sefer zikaron* [Dubno; a memorial to the Jewish community of Dubno, Wolyn*]. Ed.: Y. Adini. Tel Aviv, Dubno Organization in Israel, 1956. 752 columns, ports., maps, facsims. (H,Y)

Dubossary (R). *Dubossary; sefer zikaron* [Dubossary memorial book]. Ed.: Y. Rubin. Tel Aviv, Association of Former Residents of Dubossary in America, Argentina and Israel, 1965. 377 p., ports., maps, music (H,Y)

Dubrovitsa (R) see Dabrowica

Dukszty (R) see under Swieciany

Dumbraveny (R). *Sefer Dombroven; ner-zikaron le-moshava ha-haklait ha-yehudit ha-rishonah be-Bessarabia* [Dombroven book; memorial to the first Jewish agricultural colony in Bessarabia]. Ed.: Haim Toren. Jerusalem, Dombroven Societies in Israel and The Diaspora, 1974. 8, 252 p., illus. (H,Y)

Dunajska Streda (AH) see Dunaszerdahely

Dunaszerdahely (AH). *Sefer zikaron le-kehilat Dunaszerdahely* [A memorial to the Jewish community of Dunaszerdahely (Dunajska Streda)*]. [By] Abraham (Alfred) Engel. Israel, Committee of Dunaszerdahely Emigrants, 1975. 429, 157 p., illus. (H,Hu)

Dunilowicze (R) see under Glebokie

Dusetos (R). *Ayarah hayetah be-Lita: Dusiat bi-re'i ha-zikhronot* [There was a shtetl in Lithuania: Dusiat reflected in reminiscences*]. Ed.: Sara Weiss-Slep. Tel Aviv, Society of Former Residents of Dusiat, 1989. 421 p., illus., maps, ports. (H)

Dvart (R) see Warta

Dvinsk (R) see Daugavpils

Dyatlovo (R) see Zdzieciol

Dynow (AH). *Khurbn Dynow, Sonik, Dibetsk* [The destruction of Dynow, Sanok, Dubiecko]. [By] David Moritz. New York, [1949/50]. 156 p., illus. (Y)

Dynow (AH). *Sefer Dynow; sefer zikaron le-kedoshei kehilat Dynow she-nispu ba- shoa ha-natsit* [The memorial book of Jewish Dinov*]. Eds.: Yitzhak Kose, Moshe Rinat. Tel Aviv, Dynow Society, 1979. 324 p., illus., map (H,Y)

Dzerzhinsk (R) see Koidanovo

Dzialoszyce (R). *Sefer yizkor shel kehilat Dzialoszyce ve-ha-seviva* [Yizkor book of the Jewish community in Dzialoszyce and surroundings*]. Tel Aviv, Hamenora, 1973. 44, 423 p., illus. (H,Y,E)

Dziewieniszki (R). *Sefer Divenishok; yad vashem le-ayara yehudit* [Devenishki book; memorial book*]. Ed.: David Shtokfish. Israel, Divenishok Societies in Israel and the United States, 1977. 536 p., illus. (H,Y)

Dzikow (AH) see Tarnobrzeg

Dzisna (R). *Disna; sefer zikaron le-kehila* [Disna; memorial book of the community]. Eds.: A. Beilin *et al.* Tel Aviv, Former Residents of Disna in Israel and the USA, 1969. 277 p., ports., facsims. (H,Y)

Edineti (R) see Yedintsy

Eger (AH). *Yehudei Erlau* [The Jews of Eger]. Eds.: Arthur Abraham Ehrenfeld-Elkay, Tibor Meir Klein-Z'ira. Jerusalem, Eger Commemorative Committee, 1975. 64, 36, 100 p., illus. (H,Hu)

Ejszyszki (R). *"Aishishuk"; its history and its destruction: documentaries, memories and illustrations.* Compiled and edited by Peretz Alufi, Shaul Barkali; translated by Shoshanna Gavish. [U.S.A.?], 1980. 81 p. (E)

Ejszyszki (R). *Eishishok, koroteha ve-hurbana* [Ejszyszki, its history and destruction]. Ed.: Sh. Barkeli. Jerusalem, Committee of the Survivors of Ejszyszki in Israel, 1960. 136 p., ports. (H,Y)

Ekaterinoslav (R) see Yekaterinoslav

Erlau (AH) see Eger

Falenica (R). *Sefer Falenica* [Falenica book*]. Ed.: D. Shtokfish. Tel Aviv, Former Residents of Falenica in Israel, 1967. 478 p., ports., facsims. (H,Y)

Falenica (R) see also under Otwock

Fehergyarmat (AH). *Ayaratenu le-she-avar Fehergyarmat* [Our former city Fehergyarmat]. [By] J. Blasz. Bnei Brak, 1965. 44, 52 p., ports., music, facsims. (H,Hu)

Felshtin (R). *Felshtin; zamlbukh lekoved tsum ondenk fun di Felshtiner kdoyshim* [Felshtin; collection in memory of the martyrs of Felshtin]. New York, First Felshtiner Progressive Benevolent Association, 1937. 670 p., illus. (Y,E)

Filipow (R) see under Suwalki

Frampol (Lublin) (R). *Sefer Frampol* [Frampol book*]. Ed.: D. Shtokfish. Tel Aviv, [Book Committee], 1966. 414 p., ports. (H,Y)

Frampol (Podolia) (R) see under Kamenets-Podolskiy

Gabin (R). *Gombin; dos lebn un umkum fun a yidish shtetl in Poyln* [Gombin; the life and destruction of a Jewish town in Poland*]. Eds.: Jack Zicklin *et al.* New York, Gombin Society in America, 1969. 228, 162 p., illus. (Y,E)

Gargzdai (R). *Sefer Gorzd (Lita); ayara be-hayeha u-be-hilayona* [Gorzd book; a memorial to the Jewish community of Gorzd*]. Ed.: Yitzhak Alperovitz. Tel Aviv, The Gorzd Society, 1980. 79, 417 p., illus. (H,Y,E)

Garwolin (R). *Garwolin yisker-bukh* [Garwolin memorial book]. Eds.: Moshe Zaltsman, Baruch Shein. Tel Aviv, New York, Garwolin Societies, 1972. 304 p., illus. (H,Y)

Ger (R) see Gora Kalwaria

Gherla (AH) see Szamosujvar

Glebokie (R). *Khurbn Glubok. . . Koziany* [The destruction of Glebokie. . . Koziany]. [By] M. and Z. Rajak. Buenos Aires, Former Residents' Association in Argentina, 1956. 426 p., ports. (Y)

Glebokie (R) see also under Vilna (*Vilner zamlbukh. . .*)

Glina (AH) see Gliniany

Gliniany (AH). *Kehilat Glina 1473-1943; toldoteha ve-hurbana* [The community of Glina 1473–1943; its history and destruction]. [By] Asher Korech. Jerusalem, 1950. 138 p., illus. (H)

Gliniany (AH). *Khurbn Glinyane* [The tragic end of our Gliniany*]. New York, Emergency Relief Committee for Gliniany and Vicinity, 1946. [52] p. (Y,E)

Gliniany (AH). *Megiles Gline* [The book of Gline*]. Ed.: H. Halpern. New York, Former Residents of Gline, 1950. 307 p. (Y)

Glinojeck (R). *Mayn shtetele Glinovyetsk; un di vayterdike vandlungen Plotsk-Wierzbnik, zikhroynes* [My town Glinojeck. . .]. [By] Shlomo Moshkovich. Paris, 1976. 335 p., illus. (Y)

Glubok (R) see Glebokie

Glusk (R) see under Bobruisk; Slutsk

Gniewaszow (R). *Sefer Gniewaszow* [Memorial book Gniewashow*]. Ed.: D. Shtokfish. Tel Aviv, Association of Gniewashow in Israel and the Diaspora, 1971. 533, 19 p., ports. (H,Y,E)

Golub (R) see under Dobrzyn (*Ayarati*)

Gombin (R) see Gabin

Gomel (R) see under *Arim ve-imahot,* vol. 2

Goniadz (R). *Sefer yizkor Goniadz* [Our hometown Goniondz*]. Eds.: J. Ben-Meir (Treshansky), A. L. Fayans. Tel Aviv, The Committee of Goniondz Association in the USA and in Israel, 1960. 808, xix p., ports., maps (H,Y,E)

Gora Kalwaria (R). *Megiles Ger.* Ed.: Gregorio Sapoznikow. Buenos Aires, Ger Societies in Argentina, Israel and the United States, 1975. 512 p., illus. (Y)

Gorlice (AH). *Sefer Gorlice; ha-kehila be-vinyana u-be-hurbana* [Gorlice book; the community at rise and fall*]. Ed.: M. Y. Bar-On. [Association of Former Residents of Gorlice and Vicinity in Israel], 1962. 338 p., ports., map, facsims. (H,Y)

Gorodnitsa (R) see under Novograd-Volynskiy

Gorzd (R) see Gargzdai

Gostynin (R). *Pinkes Gostynin; yisker-bukh* [Pinkas Gostynin; book of Gostynin*]. Ed.: J. M. Biderman. New York, Gostynin Memorial Book Committees, 1960. 358 p., ports. (Y)

Goworowo (R). *Goworowo; sefer zikaron* [Govorowo memorial book*]. Eds.: A. Burstin, D. Kossovsky. Tel Aviv, The Govorover Societies in Israel, the USA and Canada, 1966. 496, xvi p., ports., facsims. (H,Y,E)

Grabowiec (R). *Sefer zikaron le-kehilat Grabowiec* [Memorial book Grabowitz*]. Ed.: Shimon Kanc. Tel Aviv, Grabowiec Society, 1975. 432, 5, 26 p., illus. (H,Y,E)

Grajewo (R). *Grayeve yisker-bukh* [Grayewo memorial book]. Ed.: Dr. G. Gorin. New York, United Grayever Relief Committee, 1950. 51, [38], 311 p., illus. (Y,E)

Greiding (AH) see Grodek Jagiellonski

Gritsa (R) see Grojec

Grodek (near Bialystok) (R). *Sefer zikaron le-kehilat Horodok* [Horodok; in memory of the Jewish community*]. Ed.: M. Simon (Shemen). Tel Aviv, Associations of Former Residents of Grodek in Israel and Argentina, 1963. 142 p., ports., facsims. (H,Y)

Grodek Jagiellonski (AH). *Sefer Grayding* [Book of Griding, Grodek Jagiellonski*]. Ed.: Yehuda Leibish Margel. Tel Aviv, Society of Grayding Emigrants, 1981. 120, 8 p., illus. (H,Y,E)

Grodno (R). *Grodno* [Grodno*]. Ed.: Dov Rabin. Jerusalem, Grodno Society; The Encyclopaedia of the Jewish Diaspora, 1973. 744 columns, illus. (H,Y)

Grodno (R). *Kovets Grodna-Zaml-heft Grodne* [Grodno collection]. Ed.: Yitzhak Yelin. Tel Aviv, Grodner Association of Israel, Dec. 1958. no. 1: 50 p., illus. (H,Y)

Grojec (R). *Megilat Gritse* [Megilat Gritze*]. Ed.: I. B. Alterman. Tel Aviv, Gritzer Association in Israel, 1955. iv, 408 p., ports. (H,Y)

Gross Magendorf (Nagymagyar) (AH) see under Dunaszerdahely

Grosswardein (AH) see Oradea

Grozovo (R) see under Slutsk

Gusiatyn (R) see Husiatyn (R)

Gwozdziec (AH). *Sefer zikaron Gwozdziec ve-ha-sevivah* [Memorial book for Gwozdziec and vicinity]. Ed.: Mendel Zilber. Ramat-Gan, 1974.

Gyor (AH). *Le-zekher kedoshei Gyor* [In memory of the martyrs of Gyor]. Ed.: Hana Spiegel. Haifa, [197–/8–]. 36 p., illus., maps (H)

Hajdunanas (AH) see under Debrecen

Hajdusamson (AH) see under Debrecen

Halmi (AH). *Zikhron netsah le-kehilot ha-kedoshot Halmin-Turcz ve-ha-seviva asher nehrevu ba-shoa* [In memory of the communities of Halmin-Turcz and vicinity]. Ed.: Yehuda Shvartz. Tel Aviv, Halmin-Turcz and Vicinity Society, [1968]. 138 p., illus. (H)

Harlau (Romania). *Der khoyv fun zikorn; mayn moldevish shtetl Harloy* [The duty of memory; my Moldavian town Harlau]. [By] Khayim Zaydman. Jerusalem, Yidishe kultur-gezelshaft, 1982. 398 p., illus., ports. (Y)

Haydutsishok (Hoduciszki) (R) see under Swieciany

Hivniv (AH) see Uhnow

Hlusk (Glusk) (R) see under Slutsk

Hoduciszki (R) see under Swieciany

Holojow (Cholojow) (AH) see under Radziechow

Holszany (R). *Lebn um umkum fun Olshan* [The life and destruction of Olshan]. Tel Aviv, Former Residents of Olshan in Israel, 1965. 431, 136 p., ports., facsims. (H,Y)

Holynka (R) see under Dereczyn

Homel (Gomel) (R) see under *Arim ve-imahot,* vol. 2

Horochow (R). *Sefer Horochow* [Horchiv memorial book*]. Ed.: Y. Kariv. Tel Aviv, Horchiv Committee in Israel, 1966. 357, 79 p., ports., map, facsims. (H,Y,E)

Horodec (R). *Horodets; a geshikhte fun a shtetl, 1142–1942* [Horodec;

history of a town, 1142–1942]. Ed.: A. Ben-Ezra. "Horodetz" Book Committee, 1949. 238 p., ports., map, facsims. (Y)

Horodenka (AH). *Sefer Horodenka* [The book of Horodenka]. Ed.: Sh. Meltzer. Tel Aviv, Former Residents of Horodenka and Vicinity in Israel and the USA, 1963. 425, vii p., ports., map, facsims. (H,Y)

Horodlo (R). *Di kehile fun Horodlo; yisker-bukh. . .* [The community of Horodlo; memorial book. . .]. Ed.: Y. Ch. Zawidowitch. Tel Aviv, Former Residents of Horodlo in Israel, 1962. 324 p., ports., facsims. (Y)

Horodlo (R). *Kehilat Horodlo; sefer zikaron le-kedoshei Horodlo (Polin) ve-li- kedoshei ha-kefarim ha-semukhim* [The community of Horodlo; memorial book. . .]. Ed.: Y. Ch. Zawidowitch. Tel Aviv, Former Residents of Horodlo in Israel, 1959. 260 p., ports., facsims. (H)

Horodno (R) see under Stolin

Horodok (R) see Grodek (near Bialystok)

Horyngrod (R) see under Tuczyn

Hoszcza (R). *Hoshtsh; sefer zikaron* [Hoshtch-Wolyn; in memory of the Jewish community*]. Eds.: B. H. Ayalon-Baranicka, A. Yaron-Kritzmar. Tel Aviv, Former Residents of Hoshtch in Israel, 1957. 269 p., ports., facsims. (H)

Hoszcza (R). *Sefer Hoshtsh; yisker-bukh* [The book of Hosht—in memoriam*]. Ed.: R. Fink. New York and Tel Aviv, Society of Hosht, 1957. xvi, 294 p., ports., facsims. (Y)

Hotin (R) see Khotin

Hrubieszow (R). *Pinkas Hrubieszow* [Memorial book of Hrubieshov*]. Ed.: B. Kaplinsky. Tel Aviv, Hrubieshov Associations in Israel and the USA, 1962. 811, xviii columns, ports. (H,Y,E,P)

Hrubieszow (R). *Shorashim shelanu: le-zekher kedoshei Hrubieszow* [Our roots: in memory to the Jewish victims of the Holocaust 1939–1945*]. Tel Aviv, Organization of Former Jewish Inhabitants of Hrubieszow in Israel, 1990–1992. 2 vols., illus., ports. (H,Y,E,P)

Huedin (AH). *Zikhronotai me-Banfi-Hunyad; sefer zikaron li-yehude Banfi-Hunyad* [Igyemlekszem Huedin/Banffy-Hunyadra*=My memories of Banffy-Hunyadi]. [By] Eliezer Laci Klepner. Tel Aviv, Author, 1990. 38, 19, [13], 100 p., illus., maps, ports. (H,Hu)

Husiatyn (R). *Husiatyn; Podoler Gubernye* [Husiatyn; Podolia-Ukraine*]. Ed.: B. Diamond. New York, Former Residents of Husiatyn in America, 1968. 146, [40], 123 p., ports. (Y,E)

Husiatyn (AH). *Kehilatiyim: Husiatyn ve-Kopyczynce* [Two communities: Husiatyn and Kopyczynce*]. [By] Abraham Backer. Tel Aviv, Husiatyn Society, 1977. 286 p., illus. (H,Y)

Husiatyn (AH). *Mibet aba; pirkei zikhronot mi-yemei yaldut be-ayarat moladeti Husiatyn* [From my parents' home; memorial chapter. . .]. [By] A. Y. Avitov (Birnbojm). Tel Aviv, The author, 1965, 155 p., ports. (H)

Husiatyn (AH). *Sefer zikaron Husiatyn ve-ha-seviva* [Memorial book of

Husiatyn and the surrounding region]. Ed.: Abraham Backer. Tel Aviv, Husiatyn-Galicia Society, 1976. 499 p., illus. (H,Y)

Iampol (R) see Yampol

Ignatowka (R) see under Zofiowka

Iklad (AH) see under Szamosujvar

Ileanda (Nagyilonda) (AH) see under Des

Ilja (R). *Kehilat Ilja; pirkei hayim ve-hashmada* [The community of Ilja; chapters of life and destruction]. Ed.: A. Kopilevitz. [Tel Aviv], Association of Former Residents of Ilja in Israel, 1962. 466 p., ports., facsims. (H,Y)

Indura (R). *Amdur, mayn geboyrn-shtetl* [Amdur, my hometown]. [By] Iedidio Efron. Buenos Aires, 1973. 252, 33 p., illus. (Y,S)

Istrik (Ustrzyki Dolne) (AH) see under Lesko

Ivano-Frankovsk (Stanislawow) (AH) see under *Arim ve-imahot,* vol. 5

Ivanovo (R) see Janow (near Pinsk)

Iwacewicze (R) see under Byten

Iwie (R). *Sefer zikaron le-kehilat Iwie* [Ivie; in memory of the Jewish community*]. Ed.: M. Kaganovich. Tel Aviv, Association of Former Residents of Ivie in Israel and "United Ivier Relief" in America, 1968. 738 p., ports., map (H,Y)

Iwieniec (R). *Sefer Iwieniec, Kamien ve-ha-seviva; sefer zikaron* [The memorial book of Iwieniec, Kamien, and the surrounding region]. Tel Aviv, Iwieniec Societies in Israel and the Diaspora, 1973. 484 p., illus. (H,Y)

Jablonka (AH) see under Nowy Targ

Jadow (R). *Sefer Jadow* [The book of Jadow*]. Ed.: A. W. Jassni. Jerusalem, The Encyclopaedia of the Jewish Diaspora, 1966. 472, xxiii p., ports. (H,Y,E)

Jaisi (Jejsa) (R) see under Braslaw

Janova (R) see Jonava

Janow (near Pinsk) (R). *Janow al yad Pinsk; sefer zikaron* [Janow near Pinsk; memorial book*]. Ed.: M. Nadav (Katzikowski). Jerusalem, Assoc. of Former Residents of Janow near Pinsk in Israel, 1969. 420 p., ports. (H,Y)

Janow (near Trembowla) (AH) see under Budzanow; Trembowla

Jaroslaw (AH). *Sefer Jaroslaw* [Jaroslav book*]. Ed.: Yitzhak Alperowitz. Tel Aviv, Jaroslaw Society, 1978. 371, 28 p., illus. (H,Y,E)

Jaryczow Nowy (AH). *Khurbn Jaryczow bay Lemberg; sefer zikaron le-kedoshei Jaryczow u-sevivoteha* [Destruction of Jaryczow; memorial book to the martyrs of Jaryczow and surroundings]. [By] Mordekhai Gerstl. New York, A. Boym, 1948. 78 p., ports. (Y)

Jaslo (AH). *Toldot yehudei Jaslo; me-reshit hityashvutam be-tokh ha-ir ad yemei ha-hurban al yedei ha-natsim. . .* [History of the Jews of Jaslo. . .]. [By] Moshe Natan Even-Hayim. Tel Aviv, Jaslo Society, 1953. 360 p., map, ports., illus. (H)

Jaworow (AH). *"Judenstadt Jaworow;" der umkum fun Yavorover idn*

[Swastika over Jaworow*]. [By] S. Druck. New York, First Jaworower Indep. Ass'n, 1950. 69, iv, 35 p., ports. (Y,E)

Jaworow (AH). *Matsevet zikaron le-kehilat Jaworow ve-ha-seviva* [Monument to the community of Jaworow and the surrounding region]. Ed.: Michael Bar-Lev. Haifa, Jaworow Societies in Israel and the United States, 1979. 252 p., illus. (H,Y)

Jedrzejow (R). *Sefer ha-zikaron le-yehudei Jedrzejow* [Memorial book of the Jews of Jedrzejow]. Ed.: Sh. D. Yerushalmi. Tel Aviv, Former Residents of Jedrzejow in Israel, 1965. 490 p., ports., facsims. (H,Y)

Jedwabne (R). *Sefer Jedwabne; historiya ve-zikaron* [Yedwabne; history and memorial book*]. Eds.: Julius L. Baker, Jacob L. Baker; assisted by Moshe Tzinovitz. Jerusalem-New York, The Yedwabner Societies in Israel and in the United States of America, 1980. 121, 110 p., illus. (H,Y,E)

Jeremicze (R) see under Turzec

Jezierna (AH) *Sefer Jezierna* [Memorial book of Jezierna*]. Ed.: J. Sigelman. Haifa, Committee of Former Residents of Jezierna in Israel, 1971. 354 p., ports. (H,Y)

Jezierzany (AH). *Sefer Ozieran ve-ha-seviva* [Memorial book; Jezierzany and surroundings*]. Ed.: M. A. Tenenblatt. Jerusalem, The Encyclopaedia of the Jewish Diaspora, 1959. 498 columns, ports. (H,Y)

Jeznas (R). *Le-zikhram shel kedoshei kehilat Jezna she-nispu bi-shnat 1941* [Memorial book of the martyrs of Jeznas who perished in 1941]. Ed.: D. Aloni. Jerusalem, Former Residents of Jeznas in Israel, 1967. 105 p., ports., maps, facsims. (H), mimeo.

Jod (Jody) (R) see under Braslaw

Jonava (R). *Yanove oyf di breges fun Vilye; tsum ondenk fun di khorev-gevorene yidishe kehile in Yanove* [Yizkor book in memory of the Jewish community of Yanova*]. Ed.: Shimeon Noy. Tel Aviv, Jonava Society, 1972. 35, 429 p., illus. (Y,E)

Jordanow (AH) see under Nowy Targ

Jozefow (R). *Sefer zikaron le-kehilat Jozefow ve-le-kedosheha* [Memorial book to the community of Jozefow and its martyrs]. Ed.: Azriel Omer-Lemer. Tel Aviv, Jozefow Societies in Israel and the U.S.A., 1975. 462 p., illus. (H,Y)

Jurbarkas (R). *Sefer ha-zikaron le-kehilat Yurburg-Lita* [Memorial book for the community of Yurburg, Lithuania]. Ed.: Zevulun Poran. Jerusalem, Society of Yurburg Emigrants in Israel, 1991. 524 p., illus., ports. (H,Y; introd.:E)

Kadzidlo (R) see under Ostroleka

Kalarash (R). *Sefer Kalarash; le-hantsahat zikhram shel yehudei ha-ayara she- nehreva bi-yemei ha-shoa* [The book of Kalarash in memory of the town's Jews, which was destroyed in the Holocaust]. Eds.: N. Tamir *et al.* Tel Aviv, 1966. 533 p., ports., facsims. (H,Y)

Kalisz (R). *The Kalish book.* Ed.: I. M. Lask. Tel Aviv, The Societies of Former Residents of Kalish and the Vicinity in Israel and the USA, 1968. 327 p. (E)

Kalisz (R). *Kalisz she-hayeta; ir ve-em be-yisrael be-medinat "Polin-Gadol"* [The Kalisz that was. . .]. Haifa, Bet ha-sefer ha-reali ha-ivri and The Kalisz Society, [1979/80]. 136 p., illus., ports., maps (H)

Kalisz (R). *Sefer Kalish* [The Kalish book *]. Tel Aviv, The Israel-American Book Committee, 1964–1968. 2 vols. (624, 598 p.), ports., facsims. (H,Y)

Kalisz (R). *Toldot yehude Kalisz* [History of the Jews of Kalisz]. [By] Yisrael David Beth-Halevy. Tel Aviv, Author, [1960/61]. 448 p., illus., map, ports. (H)

Kalov (AH) see Nagykallo

Kalusz (AH). *Kalusz; hayeha ve-hurbana shel ha-kehila* [Kalusz; the life and destruction of the community]. Eds.: Shabtai Unger, Moshe Ettinger. Tel Aviv, Kalusz Society, 1980. 325, 330, 15 p., illus. (H,Y,E)

Kaluszyn (R). *Kehilat Kaluszyn* [The community of Kaluszyn]. Translated from Yiddish: Yitzhak Shoshani. Tel Aviv, I.L. Peretz and Society of Kaluszyn Emigrants in Israel, 1977—-1978. 2 vols. (H)

Kaluszyn (R). *Sefer Kaluszyn; geheylikt der khorev gevorener kehile* [Memorial book of Kaluszyn]. Eds.: A. Shamir, Sh. Soroka. Tel Aviv, Former Residents of Kaluszyn in Israel, 1961. 545, [15] p., ports., facsims. (Y)

Kalwaria (AH) see under Wadowice

Kamenets-Litovsk (R) see Kamieniec Litewski

Kamenets-Podolskiy (R). *Kamenets-Podolsk u-sevivata* [Kamenets-Podolsk and its surroundings]. Eds.: A. Rosen, Ch. Sharig, Y. Bernstein. Tel Aviv, Association of Former Residents of Kamenets-Podolsk and Its Surroundings in Israel, 1965. 263 p., ports., facsims. (H)

Kamenets-Podolskiy (R). *Kamenetz-Podolsk, a memorial to a city annihilated by the Nazis.* Ed.: Leon S. Blatman. New York, published by the Sponsors of the Kamenetz-Podolsk Memorial Book, 1966. 133 p., illus., ports. (E)

Kamenets-Podolskiy (R). *Kaminits-Podolsk; excerpts from Kaminits-Podolsk u-sevivatah, a memorial book.* Translated by Bonnie S. Sohn. Washington, D.C., 1990. iii, 134 p. (E)

Kamien (R) see under Iwieniec

Kamien Koszyrski (R). *Sefer ha-zikaron le-kehilat Kamien Koszyrski ve-ha-seviva. . .* [Kamin Koshirsky book; in memory of the Jewish community*]. Eds.: A. A. Stein *et al.* Tel Aviv, Former Residents of Kamin Koshirsky and Surroundings in Israel, 1965. 974 columns, ports. (H,Y)

Kamieniec Litewski (R). *Sefer yizkor le-kehilot Kamenits de-Lita, Zastavye ve-ha-koloniyot* [Kamenetz Litovsk, Zastavye, and colonies memorial book*]. Eds.: Shmuel Eisenstadt, Mordechai Gelbart. Tel Aviv, Kamieniec and Zastavye Committees in Israel and the United States, 1970. 626, 185 p., illus., map (H,Y,E)

Kamiensk (R) see under Radomsko

Kammeny Brod (R) see under Novograd-Volynskiy

Kapreshty (R). *Kapresht ayaratenu—undzer shtetele Kapresht; sefer zikaron le-kehila yehudit be-Bessarabia* [Kapresht, our village; memorial book for the

Jewish community of Kapresht, Bessarabia*]. Eds.: M. Rishpy, Av. B. Yanowitz. Haifa, Kapresht Society in Israel, 1980. 496 p., map, illus. (H,Y)

Kapsukas (R) see Marijampole

Kapulye (Kopyl) (R) see under Slutsk

Karcag (AH). *Toldot kehilat Karcag ve-kehilot mehoz Nagykunsag* [History of the community of Karcag and the communities of the district of Nagykunsag]. [By] Moshe Hershko. Jerusalem, Karcag Society, 1977. 53, 219 p., illus. (H,Hu)

Karczew (R) see under Otwock

Kartuz-Bereze (Bereza Kartuska) (R) see under Pruzana

Kaszony (AH) see Kosyno

Kazimierz (R). *Pinkas Kuzmir* [Kazimierz—memorial book*]. Ed.: D. Shtokfish. Tel Aviv, Former Residents of Kazimierz in Israel and the Diaspora, 1970. 655 p., ports., facsims. (H,Y)

Kedainiai (R). *Keydan; sefer zikaron* [Keidan memorial book*]. Ed.: Josef Chrust. Tel Aviv, Keidan Societies in Israel, South America, and the United States, 1977. 39, 313 p., illus. (H,Y,E)

Kelts (R) see Kielce

Keydan (R) see Kedainiai

Khmelnitskii (R) see Proskurov

Kholm (R) see Chelm

Khotin (R). *Sefer kehilat Khotin (Bessarabia)* [The book of the community of Khotin (Bessarabia)]. Ed.: Shlomo Shitnovitzer. Tel Aviv, Khotin (Bessarabia) Society, 1974. 333 p., illus. (Y)

Khozhel (R) see Chorzele

Kibart (R) see Kybartai

Kielce (R). *Al betenu she-harav—Fun der khorever heym* [About our house which was devastated*]. Ed.: David Shtokfish. Tel Aviv, Kielce Societies in Israel and in the Diaspora, 1981. 246 p., illus., ports. (H,Y,P,E)

Kielce (R). *Sefer Kielce; toldot kehilat Kielce* [The history of the community of Kielce]. [By] P. Zitron. Tel Aviv, Former Residents of Kielce in Israel, 1957. 328 p., ports. (H,Y)

Kiemieliszki (R) see under Swieciany

Kiernozia (R) see under Lowicz

Kikol (R) see under Lipno

Kislowszczyzna (R) see under Braslaw

Kisvarda (AH). *Sefer yizkor le-kehilat Kleinwardein ve-ha-seviva* [Memorial book of Kleinwardein and vicinity]. Tel Aviv, Kleinwardein Society, 1980. 79, 190 p., illus. (H,Hu,E)

Kitai-Gorod (R) see under Kamenets-Podolskiy

Kitev (AH) see Kuty

Klausenburg (AH) see Kolozsvar

Kleck (R). *Pinkas Kletsk* [Pinkas Klezk; a memorial to the Jewish community of Klezk-Poland*]. Ed.: E. S. Stein. Tel Aviv, Former Residents of Klezk in Israel, 1959. 385 p., ports., map, facsims. (H,Y)

Kleinwardein (AH) see Kisvarda

Klobucko (R). *Sefer Klobutsk; mazkeret kavod le-kehila ha-kedosha she-hushmeda* [The book of Klobucko; in memory of a martyred community that was destroyed]. Tel Aviv, Former Residents of Klobucko in Israel, 1960. 439 p., ports., facsims. (Y)

Klosowa (R). *Sefer Klosowa; kibuts hotsvei avanim a(l) sh(em) Yosef Trumpeldor be-Klosowa u-flugotav, measef* [The story of Kibbutz Klosova*]. Ed.: Haim Dan. Beit Lohamei Hagetaot, Ghetto Fighters House, 1978. 405 p., illus. (H)

Knenitsh (Knihynicze) (AH) see under Rohatyn

Knihynicze (AH) see under Rohatyn

Kobryn (R). *The book of Kobrin; the scroll of life and destruction.* Eds.: Betzalel Shwartz, Israel Chaim Bil[e]tzki; translated from the Hebrew by Nilli Avidan and Avner Perry; edited and printed by Joel Neuberg for HCNC. San Francisco, Holocaust Center of Northern California, 1992. iv, 447 p., illus., map, ports. (E)

Kobryn (R). *Kobryn; zamlbukh (an iberblik ibern yidishn Kobryn)* [Kobryn; collection (an overview of Jewish Kobryn)]. Ed.: Melech Glotzer. Buenos Aires, Kobryn Book Committee, 1951. 310 p., illus. (Y)

Kobryn (R). *Sefer Kobryn; megilat hayim ve-hurban* [Book of Kobryn; the scroll of life and destruction]. Eds.: B. Schwartz, Y. H. Biletzky. Tel Aviv, 1951. 347 p., ports. (H)

Kobylnik (R). *Sefer Kobylnik* [Memorial book of Kobilnik*]. Ed.: I. Siegelman. Haifa, Committee of Former Residents of Kobilnik in Israel, 1967. 292 p., ports., map (H,Y)

Kock (R). *Sefer Kotsk* [Memorial book of Kotsk]. Ed.: E. Porat. Tel Aviv, Former Residents of Kotsk in Israel. . . , 1961. 424 p., ports., map, facsims. (H,Y)

Koidanovo (R). *Koydenov; zamlbukh tsum ondenk fun di Koydenover kdoyshim* [Koidanov; memorial volume of the martyrs of Koidanov]. Ed.: A. Reisin. New York, United Koidanover Assn., 1955. 216, [41], 207 p., ports., facsims. (Y)

Kolarovgrad (Bulgaria) see Shumla

Kolbuszowa (AH). *Pinkas Kolbishov (Kolbasov)* [Kolbuszowa memorial book*]. Ed.: I. M. Biderman. New York, United Kolbushover, 1971. 793, 88 p., ports. (H,Y,E)

Kolki (R). *Fun ash aroysgerufn* [Summoned from the ashes]. [By] Daniel Kac. Warsaw, Czytelnik, Zydowski Instytut Historyczny w Polsce, 1983. 399 p., illus., map, ports. (Y)

Kolno (R). *Sefer zikaron le-kehilat Kolno* [Kolno memorial book*]. Eds.: A. Remba, B. Halevy. Tel Aviv, The Kolner Organization and Sifriat Poalim, 1971. 680, 70 p., ports., facsims. (H,Y,E)

Kolo (R). *Azoy zenen zey umgekumen-Kakh hem nispu* [This is how they perished*]. [By] A. M. Harap. Israel, Memorial Book Committee and the Author, 1974. 169, 8 p., illus. (Y,H,E)

Kolo (R). *Sefer Kolo* [Memorial book of Kolo]. Ed.: M. Halter. Tel Aviv, Former Residents of Kolo in Israel and the USA, 1958. 408 p., ports. (H,Y)

Kolomyja (AH). *Pinkes Kolomey* [Memorial book of Kolomey]. Ed.: Sh. Bickel. New York, 1957. 448 p., ports. (Y)

Kolomyja (AH). *Sefer zikaron le-kehilat Kolomey ve-ha-seviva* [Kolomeyer memorial book*]. Eds.: D. Noy, M. Schutzman. [Tel Aviv], Former Residents of Kolomey and Surroundings in Israel, [1972]. 395 p., ports., facsims. (H)

Kolonia Synajska (R) see under Dereczyn

Kolozsborsa (AH) see Borsa

Kolozsvar (AH). *Sefer zikaron le-yahadut Kluzh-Kolozsvar* [Memorial volume of the Jews of Cluj-Kolozsvar*]. Ed.: M. Carmilly-Weinberger. New York, 1970. 156, 313 p., ports., facsims. (H,E,Hu)

Kolozsvar (AH). *Zikaron netsah le-kehila ha-kedosha Kolozhvar-Klauzenburg asher nehreva ba-shoa* [Everlasting memorial of the martyred community Kolozsvar-Klausenburg, which perished in the Holocaust]. [Eds.]: Sh. Zimroni, Y. Schwartz. Tel Aviv, Former Residents of Kolozsvar in Israel, 1968. 118 p. (H,Hu), mimeo.

Koltyniany (R) see under Swieciany

Komarno (AH). *Bet Komarno; korot ha-'ir ve-toldotehah, me-hivsadah ve-'ad hurbanah: rabanehah, gedolehah ve-admore" ha, ishehah, hayehem ve-khilayonam* [The house of Komarno; history of the town, from its founding until its destruction]. [By] Barukh Yashar (Shlikhter). Jerusalem, Author, 1965. 204 p., illus., ports. (H)

Konin (R). *Kehilat Konin be-ferihata u-ve-hurbana* [Memorial book Konin*]. Ed.: M. Gelbart. Tel Aviv, Assoc. of Konin Jews in Israel, 1968. 772, 24 p., map, facsims. (H,Y,E)

Konyar (AH) see under Debrecen

Kopin (R) see under Kamenets-Podolskiy

Koprzywnica (R). *Sefer Pokshivnitsa* [Memorial book of Koprzywnica]. Ed.: E. Erlich. Tel Aviv, Former Residents of Koprzywnica in Israel, 1971. 351 p., ports., facsims. (H,Y)

Kopyczynce (AH) see under Husiatyn (*Kehilatiyim*)

Kopyl (R) see under Slutsk

Korczyna (AH). *Korczyna; sefer zikaron* [Korczyna memorial book*]. New York, Committee of the Korczyna Memorial Book, 1967. 495 p., ports. (H,Y)

Korelicze (R). *Korelits; hayeha ve-hurbana shel kehila yehudit* [Korelitz; the life and destruction of a Jewish community*]. Ed.: Michael Walzer-Fass. Tel Aviv, Korelicze Societies in Israel and the U.S.A., 1973. 61, 357 p., illus. (H,Y,E)

Korelicze (R) see also under Nowogrodek

Korets (R) see Korzec

Koriv (R) see Kurow

Korzec (R). *Korets (Wolyn); sefer zikaron le-kehilatenu she-ala aleha ha-koret* [The Korets book; in memory of our community that is no more*]. Ed.: E. Leoni. Tel Aviv, Former Residents of Korets in Israel, 1959. 791 p., ports., facsims. (H,Y)

Kosice (AH). *Divrei yemei kehilot Kosice* [The story of the Jewish community of Kosice*]. Hebrew version: Yehuda Schlanger; translated from the Hebrew: Gabriela Williams. [Yiddish title-page: *500 yor in Kashoy-Kosice: kurtse historishe faktn* [By] Shraga Peri; Hungarian title-page: *A kassai zsidosag tortenete es galleriaja* [By] Gorog Artur.] Bne-Brak, 1993. vi, 340, [18], 92 p., illus., ports. (H,Y,E,Hu)

Kosow (East Galicia) (AH). *Sefer Kosow-Galicia ha-mizrahit* [Memorial book of Kosow—Kosow Huculski*]. Eds.: G. Kressel, L. Oliczky. Tel Aviv, Former Residents of Kosow and Vicinity in Israel, 1964. 430 p., ports., facsims. (H,Y)

Kosow (East Galicia) (AH). *Megiles Kosow* [The scroll of Kosow]. [By] Yehoshua Gertner. Tel Aviv, Amkho, 1981. 156 p. (Y)

Kosow (Polesie) (R). *Pinkas kehilat Kosow Poleski* [Memorial book of Kosow Poleski]. Jerusalem, Relief Org. of Former Residents of Kosow Poleski in Israel, 1956. 81 p., ports. (H)

Kosow Lacki (R). *Kosow Lacki.* General ed.: Jacob Boas. San Francisco, Holocaust Center of Northern California, 1992. 75 p., illus., ports. (E,Y)

Kostopol (R). *Sefer Kostopol; hayeha u-mota shel kehila* [Kostopol; the life and death of a community*]. Ed.: A. Lerner. Tel Aviv, Former Residents of Kostopol in Israel, 1967. 386 p., ports. (H)

Kosyno (AH). *The Jews of Kaszony, Subcarpathia.* By Joseph Eden (Einczig). New York, 1988. v, 131 p., illus., map, ports. (E,H,Hu)

Kotsk (R) see Kock

Kowal (R) see under Wloclawek

Kowel (R). *Kowel; sefer edut ve-zikaron le-kehilatenu she-ala aleha ha-koret* [Kowel; testimony and memorial book of our destroyed community]. Ed.: E. Leoni-Zopperfin. Tel Aviv, Former Residents of Kowel in Israel, 1959. 539 p., ports. (H,Y)

Kowel (R). *Pinkes Kowel* [Memorial book of Kowel]. Ed.: B. Baler. Buenos Aires, Former Residents of Kowel and Surroundings in Argentina, 1951. 511 p., ports., facsims. (Y)

Kozangrodek (R) see under Luniniec; Polesie (region)

Koziany (R) see under Glebokie; Swieciany

Kozieniec (R). *The book of Kozienice.* Ed.: B. Kaplinsky. Tel Aviv-New York, The Kozienice Organization, 1985. xxxvi, 677 p., illus. (E)

Kozieniec (R). *Sefer zikaron le-kehilat Kozieniec* [Memorial book of the community of Kozieniec]. Ed.: B. Kaplinsky. Tel Aviv, Former Residents of Kozieniec in Israel. . . , 1969. 516 p., ports., map, music, facsims. (H,Y)

Krakinovo (R) see Krekenava

Krakow (AH). *Dape hantsahat le-kehilat Krakow* [Memorial pages (dapeh hantzacha) dedicated to kehilat Cracow*]. Ed.: Avshalom Kor. Tel Aviv, The Municipal Secondary School No. 5, 1969. 91 p., illus., ports., map. (H)

Krakow (AH). *Sefer Kroke, ir va-em be-yisrael* [Memorial book of Krakow, mother and town in Israel]. Eds.: A. Bauminger *et al.* Jerusalem, The Rav Kuk Inst. and Former Residents of Krakow in Israel, 1959. 429 p., ports., facsims. (H)

Krakow (AH) see also under *Arim ve-imahot,* vol. 2

Krakowiec (AH) see under Jaworow (*Matsevet zikaron le-kehilat Jaworow. . .*)

Krasnik (R). *Sefer Krasnik.* Ed.: David Shtokfish. Tel Aviv, Krasnik Societies in Israel and the Diaspora, 1973. 673 p., illus. (H,Y)

Krasnobrod (R). *Krasnobrod; sefer zikaron* [Krasnobrod; a memorial to the Jewish community*]. Ed.: M. Kushnir. Tel Aviv, Former Residents of Krasnobrod in Israel, 1956. 526 p., ports., facsims. (H,Y)

Krasnystaw (R). *Yisker tsum ondenk fun kdoyshey Krasnystaw* [Memorial book of the martyrs of Krasnystaw]. Ed.: A. Stunzeiger. Munich, Publ. "Bafrayung"—Poalei Zion, 1948. 150 p., ports. (Y)

Krekenava (R). *Krakenowo; our town in Lithuania, the story of a world that has passed.* Johannesburg, Krakenowo Sick Benefit and Benevolent Society, 1961. 48 p., illus., facsims. (Y,E)

Krememits (R) see Krzemieniec

Kripa (Horyngrod) (R) see under Tuczyn

Krivitsh (R) see Krzywicze

Kroscienko (AH) see under Nowy Targ

Kroshnik (R) see Krasnik

Krosniewiec (R) see under Kutno

Krynki (R). *Krinik in khurbn: memuarn* [Krinki en ruines*]. [By] Alex Sofer. Montevideo, Los Comites de Ayuda a los Residentes de Krinki de Montevideo y Buenos Aires, 1948. 269, [27] p., illus., map, ports. (Y)

Krynki (R). *Pinkas Krynki* [Memorial book of Krynki]. Ed.: D. Rabin. Tel Aviv, Former Residents of Krynki in Israel and in the Diaspora, 1970. 373 p., ports., map, facsims. (H,Y)

Krzemienica (R) see under Wolkowysk (*Volkovisker yisker-bukh*)

Krzemieniec (R). *Kremenits, Vishgorodek un Pitshayev; yisker-bukh* [Memorial book of Krzemieniec]. Ed.: P. Lerner. Buenos Aires, Former Residents of Kremenits and Vicinity in Argentina, 1965. 468 p., ports., facsims. (Y)

Krzemieniec (R). *Pinkas Kremenits; sefer zikaron* [Memorial book of Krzemieniec]. Ed.: A. S. Stein. Tel Aviv, Former Residents of Krzemieniec in Israel, 1954. 450 p., ports., facsims. (H,Y)

Krzywicze (R). *Ner tamid; yizkor le-Krivitsh* [Kryvitsh yizkor book*]. Ed.: Matityahu Bar-Ratzon. Tel Aviv, Krivitsh Societies in Israel and the Diaspora, 1977. 724 p., illus. (H,Y)

Kshoynzh (Ksiaz Wielki) (R) see under Miechow

Ksiaz Wielki (R) see under Miechow

Kunow (R) see under Ostrowiec

Kurow (R). *Yisker-bukh Koriv; sefer yizkor, matsevet zikaron la-ayaratenu Koriv* [Yizkor book in memoriam of our hometown Kurow*]. Ed.: M. Grossman. Tel Aviv, Former Residents of Kurow in Israel, 1955. 1148 columns, ports., facsims. (Y)

Kurzeniec (R). *Megilat Kurenits; ayara be-hayeha u-ve-mota* [The scroll of Kurzeniec; the town living and dead]. Ed.: A. Meyerowitz. Tel Aviv, Former Residents of Kurzeniec in Israel and in the USA, 1956. 335 p., ports. (H)

Kutno (R). *Kutno ve-ha-seviva* [Kutno and surroundings book*]. Ed.: D. Shtokfish. Tel Aviv, Former Residents of Kutno and Surroundings in Israel and the Diaspora, 1968. 591 p., ports., facsims. (H,Y)

Kuty (AH). *Kitever yisker bukh* [Kitever memorial book]. Ed.: E. Husen. New York, Kitever Sick and Benevolent Society in New York, 1958. 240 p., ports. (Y)

Kuzmir (R) see Kazimierz

Kybartai (R). *Kibart (Lita)*. By Yosef Rosin. Haifa, Executive Committee of the Society of Former Residents of Kibart, 1988. 2, 62, [20] p., illus., map, ports., facsims. (H)

Lachowicze (R). *Lachowicze; sefer zikaron* [Memorial book of Lachowicze]. Ed.: J. Rubin. Tel Aviv, Assoc. of Former Residents of Lachowicze, [1948/49]. 395 p., ports. (H,Y)

Lachwa (R). *Rishonim la-mered; Lachwa* [First ghetto revolt, Lachwa*]. Eds.: H. A. Malachi *et al.* Jerusalem, The Encyclopaedia of the Jewish Diaspora, 1957. 500 columns, ports., facsims. (H,Y)

Lachwa (R) see also under Polesie (region)

Lancut (AH). *Lancut; hayeha ve-hurbana shel kehila yehudit* [Lancut; the life and destruction of a Jewish community*]. Eds.: M. Waltzer, N. Kudish. Tel Aviv, Associations of Former Residents of Lancut in Israel and USA, 1963. 465, lix p., ports., facsims. (H,Y,E)

Lanovits (R) see Lanowce

Lanowce (R). *Lanovits; sefer zikaron le-kedoshei Lanovits she-nispu be-shoat ha-natsim* [Lanowce; memorial book of the martyrs of Lanowce who perished during the Holocaust]. Ed.: H. Rabin. Tel Aviv, Association of Former Residents of Lanowce, 1970. 440 p., ports. (H,Y)

Lapichi (R) see under Bobruisk

Lask (R). *Lask; sefer zikaron* [Memorial book of Lask]. Ed.: Z. Tzurnamal. Tel Aviv, Assoc. of Former Residents of Lask in Israel, 1968. 737, 164 p., ports., facsims. (H,Y,E)

Lask (R) see also under Pabianice

Laskarzew (R). *Sefer Laskarzew-Sobolew* [Laskarzew-Sobolew*]. Ed.: Moshe Levani. Paris, La Société de Laskarzew-Sobolew en France, [197–/8–]. 708 p., illus., map, ports. (Y)

Leczyca (R). *Sefer Linshits* [Memorial book of Leczyca]. Ed.: J. Frenkel. Tel Aviv, Former Residents of Leczyca in Israel, 1953. 223 p., ports. (H)

Lemberg (AH) see Lwow

Lenin (R). *Kehilat Lenin; sefer zikaron* [The community of Lenin; memorial book]. Ed.: M. Tamari. Tel Aviv, Former Residents of Lenin in Israel and in the USA, 1957. 407 p., ports. (H,Y)

Leonpol (R) see under Druja (*Sefer Druja*)

Lesko (AH). *Sefer yizkor; mukdash le-yehudei ha-ayarot she-nispu ba-shoa be-shanim 1939-44, Linsk, Istrik. . . ve-ha-seviva* [Memorial book; dedicated to the Jews of Linsk, Istrik. . . and vicinity who perished in the Holocaust in the years 1939–44]. Eds.: N. Mark, Sh. Friedlander. [Tel Aviv], Book Committee of the "Libai" Organization, [1965]. 516 p., ports. (H,Y)

Levertev (R) see Lubartow

Lezajsk (AH). *Lizhensk; sefer zikaron le-kedoshei Lizhensk she-nispu be-shoat ha-natsim* [Memorial book of the martyrs of Lezajsk who perished in the Holocaust]. Ed.: H. Rabin. Tel Aviv, Former Residents of Lezajsk in Israel, [1970]. 495 p., ports., facsims. (H,Y)

Libovne (R) see Luboml

Lida (R). *Sefer Lida* [The book of Lida*]. Eds.: A. Manor *et al.* Tel Aviv, Former Residents of Lida in Israel and the Relief Committee of the Lida Jews in the USA, 1970. 438, xvii p., ports., maps, facsims. (H,Y,E)

Likeva (R) see Lukow

Linshits (R) see Leczyca

Linsk (AH) see Lesko

Lipkany (R). *Kehilat Lipkany; sefer zikaron* [The community of Lipkany; memorial book]. Tel Aviv, Former Residents of Lipkany in Israel, 1963. 407 p., ports. (H,Y)

Lipkany (R). *Lipkan fun amol* [Lipcan of old*]. By Aaron Shuster. Montreal, Author, 1957. 217 p., illus., ports. (Y)

Lipniszki (R). *Sefer zikaron shel kehilat Lipnishok* [Memorial book of the community of Lipniszki]. Ed.: A. Levin. Tel Aviv, Former Residents of Lipniszki in Israel, 1968. 206 p., ports., map (H,Y)

Lipno (R). *Sefer Lipno, Skepe, Lubicz, Kikol ve-ha-sevivah* [Sepher Lipno—The Lipno book*]. Ed.: Shmuel Alon (Domb). Tel Aviv, Society of Former Residents of Lipno and Vicinity, 1988. viii, 327 p., illus., maps, ports. (H,Y,E)

Litevisk (Lutowiska) (AH) see under Lesko

Lizhensk (AH) see Lezajsk

Lodz (R). *Kehilat Lodz; ir ve-em be-yisrael* [The community of Lodz; a Jewish mother-city]. [By] Aaron Ze'ev Aescoly. Jerusalem, Ha-Mahlakah le-inyanei ha-no'ar shel ha-Histadrut ha-Tsiyonit [Youth Section of the Zionist Organization], [1947/48]. 238 p. (H)

Lodz (R). *Lodzer yisker-bukh* [Lodzer yizkor book*]. New York, United Emergency Relief Committee for the City of Lodz, 1943. Various pagings, ports. (Y)

Lodz (R). *Yiddish Lodz; a yizkor book.* Melbourne, Lodzer Center, 1974. 13, 243 p., illus. (Y,E)

Lokacze (R). *Sefer yizkor le-kehilat Lokatsh (Polin)— Gedenk bukh far di shtetl Lokatsh* [Lokatch (Poland) memorial book*]. Comp.: Eliezer Verba; ed.: Shimon Matlofsky. Jerusalem, Shimon Matlofsky, 1993. 98, [34] p., illus., map, ports. (H,Y; intro.: E)

Lomza (R). *Lomzhe; ir oyfkum un untergang* [The rise and fall of Lomza]. Ed.: H. Sabatka. New York, American Committee for the Book of Lomza, 1957. 371 p., ports., facsims. (Y)

Lomza (R). *Sefer zikaron le-kehilat Lomza* [Lomza—In memory of the Jewish community*]. Ed.: Y. T. Lewinski. Tel Aviv, Former Residents of Lomza in Israel, 1952. 337 p., ports., facsims. (H)

Lopatyn (AH) see under Radziechow

Losice (R). *Loshits; lezeykher an umgebrakhte kehile* [Losice; in memory of a Jewish community, exterminated by Nazi murderers*]. Ed.: M. Shener. Tel Aviv, Former Residents of Losice in Israel, 1963. 459 p., ports., facsims. (H,Y)

Lowicz (R). *Lowicz; ir be-Mazovia u-seviva, sefer zikaron* [Lowicz; a town in Mazovia, memorial book*]. Ed.: G. Shaiak. [Tel Aviv], Former Residents of Lowicz in Melbourne and Sydney, Australia, 1966. 395, xxii p., ports., facsims. (H,Y,E)

Lozisht (Ignatowka) (R) see under Zofiowka

Lubartow (R). *Khurbn Levartov* [The destruction of Lubartow]. Ed.: B. Tshubinski. Paris, Association of Lubartow, 1947. 117 p., ports., facsims. (Y)

Lubcza (R). *Lubtsh ve-Delatitsh; sefer zikaron* [Lubtch ve-Delatich; in memory of the Jewish community*]. Ed.: K. Hilel. Haifa, Former Residents of Lubtsh-Delatitsh in Israel, 1971. 480 p., ports., map, facsims. (H,Y)

Lubenichi (R) see under Bobruisk

Lubicz (R) see under Lipno

Lublin (R). *Dos bukh fun Lublin* [The memorial book of Lublin]. Paris, Former Residents of Lublin in Paris, 1952. 685 p., ports., facsims. (Y)

Lublin (R). *Lublin* [Lublin volume*]. Eds.: N. Blumenthal, M. Korzen. Jerusalem, The Encyclopaedia of the Jewish Diaspora, 1957. 816 columns, ports., map, facsims. (H,Y)

Luboml (R). *Sefer yizkor le-kehilat Luboml* [Yizkor book of Luboml*]. Ed.: Berl Kagan. Tel Aviv, 1974. 390, 18 p., illus. (H,Y,E)

Lubraniec (R) see under Wloclawek

Luck (R). *Sefer Lutsk* [Memorial book of Lutsk]. Ed.: N. Sharon. Tel Aviv, Former Residents of Lutsk in Israel, 1961. 608 p., ports., facsims. (H,Y)

Ludmir (R) see Wlodzimierz

Ludwipol (R). *Sefer zikaron le-kehilat Ludwipol* [Ludvipol-Wolyn; in memory of the Jewish community*]. Ed.: N. Ayalon. Tel Aviv, Ludvipol Relief Society of Israel, 1965. 335 p., ports., map, facsims. (H,Y)

Lukow (R). *Sefer Lukow; geheylikt der khorev gevorener kehile* [The book of Lukow; dedicated to a destroyed community]. Ed.: B. Heller. Tel Aviv, Former Residents of Lukow in Israel and the USA, 1968. 652 p., ports., facsims. (H,Y)

Luniniec (R). *Yizkor kehilot Luniniec/Kozhanhorodok* [Memorial book of the communities of Luniniec/Kozhanhorodok]. Eds.: Y. Zeevi (Wilk) *et al.* Tel Aviv, Assoc. of Former Residents of Luniniec/Kozhanhorodok in Israel, 1952. 268 p., ports. (H,Y)

Luniniec (R) see also under Polesie (region)

Lutowiska (AH) see under Lesko

Lutsk (R) see Luck

Lvov (AH) see Lwow

Lwow (AH). *Lwow* [Lwow volume*], part I. Ed.: N. M. Gelber. Jerusalem, The Encyclopaedia of the Jewish Diaspora, 1956. 772 columns, ports., facsims. (H)

Lwow (AH) see also *Arim ve-imahot,* vol. 1

Lyngmiany (R) see under Stolin

Lynki (R) see under Stolin

Lyntupy (R) see under Swieciany

Lyskow (R) see under Wolkowysk (*Volkovisker yisker-bukh*)

Lyszkowice (R) see under Lowicz

Lyuban (R) see under Slutsk

Mad (AH). *Ha-kehilah ha-yehudit shel Mad, Hungaria* [The Jewish community of Maad, Hungary*]. Ed.: Arieh Lewy. Jerusalem, Mad Commemorative Committee, 1974. 154, 31 p., illus. (H,E,Hu)

Magyarlapos (AH) see under Des

Makow-Mazowiecki (R). *Sefer zikaron le-kehilat Makow-Mazowiecki* [Memorial book of the community of Makow-Mazowiecki]. Ed.: J. Brat. Tel Aviv, Former Residents of Makow-Mazowiecki in Israel, 1969. 505 p., ports., facsims. (H,Y)

Makow Podhalanski (AH) see under Nowy Targ

Malecz (R) see under Pruzana

Margareten (AH) see Margita

Margita (AH). *Sefer yizkor le-kehilat Margareten ve-ha-seviva* [Memorial book of the community of Margareten and the surrounding region]. Ed.: Aharon Kleinmann. Jerusalem, Hayim Frank, 1979. 200, 275 p. (H,Hu)

Marijampole (R). *Marijampole al gedot ha-nahar Sheshupe (Lita)* [Marijampole on the river Sheshupe (Lithuania)*]. Ed.: Avraham Tory-Golub. Tel Aviv, Committee of Survivors from Marijampole in Israel, 1983. 74, 245 p., illus., map, ports. (H,Y,E)

Markuleshty (R). *Markuleshty; yad le-moshava yehudit be-Bessarabia* [Markuleshty; memorial to a Jewish colony in Bessarabia]. Eds.: Leib Kuperstein, Meir Kotik. Tel Aviv, Markuleshty Society, 1977. 272 p., illus. (H,Y)

Markuszow (R). *Hurbana u-gevurata shel ha-ayara Markuszow* [The destruction and heroism of the town of Markuszow]. Ed.: D. Shtokfish. Tel Aviv, Former Residents of Markuszow in Israel, 1955. 436 p., ports. (Y)

Marosvasarhely (AH). *Korot yehudei Marosvasarhely ve-ha-seviva* [History of the Jews in Marosvasarhely]. [By] Yitzhak Perri (Friedmann). Tel Aviv, Ghetto Fighters House, Ha-Kibbutz ha-Meuhad, 1977. (H)

Marvits (Murawica) (R) see under Mlynow

Medenice (AH) see under Drohobycz

Melits (AH) see Mielec

Meretsh (R) see Merkine

Merkine (R). *Meretsh; ayara yehudit be-Lita* [Merkine*]. Ed.: Uri Shefer. Tel Aviv, [Society of Meretsh Immigrants in Israel], 1988. 195 p., illus., map, ports. (H)

Meytshet (R) see Molczadz

Mezhirechye (R) see Miedzyrzec-Wolyn

Mezritsh (R) see Miedzyrzec

Miava (AH) see under Postyen

Michalovce (AH) see Nagymihaly

Michow (R). *Michow (Lubelski); sefer zikaron le-kedoshei Michow she-nispu be-shoat ha-natsim ba-shanim 1939–1942* [Memorial book to the martyrs of Michow who perished in the Holocaust. . .]. Ed.: Hayim Rabin. [Israel], Former Residents of Michow, 1987. 343 p., illus., map, ports. (H,Y)

Miechow (R). *Sefer yizkor Miechow, Charsznica, Ksiaz* [Miechov memorial book, Charshnitza and Kshoynge*]. Eds.: N. Blumenthal, A. Ben-Azar (Broshy). Tel Aviv, Former Residents of Miechov, Charshnitza and Kshoynzh, 1971. 314, [4] p., ports., facsims. (H,Y)

Miedzyrzec (R). *Mezritsh; zamlbukh* [The Mezritsh volume]. Ed.: Y. Horn. Buenos Aires, Assoc. of Former Residents of Mezritsh in Argentina, 1952. 635 p., ports., facsims. (Y)

Miedzyrzec (R). *Sefer Mezritsh; lezeykher di kdoyshim fun undzer shtot* [Mezritsh book, in memory of the martyrs of our city]. Eds.: Binem Heller, Yitzhak Ronkin. Israel, Mezritsh Societies in Israel and the Diaspora, 1978. 821 p., illus. (H,Y)

Miedzyrzec (R). *Di yidn-shtot Mezritsh; fun ir breyshis biz erev der velt-milkhome* [Historia de Mezritch (Mezritch Podlasie); su población judía*]. [By] Meir Edelboim. Buenos Aires, Sociedad de Residentes de Mezritch en la Argentina, 1957. 424 p., facsims. (Y)

Miedzyrzec-Wolyn (R). *Mezeritsh gadol be-vinyana u-be-hurbana* [Mezhiritch-Wolyn; in memory of the Jewish community*]. Ed.: B. H. Ayalon-Baranick. Tel Aviv, Former Residents of Mezhiritch, 1955. 442 columns, ports., facsims. (H,Y)

Miedzyrzec-Wolyn (R). *Pinkas ha-kehila Mezhirits* [Memorial book of Mezhirits]. Ed.: Natan Livneh. Tel Aviv, Committee of Former Residents of Mezhirits in Israel, 1973. 71 p., illus. (H,Y)

Mielec (AH). *Melitser yidn* [Mielec Jews]. [By] Shlomo Klagsbrun. Tel Aviv, Nay-Lebn, 1979. 288 p., illus. (Y)

Mielec (AH). *Sefer zikaron le-kehilat Mielec; sipur hashmadat ha-kehila ha- yehudit* [Remembering Mielec; the destruction of the Jewish community*]. [New York], Mielec Yizkor-Book Committee, 1979. 84, 122 p., illus., ports. (H,Y,E)

Mielnica (R) see under Kowel (*Pinkes Kowel*)

Mikepercs (AH) see under Debrecen

Mikolajow (AH) see under Radziechow

Mikulince (AH). *Mikulince; sefer yizkor* [Mikulince yizkor book*]. Ed.: Haim Preshel. [Israel], The Organisation of Mikulincean Survivors in Israel and in the United States of America, 1985. 356, 266 p., illus., ports. (H,E)

Mikulov (Nikolsburg) (AH) see under *Arim ve-imahot,* vol. 4

Milosna (R) see under Rembertow

Minkovtsy (R) see under Kamenets-Podolskiy

Minsk (R). *Albom Minsk* [The Minsk album; selected pictures collected by David Cohen from the two volumes of the book "The Jewish Mother-City Minsk"*]. Eds.: Shlomo Even-Shoshan, Nehemiya Maccabee. [Israel], Association of Olim from Minsk and its Surroundings in Israel, Hakibbutz Hameuchad Publishing House, 1988. 71 p., illus., maps, ports. (H,E)

Minsk (R). *Minsk ir ve-em* [Minsk; Jewish mother city: a memorial anthology*]. Ed.: Shlomo Even-Shushan. Jerusalem, Association of Olim from Minsk and its Surroundings in Israel; Ghetto Fighters' House; Kiryat Sefer, 1975—-1985. 2 vols., illus., ports. (H)

Minsk-Mazowiecki (R). *Sefer Minsk-Mazowiecki* [Minsk-Mazowiecki memorial book*]. Ed.: Ephraim Shedletzky. Jerusalem, Minsk-Mazowiecki Societies in Israel and Abroad, 1977. 6, 633 p., illus. (H,Y,E)

Miory (R) see under Druja (*Sefer Druja*)

Mir (R). *Sefer Mir* [Memorial book of Mir]. Ed.: N. Blumenthal. Jerusalem, The Encyclopaedia of the Jewish Diaspora, 1962. 768, 62 columns, ports. (H,Y,E)

Miskolc (AH). *Kedoshei Miskolc ve-ha-seviva; ha-kehilot me-Hidasnemeti ad Mezokovesd u-me-Ozd ad Szerencs* [The martyrs of Miskolc and vicinity; the communities from Hidasnemeti to Mezokovesd and from Ozd to Szerencs]. [By] Slomo Paszternak. Bnei Brak, 1970. 14, 38, 277 p., illus., ports. (Hu,E,H)

Mizocz (R). *Mizocz; sefer zikaron* [Memorial book of Mizocz]. Ed.: A. Ben-Oni. Tel Aviv, Former Residents of Mizocz in Israel, 1961. 293, [24] p., ports., facsims. (H)

Mlawa (R). *Mlawa ha-yehudit; koroteha, hitpathuta, kilayona —Di yidishe Mlave; geshikhte, oyfshtand, umkum* [Jewish Mlawa; its history, development, destruction*]. Ed.: David Shtokfish. [Israel], Mlawa Societies in Israel and in the Diaspora, 1984. 2 vols. (536, 584 p.), illus., maps, ports. (H,Y,E)

Mlawa (R). *Pinkes Mlave* [Memorial book of Mlawa]. New York, World Assoc. of Former Residents of Mlawa, 1950. 483, 63 p., ports. (Y)

Mlynow (R). *Sefer Mlynow-Marvits* [Mlynov-Muravica memorial book*]. Ed.: J. Sigelman. Haifa, Former Residents of Mlynov-Muravica in Israel, 1970. 511 p., ports. (Y,H)

Modrzyc (R) see Deblin

Mogielnica (R) *Sefer yizkor Mogielnica-Bledow* [Memorial book of Mogielnica-Bledow]. Ed.: Yisrael Zonder. Tel Aviv, Mogielnica and Bledow Society, 1972. 808 p., illus., map, ports. (H,Y)

Molczadz (R). *Sefer-zikaron le-kehilat Meytshet* [Memorial book of the community of Meytshet]. Ed.: Benzion H. Ayalon. Tel Aviv, Meytshet Societies in Israel and Abroad, 1973. 460, 12 p., illus. (H,Y)

Monasterzyska (AH). *Sefer Monastrishtz* [Monasterzyska; a memorial book*]. Ed.: M. Segal. Tel Aviv, Monasterzyska Association, 1974. 126 p., illus. (H,Y,E)

Monastir (Turkey). *Ir u-shema Monastir* [A city called Monastir]. [By] Uri Oren. Tel Aviv, Naor, 1972. 167 p., illus. (H)

Monastir (Turkey). *A town called Monastir.* [By] Uri Oren; translated from the Hebrew by Mark Segal. Tel Aviv, Dror Publications, 1971. 240 p., illus., ports. (E)

Mosty (R) see under Piaski

Mosty-Wielkie (AH). *Mosty-Wielkie—Most Rabati, sefer zikaron* [Mosty-Wielkie memorial book*]. Eds.: Moshe Shtarkman, Abraham Ackner, A.L. Binot. Tel Aviv, Mosty Wielkie Societies in Israel and the United States, 1975—-1977. 2 vols., illus. (H,Y,E)

Motele (R) see Motol

Motol (R). *Hurban Motele* [The destruction of Motele]. [By] A. L. Poliak. Jerusalem, Council of Motele Immigrants, 1957. 87 p. (H)

Mszczonow (R) see under Zyrardow

Mukacevo (Munkacs) (AH) see under *Arim ve-imahot,* vol. 1

Munkacs (AH) see under *Arim ve-imahot,* vol. 1

Murawica (R) see under Mlynow

Myjava (Miava) (AH) see under Postyen

Mysleniec (R) see under Wadowice

Myszyniec (R) see under Ostroleka

Nadarzyn (R) see under Pruszkow

Nadworna (AH). *Nadworna; sefer edut ve-zikaron* [Nadworna, Stanislav district; memorial and records*]. Ed.: Israel Carmi (Otto Kramer). Tel Aviv, Nadworna Societies in Israel and the United States, 1975. 281, 67 p., illus. (H,Y,E)

Nadzin (Nadarzyn) (R) see under Pruszkow

Nagybanya (AH). *Nagybanya ve-ha-seviva* [Nagybanya and the surrounding region]. Ed.: Naftali Stern. Bne Brak, 1976. 245, 175 p., illus. (H,Hu)

Nagyilonda (AH) see under Des

Nagykallo (AH). *Ha-tsadik me-Kalov ve-kehilato; tsiyun le-nefesh hayeha zts"l ve-le-kehila nihahedet. . .* [The tsadik of Kalov and his community. . .]. [By] Tuvia (Laszlo) Szilágyi-Windt; translated from Hungarian and edited: Yehuda Edelshtein. Haifa, [1970?]. 208 p., facsims., illus., ports. (H)

Nagymagyar (AH) see under Dunaszerdahely

Nagymihaly (AH). *Sefer Michalovce ve-ha-seviva* [The book of Michalovce*]. Ed.: M. Ben-Zeev (M. Farkas). Tel Aviv, Committee of Former Residents of Michalovce in Israel, 1969. 240, 64, 103 p., ports., facsims. (H,E,Hu)

Nagyszollos (AH). *Sefer zikaron le-kehilat Selish ve-ha-seviva* [A memorial to the Jewish community of Sevlus (Nagyszollos) District*]. Ed.: Shmuel ha-Kohen Weingarten. Israel, Selish Society, 1976. 326 p., illus. (H)

Nagyszollos (AH). *Sefer zikaron. . .* [Memorial book*]—Musaf [Addenda]. Eds.: J. H. Klein, J. M. Hollander. Israel, The Committee of Olei Nagyszollos and Vicinity in Israel, 1981. 94 p., ports. (H,E)

Nagytapolcsany (AH) see Topolcany

Nagyvarad (AH) see Oradea

Naliboki (R). *Ayaratenu Nalibok, hayeha ve-hurbana* [Our town Nalibok, its existence and destruction*]. Tel Aviv, Former Residents of Nalibok, 1967. 239 p., ports., map (H,Y)

Naliboki (R) see also under Stolpce

Narajow (AH) see under Brzezany

Navaredok (R) see Nowogrodek

Naymark (AH) see Nowy Targ

Nemirov (R) see under *Arim ve-imahot,* vol. 2

Nestilye (R) see Uscilug

Neumarkt (AH) see Nowy Targ

Nevel (R) see under Vitebsk (*Sefer Vitebsk*)

Nieswiez (R). *Sefer Nieswiez.* Ed.: David Shtokfish. Tel Aviv, Nieswiez Societies in Israel and the Diaspora, 1976. 531 p., illus. (H,Y)

Nieszawa (R) see under Wloclawek

Nikolsburg (AH) see under *Arim ve-imahot,* vol. 4

Novograd-Volynskiy (R). *Zvhil-Novogradvolinsk.* Eds.: A. Ori, M. Bone.

Tel Aviv, Association of Former Residents of Zvhil and the Environment, 1962. 354, 232, 16 p., ports. (H,Y,E)

Novo Minsk (R) see Minsk Mazowiecki

Novyi Vitkov (Witkow Nowy) (AH) see under Radziechow

Novyi Yarichev (AH) see Jaryczow Nowy

Nowe Miasto (R) see under Plonsk

Nowogrod (R) see under Lomza (*Lomzhe; ir oyfkum un untergang*)

Nowogrodek (R). *Pinkas Navaredok* [Navaredok memorial book*]. Eds.: E. Yerushalmi *et al.* Tel Aviv, Alexander Harkavy Navaredker Relief Committee in the USA and. . . in Israel, 1963. 419 p., ports., maps, facsims. (H,Y)

Nowo-Swieciany (R) see under Swieciany

Nowy Dwor (near Warszawa) (R). *Pinkas Nowy Dwor* [Memorial book of Nowy-Dwor]. Eds.: A. Shamri, D. First. Tel Aviv, Former Residents of Nowy-Dwor in Israel, USA, Argentina. . . , 1965. 556, xix p., ports., map, facsims. (H,Y,E)

Nowy Dwor (R). *Ondenk bukh fun Nowy Dwor* [Memorial book of Nowy Dwor]. Los Angeles, Nowy Dwor Relief Committee, [1947]. 60 p., illus., ports. (Y)

Nowy Dwor (R) see also under Szczuczyn (*Sefer zikaron le-kehilot Szczuczyn, Wasiliszki. . .*)

Nowy Sacz (AH). *Le-zekher kehilat Tsants* [In memory of the community of Tsants]. Ed.: Ya'akovi Tefuhah. Jerusalem, Bet ha-sefer ha-tikhon ha-dati la-banot Oylinah di Rotshild, [1967/68]. 174 p., illus., facsims., music, ports. (H)

Nowy Sacz (AH). *Sefer Sants* [The book of the Jewish community of Nowy Sacz*]. Ed.: R. Mahler. New York, Former Residents of Sants in New York, 1970. 886 p., ports., facsims. (H,Y)

Nowy Targ (AH). *Sefer Nowy Targ ve-ha-seviva* [Remembrance book Nowy Targ and vicinity*]. Ed.: Michael Walzer-Fass. Tel Aviv, Townspeople Association of Nowy Targ and Vicinity, 1979. 301 p., illus. (H,Y,E)

Nowy Zagorz (AH) see under Sanok

Odessa (R) see under *Arim ve-imahot,* vol. 2

Okmieniec (R) see under Braslaw

Okuniew (R) see under Rembertow

Olkeniki(R). *Ha-ayara be-lehavot; sefer zikaron le-kehilat Olkenik pelekh Vilna* [Olkeniki in flames; a memorial book*]. Ed.: Sh. Farber. Tel Aviv, Association of Former Residents of Olkeniki and Surroundings, 1962. 287, [4] p., ports. (H,Y)

Olkusz (AH). *Olkusz (Elkish); sefer zikaron le-kehila she-huhehada ba-shoa* [Olkusz; memorial book to a community that was exterminated during the Holocaust]. Ed.: Zvi Yashiv. Tel Aviv, Olkusz Society, [1971/72]. 280 p., map, illus. (H,Y)

Olshan (R) see Holszany

Olyka (R). *Pinkas ha-kehila Olyka; sefer yizkor* [Memorial book of the community of Olyka]. Ed.: Natan Livneh. Tel Aviv, Olyka Society, 1972. 397 p., illus. (H,Y)

Opatow (R). *Apt (Opatow); sefer zikaron le-ir va-em be-yisrael* [Apt; a town which does not exist any more*]. Ed.: Z. Yasheev. Tel Aviv, The Apt Organization in Israel, USA, Canada and Brazil, 1966. 441, [3], 20 p., ports. (H,Y,E)

Opatow (R) see also under Ostrowiec (*Ostrovtse; geheylikt dem ondenk. . .*)

Opoczno R). *Sefer Opotshnah; yad vashem le-kehilah she-harvah* [The book of Opoczno]. Ed.: Yitshak Alfasi. Tel Aviv, Association of Emigrants from Opoczno and Vicinity, 1989. 394, 21 p., illus., ports., diagrams (H,Y,E)

Opole (R). *Sefer Opole-Lubelski* [Memorial book of Opole-Lubelski*]. Ed.: David Shtokfish. Tel Aviv, Opole Societies in Israel and the Diaspora, 1977. 467 p., illus. (H,Y)

Opsa (R) see under Braslaw

Oradea (AH). *A tegnap városa; a nagyváradi zsidóság emlékkönyve* [Ir veetmol; sefer zikaron le-yehudei Grosswardein* = A city and yesterday; memorial book to the Jews of Grosswardein]. Eds.: Schön Dezsö *et al.* Tel Aviv, 1981. 446 p., illus., maps, ports. (Hu)

Oradea (AH). *Sefer zikaron le-yahadut Grosswardein-Oradea-Nagyvarad ve-ha-seviva, mishnat yisoda ve-ad-hurbana* [Memorial book to the Jews of Grosswardein-Oradea-Nagyvarad and vicinity. . .]. Ed.: Zvi Grossman. Tel Aviv, Grosswardein Society in Israel, 1984. 451, 67 p., illus., maps, ports. (H)

Orgeyev (R). *Orheyev be-vinyana u-be-hurbana* [Orheyev alive and destroyed]. Eds.: Y. Spivak *et al.* Tel Aviv, Committee of Former Residents of Orheyev, 1959. 216 p., ports. (H,Y)

Orhei (R) see Orgeyev

Orlowa (R) see under Zoludek

Oshmena (R) see Oszmiana

Oshpitsin (AH) see Oswiecim

Osiek (R) see under Staszow

Osipovichi (R) see under Bobruisk

Ostra (R) see Ostrog

Ostrog (R). *Le-zekher kehilat Ostrah; hantsahat kehilat Ostrah* [In memory of the Jewish community of Ostrog]. Ramat-Hasharon, Bet-sefer "Oranim," 1969. 55 p., illus. (H)

Ostrog (R). *Ostrog.* [By] Judah Loeb Levin. Jerusalem-Tel Aviv, Yad Yahadut Polin, 1966. 111 p., map, ports., illus. (H)

Ostrog (R). *Pinkas Ostra; sefer zikaron. . .* [Ostrog-Wolyn; in memory of the Jewish community*]. Ed.: H. Ayalon-Baranick. Tel Aviv, Association of Former Residents of Ostrog, 1960. 640 columns, ports., maps, facsims. (H,Y)

Ostrog (R). *Sefer Ostrog (Vohlin); matsevet zikaron le-kehila kedosha* [Ostrog book; a memorial to the Ostrog holy community*]. Ed.: Yitzhak Alperowitz; Chief Coordinator: Chaim Finkel. Tel Aviv, The Ostrog Society in Israel, 1987. 402, 34 p., illus., ports., map (H,Y,E,P)

Ostrog (R). *Ven dos lebn hot geblit* [When life was blooming]. [By] M. Grines. Buenos Aires, 1954. 471 p., ports. (Y)

Ostrog (R) see also under *Arim ve-imahot,* vol. 1

Ostroleka (R). *Sefer kehilat Ostrolenka* [Book of kehilat Ostrolenka*]. Ed.: Y. Ivri. Tel Aviv, Association of Former Residents of Ostrolenka, 1963. 579 p., ports. (H,Y)

Ostrowiec (R). *Ostrovtse; geheylikt dem ondenk. . . fun Ostrovtse, Apt. . .* [Ostrovtse; dedicated to the memory of Ostrovtse, Apt. . .]. Buenos Aires, Former Residents of Ostrovtse. . . in Argentina, 1949. 217, [3] p., ports. (Y)

Ostrowiec (R). *Ostrovtse; a denkmol oyf di khurves fun a farnikhtete yidishe kehile* [Ostrowiec; a monument on the ruins of an annihilated Jewish community*]. Eds.: Gershon Silberberg, M. S. Geshuri. Tel Aviv, Society of Ostrovtser Jews in Israel, with the cooperation of the Ostrovtser Societies in New York and Toronto, [197–/8–]. 560, [106], 134 p., illus., maps, ports. (Y,H,E)

Ostrow-Lubelski (R). *Sefer-yizkor Ostrow-Lubelski — Yisker-bukh Ostrow- Lubelski* [Memorial-book Ostrow-Lubelski*]. Ed.: David Shtokfish. Israel, Association of Former Residents of Ostrow-Lubelski in Israel, 1987. 422 p., illus., ports. (H,Y,E)

Ostrow-Mazowiecka (R). *Ostrow Mazowiecka.* [By] Judah Loeb Levin. Jerusalem-Tel Aviv, Yad Yahadut Polin, 1966. 164 p., ports., illus. (H)

Ostrow-Mazowiecka (R). *Sefer ha-zikaron le-kehilat Ostrov-Mazovyetsk* [Memorial book of the community of Ostrow-Mazowiecka]. Ed.: A. Margalit. Tel Aviv, Association of Former Residents of Ostrow-Mazowieck, 1960. 653 p., ports. (H,Y)

Ostryna (R) see under Szczuczyn (*Sefer zikaron le-kehilot Szczuczyn, Wasiliszki. . .*)

Oswiecim (AH). *Sefer Oshpitsin* [Oswiecim-Auschwitz memorial book*]. Eds.: Ch. Wolnerman, A. Burstin, M. S. Geshuri. Jerusalem, Oshpitsin Society, 1977. 622 p., illus. (H,Y)

Oszmiana (R). *Sefer zikaron le-kehilat Oshmana* [Oshmana memorial book*]. Ed.: M. Gelbart. Tel Aviv, Oshmaner Organization in Israel and the Oshmaner Society in the USA, 1969. 659, 109 p., ports. (H,Y,E)

Otvotsk (R) see Otwock

Otwock (R). *Khurbn Otvotsk, Falenits, Kartshev* [The destruction of Otvotsk, Falenits, Kartshev]. [By] B. Orenstein. [Bamberg], Former Residents of Otvotsk, Falenits and Kartshev in the American Zone in Germany, 1948. 87 p., ports. (Y)

Otwock (R). *Yisker-bukh; Otvotsk-Kartshev* [Memorial book of Otvotsk and Kartshev*]. Ed.: Sh. Kanc. Tel Aviv, Former Residents of Otvotsk-Kartshev, 1968. 1086 columns, ports. (H,Y)

Ozarow (R) see under Ostrowiec

Ozieran (AH) see Jezierzany

Ozorkow (R). *Ozorkow.* [By] Judah Loeb Levin. Jerusalem, Yad Yahadut Polin, 1966. 128 p., illus. (H)

Pabianice (R). *Sefer Pabianice* [Memorial book of Pabianice]. Ed.: A. W. Yassni. Tel Aviv, Former Residents of Pabianice in Israel, 1956. 419 p., ports., facsims. (H,Y)

Paks (AH). *Mazkeret Paks* [Paks memorial book]. Ed.: D. Sofer. Jerusalem, 1962– [1972/73]. 3 vols., ports., facsims. (H)

Papa (AH). *Sefer zikaron Papa; le-zekher kedoshei ha-kehila ve-yishuvei ha-seviva* [Memorial book of Papa. . .]. [By] Jehuda-Gyula Lang. Israel, Papa Memorial Committee, [197–]. 28, 188 p., illus., ports. (H,Hu)

Parafianowo (R) see under Dokszyce

Parczew (R). *Parczew—sefer zikaron le-kedoshei Parczew ve-ha-seviva* [Parczew—memorial book of the martyrs of Parczew and vicinity]. Eds.: Sh. Zonnenshein *et al.* Haifa, Association of Former Residents of Parczew in Israel, 1977. 328 p., ports. (H,Y)

Parichi (R) see under Bobruisk

Parysow (R). *Sefer Porisov* [Parysow; a memorial to the Jewish community of Parysow, Poland*]. Ed.: Y. Granatstein. Tel Aviv, Former Residents of Parysow in Israel, 1971. 625 p., ports. (H,Y)

Perehinsko (AH) see under Rozniatow

Petrikov (R) see Piotrkow Trybunalski

Piaski (R). *Pyesk ve-Most; sefer yizkor* [Piesk and Most, a memorial book*]. Tel Aviv, Piesk and Most Societies in Israel and the Disapora, 1975. 657, 17, 52 p., illus. (H,Y,E)

Piatnica (R) see under Lomza (*Lomzhe, ir oyfkum un untergang*)

Piesk (R) see Piaski

Piestany (AH) see Postyen

Pilev (R) see Pulawy

Pinczow (R). *Sefer zikaron le-kehilat Pintshev; in Pintshev togt shoyn nisht* [A book of memory of the Jewish community of Pinczow, Poland*]. Ed.: M. Shener. Tel Aviv, Former Residents of Pinczow in Israel and in the Diaspora, 1970. 480 p., ports. (H,Y)

Pinsk (R). *Pinsk sefer edut ve-zikaron le-kehilat Pinsk-Karlin* [Pinsk*]. Ed.: N. Tamir (Mirski). Tel Aviv, Former Residents of Pinsk-Karlin in Israel, 1966—-1977. 3 vols., ports., facsims. (H,Y)

Pinsk (R). *Toyznt yor Pinsk; geshikhte fun der shtot, der yidisher yishev, institutsyes, sotsyale bavegungen, perzenlekhkeytn, gezelshaftlekhe tuer, Pinsk iber der velt* [A thousand years of Pinsk; history of the city, its Jewish community, institutions, social movements, personalities, community leaders, Pinsk around the world]. Ed.: B. Hoffman. New York, Pinsker Branch 210, Workmen's Circle, 1941. 15, 500 p., illus. (Y)

Piotrkow Trybunalski (R). *Piotrkow Trybunalski ve-ha-seviva* [Piotrkow Trybunalski and vicinity*]. Eds.: Y. Melz, N. (Lavy) Lau. Tel Aviv, Former Residents of Piotrkow Tryb. in Israel, [1965]. 1192 columns, lxiv p., ports., facsims. (H,Y,E)

Piotrkow Trybunalski (R). *A tale of one city: Piotrkow Trybunalski.* Ed.: Ben Giladi. New York, Shengold Publishers, in cooperation with The Piotrkow Trybunalski Relief Association in New York, 1991. 494 p., illus., maps, ports. (E)

Pitshayev (R) see Poczajow

Plantsh (Polaniec) (R) see under Staszow

Plawno (R) see under Radomsko

Plintsk (R) see Plonsk

Plock (R). *Plotsk; bletlekh geshikhte fun idishn lebn in der alter heym* [Plock; páginas de historia de la vida judía de Allende el Mar*]. Ed.: Yosef Horn. Buenos Aires, Sociedad de Residentes de Plock en la Argentina, 1945. 255 p., illus., ports. (Y)

Plock (R). *Plotsk; toldot kehila atikat yomin be-Polin* [Plotzk; a history of an ancient Jewish community in Poland*]. Ed.: E. Eisenberg. Tel Aviv, World Committee for the Plotzk Memorial Book, 1967. 684, 96 p., ports., maps, facsims. (H,Y,E)

Plock (R). *Yidn in Plotsk* [Jews in Plotzk*]. [By] S. Greenspan. New York, 1960. 325 p., ports. (Y)

Plonsk (R). *Sefer Plonsk ve-ha-seviva* [Memorial book of Plonsk and vicinity]. Ed.: Sh. Zemah. Tel Aviv, Former Residents of Plonsk in Israel, 1963. 775 p., ports., map, facsims. (H,Y)

Plotsk (R) see Plock

Plusy (R) see under Braslaw

Poczajow (R). *Pitshayever yisker-bukh* [Memorial book dedicated to the Jews of Pitchayev-Wohlyn executed by the Germans*]. Ed.: H. Gelernt. Philadelphia, The Pitchayever Wohliner Aid Society, 1960. 311 p., ports. (Y)

Poczajow (R) see also under Krzemieniec

Podbrodzie (R) see under Swieciany

Podhajce (AH). *Sefer Podhajce.* Ed.: M. S. Geshuri. Tel Aviv, Podhajce Society, 1972. 295, 17 p., illus. (H,Y,E)

Podwoloczyska (AH). *Sefer Podwoloczyska ve-ha-sevivah* [The book of Podwoloczyska and environment; Podvolocisk book*]. Eds.: Zunyu Levinson, Dov Brayer, Avraham Ahuviah. Haifa, Podwoloczyska Community in Israel, 1988. 207 p., illus., ports., maps (H; introd.: E)

Pogost (R) see under Slutsk

Pohost (Pogost) (R) see under Slutsk

Pokshivnitsa (R) see Koprzywnica

Polaniec (R) see under Staszow

Poligon (R) see under Swieciany

Polonnoye (R) see under Novograd-Volynskiy

Porcsalma (AH) see under Csenger

Porisov (R) see Parysow

Porozow (R) see under Wolkowysk (*Volkovisker yisker-bukh*)

Postawy (R) see under Glebokie

Postyen (AH). *Gedenkbuch der Gemeinden Piestany und Umgebung.* [By] Sh. Grunwald. Jerusalem, 1969. 111, [10] p., ports. (G)

Pozsony (AH) see *Arim ve-imahot,* vol. 7

Praga (R). *Sefer Praga; mukdash le-zekher kedoshei irenu* [Praga book; dedicated to the memory of the martyrs of our town]. Ed.: Gabriel Weisman. Tel Aviv, Praga Society, 1974. 563 p., illus. (H,Y)

Premisle (AH) see Przemysl

Pressburg (Pozsony) (AH) see under *Arim ve-imahot,* vol. 7

Proshnits (R) see Przasnysz

Proskurov (R). *Khurbn Proskurov; tsum ondenken fun di heylige neshomes vos zaynen umgekumen in der shreklikher shkhite, vos iz ongefirt gevoren durkh di haydamakes* [The destruction of Proskurov; in memory of the sacred souls who perished during the terrible slaughter of the Haidamaks]. New York, 1924. 111 p., illus. (Y,H)

Pruszkow (R). *Sefer Pruszkow, Nadzin ve-ha-seviva* [Memorial book of Pruszkow, Nadzin and vicinity]. Ed.: D. Brodsky. Tel Aviv, Former Residents of Pruszkow in Israel, 1967. 334 p., ports., facsims. (H,Y)

Pruzana (R). *Pinkas me-hamesh kehilot harevot. . .* [Memorial book of five destroyed communities. . .]. Ed.: M. W. Bernstein. Buenos Aires, Former Residents of Pruzana. . . , 1958. 972 p., ports., facsims. (Y)

Pruzana (R). *Pinkas Pruzhany ve-ha-seviva; edut ve-zikaron le-kehilot she-hushmedu ba-shoa* [Pinkas Pruz'any and its vicinity (Bereze, Malch, Shershev, Seltz and Lineve); chronicle of six communities that perished in the Holocaust*]. Ed.: Joseph Friedlaender. Tel Aviv, United Pruziner and Vicinity Relief Committee in New York and in Philadelphia and the Pruz'ana Landshaft Association in Israel, 1983. 542, 169 p., illus., maps, ports. (H,E)

Przasnysz (R). *Sefer zikaron kehilat Proshnits* [Memorial book to the community of Proshnitz*]. Ed.: Shlomo Bachrach. Tel Aviv, Proshnitz Society, 1974. 273 p., illus. (H,Y,E)

Przeclaw (AH) see under Radomysl Wielki

Przedborz (R). *Przedborz—33 shanim le-hurbana* [Przedborz memorial book*]. Ed.: Shimon Kanc. Tel Aviv, Przedborz Societies in Israel and America, 1977. 84, 548 p., illus. (H,Y,E)

Przedborz (R) see also under Radomsko

Przedecz (R). *Sefer yizkor le-kedoshei ir Pshaytsh korbanot ha-shoa* [Memorial book to the Holocaust victims of the city of Pshaytsh]. Eds.: Moshe

Bilavsky *et al.* Tel Aviv, Przedecz Societies in Israel and the Diaspora, 1974. 400 p., illus. (H,Y)

Przemysl (AH). *Sefer Przemysl* [Przemysl memorial book*]. Ed.: A. Menczer. Tel Aviv, Former Residents of Przemysl in Israel, 1964. 522 p., ports., facsims. (H,Y)

Przytyk (R). *Sefer Przytyk.* Ed.: David Shtokfish. Tel Aviv, Przytyk Societies in Israel, France and the USA, 1973. 7, 461 p., illus. (H,Y)

Pshaytsh (R) see Przedecz

Pshedbozh (R) see Przedborz

Pshemishl (AH) see Przemysl

Pshetslav (Przeclaw) (AH) see under Radomysl Wielki

Pshitik (R) see Przytyk

Pulawy (R). *Yisker-bukh Pulawy* [In memoriam—the city of Pulawy*]. Ed.: M. W. Bernstein. New York, Pulawer Yizkor Book Committee, 1964. 494 p., ports., maps, facsims. (Y)

Pultusk (R). *Pultusk; sefer zikaron* [Pultusk memorial book]. Ed.: Yitzhak Ivri. Tel Aviv, Pultusk Society, 1971. 683 p., illus. (H,Y)

Punsk (R) see under Suwalki

Raab (AH) see Gyor

Rabka (AH) see under Nowy Targ

Rachev (R) see under Novograd-Volynskiy

Rachov (R) see under Annopol

Raciaz (R). *Galed le-kehilat Raciaz* [Memorial book of the community of Racionz*]. Ed.: E. Tsoref. Tel Aviv, Former Residents of Raciaz, 1965. 446, 47 p., ports., facsims. (H,Y,E)

Raczki (R) see under Suwalki

Radikhov (AH) see Radziechow

Radom (R). *Dos yidishe Radom in khurves; ondenkbukh* [The havoc of Jewish Radom*]. Stuttgart, The Committee of Radom Jews in Stuttgart, 1948. l vol., illus. (Y)

Radom (R). *Radom* [Radom; a memorial to the Jewish community of Radom, Poland*]. Ed.: A. Sh. Stein. Tel Aviv, Former Residents of Radom in Israel and in the Diaspora, 1961. 346, [20] p., ports., facsims. (H)

Radom (R). *Sefer Radom* [The book of Radom; the story of a Jewish community in Poland destroyed by the Nazis*]. Ed.: Y. Perlow; [English section]: Alfred Lipson. Tel Aviv, Former Residents of Radom in Israel and the USA, 1961. 451, [23], lxxviii, 120 p., illus., ports. (Y,E)

Radomsko (R). *Sefer yizkor le-kehilat Radomsk ve-ha-seviva* [Memorial book of the community of Radomsk and vicinity]. Ed.: L. Losh. Tel Aviv, Former Residents of Radomsk. . . , 1967. 603 p., ports., music, facsims. (H,Y)

Radomysl Wielki (AH). *Radomysl Rabati ve-ha-seviva; sefer yizkor* [Radomysl Wielki and neighbourhood; memorial book*]. Eds.: H.

Harshoshanim *et al.* Tel Aviv, Former Residents of Radomysl and Surroundings in Israel, 1965. 1065, liii p., ports., map, facsims. (H,Y,E)

Radoszkowice (R). *Radoshkovits; sefer zikaron* [Radoshkowitz; a memorial to the Jewish community*]. Eds.: M. Robinson *et al.* Tel Aviv, Former Residents of Radoshkowitz in Israel, 1953. 222 p., ports. (H)

Radzanow (R) see under Szransk

Radziechow (AH). *Sefer zikaron le-kehilot Radikhov, Lopatyn, Witkow Nowy, Cholojow, Toporow, Stanislawcyzk, Stremiltsh, Shtruvits, ve-ha-kefarim Ubin, Barylow, Wolica-Wygoda, Skrilow, Zawidcze, Mikolajow, Dmytrow, Sienkow, ve-od* [Memorial book of Radikhov, Lopatyn, Witkow Nowy, Cholojow, Toporow, Stanislawcyzk, Stremiltsh, Shtruvits, and the villages Ubin, Barylow, Wolica-Wygoda, Skrilow (i.e., Sknilow?), Zawidcze, Mikolajow, Dmytrow, Sienkow, etc.]. Ed.: G. Kressel. Tel Aviv, Society of Radikhov, Lopatyn and Vicinity, 1976. 656 p., illus. (H,Y)

Radzin (R). *Radzin 1939-—1943.* Ed.: Y. Rosenkrantz. Tel Aviv, Committee of Former Residents of Radzin and Pudel in Israel. 17 p. (H), mimeo.

Radzin (R). *Sefer Radzin* [The book of Radzin]. Ed.: I. Siegelman. Tel Aviv, Council of Former Residents of Radzin (Podolsky) in Israel, 1957. 358 p. (H,Y)

Radziwillow (R). *Radziwillow; sefer zikaron* [A memorial to the Jewish community of Radziwillow, Wolyn*]. Ed.: Y. Adini. Tel Aviv, The Radziwillow Organization in Israel, 1966. 438, [15] p., ports., map, facsims. (H,Y)

Radzymin (R). *Sefer zikaron le-kehilat Radzymin* [Le livre du souvenir de la communauté juive de Radzymin*]. Ed.: Gershon Hel. Tel Aviv, The Encyclopaedia of the Jewish Diaspora, 1975. 389 p., illus. (H,Y,F)

Rakhov (R) see Annopol

Rakishok (R) see Rokiskis

Rakospalota (AH). *Toldot kehilat Rakospalota* [History of the Rakospalota community]. [By] Rachel Aharoni. Tel Aviv, 1978. 52, 204 p., illus. (H,Hu)

Rakow (R). *Sefer zikaron le-kehilat Rakow* [Memorial book of the community of Rakow]. Ed.: H. Abramson. Tel Aviv, Former Residents of Rakow in Israel and the USA, 1959. 184, [13] p., ports., facsims. (H,Y)

Ratno (R). *Ratne; sipura shel kehila yehudit she-hushmeda* [Ratne; the story of a Jewish community that was destroyed]. Ed.: Nahman Tamir. Tel Aviv, Ratno Society in Israel, 1983. 331 p., illus., map, ports. (H)

Ratno (R). *Yisker-bukh Ratne; dos lebn un umkum fun a yidish shtetl in Volin* [Memorial book of Ratno; the life and destruction of a Jewish town in Wolyn]. Eds.: Y. Botoshansky, Y. Yanasovitsh. Buenos Aires, Former Residents of Ratno in Argentina and the USA, 1954. 806 p., ports., map (Y)

Rawa Ruska (AH). *Sefer zikaron le-kehilat Rawa Ruska ve-ha-seviva* [Rawa Ruska memorial book*]. Eds.: A. M. Ringel, I. Z. Rubin. Tel Aviv, Rawa Ruska Society, 1973. 468 p., illus. (H,Y,E)

Raysha (AH) see Rzeszow

Rayvits (R) see Rejowiec

Rejowiec (R). *"Shtil vi in Rayvits. . ."; oyfn khurbn fun mayn heym* ["As silent as in Rayvits. . ."; on the destruction of my home]. [By] Shmuel Drelikhman. Bergen-Belsen, 1947. 46 p., ports. (Y)

Rembertow (R). *Sefer zikaron le-kehilot Rembertow, Okuniew, Milosna* [Yizkor book in memory of Rembertov, Okuniev, Milosna*]. Ed.: Shimon Kanc. Tel Aviv, Rembertow, Okuniew and Milosna Societies in Israel, the USA, France, Mexico City, Canada, Chile and Brazil, 1974. 16, 465 p., illus. (H,Y)

Retteg (AH) see under Des

Rietavas (R). *Sefer Ritova; gal-ed le-zekher ayaratenu* [Memorial book: the Ritavas Community; a tribute to the memory of our town*]. Ed.: Alter Levite. Tel Aviv, Ritova Societies in Israel and the Diaspora, 1977. 37, 223 p., illus. (H,Y,E)

Rimszan (Rymszany) (R) see under Braslaw

Riskeva (R) see Ruscova

Rohatyn (AH). *Kehilat Rohatyn ve-ha-seviva* [Rohatyn; the history of a Jewish community*]. Ed.: M. Amihai. Tel Aviv, Former Residents of Rohatyn in Israel, 1962. 362, [15], 62 p., ports., facsims. (H,Y,E)

Rokiskis (R). *Yisker-bukh fun Rakishok un umgegnt* [Yizkor book of Rakishok and environs*]. Ed.: M. Bakalczuk-Felin. Johannesburg, The Rakishker Landsmanshaft of Johannesburg, 1952. 626 p., ports., facsim. (Y)

Rokitno (R). *Rokitno (Volin) ve-ha-seviva; sefer edut ve-zikaron* [Rokitno-Wolyn and surroundings; memorial book and testimony]. Ed.: E. Leoni. Tel Aviv, Former Residents of Rokitno in Israel, 1967. 459 p., ports., maps (H,Y)

Romanova (R) see under Slutsk

Rotin (AH) see Rohatyn

Rovno (R) see Rowne

Rowne (R). *A zikorn far Rowne* [In memory of Rowne]. Eds.: Y. Margulyets, Z. Finkelshteyn, Y. Shvartsapel. [Munich], Rowne Landsmannschaft in Germany, [1947?]. 43 p., ports. (Y), mimeo.

Rowne (R). *Rowne; sefer zikaron* [Rowno; a memorial to the Jewish community of Rowno, Wolyn*]. Ed.: A. Avitachi. Tel Aviv, "Yalkut Wolyn"—Former Residents of Rowno in Israel, 1956. 591 p., ports., map, facsims. (H)

Rozan (R). *Sefer zikaron le-kehilat Rozan (al ha-Narew)* [Rozhan memorial book*]. Ed.: Benjamin Halevy. Tel Aviv, Rozhan Societies in Israel and the USA, 1977. 518, 96 p., illus. (H,Y,E)

Rozana (R). *Rozhinoy; sefer zikaron le-kehilat Rozhinoy ve-ha-seviva* [Rozana; a memorial to the Jewish community*]. Ed.: M. Sokolowsky. Tel Aviv, Former Residents of Rozhinoy in Israel, 1957. 232 p., ports. (H,Y)

Rozanka (R) see under Szczuczyn (*Sefer zikaron le-kehilot Szczuczyn, Wasiliszki. . .*)

Rozhan (R) see Rozan

Rozhinoy (R) see Rozana

Rozniatow (AH). *Sefer zikaron le-kehilat Rozniatow, Perehinsko, Broszniow, Swaryczow ve-ha-seviva* [Yizkor-book in memory of Rozniatow, Perehinsko, Broszniow, Swaryczow and environs*]. Ed.: Shimon Kanc. Tel Aviv, Rozniatow, Perehinsko, Broszniow and Environs Societies in Israel and the USA, 1974. 58, 537 p., illus. (H,Y,E)

Rozprza (R) see under Piotrkow Trybunalski

Rozwadow (AH). *Sefer yizkor Rozwadow ve-ha-seviva* [Rozwadow memorial book*]. Ed.: N. Blumental. Jerusalem, Former Residents of Rozwadow in Israel. . . , 1968. 349 p., ports. (H,Y,E)

Rozyszcze (R). *Rozyszcze ayarati* [Rozyszcze my old home*]. Ed.: Gershon Zik. Tel Aviv, Rozyszcze Societies in Israel, the United States, Canada, Brazil, and Argentina, 1976. 482, 76 p., illus. (H,Y,E)

Rubeshov (R) see Hrubieszow

Rubiel (R) see under Polesie (region)

Rubiezewicze (R). *Sefer Rubizhevitsh, Derevne ve-ha-seviva* [Rubiezewicze and surroundings book*]. Ed.: D. Shtokfish. Tel Aviv, 1968. 422 p., illus. (Y,H)

Rubiezewicze (R) see also under Stolpce

Rudki (AH). *Rudki; sefer yizkor le-yehudei Rudki ve-ha-seviva* [Rudki memorial book; of the Jews of Rudki and vicinity*]. Ed.: Joseph Chrust. Israel, Rudki Society, 1978. 374 p., illus. (H,Y,E)

Ruscova (AH). *Sefer le-zikaron kedoshei Ruskova ve-Soblas, mehoz Marmarosh* [Memorial book of the martyrs of Ruskova and Soblas, Marmarosh District]. Ed.: Y. Z. Moskowits. Tel Aviv, Former Residents of Ruskova and Soblas in Israel and in the Diaspora, 1969. 126 p., ports., facsims. (H,Y)

Ryki (R). *Yisker-bukh tsum fareybikn dem ondenk fun der khorev-gevorener yidisher kehile Ryki* [Ryki; a memorial to the community of Ryki, Poland*]. Ed.: Shimon Kanc. Tel Aviv, Ryki Societies in Israel, Canada, Los Angeles, France, and Brazil, 1973. 611 p., illus. (H,Y)

Rypin (R). *Hantsahat kehilat Rypin-Polin* [Dedicated to the Jewish community of Rypin, Poland]. [By a group of students.] Bene Berak, Bet ha-sefer "Komemiyut," [1966]. 64 p., illus., map, ports. (H)

Rypin (R). *Sefer Rypin* [Ripin; a memorial to the Jewish community of Ripin—Poland*]. Ed.: Sh. Kanc. Tel Aviv, Former Residents of Ripin in Israel and in the Diaspora, 1962. 942, 15 p., ports., facsims. (H,Y,E)

Rytwiany (R) see under Staszow

Rzeszow (AH). *Kehilat Raysha; sefer zikaron* [Rzeszow Jews; memorial book*]. Ed.: M. Yari-Wold. Tel Aviv, Former Residents of Rzeszow in Israel and the USA, 1967. 620, 142 p., ports., maps, facsims. (H,Y,E)

Saloniki (Turkey). *Saloniki; ir va-em be-yisrael* [Salonique, ville-mère en

Israël*]. Jerusalem-Tel Aviv, Centre de recherches sur le Judaisme de Salonique, Union des Juifs de Grèce, 1967. 358, xviii p., ports., maps, facsims. (H,F)

Saloniki (Turkey). *Zikhron Saloniki; gedulata ve-hurbana shel Yerushalayim de-Balkan* [Zikhron Saloniki; grandeza i destruyicion de Yeruchalayim del Balkan*]. Tel Aviv, Committee for the Publication of the Saloniki Book, [1971/72–1985/86]. 2 vols., illus., facsims., ports. (H,J)

Sambor (AH). *Sefer Sambor-Stary Sambor; pirkei edut ve-zikaron le-kehilot Sambor-Stary Sambor mi-reshitan ve-ad hurbanan* [The book of Sambor and Stari Sambor; a memorial to the Jewish communities of Sambor and Stari Sambor, the story of the two Jewish communities from their beginnings to their end*]. Ed.: Alexander Manor. Tel Aviv, Sambor/Stary Sambor Society, 1980. xlvi, 323 p., illus. (H,Y,E)

Sammerein (Somorja) (AH) see under Dunaszerdahely

Samorin (Somorja) (AH) see under Dunaszerdahely

Sanok (AH). *Sefer zikaron le-kehilat Sanok ve-ha-seviva* [Memorial book of Sanok and vicinity]. Ed.: E. Sharvit. Jerusalem, Former Residents of Sanok and Vicinity in Israel, 1970. 686 p., ports., facsims. (H,Y)

Sanok (AH) see also under Dynow (*Khurbn Dynow*)

Sants (AH) see Nowy Sacz

Sarkeystsene (Szarkowszczyna) (R) see under Glebokie

Sarnaki (R). *Sefer yizkor le-kehilat Sarnaki* [Memorial book of the community of Sarnaki]. Ed.: D. Shuval. Haifa, Former Residents of Sarnaki in Israel, 1968. 415 p., ports. (H,Y)

Sarny (R). *Sefer yizkor le-kehilat Sarny* [Memorial book of the community of Sarny]. Ed.: Y. Kariv. Tel Aviv, Former Residents of Sarny and Vicinity in Israel, 1961. 508, 32 p., ports., facsims. (H,Y)

Sarny (R) see also under Polesie (region)

Sasow (AH). *Mayn shtetl Sasow* [My town Sasow]. [By] Moshe Rafael. Jerusalem, 1979. (Y)

Satmar (AH) see Satu Mare

Satorujhely (AH) see under Zemplenmegye

Satu Mare (AH). *Zekhor et Satmar; sefer ha-zikaron shel yehudei Satmar* [Remember Satmar; the memorial book of the Jews of Satmar]. Ed.: Naftali Stern. Bnei Brak, 1984. 160, 240 p., illus., maps, ports. (H,Hu)

Schodnica (AH) see under Drohobycz

Schutt Szerdahely (AH) see Dunaszerdahely

Secureni (R) see Sekiryany

Sedziszow (R) see under Wodzislaw

Sekiryani (R). *Sekurian (Bessarabia) be-vinyana u-be-hurbana* [Sekiryani, Bessarabia—alive and destroyed]. Ed.: Z. Igrat. Tel Aviv, [Committee of Former Residents of Sekiryani], 1954. 260 p., ports. (H)

Selib (Wsielub) (R) see under Nowogrodek

Selish (AH) see Nagyszollos

Selts (Sielec) (R) see under Pruzana

Semyatichi (R) see Siemiatycze

Sendishev (Sedziszow) (R) see under Wodzislaw

Serock (R). *Sefer Serotsk* [The book of Serock]. Ed.: M. Gelbart. Former Residents of Serock in Israel, 1971. 736 p., ports. (H,Y)

Sevlus (AH) see Nagyszollos

Shchedrin (R) see under Bobruisk

Shebreshin (R) see Szczebrzeszyn

Shedlets (R) see Siedlce

Shelib (Wsielub) (R) see under Nowogrodek

Sherpts (R) see Sierpc

Shidlovtse (R) see Szydlowiec

Shimsk (R) see Szumsk

Shkud (R) see Skuodas

Shpola (R). *Shpola; masekhet hayei yehudim ba-ayara* [Shpola; a picture of Jewish life in the town]. [By] David Cohen. [Haifa], Association of Former Residents of Shpola (Ukraine) in Israel, 1965. 307 p., ports. (H)

Shransk (R) see Szransk

Shtruvits (Szczurowice) (AH) see under Radziechow

Shumen (Bulgaria) see Shumla

Shumla (Bulgaria). *Yehudei Bulgaria—Kehilat Shumla* [The Jews in Bulgaria—The community in Shumla*]. [By] Benjamin J. Arditti. Tel Aviv, Community Council, 1968. 179 p., ports. (H)

Siedlce (R). *Oyf di khurves fun mayn heym (khurbn Shedlets)* [On the ruins of my home; the destruction of Siedlce]. [By] M. Fainzilber. Tel Aviv, Committee of Townspeople, 1952. 260 p., illus., map, ports. (Y)

Siedlce (R). *Sefer yizkor le-kehilat Shedlets* [Memorial book of the community of Siedlce]. Ed.: A. W. Yassni. Buenos Aires, Former Residents of Siedlce in Israel and Argentina, 1956. xvi, 813 p., ports., facsims. (H,Y)

Siedliszcze (R). *Sefer zikaron le-kehilat Siedliszcze ve-ha-seviva* [Memorial book of the community of Siedliszcze and vicinity]. Ed.: B. Haruvi. Tel Aviv, Former Residents of Siedliszcze in Israel, 1970. 360 p., ports., facsims. (H,Y)

Sielec (R) see under Pruzana

Siemiatycze (R). *Kehilat Semiatycze* [The community of Semiatich*]. Ed.: E. Tash (Tur-Shalom). Tel Aviv, Assoc. of Former Residents of Semiatich in Israel and the Diaspora, 1965. 449 p., ports., map, facsims. (H,Y,E)

Sienkow (AH) see under Radziechow

Sierpc (R). *Kehilat Sierpc; sefer zikaron* [The community of Sierpc; memorial book]. Ed.: E. Talmi (Wloka). Tel Aviv, Former Residents of Sierpc in Israel and Abroad, 1959. 603 p., ports., map, facsims. (H,Y)

Sierpc (R). *Khurbn Sierpc 1939–1945; zikhroynes fun di ibergeblibene landslayt vos gefinen zikh in der Amerikaner Zone in Daytshland* [The destruction of Sierpc 1939–1945; memories of the remnants of the community of Sierpc in the American Zone in Germany]. Eds.: A. Meirantz, H. Nemlich. Munich, Committee of the Former Residents of Sierpc in the American Zone in Germany, 1947. 55 p., ports. (Y)

Sierpc (R). *Zaml-bukh fun Sherptser sheyres ha-khurbn, 1939–1945* [Collection of Sierpc Holocaust survivors, 1939–1945]. [Germany], Sherpcer Jewish Committee (U.S. Zone, Germany), 1948. 93 p., illus., ports. (Y)

Siniawka (R) see under Kleck

Sislevitsh (R) see Swislocz

Skala (AH). *Sefer Skala.* Ed.: Max Mermelstein (Weidenfeld). New York-Tel Aviv, Skala Benevolent Society, 1978. 98, 261 p., illus. (H,Y,E)

Skalat (AH). *Es shtarbt a shtetl; megiles Skalat* [Skalat destroyed*]. [By] Abraham Weissbrod. Ed.: I. Kaplan. Munich, Central Historical Commission of the Central Committee of Liberated Jews in the U.S. Zone of Germany, 1948. 184 p., maps, ports. (Y)

Skalat (AH). *Skalat; kovets zikaron le-kehila she-harva ba-shoa* [Skalat; memorial volume of the community which perished in the Holocaust]. Ed.: H. Bronstein. Tel Aviv, The Yaacov Krol School in Petah-Tikva and Former Residents of Skalat in Israel, 1971. 160 p., ports., facsims. (H)

Skarzysko-Kamienna (R). *Skarzysko-Kamienna sefer zikaron* [The "yischor" book in memoriam of the Jewish community of Skarzysko and its surroundings*]. Tel Aviv, Skarzysko Society, 1973. 260 p., illus. (H,Y)

Skepe (R) see under Lipno

Skierniewice (R). *Sefer Skierniewice* [The book of Skierniewice]. Ed.: J. Perlow. Tel Aviv, Former Residents of Skierniewice in Israel, 1955. 722 p., ports., facsims. (Y)

Sknilow (AH) see under Radziechow

Skole (AH). *Le-zekher kedoshe Skolah veha-sevivah* [In memorium to the Jewish community of Skole and neighbouring villages who perished in the Holocaust*]. [Israel], Jewish Committee of Skole in Israel, 1986. 180 p., illus. (H)

Skole (AH) see also under Galicia (*Gedenkbukh Galicia*)

Skuodas (R). *Kehilat Shkud; kovets zikaron* [Memorial book of Skuodas]. Tel Aviv, Former Residents of Skuodas, 1948. 68 p., ports., facsims. (H,Y)

Slobodka (R) see under Braslaw

Slonim (R). *Pinkas Slonim* [Memorial book of Slonim]. Ed.: K. Lichtenstein. Tel Aviv, Former Residents of Slonim in Israel, [1962—-1979]. 4 vols., illus., ports. (H,Y,E)

Slupia (R) see under Ostrowiec

Slutsk (R). *Pinkas Slutsk u-benoteha* [Slutsk and vicinity memorial book*]. Eds.: N. Chinitz, Sh. Nachmani. Tel Aviv, Yizkor-Book Committee, 1962. 450 p., ports., maps, facsims. (H,Y,E)

Sluzewo (R) see under Wloclawek

Smorgonie (R). *Smorgon mehoz Vilno; sefer edut ve-zikaron* [Smorgonie, District Vilna; memorial book and testimony]. Ed.: E. Tash (Tur-Shalom). [Tel Aviv], Assoc. of Former Residents of Smorgonie in Israel and USA, 1965. 584 p., ports., facsims. (H,Y)

Smotrich (R) see under Kamenets-Podolskiy

Soblas (AH) see under Ruscova

Sobolew (R) see under Laskarzew

Sobota (R) see under Lowicz

Sochaczew (R). *Pinkas Sochaczew* [Memorial book of Sochaczew]. Eds.: A. Sh. Stein, G. Weissman. Jerusalem, Former Residents of Sochaczew in Israel, 1962. 843 p., ports. (H,Y)

Sofyovka (R) see Zofiowka

Sokal (AH). *Sefer Sokal, Tartakow. . . ve-ha-seviva* [Memorial book of Sokal, Tartakow. . . and surroundings]. Ed.: A. Chomel. Tel Aviv, Former Residents of Sokal and Surroundings, 1968. 576 p., ports., facsims. (H,Y)

Sokolka (R). *Sefer Sokolka* [Memorial book of Sokolka]. Jerusalem, The Encyclopaedia of the Jewish Diaspora, 1968. 768 columns, ports., facsims. (H,Y)

Sokolovka (Yustingrad) (R) see Yustingrad

Sokolow (R). *In shotn fun Treblinka (khurbn Sokolow-Podlaski)* [In the shadow of Treblinka*]. [By] Symcha Polakiewicz. Tel Aviv, Sokolow-Podlaski Society, 1957. 167 p. (Y)

Sokolow (R). *Mayn khorev shtetl Sokolow; shilderungen, bilder un portretn fun a shtot umgekumene yidn* [My destroyed town of Sokolow]. [By] Peretz Granatstein. Buenos Aires, Union Central Israelita Polaca en la Argentina, 1946. 188 p., illus. (Y)

Sokolow (R). *Sefer ha-zikaron; Sokolow-Podlask* [Memorial book Sokolow-Podlask]. Ed.: M. Gelbart. Tel Aviv, Former Residents of Sokolow-Podlask in Israel and. . . in the USA, 1962. 758, [55] p., ports. (Y,H)

Sokolow (R). *Yoyvl-bukh gevidmet dem ondenken fun di kdoyshim un martirer fun Sokolow* [Jubilee book dedicated to the memory of the hallowed martyrs of Sokolow*]. Ed.: A. S. Lirick. New York, Sokolower Society in New York, 1946. 20, 180 p., illus., ports. (Y,E)

Sokoly (R). *Sefer zikaron le-kedoshei Sokoly* [Memorial book of the martyrs of Sokoly]. Ed.: M. Grossman. Tel Aviv, Former Residents of Sokoly, 1962. 625 p., ports. (Y)

Sokoly (R). *Sokoly—be-ma'avak le-hayim* [Sokoly—in a struggle for survival]. Trans. and ed.: Shmuel Klisher. Tel Aviv, Sokoly Society, 1975. 438 p., illus. (H)

Sombor (AH) see Zombor

Somorja (AH) see under Dunaszerdahely

Sompolno (R). *Dapei ed shel sarid ha-ayara Sompolno* [Pages of witness of the remnants of the town Sompolno]. [By] Yitzhak Kominkovski. Tel Aviv, Alef, 1981. 103 p., illus., ports. (H)

Sonik (AH) see Sanok

Sopockinie (R). *Korot ayara ahat; megilat ha-shigshug ve-ha-hurban shel kehilat Sopotkin* [Sopotkin; in memory of the Jewish community*]. [By] Alexander Manor (Menchinsky). [Tel Aviv], Sopotkin Society, 1960. 124 p., illus. (H)

Sopotkin (R) see Sopockinie

Sosnovoye (R) see Ludwipol

Sosnowiec (AH). *Sefer Sosnowiec ve-ha-seviva be-Zaglembie* [Book of Sosnowiec and the surrounding region in Zaglebie]. Ed.: Meir Shimon Geshuri (Bruckner). Tel Aviv, Sosnowiec Societies in Israel, the United States, France, and other countries, 1973–1974. 2 vols., illus. (H,Y)

Stanislawczyk (AH) see under Radziechow

Stanislawow (AH). *Al horvotayikh Stanislawow; divrei edut le-kilayon kehilat Stanislawow ve-sevivata mipi adei-riah ve-al-pi teudot* [On the ruins of Stanislawow; concerning the annihilation of the community of Stanislawow and vicinity. . .]. [By] Ami Weitz. Tel Aviv, 1947. 113 p. (H)

Stanislawow (AH) see also under *Arim ve-imahot,* vol. 5

Starachowice (R) see under Wierzbnik

Starobin (R) see under Slutsk

Stary Sambor (AH) see under Sambor

Starye Dorogi (R) see under Slutsk

Staszow (R). *Sefer Staszow* [The Staszow book*]. Ed.: E. Erlich. Tel Aviv, Former Residents of Staszow in Israel. . . and in the Diaspora, 1962. 690 p., ports., facsims. (H,Y,E)

Stavische (R). *Stavisht.* Ed.: A. Weissman. Tel Aviv, The Stavisht Society, New York, 1961. 252 columns, ports. (H,Y)

Stawiski (R). *Stawiski; sefer yizkor* [Stawiski memorial book]. Ed.: I. Rubin. Tel Aviv, Stavisk Society, 1973. 379, 5 p., illus. (H,Y,E)

Stefanesti (AH). *Mi-Stefanesti le-erets-yisrael: sipurah shel ayarah* [Din Stefanesti spre Eretz-Israel: saga unui orasel*]. [By] Idel Nachberg-Evron. Haifa: Author, 1989. 181 p., illus., map, ports. (H)

Stepan (R). *Ayaratenu Stepan* [The Stepan Story; excerpts*]. Ed.: Yitzchak Ganuz. Tel Aviv, Stepan Society, 1977. 4, 364 p., illus. (H,E)

Steybts (R) see Stolpce

Stiyanev (Stojanow) (AH) see under Sokal

Stoczek-Wegrowski (R). *Pinkes Stok (bay Vengrov); matsevet netsah* [Memorial book of Stok, near Wegrow]. Ed.: I. Zudicker. Buenos Aires, Stok

Societies in Israel, North America and Argentina, 1974. 654 p., illus. (H,Y)

Stojaciszki (R) see under Swieciany

Stojanow (AH) see under Sokal

Stok (R) see Stoczek-Wegrowski

Stolin (R). *Albom Stolin* [Stolin album]. Eds.: Phinehas Doron, Z. Blizovski. Jerusalem, 1960. 88 p., illus., ports. (H,Y)

Stolin (R). *Stolin; sefer zikaron le-kehilat Stolin ve-ha-seviva* [Stolin; a memorial to the Jewish communities of Stolin and vicinity*]. Eds.: A. Avatichi, Y. Ben-Zakkai. Tel Aviv, Former Residents of Stolin and Vicinity in Israel, 1952. 263 p., ports. (H)

Stolin (R) see also under Polesie (region)

Stolpce (R). *Sefer zikaron; Steibts-Sverzhnye ve-ha-ayarot ha-semukhot. . .* [Memorial volume of Steibtz-Swerznie and the neighbouring villages. . . *]. Ed.: N. Hinitz. Tel Aviv, Former Residents of Steibtz in Israel, 1964. 537, xxiii p., ports., map, facsims. (H,Y,E)

Stramtura (AH). *Agadot Strimtera; sipura shel kehilat yehudit me-reshita ve-ad ahrita* [Tales of Strimtera; the story of a Jewish community from beginning to end]. [By] Sh. Avni. Tel Aviv, Reshafim, [1985/86]. 270 p. (H)

Stremiltsh (Strzemilcze) (AH) see under Radziechow

Strimtera (AH) see Stramtura

Strusow (AH) see under Trembowla

Stryj (AH). *Sefer Stryj* [Memorial book of Stryj]. Eds.: N. Kudish *et al.* Tel Aviv, Former Residents of Stryj in Israel, 1962. 260, 68 p., ports., facsims. (H,Y,E)

Strzegowo (R). *Strzegowo yisker-bukh* [Memorial book of Strzegowo]. New York, United Strzegower Relief Committee, 1951. 135, [18] p., ports., facsims. (H,Y,E)

Strzemilcze (AH) see under Radziechow

Strzyzow (AH). *Sefer Strizhuv ve-ha-seviva* [Memorial book of Strzyzow and vicinity]. Eds.: J. Berglas, Sh. Yahalomi (Diamant). Tel Aviv, Former Residents of Strzyzow in Israel and Diaspora, 1969. 480 p., ports., facsims. (H,Y)

Strzyzow (AH). *The book of Strzyzow and vicinity.* Eds.: Itzhok Berglass, Shlomo Yahalomi-Diamond; trans.: Harry Langsam. Los Angeles, Harry Langsam, [1990]. viii, 560 p., illus., ports., facsims. (E)

Stutshin (R) see Szczuczyn

Sucha (AH) see under Wadowice

Suchocin (R) see under Plonsk

Suchowola (R). *Khurbn Sukhovolye; lezikorn fun a yidish shtetl tsvishn Bialystok un Grodne* [The Holocaust in Suchowola; in memory of a Jewish shtetl between Bialystok and Grodno]. Description by Lazar Simhah; ed. by Sh. Zabludovski. Mexico, published by a group of Suchowola Landslayt in Mexico, 1947. 72 p., illus., ports. (Y)

Suchowola (R). *Sefer Suchowola* [Memorial book of Suchowola]. Eds.:

H. Steinberg *et al.* Jerusalem, The Encyclopaedia of the Jewish Diaspora, 1957. 616 columns, [2] p., ports., map, facsims. (H,Y)

Suprasl (R). *Hayim ve-mavet be-tsel ha-ya'ar: sipurah shel Suprasl ha-yehudit, 'ayarah be-mizrah Polin* [Life and death in shadow of the forest: the story of Suprasl, a shtetl in Eastern Poland*]. [By] Yaacov Patt. [Israel], Committee of Former Supraslers, 1991. 182, 60 p., illus., maps, ports. (H,Y,E)

Suwalki (R). *Sefer kehilat Suvalk u-benotehah* [Jewish community book Suwalk and vicinity. . . *]. Eds.: Yehuda Alroi, Yosef Chrust. Tel Aviv, The Yair-Abraham Stern Publishing House, 1989. 446, 86 p., illus., maps, ports. (H,E)

Suwalki (R). *Yisker-bukh Suvalk* [Memorial book of Suvalk]. Ed.: B. Kahan [Kagan]. New York, The Suvalk and Vicinity Relief Committee of New York, 1961. 825 columns, ports., facsims. (Y)

Swaryczow (AH) see under Rozniatow

Swieciany (R). *Sefer zikaron le-esrim ve-shalosh kehilot she-nehrevu be-ezor Svintsian* [Svintzian Region; memorial book of twenty-three Jewish communities*]. Ed.: Sh. Kanc. Tel Aviv, Former Residents of the Svintzian District in Israel, 1965. 1954 columns, ports., maps, music, facsims. (H,Y)

Swierzen (R) see under Stolpce

Swir (R). *Ayaratenu Swir* [Our townlet Swir*]. Ed.: Ch. Swironi (Drutz). Tel Aviv, Former Residents of Swir in Israel and. . . in the United States, 1959. 240 p., ports., map (H,Y)

Swir (R). *Haya hayeta ayarat Swir; ben shtei milhamot ha-olam* [There once was a town Swir; between the two world wars]. [By] Herzl Vayner. [Israel], Swir Society, 1975. 227 p., illus. (H,Y)

Swislocz (R). *Kehilat Swisiocz pelekh Grodno* [The community of Swisocz, Grodno District]. Ed.: H. Rabin. Tel Aviv, Former Residents of Swislocz in Israel, 1961. 159 p., ports. (H,Y)

Swislocz (R). *Sefer Swislocz* [Swislocz book], [vol.] 2. Ed.: Yerahmiel Lifshits. Netanya, Former Residents of Swislocz in Israel, 1984. 289 p., illus., facsims., maps, ports. (H)

Swislocz (R) see also under Wolkowysk (*Volkovisker yisker-bukh*)

Szamosujvar (AH). *Sefer zikaron shel kedoshei ayaratenu Számosujvar-Iklad ve- ha-seviva. . .* [Memorial book of the martyrs of our town Szamosujvar-Iklad and surroundings]. Eds.: M. Bar-On, B. Herskovits. Tel Aviv, Former Residents of Szamosujvar-Iklad and Surroundings in Israel, 1971. 190, 90 p., ports., facsims. (H,Hu)

Szarkowszczyzna (R) see under Glebokie

Szatmarnemeti (AH) see Satu Mare

Szczawnica (AH) see under Nowy Targ

Szczebrzeszyn (R). *Sefer zikaron le-kehilat Shebreshin* [Book of memory to the Jewish community of Shebreshin*]. Ed.: Dov Shuval. Haifa, Association of Former Inhabitants of Shebreshin in Israel and the Diaspora, 1984. xiv, 518 p., illus., maps, ports. (Y,H,E)

Szczekociny (R). *Pinkas Szczekociny* [A memorial book to the Jewish community of Szczekociny*]. Ed.: J. Schweizer. Tel Aviv, Former Residents of Szczekociny in Israel, 1959. 276 p., ports., facsims. (H,Y)

Szczuczyn (District Bialystok) (R). *Hurban kehilat Szczuczyn* [The destruction of the community of Szczuczyn]. Tel Aviv, Former Residents of Szczuczyn in Israel and. . . , 1954. 151 p., ports. (Y)

Szczuczyn (R). *Sefer zikaron le-kehilot Szczuczyn, Wasiliszki. . .* [Memorial book of the communities Szczuczyn, Wasiliszki. . .]. Ed.: L. Losh. Tel Aviv, Former Residents of Szczuczyn, Wasiliszki. . . , 1966. 456 p., ports., map, facsims. (H,Y)

Szczurowice (AH) see under Radziechow

Szereszow (R) see under Pruzana

Szikszo (AH). *Nitsutsot—mi-kehilat Szikszo ve-mehoz Abauj-Turna shenidmu; toldot hayehem ve-ad hurbanam* [Sparks; from the community of Szikszo and the region of Abauj Turna]. [By] Israel Fleishman. Bnei Brak, 1972. 96, 374 p., illus. (H,Hu)

Szkudy (R) see Skuodas

Szransk (R). *Kehilat Szransk ve-ha-seviva; sefer zikaron* [The Jewish community of Szrensk and the vicinity; a memorial volume*]. Ed.: Y. Rimon (Granat). Jerusalem, [Former Residents of Szrensk in Israel], 1960. 518, 70 p., ports., maps, facsims. (H,Y,E)

Szumsk (R). *Szumsk. . . sefer zikaron le-kedoshei Szumsk. . .* [Szumsk. . . memorial book of the martyrs of Szumsk. . .]. Ed.: H. Rabin. [Tel Aviv, Former Residents of Szumsk in Israel, 1968]. 477 p., ports., map, facsims. (H,Y)

Szurdok (AH) see Stramtura

Szydlow (R) see under Staszow

Szydlowiec (R). *Shidlovtser yisker-bukh* [Yizkor book Szydlowiec*]. Ed.: Berl Kagan. New York, 1974. 7, 912, 22 p., illus. (Y,E)

Szydlowiec (R). *Szydlowiec memorial book.* Ed.: Berl Kagan; trans. from Yiddish: Max Rosenfeld. New York, Shidlowtzer Benevolent Association in New York, 1989. 349, [134] p., illus., map, ports. (E)

Targowica (R). *Sefer Trovits* [Memorial book of Targovica*]. Ed.: I. Siegelman. Haifa, Former Residents of Targovica in Israel, 1967. 452 p., ports., map, facsims. (H,Y)

Targu-Lapus (Magyarlapos) (AH) see under Des

Targu-Mures (AH) see Marosvasarhely

Tarnobrzeg (AH). *Kehilat Tarnobrzeg-Dzikow (Galicia ha-ma'aravit)* [The community of Tarnobrzeg-Dzikow (Western Galicia)]. Ed.: Yaakov Yehoshua Fleisher. Tel Aviv, Tarnobrzeg-Dzikow Society, 1973. 379 p., illus. (H,Y)

Tarnogrod (R). *Sefer Tarnogrod; le-zikaron ha-kehila ha-yehudit shenehreva* [Book of Tarnogrod; in memory of the destroyed Jewish community].

Ed.: Sh. Kanc. Tel Aviv, Organization of Former Residents of Tarnogrod and Vicinity in Israel, United States and England, 1966. 592 p., ports. (H,Y)

Tarnopol (AH). *Tarnopol* [Tarnopol volume*]. Ed.: Ph. Korngruen. Jerusalem, The Encyclopaedia of the Jewish Diaspora, 1955. 474 columns, ports., facsims. (H,Y,E)

Tarnow (AH). *Tarnow; kiyuma ve-hurbana shel ir yehudit* [The life and decline of a Jewish city]. Ed.: A. Chomet. Tel Aviv, Association of Former Residents of Tarnow, 1954–1968. 2 vols. (xx, 928; 433 p.), ports., facsims., map (H,Y)

Tartakow (AH) see under Sokal

Tasnad (AH). *Tasnad; tei'ur le-zekher kehilat Tasnad (Transylvania) ve-ha-seviva ve-yeshivat Maharam Brisk, me-reshitan ve-ad le-aher y'mei ha-shoah* [Tasnad; description, in memory of the community of Tasnad (Transylvania) and the surrounding region, and the Brisk Yeshiva, from their beginnings until after the Holocaust]. [By] Avraham Fuks. Jerusalem, 1973. 276 p., illus. (H)

Teglas (AH) see under Debrecen

Telechany (R). *Telekhan* [Telekhan memorial book*]. Ed.: Sh. Sokoler. Los Angeles, Telekhan Memorial Book Committee, 1963. 189, 15 p., ports., map (H,Y,E)

Telenesti-Targ (R). *Ha-ayara ha-ketana she-be-Bessarabia; le-zekher Telenesti—ayaratenu* [A small town in Bessarabia; in memory of our town Telenesti]. Ed.: Rachel Fels. Kefar Habad, Bet ha-sefer li-defus "Yad ha-Hamisha," 1981. 127, [25] p., illus., map, ports. (H,Y)

Telsiai (R). *Sefer Telz (Lita); matsevet zikaron le-kehila kedosha* [Telsiai book*]. Ed.: Yitzhak Alperovitz. Tel Aviv, Telz Society in Israel, 1984. 505 p., illus., map, ports. (H,Y)

Telz (R) see Telsiai

Teplik (R). *Teplik, mayn shtetele; kapitlen fun fuftsik yor lebn* [My town Teplik; chapters from fifty years of life]. [By] Valentin Chernovetzky. Buenos Aires, El Magazine Argentino, 1946–1950. 2 vols., illus. (Y)

Terebovlya (AH) see Trembowla

Ternovka (R). *Ayaratenu Ternovka; pirkei zikaron ve-matseva* [Our town Ternovka; chapters of remembrance and a monument]. [By] G. Bar-Zvi. Tel Aviv, Ternovka Society, 1972. 103 p., illus. (H)

Thessaloniki (Turkey) see Saloniki

Tighina (R) see Bendery

Tiktin (R) see Tykocin

Timkovichi (R) see under Slutsk

Tishevits (R) see Tyszowce

Tlumacz (AH). *Tlumacz-Tolmitsh; sefer edut ve-zikaron* [Memorial book of Tlumacz*]. Eds.: Shlomo Blond *et al.* Tel Aviv, Tlumacz Society, 1976. 187, 533 p., illus. (H,Y,E)

Tluste (AH). *Sefer Tluste* [Memorial book of Tluste]. Ed.: G. Lindenberg. Tel Aviv, Association of Former Residents of Tluste and Vicinity in Israel and USA, 1965. 289 p., ports., map, facsims. (H,Y)

Tluszcz (R). *Sefer zikaron le-kehilat Tluszcz* [Memorial book of the community of Tluszcz]. Ed.: M. Gelbart. Tel Aviv, Association of Former Residents of Tluszcz in Israel, 1971. 340 p. (H,Y)

Tolmitsh (AH) see Tlumacz

Tolstoye (AH) see Tluste

Tomaszow-Lubelski (R). *Sefer zikaron shel Tomaszow-Lub.* [Memorial book of Tomaszow-Lubelski]. Ed.: Moshe Gordon. Jerusalem, 1972. 28, 549 p., illus. (H)

Tomaszow Lubelski (R). *Tomashover (Lubelski) yisker-bukh* [Memorial book of Tomaszow Lubelski]. New York, Tomashover Relief Committee, 1965. 912 p., ports., facsims. (Y)

Tomaszow Mazowiecki (R). *Sefer zikaron le-kehilat Tomaszow Mazowiecki* [Tomashow-Mazowieck; a memorial to the Jewish community of Tomashow- Mazovieck*]. Ed.: M. Wajsberg. Tel Aviv, Tomashow Organization in Israel, 1969. 648 p., ports., map, facsims. (H,Y,E,F)

Topolcany (AH). *Korot mekorot le-kehila yehudit-Topolcany* [The story and source of the Jewish community of Topoltchany*]. [By] Yehoshua Robert Buchler. Lahavot Haviva, Topolcany Book Committee, 1976. 74, 64, 174 p., illus. (H,E,G)

Topolcany (AH). *Topolcany: the story of a perished ancient community.* [By] Yehoshua Robert Buchler. Lahavot Haviva, 1989. [30] p. (E)

Toporow (AH) see under Radziechow

Torczyn (R). *"Yisker" bukh fun Torczyn* [Torchin, our lost but not forgotten town*]. New York, Torchiner-Woliner Young Men's Association, 1948. 1 vol., ports., maps (E,Y)

Torna (Galicia) (AH) see Tarnow

Torna (Turna nad Bodvou) (AH) see Turna

Torun (Karpatalja) (AH). *Ayarah she-hayetah: Torun she-be-Karpatim* [A town that once was: Torun in the Carpathians]. [By] Yosef Hagalili (Fikl). Tel Aviv, Moreshet, 1956. 179 p., illus., ports. (H)

Trembowla (R). *Sefer yizkor le-kehilot Trembowla, Strusow ve-Janow ve-ha-seviva* [Memorial book for the Jewish communities of Trembowla, Strusow, Janow and vicinity*]. Bnai Brak, Trembowla Society, [1981?]. li, 379 p., illus., maps (H,E)

Trisk (R) see Turzysk

Trokhenbrod (R) see Zofiowka

Troki (R). *Troki.* Tel Aviv, [1954]. 79 p., map (H)

Trovits (R) see Targowica

Trzebinia (AH). *Kehilat Tshebin* [The community of Trzebinia*]. Eds.: P.

Goldwasser *et al.* Haifa, Committee of Trzebinians in Israel, 1969. 21, 435, 35 p., ports., map, facsims. (H,E)

Tshebin (AH) see Trzebinia

Tshekhanov (R) see Ciechanow

Tshekhanovets (R) see Ciechanowiec

Tshenstokhov (R) see Czestochowa

Tsheshanov (AH) see Cieszanow

Tshizheva (R) see Czyzewo

Tshmelev (Cmielow) (R) see under Ostrowiec

Tuczyn (R). *Sefer zikaron le-kehilat Tuczyn-Kripe* [Tutchin-Krippe, Wolyn; in memory of the Jewish community*]. Ed.: B. H. Ayalon. Tel Aviv, Tutchin and Krippe Relief Society of Israel. . . , 1967. 383 p., ports., map, facsims. (H,Y)

Tuczyn (R). *Yehude Tuczyn ve-Kripa mul rotsehehem; 'esrim ve-arba' 'eduyot* [The Jews of Tuchin and Kripa in front of their murderers*]. Comp.: Avraham Sadeh; ed.: Levi Deror. [Israel], Council of Emigrants from Tuczyn-Kripa; Moreshet, 1990. 160 p., maps, ports. (H)

Turbin (R) see Turobin

Turcz (AH) see Halmi

Turek (R). *Sefer zikaron le-kehilat Turek ve-li-kedoshehah* [Turek: a memorial to the Jewish community of Turek, Poland*]. Tel Aviv, The Turek Organization in Israel, 1982. xviii, 450 p., illus., ports., facsims. (H,Y,E)

Turets (R) see Turzec

Turka (AH). *Sefer zikaron le-kehilat Turka al nehar Stryj ve-ha-seviva* [Memorial book of the community of Turka on the Stryj River and vicinity]. Ed.: J. Siegelman. Haifa, Former Residents of Turka (Stryj) in Israel, 1966. 472 p., ports., map, facsims. (H,Y)

Turna (AH). *Torna—Turna n/Bodvou; zsidósága* [The Jews of Torna]. Ed.: Chaviva Gassner-Guttmann. [Israel, 197–/8–]. 321—-384 p., illus., ports. (Hu)

Turobin (R). *Sefer Turobin; pinkas zikaron* [The Turobin book; in memory of the Jewish community*]. Ed.: M. S. Geshuri. Tel Aviv, Former Residents of Turobin in Israel, 1967. 397 p., ports., map, facsims. (H,Y)

Turzec (R). *Kehilot Turzec ve-Jeremicze; sefer zikaron* [Book of remembrance—Tooretz-Yeremitz*]. Eds.: Michael Walzer-Fass, Moshe Kaplan. Israel, Turzec and Jeremicze Societies in Israel and America, 1978. 114, 421 p., illus. (H,Y,E)

Turzysk (R). *Pinkas ha-kehila Trisk; sefer yizkor* [Memorial book of Trisk]. Ed.: Natan Livneh. Tel Aviv, Trisk Society, 1975. 376 p., illus. (H,Y)

Tykocin (R). *Pinkes Tiktin* [Anshe Tiktin historical book; Pincus Tiktin, Tiktiner historical book*]. Ed.: Moshe Tulchin; comp.: Alter Hoffman. Chicago, Anshe Tiktin, 1949. 100, [28], 59 p., illus. (Y,E)

Tykocin (R). *Sefer Tiktin* [Memorial book of Tiktin]. Eds.: M. Bar-Yuda, Z. Ben-Nahum. Tel Aviv, Former Residents of Tiktin in Israel, 1959. 606 p., ports., facsims. (H)

Tysmienica (AH). *Tismenits; a matseyve oyf di khurves fun a farnikhteter yidisher kehile* [Tysmienica; a memorial book*]. Ed.: Shlomo Blond. Tel Aviv, Hamenora, 1974. 262 p., illus. (H,Y)

Tyszowce (R). *Pinkas Tishovits* [Tiszowic book*]. Ed.: Y. Zipper. Tel Aviv, Assoc. of Former Residents of Tiszowic in Israel, 1970. 324 p., ports., facsims. (H,Y)

Ubinie (AH) see under Radziechow

Uhnow (AH). *Hivniv (Uhnow); sefer zikaron le-kehila* [Hivniv (Uhnow); memorial book to a community]. Tel Aviv, Uhnow Society, 1981. 298, 83 p., illus. (H)

Ujhely (Satorujhely) (AH) see under Zemplenmegye

Ujpest (AH). *Sefer zikhronot shel k(ehila) k(edosha) Ujpest* [Memorial book of the community of Ujpest]. [By] Laszlo Szilagy-Windt; Hebrew translation: Menahem Miron. Tel Aviv, 1975. 27, 325 p., illus. (H,Hu)

Ungvar (AH). *Shoat yehudei rusiah ha-karpatit—Uzhorod* [The Holocaust in Carpatho-Ruthenia—Uzhorod]. [By] Dov Dinur. Jerusalem, Section for Holocaust Research, Institute of Contemporary Jewry, Hebrew University of Jerusalem; World Union of Carpatho-Ruthenian Jews; and Hebrew Schools, [1983]. 6, 123, 15 p., facsims. (H)

Ungvar (AH) see also *Arim ve-imahot,* vol. 4

Urechye (R) see under Slutsk

Uscilug (R). *Kehilat Ustila be-vinyana u-be-hurbana* [The growth and destruction of the community of Uscilug]. Ed.: A. Avinadav. Tel Aviv, Association of Former Residents of Uscilug, [1961]. 334 p., ports. (H,Y)

Ustila (R) see Uscilug

Ustrzyki Dolne (AH) see under Lesko

Utena (R). *Yisker-bukh Utyan un umgegnt* [Memorial book of Utyan and vicinity]. Tel Aviv, Nay Lebn, 1979. 296 p., illus., ports. (Y)

Utyan (R) see Utena

Uzhorod (Ungvar) (AH) see under *Arim ve-imahot,* vol. 4

Uzlovoye (Cholojow) (AH) see under Radziechow

Vamospercs (AH) see under Debrecen

Vas (AH). *Sefer zikaron mehoz Vas* [Memorial book of the region of Vas]. Ed.: Avraham Levinger. Israel, Vas Commemorative Committee, 1974. 214 p., illus. (H)

Vashilkov (R) see Wasilkow

Vashniev (Wasniow) (R) see under Ostrowiec

Vasilishok (R) see Wasiliszki

Vayslits (R) see Wislica

Velky Mager (Nagymagyar) (AH) see under Dunaszerdahely
Vengrov (R) see Wegrow
Venice (Italy) see under *Arim ve-imahot,* vol. 4
Verbo (AH) see under Postyen
Verzhbnik (R) see Wierzbnik
Vidz (R) see Widze

Vilna (R). *Bleter vegn Vilne; zamlbukh* [Pages about Vilna; a compilation]. Eds.: L. Ran, L. Koriski. Lodz, Association of Jews from Vilna in Poland, 1947. xvii, 77 p., ports., music, facsims. (Y)

Vilna (R). *Vilner zamlbukh—measef Vilna* [Vilna collection*]. Ed.: Yisrael Rudnicki. Tel Aviv, World Federation of Jews from Vilna and Vicinity in Israel, 1974. 140 p., illus., facsims. (Y,H)

Vilna (R). *Yerusholayim de-Lita* [Jerusalem of Lithuania, illustrated and documented*]. Collected and arranged by Leyzer Ran. New York, Vilna Album Committee, 1974. 3 vols., illus. (H,Y,E,R)

Vilna (R) see also under Lithuania and under *Arim ve-imahot,* vol. 1
Vilnius (R) see Vilna
Vinogradov (AH) see Nagyszollos
Vishneva (AH) see Wiszniew
Vishnevets (R) see Wisniowiec Nowy
Vishogrod (R) see Wyszogrod
Viskit (Wiskitki) (R) see under Zyrardow
Visooroszi (AH) see Ruscova
Visotsk (R) see Wysock

Vitebsk (R). *Sefer Vitebsk* [Memorial book of Vitebsk]. Ed.: B. Karu. Tel Aviv, Former Residents of Vitebsk and Surroundings in Israel, 1957. 508 columns, ports., facsims. (H)

Vitebsk (R). *Vitebsk amol; geshikhte, zikhroynes, khurbn* [Vitebsk in the past; history, memoirs, destruction]. Eds.: G. Aronson, J. Lestschinsky, A. Kihn. New York, 1956. 644 p., ports. (Y)

Vitkov (Novyy) (Witkow Nowy) (AH) see under Radziechow
Vizna (R) see under Slutsk
Vladimir Volynskiy (R) see Wlodzimierz
Vladimirets (R) see Wlodzimierzec
Vloyn (R) see Wielun
Voislavitsa (R) see Wojslawice
Volozhin (R) see Wolozyn
Voltshin (R) see under Wysokie-Litewskie
Voronovo (R) see Werenow
Voydislav (R) see Wodzislaw
Vrbove (Verbo) (AH) see under Postyen
Vurka (R) see Warka

Vysokoye (R) see Wysokie-Litewskie

Wadowice (AH). *Sefer zikaron le-kehilot Wadowice, Andrychow, Kalwarja, Myslenice, Sucha* [Memorial book of the communities Wadowice. . .] Ed.: D. Jakubowicz. Ramat Gan, Former Residents of Wadowice. . . and Masada, 1967. 454 p., ports., facsims. (H,Y)

Warez (AH) see under Sokal

Warka (R). *Vurka; sefer zikaron* [Vurka memorial book]. Tel Aviv, Vurka Societies in Israel, France, Argentina, England and the United States, 1976. 407 p., illus. (H,Y)

Warsaw (R). *Dos amolike yidishe Varshe, biz der shvel fun dritn khurbn; yisker-bletlekh nokh tayere noente umgekumene* [Jewish Warsaw that was; a Yiddish literary anthology*]. Montreal, Farband of Warsaw Jews in Montreal, 1967. 848, 56 p., facsims., illus., ports. (Y)

Warsaw (R). *Pinkes Varshe* [Book of Warsaw]. Eds.: P. Katz *et al.* Buenos Aires, Former Residents of Warsaw and Surroundings in Argentina, 1955. 1351 columns, lvi p., ports., music, maps (Y)

Warsaw (R). *Warsaw* [Warsaw volume*]. Ed.: J. Gruenbaum. Jerusalem, The Encyclopaedia of the Jewish Diaspora, 1953–1973. 3 vols., ports., maps, facsims. (H,Y)

Warsaw (R) see also under *Arim ve-imahot,* vol. 3

Warszawa (R) see Warsaw

Warta (R). *Sefer D'Vart.* Ed.: Eliezer Estrin. Tel Aviv, D'Vart Society, 1974. 567 p., illus. (H,Y)

Wasiliszki (R). *Tahat shilton ha-germani ha-shanim 1941–1945* [Under German rule in the years 1941–1945]. Tel Aviv, Former Residents of Wasiliszki in Israel, [1986/87]. 1 vol., illus. (H)

Wasiliszki (R) see also under Szczuczyn (*Sefer zikaron le-kehilot Szczuczyn, Wasiliszki*)

Wasilkow (R). *Pinkes Vashilkover yisker-bukh; a spetsyele oysgabe vegn lebn mord un toyt fun a yidishn yishev* [The Wasilkower memorial book; memories of our town Wasilkow which has been annihilated by the Nazis*]. Author and editor: Leon Mendelewicz; translated from Yiddish by Mark Langsam, Bene Gothajner. Melbourne, [Wasilkower Committee], 1990. 339, 152 p., illus., maps, ports., facsims. (Y,E)

Wasniow (R) see under Ostrowiec

Wegrow (R). *Kehilat Wegrow; sefer zikaron* [Community of Wegrow; memorial book]. Ed.: M. Tamari. Tel Aviv, Former Residents of Wegrow in Israel, 1961. 418 p., ports., facsims. (H,Y)

Werenow (R). *Voronova; sefer zikaron le-kedoshei Voronova she-nispu ba-shoat ha-natsim* [Voronova; memorial book to the martyrs of Voronova who died during the Nazi Holocaust]. Ed.: H. Rabin. Israel, Voronova Societies in Israel and the United States, 1971. 440 p., illus. (H,Y)

Widze (R). *Fertsik yor nokhn umkum fun di Vidzer Yidn z"l* [Forty years after the annihilation of the Jews of Widze]. [By] Yaakov Parmunt. Kefar Giladi, The Council of the Society of Widze Jews in the Land of Israel, [1982/83]. 8 leaves. (Y)

Widze (R) see also under Swieciany

Wieliczka (AH). *Kehilat Wieliczka; sefer zikaron* [The Jewish community of Wieliczka; a memorial book*]. Ed.: Shmuel Meiri. Tel Aviv, The Wieliczka Association in Israel, 1980. 160, [9], 93 p., illus. (H,Y,E,P)

Wielun (R). *Sefer zikaron le-kehilat Wielun* [Wielun memorial book*]. Tel Aviv, Wielun Organization in Israel and the Memorial Book Committee in USA, 1971. 534, 24 p., ports. (H,Y,E)

Wieruszow (R). *Wieruszow; sefer yizkor* [Wieruszow; memorial book]. Tel Aviv, Former Residents of Wieruszow Book Committee, 1970. 907 p., ports., maps, facsims. (H,Y)

Wierzbnik (R). *Sefer Wierzbnik-Starachowice* [Wierzbnik-Starachowitz; a memorial book*]. Ed.: Mark Schutzman. Tel Aviv, Wierzbnik-Starachowitz Societies in Israel and the Diaspora, 1973. 29, 399, 100, 83 p., illus. (H,Y,E)

Wilejka (R). *Sefer zikaron kehilat Wilejka ha-mehozit, plakh Vilna* [Memorial book of the community of Vileika*]. Eds.: Kalman Farber, Joseph Se'evi. Tel Aviv, Wilejka Society, 1972. 12, 326 p., illus. (H,Y,E)

Wilno (R) see Vilna

Wiskitki (R) see under Zyrardow

Wislica (R). *Sefer Vayslits; dos Vayslitser yisker-bukh. . .* [Book of Wislica]. Tel Aviv, Association of Former Residents of Wislica, 1971. 299 p., ports., map (H,Y,P)

Wisniowiec Nowy (R). *Wisniowiec; sefer zikaron le-kedoshei Wisniowiec she- nispu be-shoat ha-natsim* [Wisniowiec; memorial book of the martyrs of Wisniowiec who perished in the Nazi holocaust]. Ed.: H. Rabin. [Tel Aviv], Former Residents of Wisniowiec. 540 p., ports. (H,Y)

Wiszniew (AH). *Vishneva, ke-fi she-hayeta ve-enena od; sefer zikaron* [Wiszniew; as it was and is no more; memorial book]. Ed.: Hayyim Abramson. Tel Aviv, Wiszniew Society in Israel, 1972. 216 p., illus. (H,Y)

Witkow Nowy (AH) see under Radziechow

Wloclawek (R). *Wloclawek ve-ha-seviva; sefer zikaron* [Wloclawek and vicinity; memorial book*]. Eds.: K. F. Thursh, M. Korzen. [Israel], Assoc. of Former Residents of Wloclawek in Israel and the USA, 1967. 1032 columns, ports., facsims. (H,Y)

Wlodawa (R). *Wlodawa; ner zikaron* [In memory of Wlodawa]. Ed.: D. Rovner. Haifa, 1968. 211 p., ports., facsims. (H,Y,E,P), mimeo.

Wlodawa (R). *Yisker-bukh tsu Vlodave* [Yizkor book in memory of Vlodava and region Sobibor*]. Ed.: Shimon Kanc. Tel Aviv, Wlodawa Societies in Israel and North and South America, 1974. 1290, 128 columns, illus. (H,Y,E)

Wlodzimierz (R). *Pinkas Ludmir; sefer zikaron le-kehilat Ludmir* [Wladimir Wolynsk; in memory of the Jewish community*]. Tel Aviv, Former

Residents of Wladimir in Israel, 1962. 624 columns, ports., facsims. (H,Y)

Wlodzimierzec (R). *Sefer Vladimerets* [The book of Vladimerets]. Ed.: A. Meyerowitz. Tel Aviv, Former Residents of Vladimerets in Israel, [196–]. 515 p., ports., map (H,Y,E)

Wlodzimierzec (R) see also under Polesie (region)

Wodzislaw (R). *Sefer Wodzislaw-Sedziszow.* Ed.: M. Schutzman. Israel, Community Council of Wodzislaw-Sedziszow Emigrants in Israel, 1979. 437 p., illus. (H,Y)

Wojslawice (R). *Sefer zikaron Voislavitse* [Yizkor book in memory of Voislavize*]. Ed.: Sh. Kanc. Tel Aviv, Former Residents of Voislavize, 1970. 515 p., ports., facsims. (H,Y)

Wolborz (R) see under Piotrkow Trybunalski

Wolbrom (R). *Wolbrom irenu* [Our town Wolbrom]. Ed.: M. Geshuri (Bruckner). Tel Aviv, Association of Former Residents of Wolbrom in Israel, 1962. 909 p., ports., map (H,Y)

Wolczyn (R) see under Wysokie-Litewskie

Wolica-Wygoda (AH) see under Radziechow

Wolkowysk (R). *Hurban Wolkowysk be-milhemet ha-olam ha-sheniya 1939–1945* [The destruction of Wolkowysk during the Second World War 1939–1945]. Tel Aviv, Committee of Former Residents of Wolkowysk in Eretz-Israel, 1946. 96 p., ports. (H)

Wolkowysk (R). *Volkovisker yisker-bukh* [Wolkovisker yizkor book*]. Ed.: M. Einhorn. New York, 1949. 2 vols. (990 p.), ports. (Y,E)

Wolkowysk (R). *Wolkowysk: sipurah shel kehilah yehudit-tsiyonit, hushmedah ba- shoah 1941–1943* [Wolkovisk; the story of a Jewish community*]. Ed.: Katriel Lashovits. Tel Aviv, 1988. 159 p., illus., ports. (H)

Wolma (R) see under Rubiezewicze

Wolomin (R). *Sefer zikaron kehilat Wolomin* [Volomin; a memorial to the Jewish community of Volomin (Poland)*]. Ed.: Shimon Kanc. Tel Aviv, Wolomin Society, 1971. 600 p., illus. (H,Y)

Wolozyn (R). *Wolozyn; sefer shel ha-ir ve-shel yeshivat "Ets Hayim"* [Wolozin; the book of the city and of the Etz Hayyim Yeshiva*]. Ed.: E. Leoni. Tel Aviv, Former Residents of Wolozin in Israel and the USA, 1970. 679, 35 p., ports., map, facsims. (H,Y,E)

Wolpa (R) see under Wolkowysk (*Volkovisker yisker-bukh*)

Wsielub (R) see under Nowogrodek

Wysock (near Rowne) (R). *Ayaratenu Visotsk; sefer zikaron* [Our town Visotsk; memorial book]. Haifa, Association of Former Residents of Visotsk in Israel, 1963. 231 p., ports., maps (H,Y)

Wysock (R) see also under Polesie (region)

Wysokie-Litewskie (R). *Yisker zhurnal gevidmet di umgekumene fun Visoka un Voltshin* [Entertainment and ball given by the United Wisoko-Litowsker and Woltchiner Relief. . . *]. Eds.: Samuel Levine, Morris Gevirtz. New York, United

Wisoko-Litowsker and Woltchiner Relief, 1948. 1 vol., ports. (Y)

Wysokie-Mazowieckie (R). *Wysokie-Mazowieckie; sefer zikaron* [Visoka-Mazovietsk*]. Ed.: I. Rubin. Tel Aviv, Wysokie-Mazowieckie Society, 1975. 280 p., illus. (H,Y,E)

Wyszkow (R). *Sefer Wyszkow* [Wishkow book*]. Ed.: D. Shtokfish. Tel Aviv, Association of Former Residents of Wishkow in Israel and Abroad, 1964. 351 p., ports., facsims. (H,Y)

Wyszogrod (R). *Wyszogrod; sefer zikaron* [Vishogrod; dedicated to the memory. . . *]. Ed.: H. Rabin. [Tel Aviv], Former Residents of Vishogrod and. . . , [1971]. 316, 48 p., ports., facsims. (H,Y,E)

Wyzgrodek (R) see under Krzemieniec

Yagistov (R) see Augustow

Yampol (R). *Ayara be-lehavot; pinkas Yampola, pelekh Volyn* [Town in flames; book of Yampola, district Wolyn]. Ed.: L. Gelman. Jerusalem, Commemoration Committee for the Town with the Assistance of Yad Vashem and the World Jewish Congress, 1963. [154] p. (H,Y)

Yanova (R) see Jonava

Yanovichi (R) see under Vitebsk (*Vitebsk amol*)

Yartshev (AH) see Jaryczow Nowy

Yavoriv (AH) see Jaworow

Yedintsy (R). *Yad le-Yedinits; sefer zikaron le-yehudei Yedinits-Bessarabia* [Yad l'Yedinitz; memorial book for the Jewish community of Yedintzi, Bessarabia*]. Eds.: Mordekhai Reicher, Yosef Magen-Shitz. Tel Aviv, Yedinitz Society, 1973. 1022 p., illus. (H,Y)

Yedvabne (R) see Jedwabne

Yekaterinoslav (R). *Sefer Yekaterinoslav-Dnepropetrovsk.* Eds.: Zvi Harkavi, Yaakov Goldburt. Jerusalem-Tel Aviv, Yekaterinoslav-Dnepropetrovsk Society, 1973. 167 p., illus. (H)

Yendrikhov (Andrychow) (AH) see under Wadowice

Yendzheva (R) see Jedrzejow

Yurburg (R) see Jurbarkas

Yustingrad (R). *Sokolievka/Justingrad; a century of struggle and suffering in a Ukrainian shtetl, as recounted by survivors to its scattered descendants.* Eds.: Leo Miller, Diana F. Miller. New York, A Logvin Book, Loewenthal Press, 1983. 202 p., facsims., illus., maps, ports. (E,H,Y) Incl. facsim. and tr. of 1972 Mashabei Sadeh booklet.

Yustingrad (R). *Yustingrad-Sokolivka; ayara she-nihreva* [Yustingrad-Sokolivka; a town that was destroyed]. Kibbutz Mashabei Sadeh, 1972. 63, [17] p., ports., map, illus. (H)

Zablotow (AH). *Ir u-metim; Zablotow ha-melea ve-ha-hareva* [A city and the dead; Zablotow alive and destroyed]. Tel Aviv, Former Residents of Zablotow in Israel and the USA, 1949. 218 p., ports. (H,Y)

Zabludow (R). *Zabludow; dapim mi-tokh "yisker-bukh"* [Zabludow: pages from yizkor book*]. Eds.: Nehama Shavli-Shimush *et al.* Tel Aviv, Former Residents of Zabludow in Israel, [1987]. 170 p., illus., map (H)

Zabludow (R). *Zabludow yisker-bukh* [Zabludowo; in memoriam*]. Eds.: Sh. Tsesler *et al.* Buenos Aires, Zabludowo Book Committee, 1961. 507 p., ports., map, facsims. (Y)

Zagaipol (R) see Yustingrad

Zakopane (AH) see under Nowy Targ

Zaloshits (R) see Dzialoszyce

Zambrow (R). *Sefer Zambrow; Zambrove* [The book of Zambrov*]. Ed.: Y. T. Lewinsky. Tel Aviv, The Zambrover Societies in USA, Argentina and Israel, 1963. 627, 69 p., ports., facsims. (H,Y,E)

Zamekhov (R) see under Kamenets-Podolskiy

Zamosc (R). *Pinkes Zamosc; yizker-bukh* [Pinkas Zamosc; in memoriam*]. Ed.: M. W. Bernstein. Buenos Aires, Committee of the Zamosc Memorial Book, 1957. 1265 p., ports., facsims. (Y)

Zamosc (R). *Zamosc be-genona u-be-shivra* [The rise and fall of Zamosc]. Ed.: M. Tamari. Tel Aviv, Former Residents of Zamosc in Israel, 1953. 327 p., ports., facsims. (H,P)

Zamosze (R) see under Braslaw

Zaracze (R) see under Braslaw

Zareby Kowcielne (R). *Le-zikhron olam; di Zaromber yidn vos zaynen umgekumen al kidesh-hashem* [For eternal remembrance; the Jews of Zaromb. . .]. [New York], United Zaromber Relief, 1947. 68 p., ports., map, facsims. (Y)

Zarki (R). *Kehilat Zarki; ayara be-hayeha u-ve-khilyona* [The community of Zarki; life and destruction of a town]. Ed.: Y. Lador. Tel Aviv, Former Residents of Zarki in Israel, 1959. 324 p., ports. (H,Y)

Zaromb (R) see Zareby Koscielne

Zarszyn (AH) see under Sanok

Zassow (AH) see under Radomysl

Zastawie (R) see under Kamieniec Litewski

Zawidcze (AH) see under Radziechow

Zawiercie (R). *Sefer zikaron; kedoshei Zawiercie ve-ha-seviva* [Memorial book of the martyrs of Zawiercie and vicinity]. Ed.: Sh. Spivak. Tel Aviv, Former Residents of Zawiercie and Vicinity, 1948. 570 p., ports. (H,Y)

Zbaraz (AH). *Sefer Zbaraz* [Zbaraz: the Zbaraz memorial book*]. Ed.: Moshe Sommerstein. Tel Aviv, The Organization of Former Zbaraz Residents, 1983. 45, 128 p., illus., ports. (H,Y,E)

Zborow (AH). *Sefer zikaron le-kehilat Zborow* [Memorial book of the community of Zborow]. Ed.: Eliyahu (Adik) Zilberman. Haifa, Zborow Society, 1975. 477 p., illus. (H,Y)

Zdunska Wola (R). *Zdunska Wola* [The Zdunska-Wola book*]. Ed.: E. Erlich. Tel Aviv, Zdunska-Wola Associations in Israel and in the Diaspora, 1968. 718, 8, 55 p., ports., facsims. (H,Y,E)

Zdzieciol (R). *Pinkas Zhetl* [Pinkas Zetel; a memorial to the Jewish community of Zetel*]. Ed.: B. Kaplinski. Tel Aviv, Zetel Association in Israel, 1957. 482 p., ports., facsims. (H,Y)

Zelechow (R). *Yisker-bukh fun der Zhelekhover yidisher kehile* [Memorial book of the community of Zelechow]. Ed.: W. Yassni. Chicago, Former Residents of Zelechow in Chicago, 1953. 398, xxiv p., facsims. (Y)

Zelow (R). *Sefer zikaron le-kehilat Zelow* [Memorial book of the community of Zelow]. Ed.: Avraham Kalushiner. Tel Aviv, Zelow Society, 1976. 447 p., illus. (H,Y)

Zelwa (R). *Sefer zikaron Zelwa* [Zelva memorial book*]. Ed.: Yerachmiel Moorstein; English translation: Jacob Solomon Berger. Mahwah, NJ, The Zelva Committee in Israel, 1992. vii, 141 p. (E)

Zemplen (AH) see Zemplenmegye

Zemplenmegye (AH). *Mah tovu uhelekha Yaakov; korot yehudei mehoz Zemplen* [Vanished communities in Hungary; the history and tragic fate of the Jews in Ujhely and Zemplen County*]. By Meir Sas [Szasz]; translated from Hebrew by Carl Alpert. Toronto, Memorial Book Committee, 1986. 141, [56], 170, 214 p., illus., ports., maps, facsims. (H,Hu,E)

Zetel (R) see Zdzieciol

Zgierz (R). *Sefer Zgierz, mazkeret netsah le-kehila yehudit be-Polin* [Memorial book Zgierz*], vol. 1: Ed.: David Shtokfish; vol. 2: Eds: Sh. Kanc, Z. Fisher. Tel Aviv, Zgierz Society, 1975–1986. 2 vols., illus. (H,Y)

Zhelekhov (R) see Zelechow

Zhetl (R) see Zdzieciol

Zholkva (AH) see Zolkiew

Zinkov (R). *Pinkas Zinkov* [Zinkover memorial book*]. Tel Aviv-New York, Joint Committee of Zinkover Landsleit in the United States and Israel, 1966. 239, 16 p., ports. (H,Y,E)

Zloczew (Lodz) (R). *Sefer Zloczew* [Book of Zloczew]. Tel Aviv, Committee of the Association of Former Residents of Zloczew, [1971]. 432, [21] p., ports., facsims. (H,Y)

Zloczow (AH). *Der untergang fun Zloczów* [The destruction of Zloczów]. [By] Szlojme Mayer. Munich, Ibergang, 1947. 45 p., illus., ports. (Y in Latin characters)

Zloczow (AH). *Sefer kehilat Zloczow* [The city of Zloczow*]. Ed.: Baruch Karu (Krupnik). Tel Aviv, Zloczow Society, 1967. 540, 208 columns, illus. (H,E)

Zofiowka (R). *Ha-ilan ve-shoreshav; sefer korot t"l Zofiowka-Ignatowka* [The tree and the roots; the history of t.l. (Sofyovka and Ignatovka)*]. Eds.: Y. Vainer *et al.* Givataim, Beit-Tal, 1988. 572, xxxv p., illus., maps, ports. (H,Y,E)

Zolkiew (AH). *Sefer Zolkiew (kirya nisegava)* [Memorial book of Zolkiew]. Eds.: N. M. Gelber, Y. Ben-Shem. Jerusalem, The Encyclopaedia of the Jewish Diaspora, 1969. 844 columns, ports., map, facsims. (H)

Zolochev (AH) see Zloczow

Zoludek (R). *Sefer Zoludek ve-Orlowa; galed le-zikaron* [The book of Zoludek and Orlowa; a living memorial*]. Ed.: A. Meyerowitz. Tel Aviv, Former Residents of Zoludek in Israel and the USA, [196–]. 329, [5] p., ports., map (H,Y,E)

Zoludzk (R). *Ner tamid le-zekher kehilat Zoludzk* [Memorial book of the community of Zoludzk]. Ed.: A. Avinadav. Tel Aviv, Association of Former Residents of Zoludzk in Israel, 1970. 185, 3 p., ports., map (H,Y)

Zombor (AH). *Kehilat Sombor be-hurbana; dapei zikaron le-kedoshei ha-kehila* [The Sombor community in its destruction; pages of commemoration to the martyrs of the community]. [By] E. H. Spitzer. Jerusalem, 1970. 29 p., ports. (H)

Zvihil (R) see Novograd-Volynskiy

Zwiahel (R) see Novograd-Volynskiy

Zwolen (R). *Zvoliner yisker-bukh* [Zwolen memorial book]. New York, Zwolen Society, 1982. 564, 112 p., illus. (Y,E)

Zychlin (R). *Sefer Zychlin* [The memorial book of Zychlin*]. Ed.: Ammi Shamir. Tel Aviv, Zychliner Organization of Israel and America, 1974. 4, 350 p., illus. (H,Y,E,)

Zyrardow (R). *Pinkas Zyrardow, Amshinov un Viskit* [Memorial book of Zyrardow, Amshinov and Viskit]. Ed.: M. W. Bernstein. Buenos Aires, Association of Former Residents in the USA, Israel, France and Argentina, 1961. 699 p., ports., facsims. (Y)

Institutions That Collect Memorial Books

Several libraries and archives collect Memorial Books. Although these institutions *cannot* check the books for you for family or other information, they can, of course, tell you if they have them in their collections. They are:

YIVO Institute for Jewish Research
1048 Fifth Ave
New York, NY 10028

The New York Public Library
Jewish Division
42nd Street at 5th Ave
New York, NY 10018

Jewish Theological Seminary Library
3080 Broadway
New York, NY 10027

University of California Library
UCLA
Jewish Studies Collection
Los Angeles, CA 90024

Yad Vashem
P.O. Box 3477
Jerusalem, Israel

Hebrew Union College-Jewish
Institute of Religion
Klau Library
3101 Clifton Ave
Cincinnati, OH 45220

Library of Congress
Hebraic Section
101 Independence Ave S.E.
Washington, DC 20540

Brandeis University Library
Hebraic and Judaica Collection
P.O. Box 9110
Boston, MA 02254

Harvard College
Harry Elkins Widener
Memorial Library
Hebraic Collection
Cambridge, MA 02138

Yeshiva University Library
500 West 185 St
New York, NY 10033

University of Toronto
Robarts Library
Toronto, Ontario
M5S 1A5 Canada

Jewish Public Library
5151 Cote Street
Catherine Road
H3W 1MG Montreal, Quebec
Canada

Jewish National and University Library
P.O. Box 503
Jerusalem, Israel 91004

Although there are other Jewish institutions that have collections as well, these are the best. None of them will loan the books to you, but they will let you read the books and photocopy material from them at the institution. They would also answer a written inquiry as to whether they have a certain book in their collection.

How to Obtain Copies for Yourself. Once you have located a Memorial Book for yourself, you will undoubtedly want to own a copy. A Memorial Book is not the kind of publication you would find in a local bookshop, nor can a local store order a copy for you. In almost all cases, Memorial Books have been privately published and are distributed by the people who had the book printed—usually a landsmannschaft. Therefore, what you have to do is either track down the individuals (or organization) that had the book published, or find someone who will track them down for you. Keep in mind that you might have to resort to doing some extensive photocopying if you cannot locate the Memorial Books in which you are interested. But if you put effort into your search, a copy of the book you want will turn up.

Your best bet in locating Memorial Books is to track down the people who edited them. For example, when I found a Memorial Book for my father's town of Dobromil, I examined the book and found that the editors lived in New York. I looked through New York City phone books and tracked them down—finally locating a copy of the Memorial Book. Remember that many Memorial Books were published in Israel, so when you travel to Israel you will want to do the same kind of searching for editors—and it will of course be rewarding just to meet these "Landsmen." (By the way, if you do locate Memorial Books, see if you can buy more than one copy; someone else in the family might want one). And speaking of "buying" Memorial Books, quite often when I do find people who helped to edit a book, they are more than happy to give me a copy for free. They are delighted to find someone interested in their home town!

Another way of locating Memorial Books, and one that is both the most rewarding as well as the most difficult, is to track down the people or landsmannschaft that published the book in which you are interested. In this way you will also have personal contact with interesting people—and that is what it is all about. (See Locating Landsmannschaften, page 320.)

> A scattered nation that remembers its past and connects it with the present will undoubtedly have a future as a people and probably even a more glorious life than the one in the past.
>
> LEV LEVANDA

ARCHIVES, LIBRARIES AND ORGANIZATIONS

If I were to quantify all of the results of my genealogical research over the years, I am sure that the majority of what I learned was not found in archives, libraries or government offices, but were rather found in interviews with my relatives. The stories, the photos, the flavor of my family history comes from the human contact I have had with the relatives I've discovered around the world.

But although the heart and soul of my family history comes from living sources, the basic structure of my family history is made up of the names and dates and bits of information located within institutions or on documents.

Many of these institutions and documents provide information for individuals in the U. S. regardless of family background. The other government agencies that we discussed in Chapter 3 pertain to all Americans.

But some of the most important sources for Jewish genealogists can be found in uniquely Jewish archives and libraries, or in collections that are specific to Jews. The following are the most important, and will be of the greatest value to you.

AMERICAN JEWISH ARCHIVES

This archive, founded in 1947, is devoted to collecting historical documents relating to American Jewry. Of special interest to the family history researcher is their collection of family trees and family histories. The AJA also has a large collection of synagogue records (mostly Reform, though others as well, because of their affiliation with the

Reform Movement) that would be quite valuable if your family belonged to one of the synagogues whose records are deposited there.

The AJA answers inquiries through the mail and often will photocopy relevant material. You cannot expect them to do much research for you, but they are willing to make initial searches to determine whether they have something of interest. For doing research regarding a town or city in the U.S. they also have much material of worth.

If you have published a family history, town history, or even have simply drawn a family tree, it would be nice to send a copy to the AJA. Not only will this make your work available to others, but they may also print a reference to it in an issue of their publication *American Jewish Archives* alerting their readership to it. Your work will then become a part of their holdings; you can never tell when a person might check the AJA for a certain surname and it will be yours. Depositing your research at the AJA is also serving the cause of American Jewish history. The address is:

American Jewish Archives
3101 Clifton Avenue
Cincinnati, OH 45220

American Jewish Historical Society

The American Jewish Historical Society (AJHS) functions as a library, an archive, an organization and a publisher.

As a library and archive, the AJHS can be most helpful in your family history research when it comes to synagogue records, family histories that have been published, genealogies, Jewish organization records, and town histories (towns in the U.S.). The library staff is quite helpful. I have made many inquiries through the mail over the years and I always receive a prompt and thorough reply. However, it would be best to visit the society if you can, particularly if a reply through the mail indicates material of interest; you cannot expect the librarians to do too much research for you.

It would be appropriate to mention the AJHS as a good depository of Jewish records—if you have records of your own. Too often, people discard records of synagogues, charitable organizations, landsmannschaften, and the like, throwing away gems of history. If you know of any Jewish records or other items of Jewish historical interest, contact the American Jewish Historical Society or the American Jewish Archives (see previous page).

American Jewish Historical Society
2 Thornton Rd
Waltham, MA 02154

> The future of Judaism belongs to that school which can best understand the past.
>
> LEOPOLD LOWE, HUNGARIAN RABBI
>
> Research into the past, as an aim in itself, without the present, is not worth a bean.
>
> BIALIK

JEWISH HISTORICAL SOCIETIES

Many Jewish historical societies can be found around the U.S. and would be worth contacting for information concerning the regions of which they are a part. Most of these societies hold regular meetings and some publish historical material on a regular basis. If you live in the vicinity of any of these societies you may want to join. Historical societies are always looking for new members.

Jewish Historical Societies and Other Related Institutions or Organizations in the United States

ARIZONA

Arizona Jewish Historical Society
Phoenix Chapter
4143 N. 12th Street #100D
Phoenix, AZ 80514

The Jewish Historical Society of Southern Arizona
P.O. Box 57482
Tucson, AZ 85732

CALIFORNIA

Southern California Jewish Historical Society
6505 Wilshire Blvd
Suite 905
Los Angeles, CA 90048

Western Jewish History Center of the Judah L. Magnes Museum
2911 Russell St
Berkeley, CA 94705

San Diego Jewish Historical Society
1934 Pentuckett Avenue
San Diego, CA 92104

COLORADO

Rocky Mountain Jewish Historical Society
Center for Judaic Studies
University of Denver
Denver, CO 80208

CONNECTICUT

Jewish Historical Society of Greater Bridgeport
4200 Park Ave
Bridgeport, CT 06604

Jewish Historical Society of Greater Hartford
335 Bloomfield Ave
West Harford, CT 06117

Jewish Historical Society of New Haven, Inc.
c/o Home for the Aged
169 Davenport Ave
New Haven, CT 06519

Stamford Jewish Historical Society
JCC, Box 3326, Newfield Ave at Vine Rd
Stamford, CT 06905

Jewish Historical Society of Waterbury
359 Cooke St
Waterbury, CT 06710

DELAWARE

Jewish Historical Society of Delaware
505 Market St Mall
Wilmington, DE 19801

District of Columbia

Jewish Historical Society of Greater Washington
701 Third St, NW
Washington, DC 20001

Florida

Jewish Historical Society of South Florida, Inc.
4200 Biscayne Blvd
Miami, FL 33137

Georgia

Southern Jewish Historical Society
Valdosta State College, Box 179
Valdosta, GA 31698

Hawaii

Levinson Hawaii Jewish Archives
c/o Temple Emanu-El
2550 Pali Hwy
Honolulu, HI 96717

Illinois

Chicago Jewish Archives
Spertus College
618 South Michigan Ave
Chicago, IL 60605

Chicago Jewish Historical Society
618 South Michigan Ave
Chicago, IL 60605

Indiana

The Indiana Jewish Historical Society, Inc.
203 West Wayne St
Central Building, No. 310
Fort Wayne, IN 46802

Kansas

Heart of America Jewish Historical Society
9648 Walmer Lane
Overland Park, KS 66212

Louisiana

Louisiana Jewish Historical Society
6227 St. Charles Ave
New Orleans, LA 70118

Maryland

Jewish Historical Society of Annapolis, MD, Inc.
5 Sampson Pl
Annapolis, MD 21401

Jewish Historical Society & Archives of Howard County Maryland
5403 Mad River Lane
Columbus, MD 21044

Jewish Historical Society of Maryland, Inc.
Jewish Heritage Center
15 Lloyd St
Baltimore, MD 21202

Massachusetts

Berkshire Jewish Archives Council
75 Mountain Dr
Pittsfield, MA 01201

North Shore Jewish Historical Society
31 Exchange St, Suite 27
Lynn, MA 01901

Michigan

Jewish Historical Society of Michigan
6600 West Maple Rd
West Bloomfield, MI 48322

Minnesota

Jewish Historical Society of the Upper Midwest
Hamline University
1536 Hewitt Ave
St. Paul, MN 55104

Mississippi

Museum of the Southern Jewish Experience
P.O. Box 16528
Jackson, MS 39236

Missouri

St. Louis Jewish Archives
Saul Brodsky Jewish Community Library
12 Millstone Campus Dr
St. Louis, MO 63146

Nebraska

Nebraska Jewish Historical Society
333 Soluth 132nd St
Omaha, NE 68154

New Jersey

Jewish Historical Society of Central Jersey
228 Livingston Ave
New Brunswick, NJ 08901

Jewish Historical Society of MetroWest
901 Route 10 East
Whippany, NJ 07981

Jewish Historical Society of North Jersey
YM/YWHA Judaica Library
1 Pike Dr
Wayne, NJ 07470

Jewish Historical Society of Trenton
999 Lower Ferry Rd
Box 7249
Trenton, NJ 08628

NEW MEXICO

New Mexico Jewish Historical Society
P.O. Box 15598
Cielo Ct. Station
Santa Fe, NM 87506

NEW YORK

Orthodox Jewish Archives of Agudath Israel
84 William St, #1200
New York, NY 10038

Jewish Historical Society of New York, Inc.
8 West 70th St
New York, NY 10023

Westchester Jewish Historical Society
35 Sunnyridge Rd
Harrison, NY 10528

NORTH DAKOTA

Jewish Historical Project of North Dakota
P.O. Box 2431
Fargo, ND 58102

OHIO

Cleveland Jewish Archives
Western Reserve Historical Society
10825 East Blvd
Cleveland, OH 44106

Columbus Jewish Historical Society, Inc.
1175 College Ave
Columbus, OH 43209

OKLAHOMA

Tulsa Jewish Archives Project
7305 East 67th Pl
Tulsa, OK 74133

Oregon

Jewish Historical Society of Oregon
Mitteleman JCC
6651 SE Capitol Hwy
Portland, OR 97219

Pennsylvania

Jewish Museum of Eastern Pennsylvania
2300-B Mahantongo St
Pottsville, PA 17901

Jewish Archives
Historical Society of Western Pennsylvania
4338 Bigelow Blvd
Pittsburgh, PA 15213

National Museum of American Jewish History
55 North Fifth St
Philadelphia, PA 19106

Philadelphia Jewish Archives Center
Balch Institute
18 South 7th St
Philadelphia, PA 19106

Rhode Island

Rhode Island Jewish Historical Association
130 Sessions St
Providence, RI 02906

Tennessee

Jewish Historical Society of Memphis and Mid-South
163 Beale St
Memphis, TN 38103

Archives of Jewish Federation of
Nashville and Mid. Tennessee
801 Percy Warner Blvd
Nashville, TN 37205

Texas

Dallas Jewish Historical Society
7900 Northaven Rd
Dallas, TX 75230

Galveston County Jewish Historical Association
2613 Oak St
Galveston, TX 77551

Texas Jewish Historical Society
P.O. Box 10193
Austin, TX 78766

Virginia

Peninsula Jewish Historical Society
25 Stratford Rd
Newport News, VA 23601

Washington

Washington State Jewish Historical Society
2031 Third Ave
Suite 400
Seattle, WA 98121

Wisconsin

Wisconsin Jewish Archives
State Historical Society
816 State St
Madison, WI 53706

United States

American Jewish Historical Society
2 Thornton Rd
Waltham, MA 02154

Jewish Historical Societies Outside of the United States

CANADA

Canadian Jewish Congress Archives
1590 Avenue Docteur Penfield
Montreal, Quebec
Canada H3G 1C5

Canadian Jewish Historical Society
4600 Bathurst St
Willowdale, Ontario
Canada M2R 3V2

History and Archives Committee
c/o Jewish Community Council of Calgary
1607 90th Avenue SW
Calgary, Alberta
Canada T2V 4V7

History and Archives Committee
Jewish Community Council of Edmonton
7200 156th St
Edmonton, Alberta
Canada T5R 1X3

History and Archives Committee
Regina Jewish Community Center
Beth Jacob Synagogue
1640 Victoria Ave
Regina, Sasketchewan
Canada

History and Archives Commiteee
Jewish Community Center of Saskatoon
715 McKinnon Ave
Saskatoon, Saskatchewan
Canada

Jewish Historical Society of British Columbia
950 West 41st Ave
Vancouver, Br. Columbia
Canada V5Z 2N7

Jewish Historical Society of Halifax
304-1515 South Park St
Halifax, Nova Scotia
Canada B3J 2L2

Jewish Historical Society of Montreal
4903 Lacombe Ave
Montreal, Quebec
Canada 43W 1RB

Jewish Historical Society of Southern Alberta
1607 90th Ave SW
Calgary, Alberta
Canada T2V 4V7

Jewish Historical Society of Western Canada, Inc.
365 Hargrave St
Suite 404
Winnipeg, Manitoba
Canada R3B 2K3

Jewish Public Library of Montreal
Canadian Jewish Documentary Centre
5151 Cote Sainte Catherine Rd
Montreal, Quebec
Canada H3W 1M6

Ottawa Jewish Historical Society
Jewish Community Center
151 Chapel St
Ottawa, Ontario
Canada K1N 7Y2

Saint John Jewish Historical Museum
& Jewish Historical Society
29 Wellington Row
Saint John, New Brunswick
Canada E2L 3H4

Toronto Jewish Historical Society
7 Austin Crescent
Toronto, Ontario
Canada M5R 3E4

Toronto Jewish Congress Ontario Region Archives
4600 Bathurst St
Willowdale, Ontario
Canada M2R 3V2

Windsor Jewish Community Council Archives Committee
Windsor Jewish Community Center
1641 Ouellete Ave
Windsor, Ontario
Canada N8X 1K9

England

Jewish Historical Society
33 Seymour Pl
London
England W1H 5AP

Hong Kong

Jewish Historical Society of Hong Kong
3-E Cliffview Mansions
25 Conduit Rd
Hong Kong

Poland

Historic Institute of Jews in Poland
79 Swierczewskiego St
Warsaw
Poland

Scotland

Scottish Jewish Archives
3 Glenburn Rd, Giffnock
Glasgow G46 6RE
Scotland

We cannot rid ourselves of the past without destroying our present and ruining our future.

HARRY WOLFSON, "ESCAPING JUDAISM"

One of the early rabbis, Ben Azzai, translated the words of Genesis 5:1, "This is the book of the generations of man," and declared them to be "a great fundamental teaching of the Torah." As all human beings are traced back to one parent, he taught, they must necessarily be brothers.

DR. J. H. HERTZ, IN THE SONCINO, PENTATEUCH

THE CENTRAL ARCHIVES FOR THE HISTORY OF THE JEWISH PEOPLE

In 1969, the Central Archives for the History of the Jewish People was established by the Israeli government, the Jewish Agency for Israel, the Historical Society of Israel, the Israel Academy of Sciences and Humanities, the Hebrew University of Jerusalem, Tel Aviv University, and Bar-Ilan University.

The archives are in possession of "the most extensive collection of documents, pinkassim (registers), and records concerning Jewish history in the Diaspora from the Middle Ages to the present day." Although the archives staff attempts to collect original documents, it is also involved in the microfilming of historical records around the world. A unique aspect of the archives is the fact that whereas other Jewish archives specialize in one region or period of Jewish history, the Central Archives collects material from every Jewish community in the world.

The collection at the Central Archives is arranged by country and town. If you want to know what they have of interest to you, it would be best to send them a letter asking for an inventory of their holdings for a specific town or region. In their reply, they will tell you what they have. It might be a marriage register from the 1840s or a mohel book from 1909, or a record book from the community, or they might not have anything for your community. However, if they do, you can arrange to purchase microfilm of other copies of the material.

The address of the archive is:

The Central Archives for the History of the Jewish People
Hebrew University Campus
P.O.Box 1149
Jerusalem, Israel

It would also be worthwhile to write to them asking for their guide to the collection.

> I never realized, when I was very young, how much I missed by never having met either of my grandfathers. Not having known a grandfather, I had to go out looking for him, and what I will try and set out here is simply the story of the search. The trouble is that, given my own type of mind, this is bound to take me further than a few nostalgic family tales. However, if it is a little grown up for the einiklach (grandchildren) at this stage, they'll get round to it one day. Above all, they will understand, I think, that I was not just looking for my grandfather but for myself.
>
> CHAIM RAPHAEL, "ROOTS—JEWISH STYLE," MIDSTREAM

Jewish Genealogical Societies

When I first began my own personal search for my family history, there were no genealogical societies. For that matter, there were no books on the subject, no publications being issued, no organizations to give guidance. Most librarians and archivists I contacted knew little, if anything, about how a Jewish person could do successful genealogical research. The picture has changed considerably, in particular in regard to Jewish genealogical societies.

It is poignant to note that before the Holocaust there were groups that got together to share enthusiasm for Jewish genealogy. Publications were produced, meetings were held, and the pursuit of Jewish genealogy had been of keen interest to many. With the destruction of European Jewry came, of course, the end of all these activities. Today, throughout the world, a loosely connected network of Jewish Genealogical Societies exists. The first one was founded at the suggestion of Dr. Neil Rosenstein. He invited several people to his home, with the hope that we could launch a successful organization. This first meeting gave birth to the Jewish Genealogical Society, later becoming the JGS for the New York area. Quite rapidly other JGSs came into being. Some meet every month, some less frequently. Some publish newsletters (of varying quality). The New York JGS has also published a book; offers classes and beginners' seminars; and is involved in other related efforts.

Genealogists learn from each other, and the meetings of these groups have become invaluable for the swapping of new sources; mutual encouragement and support; and sharing of materials. Many groups invite guest speakers to their meetings; some maintain lending or research libraries; and all participate in the rebirth of Jewish genealogical research as an important pastime.

The following is a list of the JGSs that exist as I write this. New groups seem to spring up all the time. If there is no JGS in your area, you may want to start one. I'd suggest you contact the New York group for advice on how to start your own JGS.

I'd also like to suggest that you try to subscribe to the newsletters of these JGSs. Even though some of the newsletters are quite good and others pretty primitive, they are all filled with specialized bits of information that can often make a difference.

Another important part of the network of JGSs is the Jewish Family Finder, a computerized way of locating other individuals who are researching specific surnames or towns. If someone has been doing research on a small town that you are also interested in, chances are likely that you'll have much in common.

Jewish Genealogical Societies in the United States

ARIZONA

Arizona Jewish Historical Society
Genealogy Committee
720 West Edgewood Avenue
Mesa, AZ 85210

Southern Arizona Jewish Historical Society
Committee on Genealogy
4181 E. Pontatoc Canyon Dr
Tucson, AZ 85718

CALIFORNIA

Jewish Genealogical Society of Los Angeles
P.O. Box 55443
Sherman Oaks, CA 91343

Jewish Genealogical Society of Orange County
11751 Cherry St
Los Alamitos, CA 90720

Jewish Genealogical Society of Sacramento
2351 Wyda Way
Sacramento, CA 95825

San Diego Jewish Genealogical Society
255 South Rios Avenue
Solana Beach, CA 92075

San Francisco Bay Area—Jewish Genealogical Society
40 West 3rd Ave
San Mateo, CA 94402

South Orange County Jewish Genealogy Society
2370-1D Via Mariposa West
Laguna Hills, CA 92653

CONNECTICUT

Jewish Genealogical Society of Connecticut
25 Stoneham Rd
West Hartford, CT 06117

DISTRICT OF COLUMBIA

Jewish Genealogy Society of Greater Washington
P.O. Box 412
Vienna, VA 22183

Jewish Genealogy Society of Greater Washington
6912 Pacific Lane
Annandale, VA 22003

FLORIDA

Jewish Genealogical Society of Broward County
P.O. Box 17251
Ft. Lauderdale, FL 33318

Jewish Genealogical Society of Greater Miami
9042 SW 132 Lane
Miami, FL 33176

Jewish Genealogical Society of South Florida
1501 Cayman Way #F2
Coconut Creek, FL 33066

Georgia

Jewish Genealogical Society of Georgia
370 Lighthouse Point NW
Atlanta, GA 30328

Illinois

Illinois Jewish Genealogical Society
404 Douglas
Park Forest, IL 60466

Jewish Genealogical Society of Illinois
818 Mansfield Crt
Schaumburg, IL 60194

Kentucky

Jewish Genealogical Society of Louisville
3304 Furman Boulevard
Louisville, KY 40220

Maryland

Jewish Historical Society of Maryland
Genealogy Department
15 Lloyd St
Baltimore, MD 21202

Massachusetts

Jewish Genealogical Society of Greater Boston
P.O. Box 366
Newton Highlands, MA 02161

Michigan

Jewish Genealogical Society of Michigan
4275 Strathdale Lane
West Bloomfield, MI 48323

Missouri

Jewish Genealogy Society of St. Louis
10677 Country View Dr
St. Louis, MO 63141

Nevada

Jewish Genealogical Society of Southern Nevada
2653 Topaz Sq
Las Vegas, NV 89121

Jewish Genealogical Society of Las Vegas
P.O. Box 29342
Las Vegas, NV 89126

New Jersey

Association of Jewish Genealogical Societies
P.O. Box 1134
Teaneck, NJ 07666

Jewish Genealogical Society of North Jersey
1 Bedford Rd
Pompton Lakes, NJ 07442

New York

Albany Jewish Genealogical Society
P.O. Box 3850
Albany, NY 12203

Jewish Genealogical Society of Buffalo
174 Peppertree Drive #7
Buffalo, NY 14228

Jewish Genealogical Society of Long Island
32 Holiday Park Dr
Hauppauge, NY 11788

Jewish Genealogical Society
P.O. Box 6398
New York, NY 10128

North Carolina

Jewish Genealogical Society of Raleigh
8701 Sleepy Creek Dr
Raleigh, NC 27612

Ohio

Jewish Genealogical Society of Cleveland
996 Eastlawn Dr
Highland Heights, OH 44143

Jewish Genealogical Society of Dayton
2536 England Ave
Dayton, OH 45406

Oregon

Jewish Genealogical Society of Oregon
Mitteleman JCC
6651 SW Captitol Hwy
Portland, OR 97219

Pennsylvania

Jewish Genealogical Society of Philadelphia
332 Harrison Ave
Elkins Park, PA 19117

Jewish Genealogical Society of Pittsburgh
2131 Fifth Ave
Pittsburgh, PA 15219

Utah

Jewish Genealogical Society of Salt Lake City
3510 Fleetwood Dr
Salt Lake City, UT 84109

Virginia

Jewish Genealogical Club of Tidewater, Virginia
c/o JCCT
7300 Newport Ave
Norfolk, VA 23505

WASHINGTON

Jewish Genealogical Society of Washington
1422 NE 1st Lane
Bellevue, WA 98007

WISCONSIN

Wisconsin Jewish Genealogical Society
9280 North Fairway Dr
Milwaukee, WI 53217

Jewish Genealogical Societies Outside of the United States

CANADA

Jewish Genealogical Society of Canada
Toronto Divison P.O. Box 446, Station A
Willowdale, Ontario
Canada M2N 5T1

Jewish Genealogical Society of Montreal
5787 McAlear Ave
Cote St. Luc, Quebec
Canada H4W 2H3

ENGLAND

Jewish Genealogical Society of London
Family History Workshop of the Museum of Jewish Life
60 East End Rd
London N3 2SY
England

FRANCE

Cercle de Genealogie Juive
3 rue Richer
75009 Paris
France

Jewish Genealogical Society of Paris
38 Rue du Pere-Corentin
Paris 75014
France

HOLLAND

Nederlandse Kring voor Joodse Genealogie
Korte Prinsengracht 59
1013 GP
Amsterdam
Holland

ISRAEL

Israel Genealogical Society
50 Harav Uziel St
Jerusalem
Israel 96424

SWITZERLAND

Jewish Genealogical Society of Zurich
POB 876
CH-8021
Zurich
Switzerland

YIVO Institute for Jewish Research

The YIVO Institute for Jewish Research, located at 1048 Fifth Avenue, New York, NY 10028, is a pot of gold at the end of the rainbow for the student of Eastern European Jewry. The YIVO library and archives collections are filled with material on seemingly every aspect of the history of Eastern European Jewry. Equal to their superb collection is their helpful staff, who are aware of the fact that many of us cannot read the material in all the languages represented there and do everything they can to help the researcher. But, do not expect them to translate for you! This would be unreasonable to request.

YIVO (whose initials stand for Yidisher Visnshaftlekher Institut) was founded in Vilna in 1925. Its history is a story in itself, particularly in light of the fact that the Germans seized YIVOs collection in 1940. Much of it was recovered. Today, the institution can be found on the corner of 86th Street and Fifth Avenue in Manhattan, right down the street from the Jewish Museum. YIVO must be visited by anyone interested in the Jews of Eastern Europe.

Although YIVO cannot always be of much help when you are doing research on individual family members, there is no finer place to find background material on locations in Eastern Europe. Reference to various parts of YIVO's collection are mentioned throughout this book. Of particular note, however, are the several photography collections there, consisting of thousands of photographs, indexed by town. In other words, there is a good possibility that you can find photographs of the smallest towns at YIVO.

It would take months to discover all of the resources at YIVO, and this would be time well spent. I myself discovered the first reference to my great-great-great-grandfather, the Stropkover Rebbe, at YIVO.

In 1977, Schocken Books published a beautiful book drawn from YIVO's Polish photograph collection. Titled *Image Before My Eyes: A Photographic History of Jewish Life in Poland, 1864—1939,* the book is the result of the skillful and scholarly efforts of Lucjan Dobroszycki and Barbara Kirshenblatt-Gimblett. An historian and folklorist at YIVO, respectively, the two authors have produced a book that should be in the home library of anyone with the slightest interest in Jewish history in general, and Polish-Jewish history in particular. One of the most remarkable results of the book's publication has been the large number of people who have recognized people in the old photographs in the book.

> Yesterday did not vanish, but lives.
>
> ELISHEBA, HEBREW POET

THE LEO BAECK INSTITUTE

If any of your ancestors came from Germany, the Leo Baeck Institute at 129 East 73rd Street, New York, NY 10021 should be of interest. The institute includes a 50,000+ volume library, an archive, and is a publisher of books in the field of German Jewry, and an academic center.

Although the entire collection of the Leo Baeck Institute is fascinating and important, a few items in particular should be noted. The institute has a large collection of family trees of German Jewish families, many of which are a few centuries old. German Jews have been known to have a keen interest in genealogy, and this is reflected in the outstanding collection of material of this kind at the Leo Baeck Institute.

In addition, the institute has a collection of family histories and community histories pertaining to German Jewry, as well as a large number of unpublished memoirs.

Although the Leo Baeck Institute specializes in German Jewry, its collection also contains material related to other countries with German-speaking Jews before the Holocaust.

If you have located the town or region in Germany where your ancestors came from, you should check the institute for background information. A review of their family tree collection might also be worthwhile. Do not assume, however, that finding a family tree with a familiar surname means that it is your family, however tempting this might be.

See *Toledot: The Journal of Jewish Genealogy,* Volume 2, Number 4 (Spring 1979), for an excellent article on the genealogical resources of the Leo Baeck Institute. The article was written by Dr. Sybil Milton, Chief Archivist of the institute.

> Man lives not only in the circle of his years but also, by virtue of the subconscious, in the provinces of the generations from which he is descended, and Jewish life, to a very great extent, is based here.
>
> LEO BAECK, *THE JEW*

LDS FAMILY HISTORY LIBRARY

The Mormon Church administers what is perhaps the most ambitious genealogy archive and library in the world. The Family History Library, which is the genealogical arm of the Mormon Church, has a granite mountain in Salt Lake City, Utah, which has been carved out and has a capacity for housing six million reels of microfilm. The archive in the mountain is carefully controlled for temperature and other climate variations, and is also supposed to be able to withstand nearly every possible disaster, human- and nature-made.

To understand the Mormon interest in genealogy, one must know something about their religious beliefs. Let it be sufficient to say that the Mormons believe that people who are no longer alive can be baptized and that genealogy research uncovers unknown people for this purpose. As a religion dependent on and interested in converts, the Mormon Church is interested in *all* genealogical records.

For the Jewish researcher, there are several points of interest relating to the Mormon genealogical facilities. Simply put, the Mormons have been able to gain access to Eastern European records, including

Jewish records. The result of this is that the Mormon Church has acquired and continues to acquire Eastern European (and other) Jewish records, including census material, synagogue and Jewish communal records and other documents. Their collection already has some fascinating Polish, German and Hungarian records of Jewish interest, and they are continuing to gather more documents all the time.

At the present time, the Mormons have research projects going on in many European countries.

To gain access to the material gathered by the Mormons you need not travel to Salt Lake City. Rather, you must locate a branch library (there are many throughout the country) of the Church. Check a phone book for a branch library in your area. Look under "Church of Jesus Christ of Latter Day Saints." At the branch library you will find a microfilm copy of the index to their holdings. When you find what you want in the index, you can send for the material through the branch library at a nominal price per reel of microfilm. The index is arranged by country. If you are interested, for example, in seeing what Polish records they have, you must look up "Poland—Jews." I have also found material under the heading "Poland—Minorities—Jews," which means that their indexing system could use improvement. You might also seek material of a general nature. For example, a census taken in Hungary might have included Jews and non-Jews. Again, locate what you want by location—first by country, then by county or city.

Note: I have used the Mormon library for years and have never been approached to join the Church or to read a pamphlet. They seem to separate their religious work from their genealogical work. I would recommend using their library, but I would also suggest that you protest strongly if someone approaches you on a religious matter. The central address for their organization is:

Family History Library
35 North West Temple Street
Salt Lake City, UT 84150

An inventory of the Jewish records of the towns in Poland, Hungary and Germany that have been microfilmed by the Mormons is included in *The Encyclopedia of Jewish Genealogy* (see page 112). Also included in *The Encyclopedia of Jewish Genealogy* is a thorough explanation of the Mormon's genealogical activities and how it can be of great value to Jewish researchers.

1892 **Születési**

Folyó szám	A születés hava és napja	A gyermek neve	Neme: férfi	Neme: nő	Állapota: törvényes	Állapota: törvénytelen	Az atya neve állása v. foglalkozása és születés helye	Az anya neve és születés helye	A szülők lakása és a gyermek születésének helye
111	1892 ápril. 22.	Margit		/	/		Fülep Bertalan, mészáros, Mozalka	Keimovics Bella, Nagy Kálló	Mozalka
112	1892 ápril. 24.	György	/		/		ifj. Schwarcz Jakab, vasárus, Mozalka	Weinberger Róza, Kir. Helmecz	Mozalka
113	1892 ápril. 26.	Majer Menyhért	/		/		Schwarcz Abrahám, szűcs, Mozalka	Weisz Záni, Ó-Pályi	Mozalka
114	1892 ápril. 28.	Relli		/	/		Weinberger Sámuel, gazdálkodó, Barasznya	Braun Lina, Kisvarda	Parasznya
115	1892 máj. 2.	Heléna		/	/		Klein Márton, szeszfőző, Karász	Grünberger Háni, Mozalka	N. Bátor, Mozalka
116	1892 máj. 11.	Eszter		/	/		Friedländer József, kereskedő, Gyulaháza	Löwi Relli, Gebe	Gebe
117	1892 máj. 15.	Jolán posthuma		/	/		Czuckermann Mózes, fuvaros, Gebe	Grünstein Mária, N. Bátor	Gebe
118	1892 máj. 15.	Dezső	/		/		Zafir Jakab, gazdálkodó, Gebe	Czuckermann Czilli, Fehértó	Gebe
[illegible]	[illegible] 92	[illegible]		/	/		Winkler Abrahám, czipész	Wagner Záli	

Birth record of Helen Klein, the author's maternal grandmother (Item 115). This record was located among the Jewish material of the Mormon Church.

PROFESSIONAL GENEALOGICAL ASSISTANCE

There are several extremely talented researchers who have made themselves available for free-lance assignments. Although I would surely urge you to do as much research yourself as you can, I wouldn't want to rule out the possibility that a professional researcher can help.

Research is an art. This became clear to me when I was studying for my degree in Library Science. When a librarian is given a research question, a search strategy must be developed. Some people have minds that work like a flowchart. They can easily figure out how to put things together to get results in their research. Where one librarian will be stumped by a question, another will know what research tools are available; what questions to ask; what risks to take; and how to make progress.

The same is true for professional genealogists. Some are better, some worse. Some quick, others slow. Since they usually charge by the hour, the costs can add up. But if you locate a top-notch researcher and can clearly define the assignment and the parameters, hiring a researcher can be quite useful. I'd especially urge you to consider a researcher for very specific tasks, such as the location of particular documents from government agencies.

The following list was compiled by the Committee of Professional Jewish Genealogists. This is not an endorsement of anyone, but rather a start in the direction of locating a researcher, if you want one.

Committee of Professional Jewish Genealogists

The following list was provided to the Association of Jewish Genealogical Societies by the Committee of Professional Jewish Genealogists. Members of this committee are all members of a Jewish Genealogical Society and charge fees for their services. Each genealogist provided the information regarding his/her areas of specialization and services. If you are interested in the services of one of the professional researchers listed below, please contact him or her directly. Write a brief letter stating your research needs, and enclose a business-size (#10) self-addressed stamped envelope with your request. Researchers will respond with information about their fees and services. Telephone numbers are home numbers unless otherwise noted. Neither the Committee of Professional Jewish Genealogists not the AJGS assume any responsibility for research work contracted through this listing. For additional information about this committee, contact Marsha Saron Dennis or Eileen Polakoff, chairpersons.

Hungarian-Jewish Records at the Family History Library

Mandok	SZ	B	1886-1895	642,907
Mandok	SZ	MD	1886-1895	642,908
Marcali	SO	B	1774-1895	642,887
Marcali	SO	M	1807-1895	642,887
Marcali	SO	BMD	1845-1895	642,888
Marcali	SO	D	1851-1895	642,888
Mateszalka	ST	BMD	1863-1895	642,920
Mezobereny	BE	BMD	1879-1895	642,747
Mezocsat	BO	BMD	1851-1895	642,767
Mezogyan	BI	BMD	1878-1885	642,758
Mezokeresztes	BO	BMD	1851-1895	642,767
Mezokovesd	BO	BMD	1851-1895	642,768
Mezoladany	SZ	M	1858	642,908
Mezoladany	SZ	B	1876-1885	642,908
Mezoladany	SZ	D	1878-1885	642,908
Mezopeterd	BI	BMD	1877-1884	642,759
Mezoszilas District	VE	BMD	1854-1885	642,932
Mezoszilasve	VE	BMD	1841-1895	642,943
Mezotur	JA	BMD	1850-1895	642,832
Mihalydi	SZ	BMD	1850-1885	642,915
Mihalyfa	ZA	BMD	1866-1895	642,948
Mikepercs	HA	BMD	1886	642,759
Mindszent	BA	BMD	1851-1880	642,733
Mindszent	CS	BMD	1851-1895	642,784
Miskolc	BO	B	1836-1883	642,772
Miskolc	BO	B	1838-1881	642,769
Miskolc	BO	Cen	1848	719,823
Miskolc	BO	D	1851-1882	642,775
Miskolc	BO	M	1851-1895	642,774
Miskolc	BO	D	1871-1895	642,771
Miskolc	BO	M	1871-1875	642,770
Miskolc	BO	BMD	1879-1886	642,770
Miskolc	BO	B	1882-1895	642,770
Miskolc	BO	M	1882-1888	642,770
Miskolc	BO	D	1883-1895	642,776
Miskolc	BO	B	1884-1895	642,773
Miskolc	BO	M	1889-1895	642,771
Modor	??	Cen	1848	719,823
Mohacs	BA	Fam	1850	642,735
Mohacs	BA	BMD	1851-1895	642,735
Monor	PE	BMD	1835-1895	642,861
Monor	PE	BMD	1837-1895	642,862
Monostorpalyi	BI	BMD	1889-1895	642,759
Mor	FE	BMD	1841-1895	642,798
Moson	MO	BMD	1835-1895	601,568
Mosonmagyarovar	MO	BMD	1835-1895	601,568
Muraszombat	VA	BMD	1835-1895	642,935
Nadudvar	HA	BMD	1850-1895	642,813
Nagyabony	PE	BMD	1837-1895	642,846
Nagyatad	SO	BM	1851-1895	642,888
Nagyatad	SO	D	1851-1877	642,888
Nagyatad	SO	D	1860-1895	642,889
Nagyatad	SO	BMD	1861-1895	642,889
Nagybajom	BI	BMD	1845-1895	642,753
Nagybajom	SO	BMD	1856-1895	642,889
Nagybajom	SO	BMD	1856-1895	642,890
Nagydobos	ST	BMD	1859-1885	642,920
Nagyecsed	ST	BMD	1856-1885	642,920
Nagyharsany	BI	BMD	1877-1885	642,758
Nagykallo	SZ	BMD	1844-1895	642,909
Nagykanizsa	ZA	BMD	1835-1895	642,949
Nagykata	PE	B	1851-1895	642,862
Nagykata	PE	MD	1851-1885	642,862
Nagykata	PE	BMD	1859-1895	642,863
Nagykoros	PE	BMD	1834-1895	642,864
Nagyleta	BI	BMD	1875-1895	642,759
Nagymarton	SP	BMD	1833-1895	700,813
Nagyoroszi	NO	BMD	1850-1895	642,843
Nagyrabe	BI	BMD	1875-1895	642,759
Nagysimonyi	VA	BMD	1851-1895	642,936
Nagyszalonta	BI	B	1854-1895	642,761
Nagyszalonta	BI	D	1854-1876	642,761
Nagyszalonta	BI	M	1855/1895	642,761
Nagyszombat	??	Cen	1848	719,823
Nagyteteny	PE	B	1760-1895	642,865
Nagyteteny	PE	M	1820-1895	642,865
Nagyteteny	PE	BMD	1851-1895	642,866
Nagyteteny	PE	D	1851-1895	642,865
Nagyvarsany	SZ	BMD	1876-1885	642,918
Nagyvazsony	VE	BMD	1842-1895	642,941
Nemesdomolk	VA	BMD	1877-1895	642,933
Nemesszalok	VA	BMD	1875-1888	642,936
Nemetkeresztur	SP	BMD	1827-1895	700,836
Nemetujvar	VA	BMD	1841-1895	700,702
Nyirabrany	SZ	BMD	1867-1884	642,759
Nyiracsad	SZ	BMD	1863-1895	642,910
Nyiradony	SZ	BMD	1871-1885	642,759
Nyirbator	SZ	BMD	1845-1895	642,911
Nyirbator	SZ	BMD	1851-1895	642,912
Nyirbogat	SZ	BMD	1851-1885	642,913
Nyirderzs	ST	M	1876-1885	642,920
Nyiregyhaza	SZ	BMD	1866-1895	642,913
Nyirgelse	SZ	B	1850-1885	642,913
Nyirgelse	SZ	MD	1866-1885	642,913
Nyiribrony	SZ	BMD	1852-1880	642,913
Nyirkarasz	SZ	BMD	1876-1895	642,913
Nyirlugos	SZ	BMD	1870-1885	642,913
Nyirmada	SZ	M	1851-1895	642,914
Nyirmada	SZ	BD	1880-1895	642,914
Nyirmeggyes	ST	BMD	1853-1895	642,921
Nyirmihalydi	SZ	BMD	1850-1885	642,915
Nyirtass	SZ	BMD	1852-1895	642,915
Ocsod	BE	BMD	1850-1886	642,748
Odombovar	TO	B	1851-1895	642,924
Odombovar	TO	M	1874-1895	642,924
Odombovar	TO	D	1886-1895	642,924
Okany	BI	BMD	1877-1885	642,759
Okecske	PE	BMD	1851-1895	642,872
Olahapati	BI	BMD	1877-1882	642,759
Olaszilszka	ZE	BMD	1841-1895	642,953
Onod	BO	BMD	1851-1895	642,777
Opalyi	ST	BMD	1874-1885	642,921
Orladany	SZ	M	1858	642,908
Orladany	SZ	B	1876-1885	642,908
Orladany	SZ	D	1878-1885	642,908
Oroshaza	BE	BMD	1874-1895	642,747
Oroszvar	MO	BMD	1835-1895	601,569
Ozd	BO	BMD	1867-1895	642,777
Pacsa	ZA	BMD	1838-1895	642,950
Paks	TO	B	1830-1893	642,929
Paks	TO	BMD	1852-1895	642,931
Paks	TO	BMD	1887-1895	642,929
Pand	PE	BMD	1860-1895	642,867
Pap	SZ	BMD	1878-1894	642,915
Papa	VE	BMD	1848-1895	642,942
Papos	ST	BMD	1874-1885	642,921
Paszto	HE	BMD	1833-1895	642,822
Patahaza	GY	BMD	1839-1844	642,806
Patroha	SZ	BMD	1852-1895	642,915
Pecel	PE	BMD	1859-1884	642,867
Pecs	BA	Cen	1848	719,823
Pecs	BA	BM	1851-1895	642,736
Pecs	BA	D	1851-1895	642,737
Pecs	BA	B	1860-1895	642,737
Pecs	BA	MD	1860-1895	642,738
Pecs District	BA	BMD	1851-1885	642,738
Pecs District	BA	BMD	1864-1888	642,739

The Encyclopedia of Jewish Genealogy—Volume I, *includes a listing of Hungarian-Jewish, German-Jewish and Polish-Jewish records in the archives of the Mormon Church.*

Gad Alexander
Postfach 900 106
D-51111 Köln +49 2203-34245
Germany Fax: +49 221-247567

Nancy Arbeiter
14 Rockwood Lane
Needham, MA 02192 (617) 449-9158

Specialty: MA, New England, Amsterdam
Services: Family research/histories, record searching, lectures, consultations

Norma Arbit
4530 Woodley Ave
Encino, CA 91436 (818) 981-0590

Specialty: Russia—especially Ukraine, U.S. records
Services: Family research/histories, lectures

Jordan Auslander
309 East 90th St #7
New York, NY 10128-5282 (212) 876-6917

Specialty: Metro NYC; NYC area cemeteries; Slovak and Hungarian records; LDS research
Services: Family research, lectures, tutoring, title searches

Charles B. Bernstein
5400 S. Hyde Park Blvd 10C
Chicago, Il 60615 (312) 324-6362(H) 263-0005(O)

Specialty: Chicago, California, rabbinic genealogy
Services: Record searching (Chicago, including courthouse), book publisher (for clients)

Warren Blatt
27-1 Georgetown Drive
Framingham, MA 01701 (508) 620-0659

Specialty: Polish vital records and translations, immigration, naturalization
Services: Lectures, consultation

Philip Bloom
36 Fairfield St
Watertown, MA 02172 (617) 924-4029

Specialty: MA, RI; Hebrew, Jewish historical
Services: Family research, beginner's workshops, displays and presentations

Milton E. Botwinick
P.O. Box 13464 (215) 925-0379
Philadelphia, PA 19101-3464 Fax: (609) 869-0368

Specialty: Philadelphia, PA and Southern NJ, Jewish records, South Eastern PA, Presbyterian records
Services: Oral history, locating lost relatives, family research

Carol Clapsaddle
34 Ha-Haiell St
97891 Jerusalem, Israel (02) 322-207

Specialty: Israel; Eastern Europe; Holocaust
Services: Family and record research, search for relatives in Israel, Holocaust records, work in Hebrew and English

Sandra Cohen
102 Serpentine Lane
Albertson, NY 11507 (516) 621-6344

Services: Family research and record searching

Daphne Dennis
90 LaSalle St #13A
New York, NY 10027 (516) 678-4462

Specialty: New York City
Services: Family research/histories, record searching

Marsha Saron Dennis
885 West End Ave #3A
New York, NY 10025 (212) 749-2219

Specialty: New York City (1850 to present), USA
Services: Family research/histories, record searching, estates, searching for heirs, writing, consultations

Nancy J. Deutsch-Sinderbrand
111-32 76th Ave #3C
Forest Hills, NY 11375 (718) 544-6721

Specialty: Cleveland, New York; Czech, Slovakian and French resources; cemetery research

Services: Lectures, record searches, oral history/interviews

Alex E. Friedlander
169 Stratford Rd
Brooklyn, NY 11218 (718) 693-7169

Specialty: Polish archival records and other sources on nineteenth century Polish Jews; Suwalki Gubernia

Services: Family research, record searching, lectures

Lucille Gudis
600 West End Ave
New York, NY 10024 (212) 799-8660

Services: Family research, record searching, workshops

Laura Horowitz Klein
1062 S. Alvira St
Los Angeles, CA 90035 (213) 935-4838

Specialty: Polish nineteenth century, Jewish customs

Services: Classes, lectures, record searching

Simon B. Lerner
305 West End Ave #504
New York, NY 10023 (212) 288-7142

Specialty: New York State

Services: Family research, record searching, in-depth library research

Herb Mautner
6507 Longridge Ave
Van Nuys, CA 91401 (818) 761-1856

Specialty: Germany (Bavaria and Duchy of Anhalt); Bohemia (Czechoslovakia) up to 1933

Services: Family research, teaching/lectures, translations

Adele Miller
5445 No. Sheridan Rd #1605
Chicago, IL 60640 (312) 275-0941(H) 282-7600(O)

Services: Translations (Polish, Yiddish, English)

Gary Mokotoff
P.O. Box 1134 (201) 837-8300
Teaneck, NJ 07666 Fax: (201) 837-6272

Specialty: General Jewish genealogy, Holocaust research
Services: Lectures and workshops

Thomas Wolff Noy
3510 Fleetwood Dr
Salt Lake City, UT 84109 (801) 277-8752

Specialty: German Jewish
Services: Family research, record searching, some translation

Judith Persin
3018 Kadema Dr
Sacramento, CA 95864 (916) 485-7258

Specialty: Jewish genealogy and Northern California research
Services: Family research/histories, record searching

Eileen Polakoff
240 West End Ave #15-A (212) 787-4371
New York, NY 10023 Fax: (201) 837-6272

Specialty: New York City; USA; Eastern Europe
Services: Family research/histories, record searching, consultations

David Priever
1470 S. Sherbourne Dr #1
Los Angeles, CA 90035-3520 (310) 289-8701

Specialty: NY-Catskill region (Sullivan, Ulster, etc. counties); New York cemeteries; Chile and Argentina

Nicki Russler
6900 Woodland Lane
Knoxville, TN 37919 (615) 584-6422

Specialty: nineteenth century Polish records; Suwalki and environs
Services: Family research/histories, record searches

George Sackheim
9151 Crawford
Skokie, IL 60076 (708) 673-6321

Specialty: Rabbinic genealogy
Services: Family research/histories, lectures

Michelle Sandler
11751 Cherry St
Los Alamitos, CA 90720 (213) 430-7610

Specialty: Russian-Polish; Orange County, CA; U.S. Census, naturalizations and arrival records
Services: Family research, record searching, lectures

Sara Edell Schafler
1501 Beacon St #505
Brookline, MA 02146 (617) 277-5622

Specialty: General Jewish Genealogy and Rabbinic
Services: Classes, seminars, lectures, Jewish schools

Ida Cohen Selavan, PhD.
2657 Vera Ave #3
Cincinnati, OH 45237 (513) 531-8788(H) 221-1875(O)

Specialty: Eastern Europe and Western Pennsylvania
Services: Translations (Hebrew and Yiddish); library research

Leonard Spialter
2536 England Ave
Dayton, OH 45406 (513) 253-3171 or 277-3995(eves)

Specialty: Dayton, OH Jewish Community; free-form family and community databases
Services: SW Ohio family searches; computer programming

Regina Wassercier Spiszman
5921 Simpson Ave
North Hollywood, CA 91607 (818) 769-6941 or 5326

Specialty: Poland, Brazil, Australia, England; U.S.: IL, MI and NY
Services: Family research/histories, consultations, lectures

Betty Proviser Starkman
1260 Stuyvessant Rd
Birmingham, MI 48301 (313) 646-0332

Specialty: Eastern Europe; MI: all time periods; Holocaust
Services: Family histories, record searching, lectures, consultations, author (Detroit Jewish News), locate relatives

Renée Stern Steinig
37 Westcliff Dr (516) 549-9532
Dix Hills, NY 11746 Fax: (516) 673-0587

Specialty: NYC, Long Island, Holocaust, "lost" family
Services: Family research, record searches, cemetery research (Queens, Long Island), consultations

Eileen Joyce Wasserman, M.A., M.F.C.C.
1835 So. Camden Ave #308
West Los Angeles, CA 90025 (310) 479-1844

Specialty: Philadelphia, Los Angeles, Eastern Europe
Services: Research families/records, interview and locate family, teach and lecture, consultations

Miriam Weiner, C.G.
136 Sandpiper Key (201) 866-4075
Secaucus, NJ 07094 Fax: (201) 864-9222

Services: Consultations, lectures, Holocaust sources, author, "Routes to Roots" genealogy tours, customized visits to ancestral towns and research in Ukraine and Moldova archives

Geraldine Frey Winerman
4660 Varna Ave
Sherman Oaks, CA 91423 (818) 784-7277

Specialty: U.S., NY, England, Sephardic research
Services: Family research, lectures, beginning genealogy classes

Suzan Fischer Wynne
3128 Brooklawn Terrace
Chevy Chase, MD 20815 (301) 657-3389

Specialty: Galicia; Baltimore and Washington; Federal records
Services: Consultation, record searching, lecture/workshops, interviews

Jim Yarin
1063 Beacon St #6
P.O. Box 1555
Brookline, MA 02146 (617) 232-3937

Specialty: Library research: catalogs, newspapers, directories and abstracts; Boston and N.E.; Grodno Gub; unique surnames
Services: Research/histories/newsletters; missing relatives

Ten Commandments for Jewish Genealogists

Another important contribution made by Rabbi Malcolm Stern was that of a role model. Anyone who ever met him knows that he was an exceptional soul. His way with people was compassionate and sensitive. The following "Ten Commandments for Genealogists," written by Rabbi Stern, should be taken seriously. They have been created by a master genealogist.

I. *I am a genealogist dedicated to true knowledge about the families I am researching.*

II. *Thou shalt use family traditions with caution and only as clues.*

III. *Thou shalt not accept as gospel every written record or printed word.*

IV. *Thou shalt not hang nobility or royalty on your family tree without verifying with experts.*

V. *Thou shalt clearly label the questionable and the fairy tale.*

VI. *Thou shalt handle all records in such a way that the next users will find them in the same conition you did.*

VII. *Thou shalt credit those who help you and ask permission of those whose work you use.*

VIII. *Thou shalt not query any source of information without supplying postage.*

IX. *Thou shalt respect the sensitivities of the living in whatever you record but tell the truth about the dead.*

X. *Thou shalt not become a genealogical teacher or authority without appropriate training and certification.*

5

The Names in Your Family

A GOOD NAME IS RATHER TO BE CHOSEN THAN GREAT RICHES

> A good name is rather to be chosen than great riches.
>
> PROV. 22:1

Our names are links with our past, with Jewish history, and with our tradition, which each of us carries with us every moment. Both our first and surnames represent, when analyzed, a piece of history. Whether it be our first names (which in European Jewish tradition are usually in memory of beloved persons who are deceased), or our surnames (which often contain fascinating clues to help us identify our ancestors), our names are not merely labels to distinguish us from others, but rather, are special designations that place us in time and history.

Our surnames stretch back for generations. Like our heritage, our names have been passed down to us, generation to generation, until they arrived in the present. Our surnames provide us with clues about our early ancestors. At some point in time your surname was taken by (or given to) someone in your family's past, and it then continued through time to you. Of course, we must remember that although each of us has one surname, we are equally the descendants of many families with just as many surnames. Our custom has usually been to take the surname of our father, but we are just as much members of our mother's family. In addition, we are more than just the product of two families, since each of our parents is the product of two families. Therefore, it is important to keep in mind that when we discuss our surnames we are speaking of many more than one. In fact, as you discover the names of your ancestors and acknowledge the list of names that are *yours,* you will be able to understand more of your own personal history by examining the nature of your many surnames.

Although our names are usually generations old, they are not ancient. Use of surnames by Jews is a relatively recent custom considering the length of Jewish history. In the Torah, there are no surnames, nor were there any used in biblical times. It was sufficient to have one name that distinguished each member of a community from the others. In the later books of the Bible, we do find the first evidences of surnames, as in "Elijah the Tishbite" or "Uriah the Hittite." But although these names do add on place names to identify the individuals, they are not surnames as we know them today. If Uriah the Hittite moved to another location, his place name would probably change. In the same way, if Uriah the Hittite had a child, the place name would not be passed on. Rather, the child, if a male, would be called "—ben Uriah." This use of the term "ben" for "son of" or "bas" for "daughter of" is known as patronymics, and was the common way of identifying Jews for centuries before surnames as we know them today were used. But the use of additional names in biblical times, such as place names and patronymics, were precursors of later sources of surnames. A current surname like Ginzburg is a place name, and a name such as Meyerson is a patronym.

Another kind of name used in the Bible foreshadows recent surnaming customs. Descriptive names are found in the Bible, such as Hakotz in Ezra 2:61. "Ha-kotz" means "the thorn," which is a descriptive term in the same way that a surname like Klein, meaning "small," is a descriptive surname of recent days. Names in the Talmud reflect the same kind of customs, although names of locations, patronymics and occupations are used, they are still not hereditary. Vocational names, which are not found in the Bible, foreshadow modern occupation names. Talmudic examples of this are Abba Jose the Potter and Daniel the Tailor. The more recent "Snyder" is the same occupational identification of a tailor.

Patronymics in the Talmud are quite popular. Simon ben Gamliel means Simon, son of Gamliel. There are even times when we find patronymics representing two generations, such as Raba bar bar Chana, which means that Raba was the grandson of Chana. (The term "bar" and the term "ben" both mean "son of.") We find nicknames appearing in the Talmud also. Zeira the Younger is an example of this. Also in the Talmud are examples of priestly designations, known to us in modern times by the surnames Cohen or Levy. In the Talmud we find individuals such as Ishmael the High Priest and Jose Ha-kohen. But again, these names would not necessarily be passed down to children.

For centuries, surnames were not used, as we know them, by Jews. Sephardic Jews adopted surnames from the Arabs who not only used a similar patronymic, that of "ibn" to designate "son of," but who also added the father's name without the use of "ibn." But Central and Northern European Jews, even throughout the Middle Ages, generally did not use surnames. Jews were isolated from larger communities and simply did not develop the need to adopt family names. During the tenth and eleventh centuries surname usage began to become popular, because of the rise of cities and the rise of commerce, both of which stimulated the necessity for family names for practical reasons. But again, it is largely the Sephardim who were affected by this. They developed a popular use of occupational names, nicknames and place names. A famous Sephardic occupational name is Abulafia, meaning "father of medicine," and another is Gabbai, which represents a synagogue official. Among place names, we are familiar with Cardozo from Spain and Montefiore from Italy.

The isolation of the Ashkenazim, as we have said, brought the use of surnames much later. It is interesting to note that in the fourteenth century there were only about 700 Jews in Frankfort on Main and, in the sixteenth century, Prague had only 1200 Jews. From this it is easy to see that the need for surnames just did not exist among the isolated Jewish communities of Northern Europe. When an official register of a city needed to record Jews for whatever reason, the designation "the Jew" was often used. Jews themselves continued to use place names, patronymics, occupation names and other forms of family names, but these names lasted for just a generation or so rather than being kept as a permanent surname.

It was actually not until the late eighteenth century that surnames as we know them today were used commonly among Jews. This is why, as we enter the period of Jewish history before this time, it is exceedingly difficult to trace our own specific families back to these years. In all likelihood, if you are an Ashkenazi Jew, the surname that is yours today was not that of your ancestors in the 1600s or even a good part of the 1700s. This is because it was not until 1787 that Jews were first required to register last names, and this date reflects only one part of Europe, that of Austria. Switzerland, for example, did not require its Jews to register last names until 1863.

Of course, this does not mean that family names did not exist in these places before those dates. It does mean, however, that Jews were given the opportunity to change their names and register them permanently at these times. In some cases names were assigned to Jews, and at other times they had to be bought. In any case, surnames among Jews are a recent arrival, even though family names might have existed traditionally for much longer.

Jews in the Middle Ages, for example, did use names to identify their families, and many families grew attached to those names and continued to use them. A fascinating development took place in Frankfort on Main during the Middle Ages. Jews were forced to live in a special section of the city called the Judengasse, and registration was done based on the house that each family occupied. Houses at this time were not numbered but rather were labeled by signs that hung outside. The signs were colorful and represented many kinds of images, including animals, colors and fruits. A famous surname that reflects a house sign of this time is Rothschild, which means "red shield." The name Loeb might reflect the use of the image of a lion on these house signs, as Gans would reflect the sign of a goose. These sign images were often carved on the tombstones of family members, adding to the permanence of the house signs as surnames. An interesting note pertaining to the use of house signs by Jews is that when the Jews in Frankfort's Judengasse were ordered in 1776 to use numbers on their houses rather than signs, there was such resistance that the whole Jewish community was fined.

We cannot say, however, that family names tended to be kept within families. Sometimes, names were changed by individuals themselves; sometimes surnames existed, but changed from parent to child.

The year 1787 is an important date in the history of the Jewish surname, for in that year an Austrian Empire order compelled the Jews to adopt surnames. This was the first time in history that Jews were forced to take surnames. Officers were appointed to register all Jews with these names, and if any Jews refused, the officers were to force a name upon them. It was at this time that many meaningless names were assigned to individuals, and this accounts, surely, for some names which we do not know the origins at the present time.

On July 20, 1808, Napoleon issued a decree of a similar nature, insisting that Jews adopt fixed names. This was also done in Frankfort in 1807 and in Baden in 1809.

The same kind of legislation was enacted throughout Europe at different times. It happened in 1812 in Prussia, 1813 in Bavaria, 1834 in Saxony and 1845 in Russia. In each case, Jews were required to register family names. There were several reasons for these enactments. The levying of taxes was made much simpler with permanent surnames, as was the conscription of Jewish soldiers. A third reason was the effort to assimilate the Jews, at least in cases where no specific list of names to be used was issued. When lists of restricted names existed, the exact opposite purpose was intended—to single out Jews among the larger community.

An additional reason for the requirement of surnames was that it was a clever means of obtaining additional revenues for the government. This occurred when taxes were imposed for the registration of the names. It is also known that unfriendly local officials would either impose unattractive names upon Jews or threaten to do so unless a nicer name was "purchased." In response to Napoleon's decree, some of the names imposed upon Jews included Eselskopf (meaning "donkey's head"), Fresser (meaning "glutton"), and Lumpe (meaning "hoodlum"). In Austria in 1787, the unpopular names included Nussnacker (meaning "nutcracker"), and Puderbeutel (meaning "powder bag").

Those names were given with cruelty, and nicer names often came at high prices. There were also many opportunities to choose whatever name one wanted, however, and in Northeastern Germany, a series of names with "Rose" in them was common, such as Rosenzweig, Rosenthal, Rosenblum and Rosenstein.

Amusing stories of how individuals and communities obtained their names have been preserved. It is known, for example, that in one community a rabbi opened a prayer book and went word by word assigning names to people from words in the book. In another case, an official asked a person for his name. He said "Yankele." The official asked him again, to which he replied "Poshet Yankele," which means "Simply Yankele." His name thus became Poshet. In a similar case, when a family was asked its name, and they replied "Anu lo neda," meaning "We don't know," they were called Neuda.

Often, I have imagined what it might be like to be forced to choose the surname that will be in your family permanently. It must surely have been a major decision, and this is reflected, perhaps, in the time periods given to the Jews to take a name. Several months of decision were allowed in some cases. Think what it must have been like. Suddenly, you have to choose from any name or word there is (except, of course, in the cases where a limited list was provided—in which case it is a different kind of incredible decision) and be satisfied. When the edicts were enacted, people must have thought that the choice would be a permanent one. I have pretended that I was put into this situation. I suggest that you do the same. What surname would you choose?

Our surnames today come from a large variety of sources, and it is often difficult, unfortunately, to know the meaning of the word, or for that matter the reason for the name being attached to the family. It is likely that people with the family name Snyder had an ancestor who was a tailor, but it is impossible to know what the reason behind a name like Schwartz might be. Meaning "black," the word might have been a description of someone's complexion, or it could have been chosen as the name of a color, or it could have been some other etymology that will never be found.

Nevertheless, there is much we can learn from our names, and it would be useful to examine the different types of Jewish surnames to help us to identify and make tentative conclusions as to the origins of our own names. Jewish surnames can be divided into several categories, and we will now discuss each of them.

Patronymics

As we have discussed, the patronymic is an early form of name, and although patronymics were originally not used as surnames as we now use them, they were eventually adapted to modern surname usage. It is known that when Jews were ordered to take surnames, many people simply used the patronymic form that they were currently using. This way, a man named Abraham ben Isaac would become Abraham Isaacs.

The patronym was the simplest way of forming a surname, and they can be found in every language. The Austrian and German patronym would be a name ending in "sohn," such as "Abramsohn," "Isaacsohn," or "Jacobsohn." The Slavic patronym is "vitch," as in Abromovitch. Other Slavic patronymics include the suffixes "-ov," "-off," "-eff" and "-kin," which all indicate "descendant of." Examples of these would include "Malkov" and "Rivkin." It is interesting to note here that these are not patronyms but rather matronyms—named after a female name. The two examples here would mean "descendant of Malka" and "descendant of Rivka." In Germany and Austro-Hungary, the mother's name was a frequent source of the establishment of a surname. Other examples of this are "Perles," "Gitles," and "Zeldes."

Another form of surname, though not a patronym, is a name based on the first name of a wife. This kind of name has been formed by adding the suffix "mann" on to a wife's first name, as in Estermann, being the husband of Esther, and Perlmann, being the husband of Perl.

There are suffixes for other languages as well that indicate a patronymic. Thus, the suffix "-wicz" is a Slavic ending, "-vici" is Romanian, and "-witz" is another German patronymic ending.

Place Names

Perhaps the largest group of Jewish surnames is the one based on locations. We are able to learn specific information about our ancestors with place names, assuming they have surnames derived from places. If this is the case, it is fair to assume that an ancestor of yours once came from the location indicated by the name. If, for example, your surname happens to be Berliner, it would be logical to assume that someone in that line of ancestors came from Berlin.

Earlier than Ashkenazi Jews, the Sephardim often took place names as their surnames. We find Spanish surnames like "de Cordova" and "de Lima." From Portugal we have "Lisbona," from Italy there is "Lucca" and "Padua" and from Holland we find a name like DeVries derived from the location of Friesland.

Every European country has inspired Jewish surnames, reflecting the extent to which Jews migrated around the continent. Sometimes the name was as general as a country name. At other times it was as specific as the sign attached to a house. In fact, we find Jewish place-surnames as countries, regions, towns, streets and houses. There is a mystery surrounding the derivation of surnames from places. It is not known why there are some towns with no surnames representing them. Even in the cases of towns with large Jewish populations, there are some that did not seem to inspire names.

There are several suffixes that have been added to places in order to turn them into surnames. The suffix "-er" is a common one, as in the example already given: "Berliner." The suffix "-man" is also used, as in Osterman, which means "a man who comes from the east," adding the notion of what direction a person comes from to our list of place sources for surnames.

We have already discussed house signs, but it is appropriate to mention them again in the context of place names. House signs would have represented on them various images that were later adopted as permanent surnames. We have already mentioned Rothschild ("red shield") as an example. Others would include: Schwarzchild ("black shield"), Blum ("flower"), Buxbaum ("box tree"), Lachs ("salmon") and Baer ("bear"). One cannot be sure in all cases, however, whether the source of a name is actually from a house sign. Many Jewish surnames have been taken from names of flowers, fruits, plants, animals and stones, but were chosen for their beauty rather than adopted because of a house sign. There is also an amusing story behind one common name related to house signs. A Frankfort family of priestly descent had the name of Kahn, which is commonly known as such a name. However, they took as their house sign the picture of a boat, since "Kahn" is German for boat. In later years, members of the same family used the sign of a ship and their name became "Schiff." The name went from "Kahn" to "Schiff" because of a house sign.

Vocational Names

Vocational names are another type of Jewish surname that offers a concrete clue to family history. In fact, it is vocational names that give historians an insight into the kinds of occupations either held or permitted to be held by Jews at a certain time. When we examine old tombstones and see occupational names corresponding to certain dates, we add to our knowledge of what kinds of jobs were done by Jews in certain eras.

Vocational names are less common among Sephardim than among Ashkenazim. We have already offered one example of a Sephardic vocational name, "Abulafia," meaning "father of medicine." Other Sephardic vocational names would include "Almosnino," meaning "orator" in Arabic and "Mocatta," which is a "mason" also in Arabic.

Occupational names are taken not only from the exact title of the job but also from the materials used in the activity. A name such as "Leder," which means "leather," would stand for a tanner, just as a carpenter might have the name "Nagel," meaning "nail." Vocational names are also noted to range from the most common to the most highly respected types of occupations. We find names like "Dayan," meaning "judge," "Chazan," meaning "cantor" and "Spielman," meaning "player."

Descriptive Names

A large group of Jewish surnames comes under the heading of descriptive names. These, presumably, were descriptions of the original bearer of the name. These types of names can be separated into two different groups: physical descriptions and personality characteristics.

In the category of physical characteristics, we have names such as "Klein," meaning "small," "Kurtz," meaning "short" and "Geller," meaning "yellow," which we assume to be a hair color. In the same way, "Graubart," which means "gray beard," represents another general subheading of this group.

As for personality characteristics, we find names like "Selig," which means "happy," "Biederman," which means "worthy man," "Baruch," which means "blessed" and "Gottlieb," which means "God loving."

Another kind of descriptive name is the nickname, many of which have become surnames. We find names like Purim and Lustig (happy) among this category.

My own name, Kurzweil, can be seen perhaps as a descriptive name, although this name is one that might fall under any of several different types. The word "Kurzweil" literally means "short time," though as a compound word the meaning changes to "pastime." An additional definition of the word—as a German word—is an "entertainer" or someone who entertains by telling stories. An even earlier meaning of the word is that of "jester" in the more official sense of court entertainer. Therefore, although all the definitions have similar meanings, it is interesting (for me) to note that the name could be a simple word, a personal characteristic, or an occupation. I found it all the more fascinating when I discovered that there is one personal attribute that people repeated over and over in order to describe people in my family, and in particular my ancestors, and that is that Kurzweils are jokesters.

Names from Abbreviations

One of the most unusual sources for Jewish surnames is that of abbreviations. A popular surname—Katz—is not generally known to be an abbreviation but is just that. Although the source of "Katz" is commonly thought to be a form of the animal "cat," it is actually a short form of the phrase "Kohen Zedek," or "priest of righteousness." In the same way, the surname "Schatz" is an abbreviated form of "Sheliah Tzibbur," which means "minister of the congregation." Likewise the name "Segal" (also Segel, Seigel, etc.) is said to come from "segan leviyyah," meaning "assistant to the Levites."

Another form of abbreviation that resulted in surnames was that of the letters formed from a man's name and/or his father's name. So, for example, the name Schach is derived from Sabbatai Cohen. The name Bry comes from Ben Rabbi Israel, Brock is from Ben Rabbi Akiba, and Basch is the abbreviated form of Ben Shimeon.

There is another custom within the Jewish tradition concerning the abbreviation of names. During the Middle Ages, it was somewhat common to abbreviate names by initials. Although these names were not surnames, they did not become the general way of identifying the individual. The three most popular examples of this are "Rashi," who was actually Rabbi Solomon ben Isaac, "Rambam," who was Rabbi Moses ben Maimon and "Besht," which is an abbreviation of Baal Shem Tov.

A final type of surname for this category (though not truly an abbreviation or an actual surname) is the custom of referring to an individual by his *magnum opus,* his finest literary work. Perhaps the most famous of these is Israel Meir Ha-Kohen who is known as "Hafez Hayyim" after his work by that name. Two other examples of this are "Roke'ah," who is R. Eliazer b. Judah, and "Tur," who is R. Jacob b. Asher. Again, these were not surnames, but were abbreviated forms, in a sense, of lengthier names.

Matronymics

In the same way that a patronym is a name derived from a male source (usually the father), a matronym comes from a female source, usually the mother. Many Jewish surnames come from this source, and include names such as Perle, Rose, Hinde, Freude and Gutkind (from Gute).

Some Examples

In general, the origins of surnames can be determined by considering the several different sources we have discussed. However, there can be little certainty about this. Despite the fact that a surname potentially can be an excellent clue for insight into family history, a warning must be issued that this is speculation. In the same way that there are many sources for surnames, there are a great variety of circumstances that might have resulted in the establishment or adoption of a family name. Although the name "Snyder" means "tailor," we cannot be certain that there was a tailor in our past who adopted that name to reflect his profession. The name might have been imposed upon him, or he may have chosen it for other reasons.

Another issue regarding surnames within Jewish Tradition is the custom of taking the surname of one's father. Although this is common today, there have been times in our past when this was not the case universally among Jews. Often a child would adopt the maiden name of his or her mother and not his or her father. The reason for this was often as follows: When a Jewish child was born, often the parents were not married through civil law but only through Jewish law. Therefore, it was not uncommon for the civil law to refuse to recognize the legitimacy of the birth. This resulted in the child being required, by civil law, to take the name of the mother. This is something to keep in mind when doing family history research. It is not wise to assume that a surname automatically leads to the father of a child.

It should be repeated, however, that the study of surnames is a fascinating part of Jewish history and the history of your family. We are each the descendants of a countless number of families, and each of those families has its own surname. Each of those families has its own history as well, and each of those histories directly affects who you are.

Here are some examples of the meaning of some of my family names as well as some names of people close to me:

Alter	old
Aronson	son of Aaron
Blum	flower
Kaplan	priest
Billet	bank note
Steinsaltz	rock salt
Rothfarb	red colored
Engel	angel
Eisenberg	iron mountain
Gottlieb	beloved of God
Kurzweil	entertainment
Roth	red
Kaunfer	camphor
Meltsner	malt maker
Portnoy	tailor
Katz	righteous priest
Bulka	bread roll
Blech	baking tin
Schram	scratch
Schlaf	weak
Bauer	landworker
Amsel	thrush
Spack	sparrow
Pomerantz	orange

Examples of Jewish surnames that were originally nicknames or personality characteristics:

Ehrlich	honest
Kluger	wise
Frohlich	happy
Lustig	happy
Fruhling	spring
Sommer	summer

Sonntag	Sunday
Dienstag	Tuesday
Gittelson	son of good little one
Friedmann	free man
Shalom	peace
Sholem	peace
Solomon	peace
Gottschalk	God's servant
Gottlieb	God loving
Lipgott	God loving

Examples of Jewish surnames from occupations:

Becker	baker
Fleischer	butcher
Breuer	brewer
Weber	weaver
Farber	painter
Goldschmidt	goldsmith
Kramer	merchant
Wechsler	money changer
Ackermann	farmer
Brenner	distiller
Gerber	tanner
Leder	tanner (leather)
Nadel	needle (leather)
Scher	shears
Nagel	nail (carpenter)
Rabad	"Resh av beth din" (rabbi)
Babad	"ben av beth din" (son of rabbi)
Rabinovitch	son of rabbi
Schecter	slaughterer
Schochet	ritual slaughterer
Singer	cantor
Cantor	cantor
Kauffman	merchant
Drucker	printer
Bookbinder	bookbinder
Zimmerman	carpenter
Bauman	builder
Bauer	builder
Feldman	shepherd

Berger	shepherd
Schlosser	locksmith
Koster	doorkeeper
Schuster	shoemaker
Schneider	tailor
Snyder	tailor
Waldman	woodman
Sandler	cobbler
Metzger	butcher
Schnitzner	carver
Rokeach	spice merchant
Kunzler	artist

Examples of Jewish surnames from animal names:

Wolf	wolf (also Wulf, Wolk, Seiffer, Lopez)
Lowe	lion
Hirsch	stag (also Hartwig, Harris, Herschel, Herzl, Cerf)
Bar	bear (also Beerman, Berman, Berish)
Ochs	ox
Fuchs	fox
Adler	eagle
Geier	vulture
Fink	finch
Hahn	cock

Examples of Jewish surnames from physical characteristics:

Alt	old
Braun	brown
Gelber or Geller	yellow
Klein	small
Kurtz	short
Jung	young
Gross	large
Neu	new
Reise	giant
Roth	red
Schnell	fast
Schwartz	black
Schon	beautiful
Steinhart	hard as stone
Stark	strong

Personal Names

Ever since the first humans, Adam and Eve, people have had personal names. A great amount of significance has always been given to names, beginning in the Bible when we witness, among others, Abram becoming Abraham, Sarai becoming Sarah and Jacob becoming Israel. The change of one's name, in this biblical setting, symbolizes a major change in one's personality and one's being.

Throughout history we find similar examples of customs and beliefs that reflect the seriousness with which we have looked upon names. Popular in the Middle Ages and still practiced among many in modern times is the custom of changing the name of a person who is seriously ill in the hope that the Angel of Death would be confused and be unable to locate the person. One of the most popular names given at this time was Chaim, meaning "life," in order to add still another significance to names. The power of this custom is reflected in my own family. My father was renamed Chaim because he was very ill as a young child. When he grew up his parents told him of this, and he in turn has told me. This story of my father's "renaming" became a favorite of mine as a child. It was a deeply powerful story for me, inspiring my imagination to envision the Angel of Death, the renaming ceremony and a young child (who grows up to be my father) getting well after a prolonged illness. Stories, as well as names, can have a profound effect on a person. This custom, which is known as "meshanneh shem," can be found in the Talmud.

The same type of belief is found in a custom that was, in all probability, begun by Judah the Pious. He forbade his immediate descendants from bearing his name or the name of his father during their lifetime in the belief that since a man's soul was bound up with his name, the soul would be deprived of its rest if someone else bore it. Although this is not a universally accepted custom, it is generally true that children are not named after living relatives. Among the reasons for this custom is that the Angel of Death might be unnecessarily confused and might take the wrong person. Finally, the custom of naming children after relatives who are deceased is based on the notion that to do this would be an honor to the deceased. It is also an attempt to "inject" the child with the qualities of the deceased.

It has been customary to name children after deceased relatives or other individuals who are greatly respected. It is common, for example, to name a child after a man's teacher. In European Jewish communities it also became common to name the eldest son after the paternal or maternal grandfather. Because of this, it is curious to examine the repetition of certain few names within many generations. For example, in one family we find the following: Meshullam b. Moses b. Ithiel b. Moses b. Kalonymus b. Meshullam b. Kalonymus b. Moses b. Kalonymus b. Jekuthiel b. Moses b. Meshullam b. Ithiel b. Meshullam. The interesting aspect of this genealogy is that among the fourteen people who span three centuries, we find only five names.

Ever since I can remember, the notion that I was named after someone has intrigued me and captured my imagination. I learned at a young age whom I was named for (my great-grandfather Abusch) and I have been drawn to him in a somewhat mystical way. Through stories which I have solicited about my great-grandfather, I have developed a personal relationship with him that I find difficult to describe.

As we have seen in our discussion of surnames, there was a time when individuals had only one name. Then the surname was introduced and it became universal. Today, many Jews have three names: a first, a surname and an additional first name. Many Jews have secular and Hebrew first names. At various points in history, depending on the location, Jews began to use secular first names. This inspired the custom of giving Jewish children separate Hebrew first names to use during religious ceremonies and for religious purposes. Naming ceremonies have developed for just this purpose.

In modern times, two occurrences of note relating to names have been witnessed among Jews. The first is the changing of names, usually without the consent of the individual, during the days of great immigration at U.S. ports. There are many stories of name changes that occurred when an immigration official "renamed" a Jewish immigrant by mistake, or on purpose. Of course, it often happened that immigrants would change their names without "assistance." The motive for this voluntary change of names might relate to another phenomenon, the adopting of new names by individuals who move to Israel. It is customary for a new Israeli to abandon his or her original name and replace it with a new one. Both of these customs may very well reflect a belief in the power of names. When a name changes, a person changes.

A CLOSE LOOK AT YOUR NAME

For Whom Were You Named?

In my family, I am named after my great-grandfather, my father is named after his great-grandfather and my grandfather is named after his grandfather. My mother was named after her great-aunt. My brother was named after another great-grandfather, and that great-grandfather was named after his own father's rebbe.

For whom were you named? What do you know about the person? Why did your parents name you after that person rather than someone else?

Speaking of being named after people, often an older relative will not remember who his or her great-grandparents were until you ask, "Who were you named after?" There's a good chance they were named after the great-grandparent whom they couldn't remember.

You can also try to figure out the names of people early in your family tree by noticing the names that keep repeating. Although you cannot come to any definite conclusions with this method, a repeating name might jolt someone's memory about an early ancestor with the same name.

> One's name has an influence on one's life.
>
> ELEAZER B. PEDAT, TALMUD: BERAKOT, 7B

WHAT IF YOUR NAME WAS CHANGED?

We have all heard stories of how Jewish names were often changed, shortened, or misspelled. If there is no one to ask or no one who remembers what the original name was, how can you find out the original name?

It is, of course, important to discover what your name was in the Old Country, because without this knowledge it will be impossible for you to bridge the ocean and find out about relatives and ancestors who never came to America.

There is a way to research your original name—assuming that it was changed from the one your family used in Europe—and this is by locating your immigrant ancestors' steamship passenger list (see page 301). Follow the directions for the various ways of obtaining the name of the ship and its date of arrival. If you send for a copy of the passenger list for your immigrant ancestor, it will contain his or her original name since these lists were usually made *before* the ship sailed—that is, before arrival in America when the name was changed.

Of course, when you get the passenger list, you will not find the name you know. Therefore, you will have to be a detective and try to determine who on the list was your ancestor. There are many ways of doing this because the lists will offer various clues to work with, including the person's place of birth, occupation, age and so on. Something ought to match—and you will then discover what your name was originally!

Names changes, both voluntary and involuntary, present obvious problems for genealogists. If a person has his or her name changed, it is almost impossible at times to locate the individual. A woman who marries and takes her husband's last name suddenly disappears from the records in her original name. An immigrant who either changes or shortens his own name or who has his name changed by an immigration official also cuts himself off from the family history. This situation is common in Israel. Huge numbers of Israelis have dropped their European names and replaced them with modern Israeli or Biblical names. Sometimes the change is as simple as translating a European word into a Hebrew word. For example, an Israeli with the European name of "Singer" has changed his name to "Zamir," which is the Hebrew word for singer.

I am against name changes because they cut off a person from his or her history. I can understand the symbolic meaning of a Black American adopting an African name or an Israeli adopting a modern Hebrew name, but it cuts the person off from his or her past. It might link that person with the distant past, but the recent past—for better or worse—is still a part of our experience. Recently, an Israeli who has maintained his European surname said to me, "I keep my old last name as my own personal memorial to the Holocaust victims in my family."

There is one kind of name change that I like, however. The well-known author Irving Wallace has a son named David Wallechinsky. Together, the two of them have coauthored *The People's Almanac* and *The People's Almanac #2*. Why do father and son have different yet similar last names? As the "About the Authors" page in *The People's Almanac #2* says, "David Wallechinsky was born in Hollywood, California, in 1948. In 1972 he adopted the original family name of his grandfather, whose name had been changed to 'Wallace' by an immigration agent at Ellis Island."

Some name changes are terrific!

> Names were changed as readily as clothes. From Yacov (Hebrew) or Yankel (Yiddish) to Jacob and finally to Jack. From Hyman to Howard, Leybel to Lester or Leon, Berel to Barnett or Barry, Chai-Sura to Sarah, Breina to Beatrice, Simcha to Seymour, Chatzkel to Haskell, Meyer to Max, Moishe to Mossir, Aaron to Allan.
>
> MILTON MELTZER, *TAKING ROOT*

> Properly, I ought to begin this account by telling when I was born. But—I am ashamed to admit it—I do not know. You see, I was only a Jewish girl, and in my day and time, in the place where I was born, female births were not recorded.
>
> REBECCA HIMBER BERG, FROM HER MEMOIR, "CHILDHOOD IN LITHUANIA"

Names Can Help You with Dates

It has been a Jewish tradition for many generations to name a child after a deceased member of the family, or a deceased member of a community who is well respected—such as a rebbe or teacher—so names can help you determine dates.

Let us illustrate this by using an example.

Look at the family tree that follows and notice the dates of birth indicated for the children named Abraham. As you can see, there is no date listed for the children's grandfather who is also named Abraham.

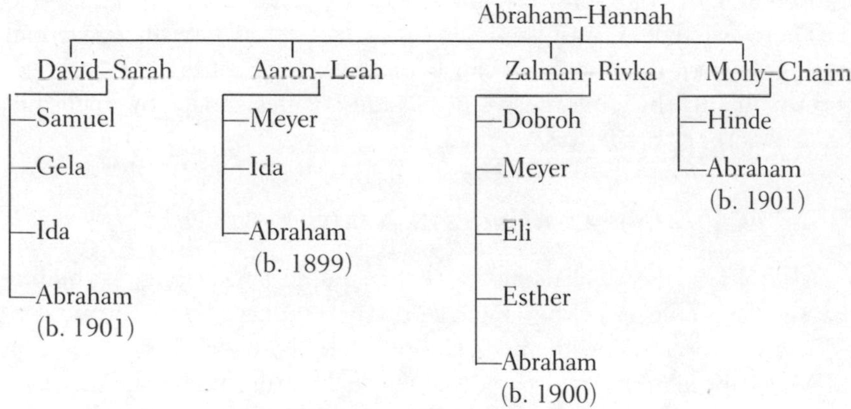

It is clear from this three-generation family tree that the four families all named a child Abraham, undoubtedly after the grandfather. They all named a child Abraham about the same time, although the earliest date was 1899. If this example represents a typical family in Europe, all four families probably named their next child after the death of Abraham. Since a child cannot, by tradition, be named after a living person, it is safe to assume that the grandfather died before 1899, and probably in that year or the year before.

Although you cannot know this for sure, nor can you know the exact date, it is reasonable to write "ca. 1899" on your family tree. The abbreviation "ca." means "circa" or "approximately."

Using this method, it is often possible to figure out older dates by the dates—and names—you already have.

> What is a good pedigree? A good name.
>
> AL-HARIZI, *TAHKEMONI*, CA. 1220

LAST NAMES FROM THE MATERNAL SIDE

Do not assume that children always took the last name of their father, or that when a couple got married they took the husband's last name.

Often the woman's surname was used. Frequently, people were married in Europe by religious ritual but not with a civil license. Because of this, the children from the marriage were not recognized as legitimate by the civil authorities (although they were legitimate as far as Jewish Law and the families were concerned!). Subsequently, the children took the mother's surname.

There existed at various times and places anti-Jewish legislation limiting Jewish marriages. Because of this, Jews often got married secretly. Again, the children were considered illegitimate by civil law, and the mother's name was adopted.

HEBREW, YIDDISH AND ENGLISH NAMES

Most Jews have two names: a secular name and a religious name. The secular name is in the language of the country where the person resides, and the religious name is Hebrew.

Many immigrants had three names: a Hebrew name, an English name, and a Yiddish name. This is because they had two names in Europe (the Yiddish was their secular name), and they adopted an additional secular name on arrival in America. My grandfather, for example, was Julius (English), Yudl (Yiddish), and Yehudah Yaakov (Hebrew-religious).

When charting your family tree, you will come across different names for the same people—sometimes even more than three when nicknames are also used. It has been my practice to record all the names used rather than to "standardize" them. I have seen Jewish genealogies where all Abes, Abbies and Abrahams became Abraham. It's more important to record a person's name as it was used from day to day than to suddenly become formal when building a family tree. Keep track of all the names used, and when deciding which name to use on a family tree, use the one that was most common, or the one that the person himself or herself liked, if you know.

> One thing is certain, I have no real feeling about my first name. I can only guess why this is. It seems to me that it may be because my parents gave it to me without any particular feeling, simply because they "liked it" (and why did they like it? because at that time it was "different"; only later were there other Franzes in the Jewish community of Cassel). It's as though my parents had seen it in a window shop, walked inside, and bought it. It has nothing traditional about it, no memory, no history, not even an anecdote, scarcely a whim—it was simply a passing fancy. A family name, a saint's name, a hero's name, a poetic name, a symbolic name, all these are good: they have grown naturally, not been bought ready-made. One should be named after somebody or something. Else a name is really only empty breath.
>
> FRANZ ROSENZWEIG

WHAT DOES YOUR NAME MEAN?

In 1977 there appeared the first book, in English, to attempt a study of Jewish surnames that included a large number of names with their meanings. *A Dictionary of Jewish Names and Their History* by Ben zion Kaganoff was the result of a hobby that Rabbi Kaganoff pursued for decades. The first half of the book is a history of Jewish surnames; the second half is a listing of nearly 1000 Jewish names with their probable meanings. Rabbi Kaganoff's book, originally published by Schocken Books, is now out of print. I would urge you to track down a copy.

In the same year as Rabbi Kaganoff's book appeared, Garland Publishing issued *Jewish and Hebrew Onomastics: A Bibliography*, by Robert Singerman. It too is out of print, but it would be a worthwhile book to consult if you were particularly interested in the subject of the origins and forms of names.

Recently, a few important books have appeared that make a significant contribution to the subject in English. I highly recommend the following two titles:

A Dictionary of Jewish Surnames from the Russian Empire, by Alexander Beider (Avotaynu, Inc., P.O. Box 900, Teaneck NJ 07666)

Once again, *Avotaynu* contributes a significant volume to help Jewish genealogists. Dayaynu! It would have been sufficient had only the incredible introduction been published. It is, without a doubt, the most informative treatise on Jewish last names available in English. The book defines 50,000 (!) Jewish surnames, gives variant spellings and other information.

Jewish Family Names and Their Origins: An Etymological Dictionary, by Heinrich W. Guggenheimer and Ave H. Guggenheimer (KTAV, 1992)

This dictionary offers the meanings of over 65,000 Jewish surnames from Ashkenazic, Sephardic, Oriental and contemporary Israeli families.

> There are men whose names are beautiful but their acts ugly.
>
> GENESIS RABBAH

SOME THOUGHTS ABOUT JEWISH NAMES

1) People with the same last name are not necessarily related to each other. If someone in your family says, "Everyone with our last name is related," the person may very well be mistaken. This goes for even the most unusual last name.
2) Most Jewish last names were *not* changed at Ellis Island. In most cases, immigration officials had the immigrant's name in writing, so most of the stories and jokes about how the official couldn't understand the name are fiction! Most names were changed voluntarily by the immigrant after arrival in this country. It was often at the encouragement of relatives who were already here, or schoolteachers' advice to new students or some such circumstance.
3) In Eastern Europe, especially among the more religious families, a child might take the surname of the mother rather than the father. This often explains why you will see that a father and a son had a different last name. The last name of the mother was often imposed by the secular authorities because of the fact that the public records did not indicate a marriage had taken place.

4) Sometimes you will find that siblings, especially boys, have different last names. Sometimes this was the result of conscription laws. For example, if the law read that the firstborn son was to be drafted, a child was represented as someone else's child to avoid the situation.
5) Never assume that there is only one way to spell your last name. You have to look for all sorts of variations. I've seen my last name spelled: Kurzweil, Kurtzweil, Kursweil, Kurzwell, Kurzwiel, Curzweil and Kirzweil, to name a few.
6) You can't assume from your name that you know where your family was from. My last name is a German word, but my family was not from Germany. Instead, my family was from the part of Europe that was once in the Austrian Empire, and it is for this reason that the name is Germanic.
7) You can't assume that just because you have the same last name as someone in history that you are a descendant. For example, if your name is Rottenberg, you can't assume that you descend from Rabbi Meir of Rothenberg.

6

Holocaust Research: To Give Them Back Their Names

SIX MILLION JEWISH PEOPLE IS ONE JEWISH PERSON—SIX MILLION TIMES

Six million Jews were murdered in the Holocaust.

That phrase, "six million," slips out of our mouths so quickly, so easily, too often even thoughtlessly. Six million. We speak the number as if we know what six million human beings means. As if we can understand such proportions of death through murder.

Six million. The number is unfathomable.

Six million Jews were murdered in the Holocaust.

That word, "murdered," is spoken without difficulty, as if we can grasp those murders, as if they are calculable. We say "murdered," but we do not mean simply murdered. Not like the killings we see so often on our televisions where life is taken every few moments without pause.

And "Holocaust." Its nine letters are supposed to add up to the six million murdered, as if a word, any word, can grasp, can include, can measure the loss, the tragedy, the meaning of what happened. We speak the word "Holocaust" often, but some things should remain nameless, since no name or word will do. No label, no phrase, no sentence, can measure the unmeasurable.

When something is named or defined, it is imprisoned by the very limitations of the combination of letters tacked on to it. As if it can now be filed away, dealt with, understood, grasped.

Six million Jews were murdered in the Holocaust.

Yes. But, no—it was more than that. So much more that to say just this is to perhaps betray the lives of the victims.

There are no graves for the victims. No markers stand as their memorials. Yes, throughout the world there are monuments, museums, posters, plaques, statues and sculptures commemorating their lives and paying tribute to them. But who were they? Who were the "six million murdered in the Holocaust"?

Some names ought to be given, some ought not.

Perhaps the deaths in total of six million Jews should remain nameless.

But the people should not remain nameless.

Have we made a mistake by naming the Event but not naming the murdered?

We have labeled the murders, added them up, written about them as if they were a phenomenon, but do most of us know the names of those in our families who were stolen from us and killed?

Education about the facts of the Jews during World War II is inferior enough. Schools often spend too little time on it; when it is discussed, the terms are broad and therefore vague. We learn about the Holocaust as a subject, as a phenomenon, as an historical event with causes and results.

What shall we tell our children? How shall we explain to those who do not remember the event, or, as time goes by, are farther and farther removed from it? In what way shall we keep the memory alive?

Elie Wiesel, a survivor of the Death Camps, taught a course at City College in New York on the Holocaust. One day, a student asked, "What shall we tell our children?"

"And what if they don't believe us?" a girl in the class added.

"They won't," a third student answered. "I'm convinced that in a few years, a few generations, it will all be forgotten."

"I am not sure I can agree," Wiesel said. "I have heard a theory, a fascinating, intriguing theory. Irving Greenberg told me this. He said that when one considers the Exodus of the Hebrews from Egypt, to those Hebrews, their exodus did not have much of an impact. But consider the impact it has had since. Consider the impact of the Exodus on Jews today. This observation might be applied to the Holocaust. Who can know? It may be the same."

"But, since we weren't there, what should we say to the next generation?" a young man asked. "You have said that we will never understand what happened. If so, how can we tell people about it?"

A member of the Kurzweil family who was murdered during the Holocaust.

"Yes," Wiesel said. "You will never know. But you will know that there was something. You will know one incident. One tear. That will be yours to tell."

Wiesel went on. "In my books, I don't like to repeat stories. Once I did. One story I told in two books."

He then told the legend, a Chassidic tale. It was a tale that contained many of the Chassidic Masters. It began with the founder of Chassidism, the Baal Shem Tov, the Master of the Good Name. It seems that when there was a disaster about to strike, the Baal Shem went into a certain spot in the woods, lit a candle and said a prayer—and the disaster was prevented. Then, a disciple of his was faced with a disaster. He knew where the special spot in the woods was located, he knew how to light the candle, but he did not know the prayer. But the disaster was averted. Then another disciple was faced with calamity. He knew where the spot in the woods was located, but he did not know how to light the candle, and he did not know the prayer. But the disaster was prevented. Then a final disciple was faced with a disaster. He did not know how to light the candle, he did not know how to say the prayer, and he did not know where the spot in the woods was located. *All he knew was how to tell the story.* And then, too, the disaster was avoided.

The Chassidic tale was instructive to the class, but Elie Wiesel wanted to be even more explicit in response to the question. So, when a student asked, "What is the story we should tell?" Wiesel responded, "In a few years, a very few years, there will not be one survivor left. Not a single survivor will be alive. Their numbers are decreasing at a very fast rate. Soon, there will be no one who was there.

"What can you tell your children? Tell them that you knew the last survivors. As the survivors were alive when it happened, you were alive to hear their story. Tell them that: You knew the last survivors.

"They will listen. And they will ask the same question: What shall we tell our children? They will tell them: We knew people who knew the last survivors. We heard the story from people who heard the last survivors. The very last.

"And the question will again be asked. And the story will be told. Again and again. It will be told."

Wiesel looked with complete seriousness at his students.

"This is what we hope for," he said. "That it will be remembered. It is up to you."

The easiest way for the Holocaust to become nothing more than one more chapter in Jewish history is to be satisfied with an impersonal approach to the understanding of it. If we allow the murders of our people to be "written up" in the history books, to be put on a shelf for future reference, we will be helping to forget. It is incumbent upon us to remember. As Jews, we are a people of memory, a people whose history should be part of each of us. We cannot let the Holocaust become

Pinchas Gottlieb, relative of the author, murdered during the Holocaust.

just another subject for books and articles and for nameless monuments in cemeteries.

We have to make a personal connection with the Holocaust. Each of us must understand the Holocaust in the most personal of terms. Who was murdered? Where were they? What are their names? How old were they? Who were in their families? Where did they die? How did they die? What is their relationship to me?

It is not enough to know that "the Jews" were killed, or that "six million were murdered," or even that "my people were slaughtered." We must try to find out who they were, these people of ours. We must know their names and their fates.

There are no gravestones for them. Our knowledge of them might be their finest memorial.

How do we discover who the victims were? How do we determine what their names were, when they were last heard from, or where they died? How do we find out what their relationship was to us?

The first step is to ask. Begin to make inquiries in your family as to who remained in Europe rather than immigrate to the U.S., Israel or some other country. You will probably discover quite quickly, sad as it is to say, that close members of your family were taken to Death Camps or murdered in their towns.

Often the best sources for this kind of information are survivors of the Holocaust. Inquire as to who in your family was there and survived, and arrange to talk to these relatives, or write to them if distance is too great. Often we are hesitant about talking to people who lived through the experience. We think that we will stir up old memories as if survivors of the Holocaust have, themselves, forgotten about it. This is obviously not the case. Often survivors are silent for other reasons. As Elie Wiesel has said, "They are either silent because they are afraid you will not understand, or they are silent because they are afraid you will understand."

Survivors of the Holocaust are also sometimes silent because they have not been asked. They feel that they do not want to volunteer the information but are waiting to be asked. Always remember the difficulty of speaking about the subject, but keep in mind its importance as well.

When you arrange to speak to a survivor in your family, ask if you can bring a tape recorder. Needless to say, a tape recording of the memories of a Holocaust survivor is important for future generations. If you become the one who helps to keep the memory of the Holocaust alive, you will be performing a fine deed.

You will discover that people in your family who have survived the Holocaust will be knowledgeable about the people in your family who did not survive. The question of "Why did I survive while they did not?" will surely have passed through many minds. Remember to tape or write down the names of the Holocaust victims in your family, and to determine what their relationship to you is. It is best to do this in the form of a family tree. Not only will this permit you to see better the relationships among relatives, but the family tree will also become a memorial to these people.

Not only survivors, but also other family members, will remember people in your family who were killed. Often after the War, families in the U.S. made inquiries to try to locate family members. It was at this time that people began to discover who did not survive. Try to locate the people in your family who were involved with these inquiries. They will be your best resources for discovering the answer to your questions. You will watch the branches of your family tree grow when you are doing this research. Never forget, however, that if not for your inquiries and your research, the names that you are gathering would be lost in another generation. You are making an effort to keep the memory of these deaths and of the Holocaust alive. It is one thing to know about "the six million," and quite another to have the names of the people in your family who were there and who were murdered.

I once naively thought that my family had escaped the Holocaust. It was my belief that since I was born in the U.S. and since my parents were in the U.S., and since even my grandparents were not in Europe during the War, our family "got out in time."

It was not until I found an old family photograph and asked my great-uncle to identify people in the picture that I realized how wrong I was. The photograph contained twenty-one people and included my great-grandfather, who also came to America, as well as my father, aunt, uncle, great-uncle and grandmother. That added up to six people of the twenty-one whom I could recognize from the photograph. Who were the others?

I didn't think much about the other people in the photograph when I first found it. After all, my grandmother and her three children were in it, and I knew all of them. Perhaps I was also preoccupied with the fact that my grandfather was not in the picture. He was already in America at the time, earning enough money to send for the rest of the family.

Yes, "the rest of the family." Since my grandmother and her three

The Kurzweil family in Dobromil, Poland. Of the 21 individuals, 14 were murdered during the Holocaust.

children were finally sent for five years after my grandfather came to America, I always thought, as I said, that we "missed it."

Today, I know the truth: In addition to the six people whom I recognized in the photograph, only one other person survived the Holocaust. The other fourteen people were murdered. Out of twenty-one family members, two-thirds were killed.

When I asked my great-uncle Sam who the other people in the picture were he said, "This is my brother Elya, his wife Dobroh, and their two children. This is my brother Hersh, his wife Anna, and their five children. And this is my sister Reisl, her husband Shimon, and their two children. Only Mechel, the oldest son of Hersh and Anna, survived. You know him. The others were all killed."

As I looked at the photograph, I thought again of my grandfather in America, working to earn the money that would bring his wife and three children, one of whom was my father, to this country. Had my grandfather stayed, had he continued his life with his brothers and sisters in the town in which they were born and raised, his family, like the others, probably would have been killed.

Belzec, Poland. Location of death camp where most of the Kurzweil family was murdered during the Holocaust.

In all, at least 103 people in the Kurzweil family alone were murdered in the Holocaust. That's just one branch of my family.

And I thought we escaped it.

HOLOCAUST RESEARCH: THE SEARCH FOR VICTIMS AND SURVIVORS

The International Tracing Service

In 1943, the Committee on Displaced Populations of the Allied Post-War Requirement Bureau, located in London, observed the obvious: As a result of the war, and particularly because of persecution, there was extensive displacement of populations. They decided, therefore, to establish the National Tracing Bureau in different countries with the aim of locating people who were missing or who had been deported. In 1944, the Supreme Headquarters of the Allied Expeditionary Forces, known as SHAEF, gave orders to register all displaced persons on index cards, to aid in the location process. By 1945, SHAEF established a tracing bureau that was given the task of collecting name lists of displaced persons as well as persons incarcerated in concentration camps.

This effort was aided by the United Nations Relief and Rehabilitation Administration (UNRRA) and was located in Versailles. Together, however, UNRRA and SHAEF relocated to Frankfort on Main.

In July of 1945, SHAEF was dissolved and the Combined Displaced Persons Executive, known as CDPX, established a collecting center for documents as well as a tracing bureau. This Central Tracing Bureau had as its goals to trace missing persons—military and civilian—of United Nations member countries, as well as to collect and preserve all documents concerning non-Germans and displaced persons in Germany. It was also given the task of assisting in the reuniting of families that had been separated by the war.

In 1946, the Central Tracing Bureau moved from Frankfort on Main to Arolsen. It was renamed the International Tracing Service, as it is still called today. At present, and since 1955, the International Tracing Service has been directed and administered by the International Committee of the Red Cross.

This organization was involved mainly with displaced persons in its beginning. However, when the ITS came into possession of concentration camp documents, the function of the organization changed. Suddenly, the ITS became involved with furnishing proof of deaths that occurred in the Death Camps. It is mainly this function of the ITS that concerns us here.

The historical background of the ITS has been provided here to offer an understanding of why the major source of information on concentration camp victims is located in Germany. The ITS continues to receive hundreds of thousands of inquiries from all over the world and provides a free research service to all interested parties.

Basically, the ITS has the most acceptable information of concentration camp victims and displaced persons in the world. Yad Vashem (see page 272), in the years 1955–1957, filmed the records that were available then and exclusively about Jewish victims of the Nazi regime. Since then, the ITS has acquired a lot of records (250 linear meters of new documentary material), especially after the political changes in Eastern Europe, so that the information at Yad Vashem no longer corresponds to that of the ITS.

The ITS has, as perhaps the most important feature in its archives, a Master Index. This index is a file, by name of individual, of all names appearing on all the documents in the archives. The reference cards include the name, personal data available and the description of the document in which the name is mentioned. At present, this Master Index contains 45,000,000 cards. It is interesting to note that the index is not filed alphabetically but rather phonetic-alphabetical in order to account for different spellings of the same surnames. Another rather remarkable resource used by ITS in this regard is a two-volume set of books listing first names and their many variations. This is obviously useful for location of individuals. The list of first names contains about 55,000 forms of names.

The Master Index is, however, just the axle about which the collections within the archives revolve. A closer look at the contents of the archives will show how useful ITS can be.

In the ITS Archives the following are contained:

Indexes and name lists of concentration camps.

Indexes and name lists of Gestapo and Sipo Offices.

Name lists of persons.

Deportation lists of Jews.

Index cards and name lists of towns and communities, district magistrate offices, labor offices, health insurance firms, etc., concerning foreigners who were registered during the war in Germany.

Index cards and name lists concerning children who had been separated from their parents or close relatives during the war or immediately after the war.

Although the holdings of ITS archives are vast, one should not think that the material is complete. For example, the concentration camp material in the archives is the largest, but it is not a collection of all concentration camp material that existed. The ITS rates the completeness of its concentration camp collection as follows:

Buchenwald	almost complete
Dachau	almost complete
Flossenburg	incomplete but quite numerous
Mauthausen	incomplete but quite numerous
Mittelbau	incomplete but quite numerous
Natzweiler	incomplete but quite numerous
Stutthof	incomplete but quite numerous
Niederhagen-Wewelsburg	incomplete but quite numerous
Ravensbruck	incomplete
Auschwitz	very incomplete
Gross-Rosen	incomplete
Sachsenhausen	incomplete

Neuengamme	incomplete
Lublin	incomplete
Krakow-Plaszow	very incomplete

According to ITS, there are literally millions of individual documents in the collection just described.

Another collection of ITS is the Post-War Documents, which generally concern displaced persons who were registered from 1945 to 1951. Included in these documents are lists of the inhabitants of the DP camps.

The Historical Section of the ITS archives is also of great value. Here are contained documents of a more general nature, including concentration camps, Jewish towns, Nuremberg trial records and information of the persecution of Jews in different countries. If you are interested in certain Jewish communities in Europe during the Holocaust, you will find these archives at the ITS to be excellent.

The ITS is currently in the process of establishing a subject index to its concentration camp material for use by researchers. They have also compiled the "Register of Concentration Camps and their Outlying Commandos under the Reichsfuhrer-SS in Germany and German-occupied Territories 1933–1945." It is for internal ITS use only.

One might think that the "tracing" function of the ITS has outlived its usefulness, but the ITS reports that the average number of tracing inquiries per year is 4000. After more than thirty years, people are still looking for lost relatives—and are sometimes finding them. It is sad to note, of course, that often the ITS offers verification regarding the concentration camp deaths of individuals.

Finally, the ITS has a staff of personnel who can make translations from the following languages into German: Croatian, Czech, Danish, Dutch, Greek, Hungarian, Italian, Latvian, Polish, Rumanian, Russian, Serbian, Spanish and Ukrainian.

If you know the name of a relative and you want to find out his or her fate during the Holocaust, write to the ITS and give them as much information about the person as you can. They require more than just a name, since their files contain so many duplicate names. The ITS usually asks for a person's name and birthdate, but if you do not know that (even an approximate date will help) then try to supply any other information that will narrow the field for the researcher.

What the ITS *will not* do is send you information on everyone in their files with a certain surname. Remember: It is a tracing service of individuals.

The ITS has all the available records kept by the Nazis at the concentration camps but, as noted, its collection is not complete. It also has a great number of other types of records. This means that its files include not only Holocaust victims who were killed, but also others who survived.

As I have mentioned, the ITS also has information concerning the fate of towns during the Holocaust. Along with your inquiry pertaining to individuals, you might want to ask about certain localities.

When you write to the ITS, simply state that you are interested in knowing whatever they have in their files on your family members and then list those individuals along with additional information as explained earlier. Again, the ITS, which is under the auspices of the International Red Cross, does not charge for its research—nor should it. Write to:

International Tracing Service
D-34444 Arolsen
Federal Republic of Germany

> The one million Jewish children murdered in the Nazi holocaust died not because of their faith, nor in spite of their faith, nor for reasons unrelated to faith. They were murdered because of the faith of their great-grandparents. Had these great-grandparents abandoned their Jewish faith, and failed to bring up Jewish children, then their fourth-generation descendants might have been among the Nazi executioners, but not among their Jewish victims. Like Abraham of old, European Jews sometime in the mid-nineteenth century offered a human sacrifice, by the mere minimal commitment to the Jewish faith of bringing up Jewish children. But unlike Abraham they did not know what they were doing, and there was no reprieve. This is the brute fact which makes all comparisons odious or irrelevant. This is the scandal of the particularity of Auschwitz which, once faced by the Jewish believer, threatens total despair.
>
> EMIL L. FACKENHEIM

Mauthausen Death Books

The National Archives in Washington, D.C., has two rolls of microfilm that contain seven volumes known as the *Mauthausen Death Books.* These books recorded the deaths of about 100,000 victims at that Nazi Death Camp. The volumes are chronological—by death (!)—

and include such personal data as name, date of birth, date of death and other comments. These volumes were introduced by the U.S. prosecution staff before the International Military Tribunal, commonly known as the Nuremberg Trials.

There is no index to these Death Books, so it is quite difficult to find specific names. However, if you have reason to believe that family members were killed in Mauthausen, and you care to do the research, these rolls of microfilm are available. You can also view these rolls of microfilm if you want to witness a frightening example of Nazi sickness.

These and other National Archives holdings are available to you on interlibrary loan. The code number for the Death Books is (T 990). Ask your local library for details concerning the interlibrary loan of these materials.

Yad Vashem

Yad Vashem is a national institution in Israel dedicated to perpetuating the memory of the victims of the Holocaust. Their stated goal is "to gather in material regarding all those Jewish people who laid down their lives, who fought and rebelled against the Nazi enemy and their collaborators, and to perpetuate their memory and that of the communities, organizations, and institutions which were destroyed because they were Jewish."

In addition to administering a museum devoted to the Holocaust, Yad Vashem is a research institution that collects material and publishes books and periodicals in Hebrew and English. Yad Vashem also aids in bringing Nazi war criminals to trial through the information it provides to legal authorities throughout the world.

Although Yad Vashem will not do research for individuals with general requests, one division of Yad Vashem is of great interest to those who wish to find information about Holocaust victims: This is the Hall of Names/Pages of Testimony Division. The primary goal of the Hall of Names at Yad Yashem is to receive, file and store Pages of Testimony. The Hall of Names, currently, has three million Pages of Testimony written by individuals who were able to provide information regarding the fate of Holocaust victims. It is the sacred goal of the Hall of Names to eventually have on file a Page of Testimony for every Jewish person who perished in the Holocaust. If you can supply the names of persons who you believe were murdered by the Nazis, or if you do not know the fate of individuals who were in Europe during the Holocaust, the Pages of Testimony Division might have information on these persons.

YAD VASHEM
Martyrs' and Heroes'
Remembrance
Authority
P.O.B. 3477 Jerusalem, Israel

דף־עד
עדות־בלאט
A Page of Testimony

אינסטיטוט צום אנדענק
פון אומקום און גבורה

THE MARTYRS' AND HEROES' REMEMBRANCE LAW, 5713—1953 determines in article No. 2 that — The task of YAD VASHEM is to gather into the homeland material regarding all those members of the Jewish people who laid down their lives, who fought and rebelled against the Nazi enemy and his collaborators, and to perpetuate their memory and that of the communities, organisations, and institutions which were destroyed because they were Jewish.

דאס געזעץ צום אנדענק פון אומקום און גבורה — יד־ושם, תשי״ג 1953

שטעלט פעסט אין פאראגראף נומ׳ 2:

די אויפגאבע פון יד־ושם איז איינזאמלען אין היימלאנד דעם אנדענק פון אלע יידן, וואס זענען געפאלן, האבן זיך מוסר נפש געווען, געקעמפט און זיך אנטקעגנגעשטעלט דעם נאצישן שונא און זיינע ארויסהעלפער, און זיי אלעמען, די קהילות, די ארגאניזאציעס און אינסטיטוציעס, וועלכע זענען חרוב געווארן צוליב זייער אנגעהעריקייט צום יידישן פאלק — שטעלן א דענקמאל.
(געזעץ־בוך נומ׳ 132, י״ז אלול תשי״ג, 28.8.1953)

בילד
Photo

1. פאמיליע־נאמען * — Family name *

2. פארנאמען (פאמיליע־נאמען פאר דער חתונה) — First Name (maiden name)

3. געבורטס־דאטע — Date of birth

4. ארט פון געבורט (שטאט, לאנד) — Place of birth (town, country)

5. נאמען פון פאטער — Name of father

6. נאמען פון מוטער — Name of mother

7. נאמען פון מאן אדער פון פרוי און איר מיידלשע־פאמיליע — Name of spouse (if a wife, add maiden name)

8. בערוף — Profession

9. סטאבילער וואוינארט — Place of residence before the war

10. וואוינערטער בעת דער מלחמה — Places of residence during the war

11. ארט, צייט און אומשטענדן פון טויט — Circumstances of death (place, date, etc.)

I, the undersigned ____________ איך, דער אונטערגעשריבענער

residing at (full address) ____________ (פולער אדרעס) וואס וואוינט

relationship to deceased ____________ קרובישאפט

hereby declare that this testimony is correct to the best of my knowledge.

דערקלער דערמיט, אז די עדות וואס איך האב דא איבערגעגעבן,
מיט אלע פרטים, איז א ריכטיקע לויט מיין בעסטען וויסן.

Place and date ____________ ארט און דאטע Signature ____________ אונטערשריפט

״...ונתתי להם בביתי ובחומותי יד ושם...אשר לא יכרת״ ישעיהו נו ה
"...even unto them will I give in mine house and within my walls a place and a name...that shall not be cut off." Isaiah, LVI, 5

* ביטע אנשרייבן יעדן נאמען פון אומגעקומענעם אויף א באזונדער בלאט.
Please inscribe the name of each victim of the Holocaust on a separate form.

Blank "Page of Testimony" in English, Yiddish and Hebrew, from Yad Vashem in Jerusalem. Yad Vashem asks individuals to testify to these forms regarding victims known to them.

A useful aspect of the Pages of Testimony is that not only is the name of the Holocaust victim on file, but so is the name, address and relationship to the deceased of the individual who made the testimony (i.e., the person who filled out the form). If you find the name of a victim of the Holocaust who was in your family, you can also find the name of someone, who is possibly still living, who knew the person who perished in the Holocaust. Relatives who lost contact with each other have found one another through a Page of Testimony's written documentation by a Holocaust survivor! For a fee of $10.00, a staff person at the Hall of Names will search for all individuals of a given surname from a particular town. For each of these surname-specific/town-specific $10.00 microfilm seaches, five photocopies of microfilm pages are provided. If additional photocopy pages are required because of the vast number of entries on file for the requested surname, an additional cost of one dollar per page will be charged. Common last names, with listings of over 300 entries, will not be searched because of current staff and time limitations. (In the words of the Director of the Page of Testimony Division, ". . . if we should search for Goldberg, with more than 4000 entries, we would spend the entire day searching, let alone ruin our eyes with the microfilm!") The creation of a computerized database for the Pages of Testimony is expected to be completed sometime after the year 2003. It is hoped that the Hall of Names staff then will be able to search for the surnames that have over 300 entries. Requests for searches should include the individual's last name, first name, birthplace or city of residence before or during the war.

To a make a request for Pages of Testimony, write to:

Yad Vashem
Pages of Testimony Division
P.O.B. 3477
Jerusalem, Israel

Note: The Pages of Testimony Division works both ways—giving information and receiving information. If you already have names and other facts about people who were murdered during the Holocaust, you will want to ask Yad Vashem for blank pages in order to send them *your* testimony.

> Everything new must have its roots in what was before.
>
> SIGMUND FREUD

Memorial Books as Sources for Learning About Holocaust Victims

If you can find a Memorial Book devoted to a town from which your family has come (see page 133), you might find a listing of Holocaust victims from that town. Often Memorial Books publish lists of individuals murdered during the Holocaust, in order to keep their memory alive. Even if you think your family left its ancestral home before the Holocaust, these listings might provide names of family members who stayed. You cannot assume that people with the same surname as yours appearing on these lists are related, but there is a good chance that they are—especially if it was a small town. If you find names in Memorial Books that are familiar, you should ask your relatives, particularly your older relatives, if they remember them.

Landsmannschaften (see page 322) can also be a good source for learning about the fate of your family and your ancestral towns during the Holocaust. Often the members of landsmannschaften are survivors and have much to share regarding this part of your family experience.

Locating Survivors

I write this section of this book with great hesitation. Although it is nearly fifty years after the Holocaust, I have met many people who still have hopes that one day they will find their relatives who have been missing since the War. Every once in a while a news item will stimulate more of this hope. "A brother and sister, separated by the Holocaust, find each other decades later." Although these stories are true, they are few and far between. Nonetheless, if the hope is there, a distant dream might one day be fulfilled.

Name	Age	Place and Time of Death	
218. Edelman, Yente	59	Skala	Sep. 1942
219. Edelman, Moses	30	Borszczow	1942
220. Edelman, Aron		Skala Forest	1943
221. Edelman, Golda	60	Borszczow	1943
222. Edelman, Liba	35	Skala	Sep. 1942
223. Edelman, Rywka	59	Borszczow	1943
224. Edelman, Moshe	35	Turylcze	1943
225. Edelman, Eli	30	Turylcze	1943
226. Edelman, Tonia	25	Turylcze	1943
227. Edelstein, Hersch	68	Borszczow	1943

228. Edelstein, Liba	64	Borszczow	1943
229. Edelstein, Dora	30	Borszczow	1943
230. Edelstein, Sara	75	Skala	Sep. 1942
231. Edelstein, Chaya	40	Skala	Sep. 1943
232. Edelstein, Alter	15	Skala	1943
233. Ehrenberg, Mendel	71	Skala	Sep. 1942
234. Ehrenberg, Ita	71	Skala	Sep. 1942
235. Ehrenberg, Dvora	45	Skala	Sep. 1942
236. Ehrlich, Meier	58	Cygany	Unkn.
237. Ehrlich, Gitel	56	Cygany	Unkn.
238. Ehrlich, Brana	19	Cygany	Unkn.
239. Ehrlich, Motio	17	Cygany	Unkn.
240. Ehrlich, Sima	16	Cygany	Unkn.
241. Eisenfeld, Mendel	67	Cygany	Unkn.
242. Eisenfeld, Ratze	63	Cygany	Unkn.
243. Eisenfeld, Zeide	70	Skala	1942
244. Eisenfeld, Szyfra	68	Skala	1942
245. Elkes, Nachum	43	Gluboczek	c.c. 1942
246. Elkes, Sosia	43	Skala	Sep. 1942
247. Elkes, Pepa	17	Skala	Sep. 1942
248. Elkes, Wolf	15	Janowska	c.c. 1942
249. Engelbach, Sima	76	Skala	Sep. 1942
250. Engelbach, Eli	42	Borki	c.c. 1942
251. Engelbach, Frima	35	Skala	Sep. 1942
252. Engelbach, Leizer	7	Skala	Sep. 1942
253. Engelbach, Chaim	72	Skala	1942
254. Engelbach, Mariem	69	Skala	Sep. 1942

From the list of more than 1400 Jews murdered by the Nazis. The "List of Martyrs" was published in the Skala Memorial Book. Lists of murdered Jews are usually included in Memorial Books.

Yet, I write this section with hesitation because I do not want to raise false hopes. I do not want to give the impression that one can easily find lost relatives. I do not want to add to the thought that "they might be alive," only to bring on greater disappointment when they are not found.

So, I ask the reader to understand the situation: Hope in finding a lost relative is very slight. Yet, if the possibility exists and if you have the strength to pursue the question, you may want to attempt the research. Finally, before I describe this next source, you should understand that the odds are great, sadly, that your missing relative is not alive and was murdered.

After the Holocaust, a major activity of Jews around the world was searching for missing relatives. The question in everyone's mind was, "Who was killed and who survived?" Immediately after the War, Jews were asked to return to their hometowns. This was, perhaps, the best way to find out the fate of one's family and friends. If everyone returned "home," even for a short time, the survivors could learn the fate of their loved ones. In addition, if any of the family's personal effects were still there, this would be an opportunity to claim them.

There are an enormous number of post-War horror stories relating to this very subject. How often a surviving Jew returned to his or her village only to be murdered—after the War!—by anti-Semites in the town. In my family, there are eyewitness accounts by many people of just this situation. A cousin of mine returned to our shtetl searching for his missing relatives and was killed by the local people.

For the Jews who returned to their homes, their experience was mixed with joy and sadness. In many cases a survivor's wildest dreams were fulfilled: Others in his family survived. But in most cases, perhaps every case, the death of many loved ones was discovered.

Not everyone returned home, however. Some refused ever to go back to the town where they were originally from—not even for a day. Others were physically unable to travel great distances to return home, or others were too ill to make the journey. Other circumstances also prevented many Jews from going "home." In addition, usually a person had family in several different towns. A survivor could not be in all places at once. Yet the survivor was desperately anxious to learn news about his or her family.

Various agencies attempted to aid in the search for missing relatives because of this situation. The Jewish Agency for Palestine in 1945 established the Search Bureau for Missing Relatives. The World Jewish Congress established the Division for Displaced Persons. Other organizations, such as the Czechoslovak Jewish Committee, the Relief Committee of Jews from Czechoslovakia, the American Federation for Lithuanian Jews, Inc., and many others, also joined in to help Jews find survivors.

The major effort of these organizations was to gather and publish information about survivors in the form of alphabetical lists of names. The Jewish Agency for Palestine's Search Bureau for Missing Relatives published a 300-page book in 1945 called *Register of Jewish Survivors*. It was a list of 58,000 Jews in Poland in June of that year.

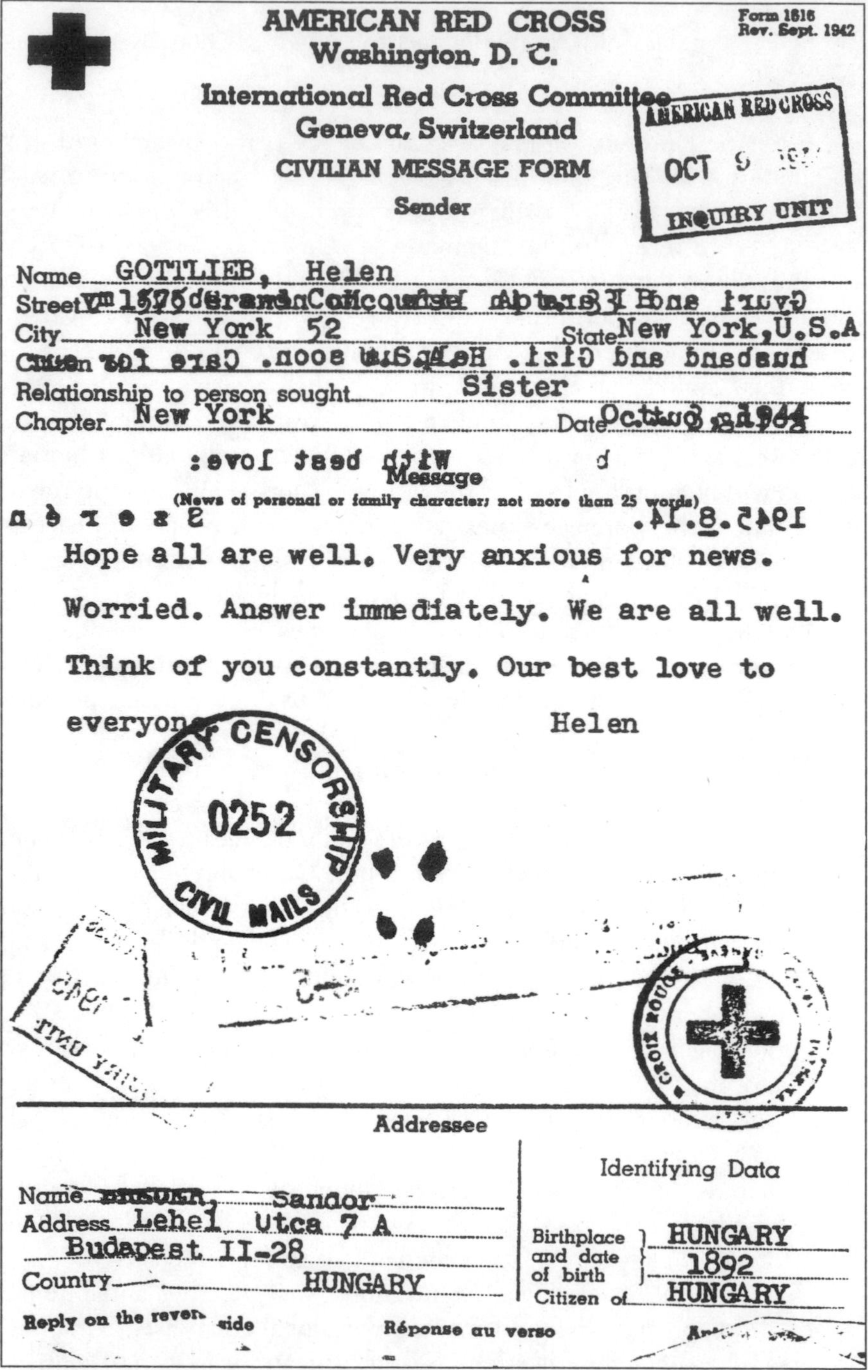

AMERICAN RED CROSS
Washington, D. C.
International Red Cross Committee
Geneva, Switzerland
CIVILIAN MESSAGE FORM
Form 1616
Rev. Sept. 1942

AMERICAN RED CROSS
OCT 9 1944
INQUIRY UNIT

Sender

Name GOTTLIEB, Helen
Street 1575 Grand Concourse Apt. 3 J
City New York 52 State New York, U.S.A
Citizen
Relationship to person sought Sister
Chapter New York Date Oct. 3, 1944

Message
(News of personal or family character; not more than 25 words)

Hope all are well. Very anxious for news.
Worried. Answer immediately. We are all well.
Think of you constantly. Our best love to
everyone. Helen

MILITARY CENSORSHIP 0252 CIVIL MAILS

Addressee

Name [illegible] Sandor
Address Lehel Utca 7 A
Budapest II-28
Country HUNGARY

Identifying Data

Birthplace and date of birth: HUNGARY 1892
Citizen of HUNGARY

Reply on the reverse side
Réponse au verso

American Red Cross message from the author's grandmother inquiring about relatives during the Holocaust.

This was just one of many such published lists, however. Here is a list of titles of some of the published lists:

Surviving Jews in Warsaw as of June 5th 1945

Surviving Jews in Lublin

List of Persons Liberated at Terezin in Early May 1945

List of Children at Terezin

Displaced Jews Resident in the Czechoslovak Republic 1948

List of Jews Residing in Riga

Jewish Refugees in Italy

Jews Liberated from German Concentration Camps Arrived in Sweden 1945–6

Surviving Jews in Yugoslavia as of June, 1945

A List of Lithuanian Jews Who Survived the Nazi Tyranny and Are Now in Lithuania, France, Italy, Sweden, Palestine, 1946

Jews Registered in Czestochowa

An Extensive List of Survivors of Nazi Tyranny Published So That the Lost May Be Found and the Dead Brought Back to Life

These are just some of the lists that were published. The titles of many of the lists are, in themselves, quite moving.

Where are these lists located? At the present time I am aware of only one place where a large collection of these books is gathered and that is at YIVO Institute for Jewish Research, 1048 5th Avenue, New York, NY 10028 (see page 224). Be aware that the YIVO staff *cannot* do research for you. They *cannot* look in these books in search of names. However important this search might be to you, the YIVO does not have the staff to do searches.

How can these lists serve you? The International Tracing Service has all available data on Holocaust victims and survivors, but I have already explained that ITS is a *tracing* service. In others words, if you give them a name of a person (and additional identification) they will check to see if they have information on the person. However, what if I am looking, for example, for information about people with the name Kurzweil? The ITS can not and will not supply me with information on every Kurzweil in their files. As they have told me through correspondence, their files have information about more than 200 Kurzweils! They cannot send me all of that information, but they can check their files if I ask them about certain specific names. Again, they are a tracing service of individuals.

This is where the lists come in. If I check the survivor lists for the surnames I am interested in, I might find people with the same surnames. The names of the towns where they registered are also listed. These towns are the ones where the people were at the time the list was compiled. Since most Jews registered in their hometowns, this is often the town where they lived before the Holocaust. If the town matches one in your family history, you *may* be on the right track in locating a relative. Once you find a listing of interest, you can photocopy the page and ask family members if they recall this person. Then you can send it to the ITS. They will check their files for the name. Finally, you can check phone books (see page 284) and you might match the name on the list with a listing in the Israeli phone books, for example, or other phone directories as well.

Once again, these lists are a way to possibly locate missing people. The lists were published more than four decades ago, but they might be an aid in discovering some valuable information. On the other hand, I must repeat that the chances are still slight, and your hopes must not be raised too high.

The Jewish Agency Search Bureau for Missing Relatives in Israel

In 1945 The Jewish Agency for Israel established the Search Bureau for Missing Relatives to help reunite family members who had been separated by the catastrophic events of World War II. At one time the Bureau had a staff of forty-five people working to help find missing relatives. Currently the work of the Bureau is done soley by its extraordinary Director, Batya Unterschatz (with the help of a part-time secretary). The Bureau receives 10,000 to 40,000 requests per year from individuals searching for missing relatives. These requests for help increase greatly every time there is a new wave of immigration, with new emigrees hoping to find their Israeli relatives. Fifteen percent of the requests the Bureau processes come from Americans and other foreigners who are researching their family history.

Batya Unterschatz feels that her mission at the Bureau, where she has worked since 1972 after immigrating from Vilna, is to bring people together. She is dedicated to the dream that her office serve as a registration center for Jews from all over the world. The search process often begins with a simple request and then the creation of an entry with the name and other personal data of the person being searched for and the name of the searcher. Until recently, a data file of more than one million index cards, with handwritten entries, was maintained in wooden boxes. This information has recently been converted to computerized data because of a donation received in 1991 from the Association of Jewish Genealogical Societies. Another source of information is an Interior Ministry listing on microfiche of every person, living or deceased, having Israeli citizenship since the state was founded. These records are current through 1984. (If you are seeking someone who became a citizen after 1984, the Interior Ministry should be contacted directly.) There are other various ways Batya pursues her searches, including checking the membership records of landsmannschaftens and professional organizations and placing ads in the Russian-language press.

Although Batya recognizes the importance of people being able to find branches of their family they may not have known about, she is sensitive to the fact that the "missing" person being sought may want to maintain his or her privacy and *not* want to be found. For this reason, when Batya has success finding the missing person, she sometimes will give the missing person information on how to contact the person doing the seeking, instead of giving the information to the person who initiated the search.

The mailing address of the Search Bureau for Missing Relatives is:

The Jewish Agency Search Bureau for Missing Relatives
P.O.B. 92
Jerusalem 91920
Israel

Deportations from France During the Holocaust

A remarkable book was published in 1978 that should be of great interest to anyone researching Holocaust victims. Titled *Le mémorial de la déportation des Juifs de France* and written and compiled by Serge Klarsfeld, this book lists all the Jews deported from France during World War II. The book contains the names, birthdates and birthplaces of nearly 80,000 Jews who were deported.

This large volume costs $25.00 dollars and is available from the *American Interfaith Institute, 401 North Broad St., Philadelphia, PA 19108.*

SPILLMAN	SIMON	12.01.20	LASK	P	UNGLIK	SZAJA	04.03.11	KLOBUCK
SZPILBERG	ABRAM	10.06.01	NADASYN	P	URMAN	NATHAN	29.12.06	PIOTROKOW
SPIRO	MELJECK	20.02.92	LUBLIN	AUT	URYN	CHILEL	28.02.02	PRYSTICK
SZPITALNIK	FAIWEL	26.08.06	PIOTRKOW	P	WACHSERGER	OSKAR	06.10.96	OPAWA
SZPRYNGER	CHALIM	18.12.03	VARSOVIE	P	WAGLESZEWSKI	SUCHER	25.10.09	KALICE
SZRAJER	MELDEL	.12	KRASNYSTEN	P	WAGNER	ABRAHANM	14.07.04	MESZERNOW
SZTEINSZNAJDER	MOWSA	09.12.04	MORDY	P	WAGNER	KALMAN	.05	OSTROWICE
SZTADTMAN	ARON	03.02.07	SIEDLEC	P	WAINTROV	SZMUL	.04	OSTROW
SZTAJNBERG	MOSZEK \	15.06.08	SWADOVICE	P	WAIS	MOSZEK	12.03.02	BRZEZNICA
SZTAJNBERG	SALOMON	02.01.22	BRZEZINY	P	WAISBLUM	MORDKA	23.03.02	OPATOW
SZTAJNBOCK	ICEK	07.11.02	RADOM	P	WAISS	EUGENIE	24.11.11	VARONGI
SZTAJNBOCK	JOSEPH	02.03.00	RADOM	P	WAJCMAN	JANKIEL	08.02.02	CZERNOWICZ
SZTAJNBOJN	CHAIM	02.08.01	VARSOVIE	P	WAJCMAN	MORDKA	.07	KRASZOW
SZTAJZALC	EZERIEL	25.03.20	VARSOVIE	P	WAJCMAN	LAIBA	27.01.09	KRASNIC
SZTAL	ISRAEL	03.11.06	STRYKOW	P	WAJL	NAFTULA	25.01.98	HEUSCHIN
SZTAL	JACQUES	20.11.01	STRYKOW	P	WAJNBAUM	SIMON	12.07.07	LUBLIN
SZTAL	MOSEK	21.05.05	STRYKOW	P	WAJNBERG	HERSZ	15.12.07	POLANICE
SZTARKMAN	LEIBUS	15.05.16	OSTROW	P	WAJNBERG	JOSEPH	11.03.02	STAL
SZTEINBERG	SZMUL	04.07.09	SIEDLEC	P	WAJNBERG	PINKUS	.02	PULKOW
SZTEINBERG	SAUL	28.12.06	LUCKOW	P	WAJNBERG	SZMUL	.02	DRZOWICA
SZTEJSZNAIJDER	CHAIM	14.03.05	MORDY	P	WAJNGLAS	HERCKA	01.05.00	POWDLOWSKA
SZTERN	ARJA	12.02.01	SLOWEN	P	WAJNGLAS	ARMAND	23.11.19	LUBLIN
SZTERN	ABA	12.03.22	CHARZWIEC	P	WAJNRYK	SZYJAN	24.06.07	PIOTRKOW
SZTERN	SLAMA	10.06.07	SLAWER	P	WAJNSZTEJN	SZMUL	15.01.16	SOKOLOW
SZTERN	JAKOB	14.02.02	SIEDLOWICE	P	WAJNSTOK	ZIMON	.07	VARSOVIE
SZTERN	SZJA	15.07.07	TOMASZOW	P	WAJNSZTOK	SLAMA	19.03.06	SAWIETZIA
SZTERNSZUS	SZCEL	03.08.07	SIEDLOVICE	P	WAJS	ABE	04.04.01	VARSOVIE
SZTIGER	DAVID	09.01.01	VARSOVIE	P	WAJSBLAT	HENRI	10.03.11	SZAKOWICE
SZTOLCMAN	IDEL	28.03.03	KALUSZYN	IND	WAJSBLAT	MOSZEK	15.10.06	LODZ
SZTUDER	ICEK	16.02.02	OZAROW	P	WAJSMAN	BENCIAN	14.12.01	BIALDOBGEZ
SZTULCMAN	HENOCH	25.05.06	RABEZYN	P	WAKSUL	ZYL	07.11.02	JANOW
SZTYKMAN	CHASKEL	27.09.00	VARSOVIE	P	WARZAUR	CHAIM	05.05.05	RADOM
SZUKSZTULSKI	HENNOCH	30.11.08	WILNO	P	WASERMAN	HERSZ	27.03.03	VARSOVIE
SZULIMOWICZ	ABRAHAM	26.12.20	RADOM	P	WASERSTAIN	MAJER	.04	SZYDLOVICE
SZYDLOWITS	RUBIN	15.06.04	SEDLICE	P	WAYS	JAKOB	29.12.03	PIOTRKOW
SZYLLER	SLAMA	.04	BENDZIN	P	WEBERSPIEL	MOSZEK	03.09.21	CHELM
SZYRMAN	PINKUS	15.04.09	VARSOVIE	P	WEIGER	LIPOT	15.07.00	BUDAPEST
SZWARC	ABRIS	15.07.00	RADOM	P	WEINTRAUB	ERNEST	30.10.01	LWOW
SZWED	HENOCH	.04	PODCEMBICE	P	WEJGLER	ARNOUX	29.12.01	BUDAPEST
SZWIMER	KUMA	19.05.10	BENDZIN	P	WEJNSZTOK	SZMUL	11.04.04	VARSOVIE
SZWERDSZAFT	ICEK	10.10.04	LUBATOW	P	WEKSBERG	JONAS	10.05.02	BENDZIN
TABAKMAN	JAKOB	15.11.07	LODZ	P	WELT	SLAMA	09.12.19	KAZIMIERS
TABAKMAN	JOSEPH	01.11.03	LODZ	P	WENGLAND	JANKIEL	08.06.02	PRZYSYCHAN
TACHNA	EFRAIM		MLAWA	P	WICHLER	LAZAR	04.02.05.	CHARKOW
TAPEL	LEIBUS	17.12.07	KRASNIC	P	WICOROWSKY	JEWNA	31.07.00	STELYN
TAIZIDER	ISRAEL	19.02.01	SWOLEN	P	WIDAWSKI	CHAIM	02.02.08	KALYSZ
TAJCHMAN	ABRAM	21.08.02	SIENNE	P	WILXZYNSKI	FAIWEL	20.12.06	RODOG
TAUB	EMMANUEL	13.06.98	BARDIOW	TC	WILK	HERSZEK	.00	MORDAI
TENENBAUM	HIRSZ	09.02.06	TOMAZOW	P	WINTERNITZ	ERNEST	30.10.88	BRNO
TENENBAUM	JOSEPH	15.03.00	SOBKOW	P	WISNIA	JOSEK	.01	KARCZAD
TENENBAUM	MAJLECK	10.03.06	SZYDOLOVICE	P	WISNIEWSKI	MORDKA	12.11.07	SZWECZOW
TENENBAUM	SYMCHA	28.08.00	VARSOVIE	P	WISTYCKI	ABRAHAM	28.06.03	VARSOVIE
TENENBAUM	SZYJA	12.08.06	RAMBERTOW	P	WITMAN	SZMULKA	04.04.02	SZYSCZE
TENEWURSEL	MOSZEK	15.04.20	TARNOPOL	P	WITTENBERG	MICHEL	26.11.05	VARSOVIE
TEPICHT	BER	24.11.01	VARSOVIE	P	WODKA	PHILIPPE	26.02.22	VARSOVIE
TER	DAVID	04.03.04	DOREDA	P	WODNICKI	LEIB	03.06.06	VARSOVIE
TOPEZA	ELYJA	02.08.02	VARSOVIE	IND	WOLF	DAVID	31.05.03	CZESTOCHOVA
TOPEZA	LEIBA	10.03.05	VARSOVIE	IND	WOLF	JAKOB	18.08.04	LODZ
TOPPER	JOSEPH	20.05.10	SZEZUCHIN	IND	WOLF	OSIAS	18.01.97	KROSENKO
TRAFIKANT	JOSEPH	15.01.05	MINSK	IND	WOLENBERG	SIMON	28.05.04	KOLO
TRAGER	ASISZ	15.04.04	RZEZOW	P	WOLKOWIZSCH	BERK	26.01.99	DAMASOFF
TREIDEL	ERIC	28.09.80	MAYENCE	F	WOLOCZYNSKI	GERSZ	14.05.06	WILNO
TROJANOWSKI	ABRAM	26.11.06	GOTSTYNYN	P	WOLONOWSKI	ISRAEL	20.10.04	PRZYAUCHA
ULLMANN	ADRIENNE	13.11.02		F	ZIFFER	ADOLPHE	05.05.04	BELZETS
ULLMAN	BERNARD	30.07.01	PARIS	F	ZIPINE	LOUIS	08.08.06	PARIS

From alphabetical lists of Jews on trains from France to Death Camps. This list includes Gersz Woloczynski, grandfather of Pamela Roth, a colleague of the author.

Death Books

At YIVO Institute for Jewish Research in New York, along with their collection of lists of survivors, are a few examples of lists of murdered Jews. There are no gravestones for the millions murdered. These lists, in effect, become their memorials.

Examples of such books are two volumes published by the Jewish Labor Committee in 1947. The titles of the two books are: *Memorial Dates of the Martyred Jews of Dachau—Jews Born in Lithuania, Latvia, Estonia and White Russia,* and *Memorial Dates of the Martyred Jews of Dachau—Jews Born in Poland.*

Both books were compiled by Jesef Lindenberger and Jacob Silberstein, themselves Dachau survivors.

These kinds of lists, although possible sources for research, also serve as a further inspiration. We must try our best to learn about those members of our families who perished during the Holocaust. We ought to know their names and to write them down on our family trees. We ought to print these family trees and distribute them to our family members so that everyone knows who perished and how we are connected to them. Their memories must live.

> Whoever teaches his son teaches not only his son but also his son's son—and so on to the end of generations.
>
> TALMUD: KIDDUSHIN, 30A

Holocaust Calendar of Polish Jewry

According to Jewish Tradition, the anniversary of the death of a family member is to be observed. On that day, each year, a candle is lit in memory of the individual who has departed.

The Holocaust, which stole six million Jews from our families, caused most of our families to observe these death anniversaries. The problem, of course, is that in most cases we do not know the exact date of death. Whole towns were often destroyed at once with nobody to recall the date. Many Jews were marched or taken to concentration camps. The precise date an individual Jew died is nearly impossible to determine.

Desiring to fulfill the religious obligation to observe the anniversary of the death, many Jews who have family members who were killed during the Holocaust will use the date that the town was attacked or evacuated as the day to remember.

In 1974, Rabbi Israel Schepansky published an 88-page book called *Holocaust Calendar of Polish Jewry.* The *Holocaust Calendar* is essentially a town-by-town list of communities in Poland. The book provides the name of the town, the population, the dates and ways of "liquidation," as the author puts it, and in many cases other information about the town. Rabbi Schepansky is a well-respected scholar, the editor of the Jewish magazine *Or Hamizrach,* and on the editorial board of the *Talmudic Encyclopedia.*

The *Holocaust Calendar* is available for $10.00 from Rabbi Israel Schepansky, 2220 Avenue L, Brooklyn, NY 11210. Be aware that the book is in Hebrew. Nonetheless, you can surely find someone who can translate for you, if Polish Jewry is your interest.

Unfortunately, there is no single reference source for the dates of other Jewish communities in Eastern Europe. Some dedicated scholar ought to do the same thing for Hungary, Czechoslovakia, etc., that Rabbi Schepansky has done for Poland.

On the other hand, as you do research on the histories of your European communities, you will find these dates and other information about your towns during the Holocaust. The day that the Nazis destroyed your town is an important date for you to remember and to keep as a part of your family history.

> Mid-nineteenth century European Jews did not know the effects of their actions upon their remote descendants when they remained faithful to Judaism and raised Jewish children. What if they had known? Could they have remained faithful? Should they? And what of us who know, when we consider the possibility of a second Auschwitz three generations hence. (Which would we rather have our great-grandchildren be—victims or bystanders and executioners?) Yet for us to cease to be Jews (and to cease to bring up Jewish children) would be to abandon our millennial post as witnesses to the God of History.
>
> EMIL L. FACKENHEIM

PRE-HOLOCAUST EUROPEAN PHONE BOOKS

The New York Public Library Research Division attempts each year to obtain current phone books from all over the world. They also save their old phone books.

One day I wondered how far back the oldest Polish phone book went in the library's collection. The New York Public Library Annex on 43rd Street keeps these books. At the annex I found two volumes of the 1936 Polish telephone directories.

Since most of my family who came to America arrived in the early part of the 1900s, and since even those who came later arrived before the Holocaust, one might wonder why these phone books would be of use to me. In addition, you might ask, "What Jews had telephones in Poland in 1936?!"

In answer to the second question, the fact of the matter is that many Jews in Poland in 1936 had phones. The myth is that every Eastern European Jew was as poor as Tevye the Dairyman. As for my family being in the U.S. before 1936, the truth is that many cousins did not come to America—and were murdered in the Holocaust.

Upon examining the 1936 Polish phone books, I discovered that the books were arranged by town. Some towns had only two phones, others had more. In one of the towns in my family history there was a listing of about twenty phones. Two of the names, to my great surprise, were slightly familiar to me. I photocopied the page and brought it to a man in the family who was from the same town and in fact had the same last name as the people listed. When I asked him if he knew who the two people listed were, he said, "Of course. One is my uncle and the other is my father."

They were both killed during the Holocaust, but in 1936 both had telephones. My cousin was then able to tell me about some of the other people who were listed as having phones in the same town. It was an excellent way to discover new people as well as to stimulate a memory to recall stories about people who had not been seen for thirty-five or more years.

The following is a listing of which pre-Holocaust telephone books can be found in the New York Public Library Annex:

Austria

Vienna, 1928–30, 1932–34, 1936–38

Niederösterreich

Burgenland

Oberösterreich

Salzburg

Steiermark

Karnten
Tirol
Vorarlberg

CZECHOSLOVAKIA

Prague, 1932–38, 1940
Bohemia, 1934/35, 1935/36, 1936/37, 1938/39
Moravia and Silesia, 1932, 1933, 1936
Slovakia and Russian Lower Carpathia, 1934, 1935

GERMANY

Berlin, 1913, 1926–38
Düsseldorf, 1931–36
Frankfurt, 1928–37
Hamburg, 1927, 1930–35
Leipzig, 1932–34
München, 1932–37
Stuttgart, 1936

(It is interesting to note that many people who do research to claim war reparations as well as to hunt Nazis use these rare pre-Holocaust German phone directories.)

HUNGARY

Budapest, 1913, 1928–34, 1936–38, 1940

POLAND

Warsaw, 1931–35, 1936/37
All districts except Warsaw, 1936

YUGOSLAVIA

Belgrade, 1934

This is an incomplete list of cities and countries, of course.

The New York Public Library also has post-Holocaust phone books that may aid in tracking down missing relatives.

> All our ancestors are in us. Who can feel himself alone?
>
> RICHARD BEER-HOFMANN, *SCHLAFIED FÜR MIRIAM,* 1898

7

Your Immigrant Ancestors

SOMEONE IN YOUR FAMILY LEFT HOME

Generally, we look at Jewish history in terms of broad categories of time. The arrival of Jewish immigrants to the U.S., for example, has been broken down into stages spanning many years for each stage. Most of us are familiar with the well-known era of American Jewish history during the years just before and after the beginning of the twentieth century, when vast numbers of Jews arrived in the Port of New York. Steamships carrying Jews from Europe arrived daily, pouring Jews into the U.S.

We see that period of history, when the Lower East Side of New York filled up with immigrants, when other cities in the U.S. saw a rapid growth of their Jewish population because of this immigration, when the U.S. emerged as a center of world Jewry, as a phenomenon. The phenomenon of Jewish immigration has been written about, studied, and celebrated literally since it began. Books appear frequently on the subjects of the Lower East Side, Jewish immigration, and related topics. As an era, as a category of history, as an event, the years we are speaking about are seen in mostly broad perspectives.

Although it is quite useful to see history in terms of the eras, stages, and time periods that are usually used, it is equally, if not more, useful to go from the general to the specific to see where, in fact, we fit into those broad descriptions of history. We know that steamships arrived in American ports daily during the active periods of immigration, but which boats brought us—meaning our ancestors—to those ports? What were the names of the ships that took our family to America? What did they look like? What route did they travel? When did they arrive? How long did it take to make the journey? Who traveled with whom? How old were your ancestors when they arrived? Where did they go when they got off the ship? Where did they live?

Again, we can understand the general history of different eras, or we can move in closer and examine details. We can see the crowd or we can examine the individuals.

As you read this, chances are you are sitting in or near your home. How long have you been living where you currently reside? How long has your family lived in the area where you are now? Whatever the answers are to those questions, if you are like most Jews in the U.S., you have not been here for too many generations. Just as the U.S. is a nation of immigrants, so too are you and your family part of that collection of people whose ancestors arrived here sometime in the recent past. Most of us live our lives as Americans, rarely remembering that the U.S. is a relatively new experience for our families.

Do you know when your family arrived in America? Perhaps you yourself are an immigrant, in which case you are well aware of the arrival of your family to the U.S. Or perhaps your parents were immigrants, in which case you might also have a good idea of the story behind your arrival in this country. Let us take a look at the Jewish immigrant experience in the U.S. and see where we fit into the large picture. Our examination of this era of Jewish history will be like a gradually moving close-up in a motion picture. We will begin with a wide-angle shot of the phenomenon of immigration. Slowly we will focus in on a more and more narrow portion of the picture until we arrive at a single detail in the original scene: you.

The United States

Jewish immigration to the U.S. can be seen in five different stages, and different branches of your family will fit into each of these time periods. Remember that unless you yourself are an immigrant, the arrival of your family to America will vary. Branches of your mother's family might have arrived in the U.S. in 1908, where your father's family—or parts of it—might have been in this country since before the Civil War.

American Jewish history can be divided into many different stages. For our purposes we will look at it from the following time periods:

1654–1825
1825–1880
1880–1929
1929–1945
1945–the present

Let us examine, in brief, each of these periods.

1654–1825

The year 1654 is a famous one in Jewish history for in that year the first Jewish settlement was established in North America. It consisted of twenty-three individuals and was located in Dutch New Amsterdam. There has been much research done concerning this group and the years that followed through the Colonial period in America. The number of Jews during that period was small, and assimilation was great. Jewish settlements appeared throughout the early Colonial period, however, and we find them quite early in Virginia, in Rhode Island, and in Maryland. By 1733 each of the thirteen colonies had Jewish populations. During this wave of settlers, most of the Jews were of Spanish descent, but after 1700, we find that German Jews were arriving in the colonies in small numbers. By 1750, the German Jews had outnumbered the Sephardic Jews. Nevertheless, the Jewish population of the U.S. by 1790 was a mere 1500.

When the American Revolution broke out, most Jews were Whigs, that is, supporters of the Revolution. Having little or no tie to England, they were much more interested in independence. A great deal of historical material exists on this early period of Jewish history in North America, including the Jewish role in the Revolution. Although the history is often fascinating, we are still aware of the fact that assimilation was the most common experience among the Jews in this period, and the reason that the Jewish population remained fairly stable was because of the balance between the Jews who faded out of the Jewish community and the trickle of Jewish immigration that continued throughout this time. By 1800, there were 2000 Jews in the U.S. and by 1826 there were approximately 6000. Most of these Jews, by this time, were native born and completely acculturated. Intermarriage was common.

1825–1880

The second period of American Jewish history is one of enormous growth. In fact, the period can be seen as the American Jewish community going from a small group of little significance to a major world Jewish community. A quick look at population figures tells the story:

1826	*6000*
1840	*15,000*
1860	*150,000*
1880	*280,000*

The increase in population was mainly the result of foreign immigration. Most of the immigrants were Germanic Jews, coming from Bohemia and Bavaria. Large numbers also came from Hungary. An interesting aspect of this migration was that many of the Jews who arrived in America did not remain on the East Coast. In fact, one of the great contributions of the Jews in America at this time was the continued opening up and development of the West. The older Jewish communities such as Charleston, South Carolina; Newport, Rhode Island; and Norfolk, Virginia, saw a decline during this westward movement across the country by Jews. Other cities began to develop Jewish communities. These included Cincinnati, Louisville, New Orleans, Chicago, St. Louis, Cleveland, Newark, Albany, Syracuse, Buffalo, Detroit, Milwaukee, and Minneapolis. Many Jews who arrived at the time of the Gold Rush traveled to California and were among the first to settle in San Francisco. By 1854, there were Jewish communities in dozens of cities across the entire country. As a result of the European revolutions of 1848–1849, the early 1850s evidenced the greatest wave of immigration of this entire period.

This was also the great era of the Jewish peddler and traveling salesman. Because of the lack of retail outlets to be found in a still-developing nation, the Jewish peddler contributed to the growth of the American economy by traveling to cities throughout the country. In fact, many major giant department stores such as Macy's, Gimbel's, and Abraham and Straus had their beginnings in this period as tiny retail outlets, sometimes in the form of a horse-drawn wagon.

The middle of the nineteenth century in American Jewish history was dominated by the German Jew. With the arrival of so many German Jews came the establishment of German theater, newspapers, cultural societies and other groups. These were often devoid of much Jewish content; however, the development of Reform Jewry as a major force in Jewish thinking took place at the same time. Major figures in the history of the Reform Movement emerged at this time, and synagogues as well as schools representing Reform Jewish ideology appeared.

Since many Jewish communities were well intact by the 1860s, Jewish participation in the Civil War was significant. Jews lived both in the North and the South and tended generally to support the war effort of the region in which they resided. After the Civil War, industrial expansion in the U.S. was great, but Jews were generally excluded from most of the industries that developed at this time, such as oil, railroads, shipping and banking. The area of business that was then wide open was retailing, and in large part this is the reason for the Jew in the U.S. being associated with retail markets.

1880–1929

In 1880, the Jewish population of the U.S. was 280,000. By 1925, it had increased to 4,500,000. Those figures, by themselves, begin to tell the story of the few decades that are a major event in Jewish history. Between 1880 and 1925, some 2,378,000 Jews arrived in the U.S.

The reasons for this huge migration of Jews from Eastern Europe, where most of them came from, are simple and at the same time complex. The simple reason is that life in Eastern Europe was becoming more and more unbearable. Pogroms were widespread during certain years, Jews were expelled from different regions and anti-Semitic violence was a constant threat. Underlying those more immediate reasons, however, were other factors: The Jewish populations in Eastern Europe grew at a pace that often made it impossible for a community to survive economically. In addition, the movement from Eastern Europe was continually building momentum. As more people arrived in the U.S., the notion of America as a land of the free made its way back to the villages of their ancestry. Eastern Europe was literally buzzing with the idea of America and this helped considerably in the migration of such masses to the U.S. The immigrants to America were mostly from Russia, Poland, Romania and Austro-Hungary during this period. It is during these years that most of our ancestors came to the U.S.

Within the years of this era, the pace of immigration increased with each decade. Between 1881–1892 approximately 19,000 Jews arrived, on the average, each year. Between 1892–1903 the annual average was 37,000. Between 1903–1914, the yearly average was 76,000. By 1918, the U.S. contained the largest Jewish community in the world.

Most of the immigrants arrived in New York. Many went to Philadelphia, Boston, Detroit, Cleveland, Chicago and other places, but the Lower East Side of New York City became the center of the world for the largest group of newly arrived Jews. With the start of World War I, immigration came to a temporary halt. After the war, a series of bills passed in the U.S. Congress also served to slow up immigration considerably.

This period in American Jewish history is perhaps the richest and most well known. It was a milestone in the history of the Jews, transplanting families from one side of the world to the other. Individuals and families left their ancestral homes of generations to establish new roots in America. The quantity of material written during and about this period is vast, and entire libraries could be filled with the story of this era.

1929–1945

The time period from the beginning of the Depression to the end of World War II can be seen as another era in American Jewish history. However, it is here where we can see that to divide history into specific eras has its problems. So much can happen within just a few years that to lump several years together does not serve much of a purpose. Although this is particularly true of this era, the same can be said of the other time periods already discussed. History is a complex unraveling of time, and hardly a generalization can be made without there being an exception quickly found.

We do see that there was very little immigration during these years, particularly in comparison with the years of the period before this one. The key date during this era is 1933, the year Nazism arrived in Germany. With the vicious anti-Semitism increasing in Germany as well as in Poland and Romania, the number of Jews driven to leave and come to the U.S. increased. Those seeking immigrant status in the U.S. came up against difficulties in this period that were unknown just a few years before. The economic situation in the U.S. coupled with anti-immigrant sentiment on the part of U.S. consuls empowered to grant visas, caused immigration to be not as great as it might have been. During the years 1933–1937, total immigration did not exceed 33,000. The rate increased between 1938 and 1941, however, and the total for this period was 124,000. The increase was the result of the extreme worsening of the situation for Jews in Germany as well as in the lands recently taken over by Germany. But by the end of 1943, Jewish immigration to the U.S. had virtually stopped.

1945–the Present

During the years 1947–1951, a little more than 119,000 Jews immigrated to the U.S. The large majority of them were Holocaust survivors, more than 63,000 of them entering the country by the Displaced Persons Act of 1949. Between 1960 and 1968, about 73,000 Jewish immigrants arrived, made up of Israelis, Cubans and Near Easterners. In recent years, many Jewish immigrants to the U.S. have come from the former Soviet Union and Israel.

Canada

Although the Jewish history of Canada parallels that of the U.S. in many ways, it would be useful to take a glimpse of Jewish migration to Canada.

The year 1759 begins the Jewish history of Canada. It was then that a permanent settlement arose in the country. At this time, the Jews were concentrated in the city of Montreal. The community was quite small, however, and by 1831 the population of Jews in Canada was only 107. In 1851, the Jewish population had increased to 248, and in 1861 there were 572 Jews in the country. By 1871, the population was 1115, split fairly evenly between Quebec and Ontario. Finally, in examining the total Jewish population of Canada just before the period of mass migration in 1881, we find that there were 2393 Jews.

The sources of these immigrants were the same as that of the U.S. immigrations. Most Jews came from Western and Central Europe with a minority coming from Eastern Europe in the middle of the nineteenth century. As in the case of the U.S., it is really after 1881 that the bulk of the Canadian Jewish population arrived. The present-day Jewish population of Canada consists mainly of families descending from the post-1881 migrations. By 1891, the Jewish population of Canada was up to 6414, and by 1920, the figure was more than 125,000.

Since the U.S. introduced a quota system for immigration after World War I, Canada saw an increase in immigration, but with the arrival of the Depression, restrictions tightened in Canada as well, limiting immigration severely. Again, as in the case of the U.S., the rise of Nazism in 1933 in Germany led to another increased effort at immigration by Jews. Pressure in Canada by its Jewish leadership attempted to keep the doors open for oppressed European Jews. But restrictions and anti-immigrant and anti-Semitic sentiment kept the figure low.

Between 1930 and 1940, 11,000 Jewish immigrants arrived in Canada. After World War II an additional wave of Jewish immigration occurred, the number totaling 40,000 between 1945 and 1960.

The major Jewish centers in Canada have been and still are Quebec and Ontario, with Montreal, Quebec, Toronto, Hamilton and Ottawa being the leading Jewish cities.

Israel

Not all European immigrants went to the U.S. In fact, there were years during which migration to the U.S. was at a standstill and other countries were sought out by those looking for a better life. Israel, or Palestine, is not merely an alternative to America; a "return to Zion" has been a part of Jewish Tradition for centuries, and whether or not individuals who migrated to Israel saw it as a Biblical "return to Zion," it remains a major destination of many Jews.

Throughout history, there have been several reasons expressed for migration to Israel. The first is the ancient notion of a "return" as we have just mentioned. A second reason has been the desire to study Torah where the Sanhedrin and the great academies were located. There has also been a belief that a person who is buried in Israel will reap "other world" benefit from this.

Another motive for migration to Israel, or aliyah as it is called, has been the belief that only in Israel can mitzvoth be fulfilled. There has also been the belief that Israel will cure illness as well as barrenness. A belief that an increased population in the Land of Israel will hasten the Messiah has been another motivation for aliyah. Finally, we find that large numbers of people went to Israel—even since the thirteenth century—to escape persecution in Europe.

In modern times, migration to Israel has been motivated by combinations of the above-mentioned reasons in addition to national and ideological factors that inspired great numbers of Jews to "make aliyah."

During the period after 1881, which as we know was the height of Jewish exit from Europe, there was considerable migration to Palestine. The stages of migration to Palestine and Israel are known by the phrases "First Aliyah," "Second Aliyah" and so on. The dates of the First Aliyah are considered 1882 through 1903. By 1903, approximately 10,000 Jews had settled in the region. The Second Aliyah was the period from 1904 through 1914, the beginning of World War I. The First and Second aliyot combined saw about 70,000 Jews migrate to the country, though it must be noted that many of them left because of the hardship of life there. There is no question but that the U.S. was the major attraction of Jews relocating during this period. Of all the Jews who were intercontinental migrants between 1881 and 1914, only 3 percent arrived in Eretz Israel.

As immigration to the U.S. slowed down considerably after World War I, aliyah picked up. Between 1919 and 1926 nearly 100,000 Jews made aliyah. When the 1930s arrived, Palestine became enormously important as a destination for Jewish migrants. Anti-Semitism was worse than ever because of the rise of Nazism, and the U.S. had slowed down acceptance of immigrants drastically. Therefore, Palestine became exceedingly important. Between 1932 and 1939, which is known as the Fifth Aliyah, almost half of the intercontinental migrants went to Palestine. In that same period, the U.S. and Canada received but a fifth of the intercontinental migrants. The period of World War II is, of course, the most tragic. Most Jews were unable to leave Europe, though between 1940 and 1945, nearly 45,000 Jews reached Palestine—where the British turned many back. The British also denied entrance to Palestine to many Jews in the years following the Holocaust, between 1945 and May, 1948. Fewer than 70,000 Jews were able to enter Palestine. In May, 1948, Palestine became the independent nation of Israel, and from that time until the present, Israel has become the most popular destination of Jewish intercontinental migrants. The U.S., Canada, and France (in the 1960s) were also the destination of many migrants of this period. But again, Israel was clearly the leader. From May, 1948, through 1951, almost 700,000 Jews went to Israel. It was only in the mid-1960s that migration to Israel began to slow down considerably.

Who Were Your Immigrant Ancestors?

The brief descriptions of Jewish migrations and population growth in the U.S., Canada and Israel are the backbone of the Jewish history of the time periods covered. Basic to the understanding of a particular history and a particular people are the answers to the questions: Where were they from? How did they get there? What did they do?

As we have said, if you examine the general periods of recent Jewish history, you should be able to place your own personal family histories in these eras. So, for example, if your great-great-grandfather was a German Jew who arrived in this country in 1852, you can easily see that this particular branch of your own family background was a part of a special era in Jewish history. Of course, in order to know this, you must know the history of your own family. It is not enough to think that your ancestors were immigrants and that they came to America one day. Your own personal history is wrapped up in the choices made by your ancestors. To lump them together in a category called "the past" is a disservice to them, their risks, their strengths, and their lives. Again, the question remains: Where do you fit into Jewish history?

One of the results of tracing your family history and creating a family tree is that at one point, for each of the branches in your direct ancestry, you will discover your immigrant ancestor. Eventually, when you follow each branch back, your mother and your father, your four grandparents, your eight great-grandparents, your sixteen great-great-grandparents and so on, one individual in each line will be an immigrant. For some of us, it may be found very soon; our own parents might be the immigrants. Or it may be just two generations back to our grandparents who were the immigrants in our families. In any case, none of us are without immigrant ancestors, obviously. That is, unless you are an immigrant.

Although each person in your family history is special for his or her own contributions to your life, your immigrant ancestors surely have a unique distinction among the others. We know that it was often hardship, anti-Semitism and fear that pushed immigrants to America, but that final decision—to make the journey—must have often taken immense courage. All you have to do to know what the experience may have been like is to imagine for yourself leaving your home, family, friends, familiar environment and everything that you have known for a lifetime, never to see it again. The result of that kind of imagining is dramatic. To envision your grandfather at age fifteen leaving his parents, his brothers and sisters and his entire life to journey by himself to America never to return is a powerful experience and an education. It strains the mind to realize the number of divided families, the number of children who said farewell to parents, the number of sisters who said goodbye to brothers, or the husbands who left behind wives and children to save enough to send for them.

Another frightening image is to think about what the fate of your family might have been (in most cases) had your ancestor not made the decision to take the risk, the journey, and leave his home. As you build your family tree, you will often notice that your direct ancestors—grandparents, great-grandparents and so on—had brothers and sisters whose decisions were quite different from each other. You will also come to understand that it was the decisions made by your direct ancestors that, in large part, are responsible for your very existence. If yours is like most Jewish families, you will undoubtedly find siblings of some of your direct ancestors who made different kinds of decisions—and their descendants were never born. This is understandable, of course. When you think of the radically different kinds of decisions that brothers and sisters make all the time, it is easy to comprehend why some lines of your family still exist and why some did not survive. But what you ought to understand above all else is how the choices made by your ancestors are so profoundly linked to your own life. If any one of your sixteen great-great-grandparents had chosen a different life from what he or she did, you might not be where you are today. You might not exist at all. Imagining this is not a senseless game, but is, rather, a serious invitation to attempt to understand the lives of your ancestors and the paths they traveled.

It is possible to enter Jewish history in a dramatic way through the history of your family as we have said and will say many times in this book. One of the most important points in the history of your family as well as in the history of the Jewish People is in the recent migrations. In the last 150 years nearly every Jewish family has made a radical move geographically. The Jewish population pockets of today are extremely different from 150 years ago, or even 100 years ago for that matter. In Eastern Europe, where the center of world Jewry existed for a few hundred years, the Jewish community today is almost nonexistent. The U.S., whose Jewish population was so small just 100 years ago, is one of the two centers of world Jewry today.

It will probably not be difficult for you to determine, for each of your family lines, who your immigrant ancestors are. Jewish migrations to this country were recent enough to make this task easy in most cases. If your family stems at all from a German-Jewish family that migrated in the 1850s, the chore might be more difficult than others, but will still be generally easy since records exist often where memories of family members fail. Along with your search for the names of your immigrant ancestors, you will want to concern yourself with other questions as well. When did each immigrant ancestor arrive in this country? What towns and countries did they come from? Let us treat each of those questions separately.

When did your immigrant ancestors arrive in this country? The answers to this question relate directly to the summaries of the different eras of Jewish history and migration we have discussed. When you know the year that an ancestor of yours arrived on America's shores, you can then link up to general Jewish history and understand your part in it. For example, let us assume that your grandfather arrived in the U.S. in 1907. From that simple piece of knowledge, you will know, from your understanding of American Jewish history, of what era and what phenomenon your grandfather was probably a part. A Jew who arrived in the U.S. in 1907 was a part of the major wave of Jewish immigration to this country, a mass migration unequaled in Jewish history. Suddenly, when you read a description of the arrival of Jewish immigrants to an American port in this era, the history is not anonymous. It is your history.

The date of arrival of a direct ancestor of yours is a special event in your own personal history regardless of how long ago it took place. It does not take much of an imagination to understand the profound impact that the decision to leave and the arrival in America had, not only on your ancestor but on you as well. There are many dates that we all have been taught are significant in history. The date of arrival of an immigrant ancestor should be among such dates for each of us. Unlike the famous dates of history shared by all, these dates are personal and meaningful to us as individuals. We each have a personal history as well as a common history. It is important to know both.

What towns and countries did they come from? This is another question of importance when pursuing our family histories. How many of us know the names of the towns left behind by our immigrant ancestors? How many of us know what the conditions were like in those towns that forced or provoked our ancestors to leave? General history tells us about the anti-Semitism, the economic hardships and other conditions that plagued Jewish communities throughout Europe. But what, specifically, was it like in the places where our families lived for generations in the Old Country? This is a question that we discuss at greater length in Chapter 8.

Once the decision was made to journey to America, money had to be saved and a steamship ticket had to be purchased. Although steamships made their way back and forth across the Atlantic throughout the years, it is hardly enough to know that the type of vehicle used to transport Jewish immigrants was, in fact, a steamship. Rather, how much more alive Jewish history and your own personal history becomes when you know the name of the ship traveled on by your ancestors, and what the ship looked like, both from the outside as well as the conditions lived in for the days of the long journey.

When the ship arrived, it landed in a port. Most often, that port was New York, though Boston, Philadelphia and other seaports were also used. Do you know where your immigrant ancestors arrived? Do you know, in addition, where your ancestors went after they arrived in America? Did they stay in the city of their port of arrival? Or did they travel to some inland city that was the location of a relative who had arrived in America earlier? Or did they go to some unexplored location? Maybe they were sent by an organization set up to aid and relocate immigrants to some rural community or to a job opportunity. The encounter that your immigrant ancestor had with his or her new country must have been what we now call "culture shock." The U.S. was very different from the Old Country. The people were different, the language odd, the customs strange. Where did they go? How did they deal with the shock of an alien culture? What organization might they have joined, or helped found, that made life in the U.S. more manageable?

There are many questions that can be asked and hopefully answered regarding the experiences of your immigrant ancestors. Suppose you discover that an ancestor settled in Richmond, Virginia, but you have lived all your life in New York. You will want to learn more about the Jewish community of Richmond at the time that your ancestor was there. Here is one more example of Jewish history coming alive through your family history: Though the history of the Jewish community of Richmond might have once been the farthest thing from your mind, it is now important for you to learn about it—in order for you to understand yourself. When was the Richmond Jewish community founded? Was there a Jewish section of the city? What synagogues existed when your ancestor lived there? Is there a Jewish cemetery there in which family members might have been buried? What occupations did Jews have at that time in Richmond? What made people go to Richmond to live and what made them leave? Are there any old photographs of the Richmond Jewish community for that time period so you can get an idea of what life was like then and there? Is there a photo of the street on which your ancestor lived? What other information can you discover about the city to add to your understanding of your ancestor's life?

The question of where your ancestors lived is not one of concern exclusively regarding your immigrant forebears. This is particularly true for families who have been in America for several generations. If some branches of your family have been in this country for many generations, you will have the same kinds of questions for each of them. Where did they live? What were their occupations? When did they arrive in the places they lived? When did they marry? What did their homes, their streets and their neighborhoods look like? Which synagogues did they belong to? For each generation before you, back to your immigrant ancestors, you will want to approach the same questions with interest and research. You will want to enter their lives as much as possible, knowing the streets in which they walked, the occupations that earned their living, and the choices that molded their lives—and yours.

Immigrants often joined and formed organizations known as landsmannschaften. A landsmannschaft, as noted earlier, is an immigrant benevolent organization formed by the ex-residents of a particular city, town, shtetl or region. For example, if you were an immigrant from Pinsk, you might belong to the Pinsk Society.

Before 1880, landsmannschaften were generally synagogues, each formed by individuals and families from the same European locality for the purpose of having a place to pray among one's "people." However, the rise in Jewish immigration after 1881 brought more secular organizations of this kind into being. These later benevolent societies often had synagogues as well, but their purposes were expanded to include other functions. Often, the landsmannschaften, as their first order of business, would raise money to buy a burial plot for the use of families of the membership. Membership would also offer other advantages, such as sick benefits, interest-free loans, aid to families during a mourning period and overseas aid to members of the town who were still in Europe. The landsmannschaften were also often instrumental in arranging for individuals and families to come to America. (It should be noted that landsmannschaften have existed and continue in some places to exist in Latin America, the U.S., Western Europe and Israel.)

Many cities throughout the U.S. had landsmannschaften. Since New York City and Chicago represent two of the largest Jewish communities in the U.S., it is understandable that they had hundreds of landsmannschaften in their midst. In 1914, there were at least 534 landsmannschaften in New York, for example. As time went on, the ancestral home of immigrants faded from their minds. This and the deaths of members over the decades has brought the existence of landsmannschaften almost to a close. Although there are still many such organizations functioning, the numbers are minute in comparison with the days when landsmannschaften were major societies. The decline of these groups was well underway by the beginning of World War II, although there was a slight revival of activity after the Holocaust when many groups published Memorial Books in honor of the destroyed towns.

The total experience of your immigrant ancestors, including their homes in the Old Country, their decision to travel to America, their journey aboard a steamship, their arrival in the U.S. or wherever else they landed, and their lives in their new home, all should have meaning for you. Most important, there are many ways in which you can learn about and document those journeys and those lives, to begin to see the experiences of your family as Jewish history, and to see yourself as a part of it as well. Enter Jewish history through the lives of your ancestors and make your own personal connections with your past and your people.

TRACING THE JOURNEY

How to Find the Ship That Brought Your Ancestors to America

The steamships on which your ancestors traveled to America and the dates of their arrival are important in the context of your family history. In the same way that the *Mayflower* was the celebrated ship that took early settlers to the American continent, so too should the steamships in your family history be noted as turning points in your own history.

It is not always easy to find the names of ships or their arrival date, but with a little detective work, you should be able to do it.

1) The first step, of course, is to ask your relatives if they remember. In cases where your family has been in this country for generations, you cannot expect anyone to know, but in families with more recent arrivals, it is possible that they know. I tried to track down the steamship of my grandmother Helen for a long time with no luck. My grandmother was one of those people (whom you will surely encounter) who did not care to talk much about family history, but one day I decided to ask her if she knew the name of the ship on which she came to America. It did not take her a second to answer, "*The Fatherland.*" This was the same woman who refused to tell me her place of birth for months! All of my research time could have been saved if I had begun by asking the immigrant herself. Since then I have asked many immigrants if they knew the name of the ship that took them to America. Most people remember—as if it were yesterday.
2) If your immigrant ancestor is alive and does not remember, ask if he or she came alone or with others. If you get names of others and they are alive, ask them. You have to become a detective, trying to locate leads wherever you can find them.
3) If you have partial information on the ship and its arrival, you might be able to narrow the field by using the *Morton Allen Directory of European Passenger Steamship Arrivals.* This volume, which is a standard book in large public and research libraries, and especially genealogy collections, includes the following information: a year-by-year listing of arrival by steamship companies, dates of arrival, ports of arrival, and the exact names of the steamships. The information is for all vessels arriving in New York between 1890 and 1930, and in Baltimore, Boston and Philadelphia between 1904 and 1926.

   How can you use this directory? Let us assume you have been told the exact date of arrival (someone might remember the day but not the ship) and the port. The *Morton Allen Directory* has an easy-to-find listing of the ships that arrived in the above-mentioned ports for each day. This will surely narrow the field to just a few. Or you may know the ship and the approximate date, but not an exact date. Again, you can narrow the possibility down considerably by using the directory. In either case, this might be helpful if you are forced to use step number 6 below.

4) One of the pieces of information often given on Petitions for Naturalization or Declarations of Intention is the name of the steamship and date of arrival for the individual who applies for citizenship. See "Naturalization Records" (page 305).
5) If you can locate the passenger list of the steamship on which your ancestors arrived in America, you can obviously identify the name of the ship. See "How to Find the Steamship Passenger Lists with Your Ancestors on Them."
6) A final means of locating this information is the most difficult and time-consuming but is certainly a good last resort. Steamship passenger lists are on microfilm at the National Archives and various genealogy libraries. If you know the approximate time of arrival and the port of arrival, you can search through the microfilm looking for the names of your ancestors. See "Your Ancestor's Steamship Passenger Lists."

How to Find the Steamship Passenger Lists with Your Ancestors on Them

One of the most intriguing documents relating to the history of your family is the actual passenger lists of the steamships on which your ancestors traveled. The National Archives has more than 11,000 reels of microfilm containing copies of most passenger lists since 1820.

If you know the name of the ship and the date of arrival for an ancestor, the National Archives will check its collection and make copies of the lists for you (and they will bill you; the current fee is $10.00 per list). Or, if you are in Washington, D.C., you can do the research yourself, provided that the ship arrived more than fifty years ago. Lists of ships that arrived since then are confidential. They can be searched, however, by the staff of the National Archives, and they will provide you with the information pertaining to your family alone.

In some cases, the passenger lists have been indexed by name, thereby relieving you of the problem of locating the name and date of the ship by yourself.

To obtain copies of passenger lists, you must fill out NATF (National Archives Trust Fund) Form 81. Send to:

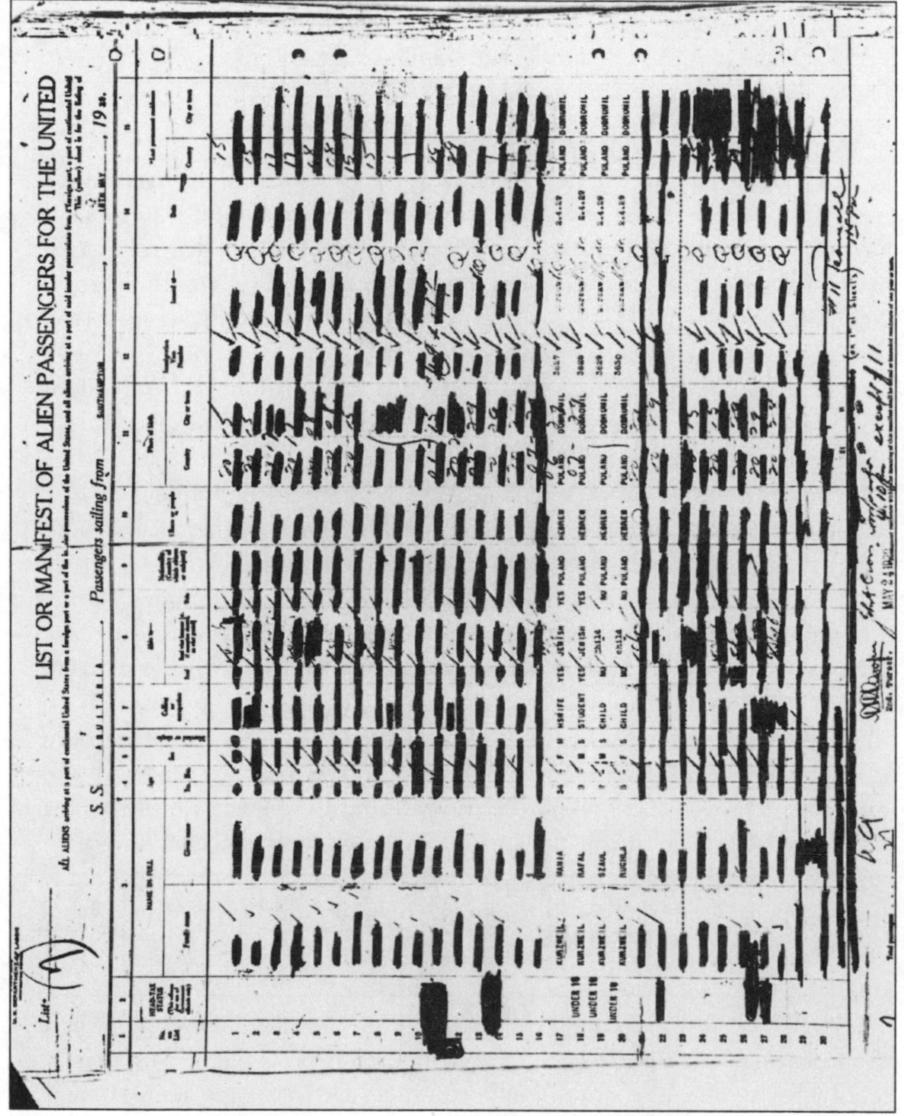

LIST OR MANIFEST OF ALIEN PASSENGERS FOR THE UNITED

S.S. AQUITANIA Passengers sailing from SOUTHAMPTON

Family name	Given name	Calling or occupation	Nationality	Race or people	Country	City or town
KURZWEIL	MANIA	HSWIFE	POLAND	HEBREW	POLAND	DOBROMIL
KURZWEIL	RAFAL	STUDENT	POLAND	HEBREW	POLAND	DOBROMIL
KURZWEIL	SZAUL	CHILD	POLAND	HEBREW	POLAND	DOBROMIL
KURZWEIL	RUCHLA	CHILD	POLAND	HEBREW	POLAND	DOBROMIL

Passenger list of the author's grandmother, father, uncles, and aunt.

General Reference Branch
National Archives and Records Administration
7th and Pennsylvania Avenue N.W.
Washington, D.C. 20408

Although the information provided on the passenger lists varies from ship to ship and year to year, some of the lists contain quite a bit of information including name, age, occupation, closest living relative at last residence, place of residence, place of birth and destination in the U.S. These and other facts will be of interest and might serve as the missing clues for additional information.

For example, many passenger lists give place of birth. You might only know the last place where an ancestor lived. This will give you an additional town where your family lived.

The Mormon Church (see page 226) has a microfilm collection of a rather unusual set of passenger lists that are worth noting. Lists were kept in Hamburg of all passengers who left from that port and went to the U.S. (and elsewhere). The lists provide each passenger's name, occupation, place of birth and residence, age, sex, name of vessel, captain's name, destination and departure date. The lists were kept from 1850 to 1934 and are indexed by year and first letter of the surname. In other words, if an ancestor of yours went through the port of Hamburg on the way to America, he or she should appear on these lists. If you know the date, you can look in the index under the first letter of the last name and hopefully find it. If you do not know the year, checking various dates would be necessary, of course. This resource is more valuable than it might seem at first since many Jews in addition to those from Germany came through Hamburg.

> Sometimes the decision to change names was not the immigrant's own. Immigration officials at the ports of entry refused to be bothered with exact transcriptions of a new arrival's difficult name. Down on the forms went totally new or easy names—Smith, Jones, Johnson, Robinson, Taylor, Brown, Black, White, Green. And then there were Jews who named themselves after old streets on the Lower East Side—Clinton, Rivington, Delancy, Rutgers, Stanton, Ludlow. Or when children went to school, teachers who found a name unpronounceable put down on the records something close enough but easier to say. After a time the parents would accept the new name the children brought home.
>
> MILTON MELTZER, *TAKING ROOT*

How to Obtain Photographs of Your Ancestors' Steamships

The ships that took our ancestors to America were often overcrowded, uncomfortable, and in poor condition, yet still a profoundly important part of our history. Therefore, an interesting and unusual addition to your family history would be photographs of the steamships themselves.

The Mariners Museum in Newport News, Virginia, has a huge collection of steamship photographs, and their collection is indexed by the name of the ship. You can either write to the museum and allow its staff to choose the photographs for you, or you can consult a large library in your area to see if it has the *Catalog of Marine Photographs* that the Mariners Museum used to publish. The Mariners Museum will sell you reproductions of its photographs. Send for their price list and details.

Another equally excellent source for these photographs as well as for additional information about steamships and their history is the Steamship Historical Society, 414 Pelton Avenue, Staten Island, New York 10310.

If you want information about the society, write to the above address. However, if you want to obtain photographs of steamships from its huge collection, write to the University of Baltimore Langsdale Library, Steamship Historical Society of America Collection, 1420 Maryland Avenue, Baltimore, Maryland 21201. The Steamship Historical Photo Bank is located at the University of Baltimore. The collection contains more than 60,000 photos.

Naturalization Records: An Important Genealogical Source

Finding naturalization records is not like looking for a needle in a haystack. It can be worse. First you have to find the haystack. (It's not easy to find the "haystacks" of naturalization records since they are scattered all over the place, look different, and are often hidden under haystacks of other kinds of documents.) Once you find the haystack, looking for the needle (the papers *you* want) requires you to have certain amounts of knowledge, skill or luck. The final problem is this: however difficult it might be to find a needle in a haystack, the saving grace is your assumption that the needle is in there somewhere, but in searching for naturalization records of an ancestor, you can never know if you will find what you are looking for. In fact, you can never be sure that the documents even exist.

2270

Form 2202
U. S. DEPARTMENT OF LABOR
NATURALIZATION SERVICE

DUPLICATE

No. 114411

UNITED STATES OF AMERICA

DECLARATION OF INTENTION

Invalid for all purposes seven years after the date hereof

State of New York,
Southern District of New York, } ss: In the District Court of the United States.

I, Samuel Leib Gottlieb, aged 32 years, occupation Salesman, do declare on oath that my personal description is: Color white, complexion dark, height 5 feet 6 inches, weight 140 pounds, color of hair brown, color of eyes brown other visible distinctive marks none, I was born in Borgo Prund, Hungary, on the 8th day of June anno Domini 1890; I now reside at 217 East 66th St., New York City, N. Y. I emigrated to the United States of America from Bremen, on the vessel Crownprinzessin Cecilie; my last foreign residence was Hungary; I am married: the name of my wife is Helen; she was born at Hungary and now resides at with me. It is my bona fide intention to renounce forever all allegiance and fidelity to any foreign prince, potentate, state, or sovereignty, and particularly to [illegible], of whom I am now a subject: I arrived at the port of N.Y., in the State of N.Y., on or about the 14th day of Jan., anno Domini 1907; I am not an anarchist; I am not a polygamist nor a believer in the practice of polygamy; and it is my intention in good faith to become a citizen of the United States of America and to permanently reside therein: SO HELP ME GOD.

X Samuel Leib Gott[illegible]
(Original signature of declarant.)

Subscribed and sworn to before me in the office of the Clerk of said Court at New York City, N. Y., this 1 day of Feb. anno Domini 1923.

[SEAL.]

[signature]
Deputy Clerk of the District Court of the United States

Declaration of Intention to become a U.S. citizen by the author's maternal grandfather.

With that pessimistic introduction, we have to attempt to tackle the problem of naturalization records, because they often are profoundly important sources of information—genealogically. One personal illustration will suffice: After sending for my great-grandfather's naturalization records, I received a reply from the Immigration and Naturalization Service that gave me my great-grandfather's birthdate, place of birth (in Europe), place of last residence (in Europe), his first wife's name (she died in Europe and never came to America), the date of his arrival (this allowed me to get a copy of the passenger list of the ship) and the names and birthdates of all his children—some of whom were killed in the Holocaust and whom I would never have been able to learn much about!

How did I get the document that provided me with so much information? I simply sent a letter to the Immigration and Naturalization Service, telling them what I wanted. They sent back a form. I filled it out. And in a few weeks I received the information.

If it's that easy, then what was the "needle in a haystack" business all about?

The answer is that it can be easy, and it can be terribly difficult, depending on when your immigrant ancestor arrived in America and petitioned to become a citizen.

Let's start at the beginning. We are looking for naturalization records, better known as citizenship papers. On your family tree, only your immigrant ancestors might have naturalization records on file. Ancestors of yours who never came to America would not have become citizens, obviously, and those ancestors (or family members) who were born in the U.S. were automatically citizens—and therefore never had to fill out papers. For your immigrant relatives, however, citizenship papers might very well be on file somewhere in the U.S. As a genealogist you should be interested in finding those records.

There are three different types of naturalization records. The first is the Declaration of Intention, which was filled out by an immigrant who wanted to become a citizen. This Declaration of Intention was commonly known as one's "first papers." Then there is the Final Petition, which was completed just prior to becoming a citizen. And finally there is the Certificate of Naturalization, which is the document given to the new citizen that declares that citizenship has been granted.

Among old family papers you can often find the Certificate of Naturalization, but this is the least valuable document in terms of information about the individual. The Declaration of Intention and the Final Petition are the most valuable because they often asked several personal

THE UNITED STATES OF AMERICA

TO BE GIVEN TO
THE PERSON NATURALIZED

No. 3889298

CERTIFICATE OF CITIZENSHIP

Petition No. 242620

Personal description of holder as of date of naturalization: Age 67 years; sex male; color white; complexion dark; color of eyes brown; color of hair brown-gr[ay]; height 5 feet 2 inches; weight 160 pounds; visible distinctive marks none
Marital status Married; former nationality Poland Austria
I certify that the description above given is true, and that the photograph affixed hereto is a likeness of me.

ORIGINAL

(Complete and true signature of holder)

UNITED STATES OF AMERICA
SOUTHERN DISTRICT OF NEW YORK } ss:

Be it known, that Abusch Kurzweil then residing at 65 Cannon Street New York City having petitioned to be admitted a citizen of the United States of America, and at a term of the District Court of The United States held pursuant to law at New York City on May 20th 1935 the court having found that the petitioner intends to reside permanently in the United States, had in all respects complied with the Naturalization Laws of the United States in such case applicable, and was entitled to be so admitted, the court thereupon ordered that the petitioner be admitted as a citizen of the United States of America.

In testimony whereof the seal of the court is hereunto affixed this 20th day of May in the year of our Lord nineteen hundred and 35 and of our Independence the one hundred and 59th

Seal

Charles Weiser.
Clerk of the U. S. District Court.
By Deputy Clerk.

DEPARTMENT OF LABOR

Certificate of Naturalization for Abusch Kurzweil, the author's paternal great-grandfather.

questions of genealogical interest, such as occupation, date and place of birth, name of ship and date of arrival and details on spouse and children.

There are a few more things to know before we discuss the locations of naturalization records. Although we may assume that immigrants became citizens (unless we know for sure that someone did not), it is possible that an immigrant ancestor of yours never applied for citizenship. Indeed, you may have a grandparent still alive who was an immigrant and who is not a citizen.

Also be aware of the fact that children under sixteen automatically became citizens when their parents were naturalized, and furthermore that until 1922 a wife automatically became a citizen either by marrying a citizen or by the naturalization of her husband.

The key date in the story of naturalization records is September 26, 1906. It was on that date that citizenship procedures became a federal function. If you are looking for the naturalization records of someone who was naturalized on or after September 26, 1906, you will usually have an easy time of searching. How do you know if your ancestor was naturalized on or after this date? You don't. But by asking a few questions within your family you will probably have a good sense of when the immigration occurred and therefore when the naturalization could possibly have taken place.

If you have reason to believe that the naturalization of interest to you took place after this date, you are advised to write to:

U.S. Immigration and Naturalization Service
Washington, D.C. 20536

Ask them for a few copies of Form G-639 (Freedom of Information Privacy Act Request). Don't write them a long letter describing your great-grandmother and her trip to America or any other information of a personal nature. No matter what you write, however long, short or interesting, if it has to do with naturalization records, they will send you Form G-639. So, you might as well ask for it right from the start. And again, ask for a few; it will save you time when you want more.

Fill out the form as best you can. Do not be alarmed when you find that you cannot fill out only 3 percent of the form. The Immigration and Naturalization Service has the nice policy of working with whatever information you can give them. If *all* you have is your ancestor's name, then fill that in and leave everything else blank. The more you can fill out, the better chance you have of locating the document—or the right document. (Once, when all I knew was the person's name, I received the papers of someone with the same name, but who was an entirely different individual.)

The INS has been flooded with requests for information because of all the recent interest in genealogy. Although they are required by law to acknowledge receipt of your request, as of this writing it can take as much as a year before you receive the information you are looking for. One thing I have yet to figure out is the Immigration and Naturalization Service policy on sending information. Sometimes I receive photocopies of the desired documents and sometimes I receive a letter that contains a transcription of the information on the original documents.

What if you are sure that a person was naturalized but the Immigration and Naturalization Service tells you they have nothing? Then, either the person was naturalized before September 26, 1906, or a clerk made a mistake (which wouldn't be the first time). As far as a clerical error is concerned, all you can do is try again (unless you want to—and are able to—examine the documents yourself, which we will discuss in a little while). The fun begins if the person was naturalized before our key date.

Before September 26, 1906, naturalizations were a local function and naturalization proceedings took place in just about any court, federal, state or local. Although naturalizations took place in courts around the country after our key date, it was only then that the courts were required to send the information to the federal government for processing and filing.

Besides the lack of centralization of these documents before 1906, the procedures also varied. Therefore, different questions were asked of the potential citizen and different records were kept. So, although the type of information on post-1906 naturalization records is basically standard, the pre-1906 information varies from next to nothing but the person's name and former country on up.

Let us say that you are looking for the naturalization records of someone who arrived in the U.S. well before September 26, 1906. I say "well before" because if the immigrant arrived shortly before that cutoff date, there is still a good chance that the naturalization took place after the 1906 date. It is here where excellent detective work is essential. What you must try to determine is where the immigrant whose papers you are looking for entered the U.S. (which port) and where he or she resided right after arrival.

Once you have determined this (to any degree of accuracy), you must try to determine which court the immigrant might have gone to to file "first papers." Of course, there is no guarantee that the immigrant filed for citizenship immediately upon arrival. He or she might have waited ten years (at which time the immigrant could have been living in another city) or he or she could have never gotten around to becoming a citizen.

We have to assume that the immigrant became a citizen, however, and we must also begin somewhere in our search. The best bet is to start at the location where the person entered the country and first resided. Finding the right court is not easy. It takes patience, time and lots of letter writing—unless you can travel to the city in mind, in which case you might either get the search done quickly or you might reach a dead end. If this all sounds very negative, it is meant to.

The process of searching for pre-1906 naturalization records can be difficult, especially if you have little information to go on. Of course, if someone entered the U.S. in Boston and then spent all of his or her life there, the search would not be too difficult. You would have the field narrowed, and it would just be a limited amount of leg work. But the more vague your information is, the more difficulty you will have.

There a exists a body of indexes of naturalization records that can save years of work, depending upon the location you are dealing with. During the Great Depression, the Works Progress Administration (WPA) put people to work doing various interesting and unusual tasks. One of them was the photocopying and indexing of pre-1906 naturalization records for certain locations. If the naturalization that you are looking for took place in the states of Maine, Massachusetts, New Hampshire or Rhode Island, or in New York City, you're in luck. The National Archives in Washington has the Soundex indexes and photocopies for these New England states.

Since New York City was not only the entering point for most Jews to the U.S. but also the home of the greatest number of Jews, it would be justified to go into more detail here regarding naturalization resources for New York City.

The National Archives Northeast Region Branch located at 201 Varick Street in New York City has an excellent collection of naturalization records for the New York City area.

The holdings there are a large, but not complete, collection of New York City naturalizations. For example, the county clerk of each county in New York has the records of those naturalizations that occurred in the State Supreme Court of that particular county. Other records are scattered elsewhere as well. In fact, this situation of the noncentralization of these records is a good example of what the researcher often has to face when trying to locate naturalization records.

A trip to this National Archives Regional Branch would be worthwhile for all people doing searches of these documents for the New York City area. If you are unable to travel here, you can write them at:

Northeast Region Branch
National Archives and Records Administration
201 Varick St
New York, NY 10014
Phone: (212) 337-1300

There is one important reason why a trip to this records center (or any archives) is worthwhile. A clerk will try to answer a specific question. However, in my opinion, you and you alone can do an adequate search. You can look for a dozen alternate spellings of a name, whereas a clerk will usually only check the spelling provided. In addition, every researcher knows that you always learn more than what you are looking for—*if* you do it yourself!

Finding naturalization records is not easy but is certainly worthwhile. Be aware, of course, that the earlier the naturalization took place, the less information there is likely to be. However, you can never know what you might find until you try.

With our despised immigrant clothing we shed our impossible Hebrew names. A committee of our friends, several years ahead of us in American experience, put their heads together and concocted American names for us all. Those of our real names that had no pleasing American equivalents they ruthlessly discarded, content if they retained the initials. My mother, possessing a name that was not easily translatable, was punished with the undignified nickname of Annie. Fetchke, Joseph and Deborah issues as Frieda, Joseph and Dora, respectively. As for poor me, I was simply cheated. The name they gave me was hardly new. My Hebrew name being Maryashe in full, Mashke for short, Russianized into Marya, my friends said that it would hold good in English as Mary; which was very disappointing, as I longed to possess a strange-sounding American name like the others.

MARY ANTIN, *THE PROMISED LAND*

The future of Judaism belongs to that school which can best understand the past.

LEOPOLD LOWE, HUNGARIAN RABBI

Research into the past, as an aim in itself, without the present, is not worth a bean.

BIALIK

Sending for Family History Documents Is Legitimate

As you send for all of the different kinds of documents available which will help you to research your family history, you might wonder whether the U.S. Government and local government agencies see your requests for information as important enough for them to help you. *Never worry.* Not only are you entitled to see the kinds of records which are described in this book, but you will also be paying for almost everything. Government documents cost generally between $2 and $10—and considering the simple process required for most document searches, it becomes a rather lucrative business for government agencies.

So, never feel that your family history is not "important" and that you will get a response only if you are on "official" business. Family history and genealogy is a legitimate and accepted endeavor.

> Everything that typified the old country, in family names as well as first names, had to go. The Russian -skis and -vitches were dropped. Levinsky became Levin, Michaelowitch, Michaels. Russian and Polish names were Anglicized: Bochlowitz to Buckley, Stepinsky to Stevens, Shidlowsky to Sheldon, Horowitz to Herrick, Willinshky to Wilson. Davidowitz became Davidson, Jacobson became Jackson. The Germanic names too were readily translated into English: Weiss-White, Preiss-Price, Reiss Rice, Rothenberg-Redmont.
>
> Milton Meltzer, *Taking Root*

THESE ARE THE GENERATIONS

As we continue to travel backward in time through Jewish history, we find it increasingly difficult to discover our individual ancestors and the lives they led. Some of us will find it impossible to trace branches of our family histories farther back than three generations. In part, this is because of the recent adoption of fixed surnames as we have discussed in Chapter 5. In part, your inability to find people who remember the histories of your families will also contribute to the difficulty of the task. But it is important that we continue to see Jewish history in terms of individuals and families. Jewish history is the story of individual Jews, not simply the "important" people. Although those "important" people had sweeping effects on our Jewish ancestors, we want to continue to examine the lives of our ancestors and how they might have lived them.

Jewish history can be seen as several overlapping layers. First there are the individuals. Individuals are connected to each other through their immediate families. Immediate families are actually small parts of larger families. The larger families come together to form the Jewish People, and if we take our progression one step farther, the Jewish People belong to the "family of humankind."

It is easy for us to view the first stage of our progression. Each of us is an individual, as are our parents and so on. We want to view the lives of as many persons as we can and to see how their lives fit into Jewish history. For example, when we view the life of your grandmother who journeyed to America in 1908, we see her as a significant part of Jewish history. When we learn about a cousin of ours who was murdered in the Holocaust, we see that as a significant part of Jewish history. Despite the fact that those experiences happened to millions of people, we enter those experiences ourselves through the lives of the people in our families.

We can also observe the history of our families. Since we, ourselves, are a part of many families, we can see the differences among them. One of our families might be more religious, another might be more Zionist, another might be more literary, and so on. Our purpose is not to generalize about people, but rather to see where they fit into the larger story of Jewish history. In my father's family, for example, there is one branch of the family tree almost all of whom went to Israel when it was still Palestine. Another branch, almost in its entirety, stayed in Europe and was killed in the Holocaust. Hardly a representative of that branch left Europe. In still another branch, nearly the whole family escaped the Holocaust and came to America. It is fascinating to examine these family branches to see how differences and decisions just like these resulted in modern Jewish history.

Can you make these same kinds of observations in your families? Can you see certain entire branches of your family tree having gone in one general direction, whereas others have taken different courses? What about your branch? When viewed from the outside, what choices have been made with your family during the last several generations that have affected you and your life—as a Jew?

There are countless stories of American families who have discovered family in Israel whom they never knew existed. Sometimes branches of a family traveled to Israel a few generations ago. In other cases, survivors of the Holocaust went to Israel and their American cousins did not know that they survived. There could be branches of your family in other countries as well. In my own family, there are branches in Israel, Australia, Poland, Hungary, South America and the U.S.

Again, however, there will come a point when it will be impossible for you to trace the tracks of your early ancestors, in which case you can focus in on the history of their community. Let us say, for example, that your family (a branch of it) can be traced to the town of Jaroslaw in Galicia. Perhaps you can even trace a few generations back in Jaroslaw with names, dates and stories. But then you can go no farther; no one remembers anyone that far back and no research was able to turn up anything about your specific family. This should not stop you from continuing to understand the Jewish community of which your family was a part. Where is Jaroslaw? What was it like? When did the Jewish community establish itself there? What is its history? Although you cannot trace individual members of your family in Jaroslaw, you can certainly begin to get an idea of Jewish community life there, and in that way enter Jewish history.

To continue with our example, we have to remember that the history of Jaroslaw had to have affected the lives of your Jaroslaw ancestors. As a part of the community, its history, its events, touch its members' lives. By quickly checking a source such as the *Encyclopedia Judaica,* we can get a glimpse of the history of Jaroslaw back to the 1600s. We learn about the famous fairs that took place there, and the meeting of the Council of the Lands of Poland that met there frequently. These meetings were important for all of Polish Jewry. We also learn that in 1738 there were 100 families living in Jaroslaw. If this was a town of yours, perhaps one of those families was yours as well. In 1737 a "blood libel" case occurred, giving us a further idea of the history of this town. This is just the beginning of the history of the Jewish community of Jaroslaw—but if it was a town of yours, you would be able to continue to learn about it and thereby enter Jewish history.

In other words, when you have traced back in your family history as far as you can go, continue to understand your history by examining the towns and regions whence you have come. If you know that your family came from Germany in the 1840s, an understanding of Germany in the decades before that date will contribute to your sense of the history of your ancestors.

Although it is not possible for everyone to take his family histories back through the Middle Ages, it is possible to begin to understand the history of the Jewish People through a history of a particular Jewish community. Again, let us take the example of the town of Jaroslaw. Two items in the brief history that we mentioned are of particular interest. The first is the Council of the Lands of Poland, and the second is the "blood libel." In order to understand the history of your ancestors' community, you will need to know about the Council of the Lands of Poland and also the history of "blood libel." In both cases, these questions will take you to other aspects of Jewish history, and again, you will find that you have entered Jewish history through the history of the community of your ancestors. This method of understanding Jewish history can be compared to setting up a long row of dominoes and then tipping over the first one. Step by step the entire row of dominoes will fall over. In the same way, once you have touched any piece of Jewish history, you will arrive quickly at the next step, until you have gone through history yourself, and begun to understand the experiences of your family. Your family is the focus of this process; in tracing their steps, you are tracing the steps of the Jewish People. In tracing the steps of the Jewish People, you will eventually arrive at the beginning of time, and also you will arrive back in the present—at yourself.

A next step would be to begin to get an understanding of the migration patterns within Jewish history. Again, if your family came from Jaroslaw, they were certainly not there since the beginning of time. The Jewish community in Jaroslaw had a beginning—before that time, there were no Jews there. Whence did the Jews of Jaroslaw come? There are general answers to this type of question, and a familiarity with migration patterns—that is, the routes taken by Jews throughout Jewish history—allows us to get a better idea of where our families came from. For example, we know that in 1492 the Jews of Spain were expelled from that country. Historical research informs us of many places where Spanish Jews fled. If the places where they fled included areas which we know our families to be from, it is reasonable to assume that parts of our families may have originated in Spain. Although we cannot be sure of this, it is reasonable speculation, and we can continue to enter Jewish history from that perspective. A branch of my family, as I mentioned earlier, whose earliest known location in Europe was the city of Przemysl, claims a family tradition that had us originate in Spain. Although our names are not Spanish (we were probably in Przemysl when surnames were first required) and we do not look Spanish, it is interesting to note that the first synagogue in Przemysl was built by two Spanish immigrants in 1560. This means that Spanish Jews did reach the east end of Galicia at that time, and that our family tradition is conceivable.

Suddenly, the expulsion of the Jews from Spain in 1492 becomes a real part of my history.

The detail of Jewish history, from the destruction of the Second Temple to modern times, is filled with tremendous variety and complexity. Although short histories of the Jewish People have been written that include the major events and areas of our history, they cannot, by definition, tell the stories of individuals and their communities in the detail that they deserve. And it is the detail that is often the most colorful, the most instructive, and the most interesting.

It is a curious fact that most of us have a good idea as to the events of Biblical history, a familiarity with the Talmudic era, and a general knowledge of recent Jewish history during the last century or so. But in between those eras, from the early days of the Diaspora to the 1800s, most of us have no more than a vague idea of Jewish life. We are familiar with biblical personalities, dramas and heroes, as we are familiar with the Holocaust and the birth of the state of Israel, but what was life in Prague like in the 1600s? How did our ancestors in Germany live in the 1700s? What was life like for our forebears in those centuries between the Talmud and the present?

> He has a great future, for he understands the past.
>
> HEINRICH HEINE

8

The Old Country

WALKING THE STREETS OF YOUR SHTETL

It is startling to realize the extent to which we are affected by the lives of our ancestors.

It is equally startling to realize the extent to which we are distant from the life-styles of those same ancestors.

The more we examine the past from which we have come, the more we make these discoveries. We find many aspects of our family histories that have survived throughout generations, and we also find many aspects of the lives of past generations that are strange to us, as if we were examining an alien culture.

Of course, the lives of our ancestors *are*, to a significant degree, alien. Life in a European shtetl was far different from, say, urban life in the U.S. Our language is different, our educations are different, the pace of our lives is different, and the structure of our communities is different. When we take a journey back through time and arrive at the places where our ancestors lived, we must be introduced to the streets, the houses and the faces as if we were strangers.

If you are like most Jews in America, it is merely a few generations ago, at most, when your parents, grandparents or great-grandparents, walked the streets of European cities, towns and villages. Of course, there are those Jewish families who have been in America for more than a century, and there are others who do not come from Europe, but generally, the Jewish community in the U.S. can find its roots in the Eastern European shtetlach that peppered the map a mere generation ago.

The Jewish towns and villages that were the homes of our ancestors for generations no longer exist in Eastern Europe. Most of the Jews in those places were murdered; many of the towns were destroyed. To imagine this is almost impossible. Millions of Jews living in thousands of towns, and suddenly, in a few years, it is all gone.

Yet we yearn to know those places, to see the streets on which our ancestors, as children, played; to see the shops in which our ancestors, as adults, earned their living. We want to see the fields, on which they tilled the soil, to enter the shuls in which they prayed to God and celebrated their Jewish lives. We want to know those places. We want to understand what it was like to live in those communities. We want to know what our ancestors wore, what issues concerned them, and how they lived their lives. We want to enter the schoolrooms and see the chairs on which we might ourselves have sat, had our families not left, or been chased out, or been destroyed. We want to know where our families lived and through them where *we* lived.

We cannot return to those places. We can take journeys to those towns and see different worlds from the ones that our ancestors left. We can walk the streets today, and wonder what the roads look like beneath the pavement that has since been laid. Often we can visit a town of our ancestors and see the synagogue that still stands, or visit the Jewish cemetery that may still be intact. But we can never return, through space, to those places of our ancestors.

Yet we can journey to them—in Time. We can travel there in our imaginations, helped along by that which has survived: facts, photographs, and tales all adding to the stories of our families, all helping us to understand from where we came.

Each Jewish community in the world, whether it be in Eastern or Western Europe, Asia, the Americas or elsewhere, has its own history, and the telling of each community history would be impractical or impossible here. Our ancestors each came from different spots on the globe, and the time in which they lived in these places will change the perspective taken to understand their lives. For example, if an ancestor lived in Germany, the history of that particular family would differ greatly depending upon what period of history we are speaking. A Jewish family in Germany in 1812 had a very different experience from a Jewish family in Germany in 1934. Another example is the shtetl where my father was born. When asked, "Where were you born?" he would answer, "Dobromil, Poland." When I ask his uncle where he was born, he would say, "Dobromil, Austria." If I had visited Dobromil before the breakup of the Soviet Union, my father's town would have been part of that nation. Today Dobromil is in the Ukraine. The same thing is true for many locations in Europe. The history of that continent is filled with border changes, sometimes so frequent that each generation finds itself in the same town, but in different countries.

But we still want to visit those places, in Time, trying to re-create what it was like for our forebears. We want to know whatever we can about the lives of our ancestors, so that the more we know of the places where they spent their lives, the more we will know about them. What has remained of those towns, cities, shtetlach and villages that were once the homes of our ancestors? What can we discover about them?

We can find photographs of these places, helping us to imagine the streets that our ancestors walked and the buildings in which they lived and worked. We can find histories that have been written about the tiniest locations where Jewish communities existed. We can learn about the religious life of the communities, discovering which rabbis taught in which communities and what these rabbis wrote and taught. This would allow us to understand some of the religious influences upon our ancestors. We can learn quite a bit about the most remote places, mostly because of the historical instinct of so many people who have come from these towns. In a vast number of cases we find examples of individuals who knew the worth of recording the present that, for us, has turned into precious history. Our Jewish libraries are filled with a wealth of information about the Jewish communities that are no longer here. It is up to us to discover those communities, to enter them in our minds, to relive those experiences, and to connect with our past.

DISCOVERING THE OLD COUNTRY

> Remember the days of old.
>
> DEUTERONOMY 32:7

MEMORBUCHS

As we have said, Memorbuchs are different from Memorial Books. They exist for many towns, and the best source is:

The Central Archives for the History of the Jewish People
The Hebrew University Campus
Sprinzak Building
P.O.B. 1149
Jerusalem, Israel

In general, it would be best to write to this archive, which is the largest Jewish archive collecting worldwide Judaica in the world, and ask them for a listing of their holdings for specific locations. For example, if you are interested in Minsk, write to the archives and ask for a listing of material in their Minsk holdings.

> To preserve the past is half of immortality.
>
> B. D'ISRAELI

BEGINNING TO DISCOVER YOUR ANCESTRAL HOMES

If you are not familiar with *Encyclopedia Judaica,* you should be. This sixteen-volume, beautifully produced set of books is a wellspring of Jewish knowledge. Though various criticisms have been lodged against the encyclopedia, it remains the finest source, in my opinion, to begin research on most Jewish subjects.

Although the smallest of villages and towns will not appear in the *EJ* unless something quite unusual happened there, you can find brief articles about hundreds of Jewish settlements throughout the world here. Volume I is the encyclopedia's index: Always check the index because you might find references to subjects that do not have their own articles.

Each article in the encyclopedia has a bibliography as well, which is useful in sending you off to more information.

> There is an uninterrupted chain of generations that makes it possible for us to regard ourselves as having descended from Abraham, Isaac, and Jacob. We may question this statement biologically; nevertheless, they were our ancestors to all intents and purposes. We are members of one mishpahah, even though our cosmology, our conception of the universe, our way of living, our whole hierarchy of values, may differ radically from theirs. Our relationship to our earliest childhood as a people is analogous to the relationship we have to our own childhood. We think and live differently from the way we did when we were children. Yet, when we think of our childhood, we maintain that we are the same persons we were before, even though there may not be a single cell in our body that has remained unchanged since we were children; but there is a continuity of personality that consists of memories, associations and habits.
>
> IRA EISENSTEIN, RABBI

Locating Landsmannschaften

Before explaining how to track down a landsmannschaft, I want to explain the usefulness in doing so.

If your family came from a certain town that still has a landsmannschaft, there is a good chance that members of the organization knew your family and could tell you about them. In addition, landsmannschaft members can give you another perspective on the European town of your ancestors. They might also have pictures of the town.

I have tracked down the landsmannschaften of two towns of my ancestors and I've gone to their meetings. In one case, I was able to purchase a copy of the town Memorial Book as well as to meet people who knew my family. In the other case, my luck was far better. I met a man who had photographs of family members of mine who were killed in the Holocaust! If not for that man and his photographs, my family would never have known what those cousins looked like. I also met a man at a landsmannschaft meeting who was a musician. He was about ninety years old, charming and friendly. He played the fiddle at my grandparents' wedding in Europe! From members of this landsmannschaft I learned the names and addresses of landsmen in Israel who knew my family from Europe. I wrote to them and received letters with still more stories about my family and their life in the shtetl.

It is extremely difficult to track down landsmannschaften. In most cases, these organizations no longer exist. For those that do exist, some have but a handful of inactive members; others, even if they do meet, do so infrequently. There are some groups that are still quite active and still meet regularly, but they too are difficult to locate. There is no central headquarters for this kind of information. Nonetheless, you can make the following attempts:

1) Contact the office of the cemetery where the landmannschaft has a plot. They will often know of a current contact person.
2) Inquire of YIVO Institute for Jewish Research. YIVO publishes a booklet called *A Guide to YIVO's Landsmannshaften Archive* by Rosaline Schwartz and Susan Milamed, New York, 1986. This index reflects the contents of YIVO's landsmannschaft archives, a collection of material of great potential interest to Jewish family historians. Since YIVO has been actively seeking material from landsmannschaften for years, they have some information on how to contact them.
3) UJA-Federation, I've been told, has a superb list of landsmann-

schaften, used by them for fund-raising. UJA is protective of their lists, but they are worth a try.

A final and more ambitious method of locating landsmannschaften, or even landsmen, is to place an ad in a Jewish newspaper. People have been known to take out an ad in a big city Jewish paper saying, "Anyone belonging to or having knowledge of a (*name of town*) landsmannschaft, please write or call:—." An ad like this can bring interesting results.

There is an excellent article on the subject of landsmannschaften in *Toledot* (see page 110). Written by Zachary M. Baker, head librarian at YIVO Institute for Jewish Research, the article is titled "Landsmannschaften and the Jewish Genealogist" and appears in the summer 1978 issue.

> The past is our cradle, not our prison, and there is danger as well as appeal in its glamour. The past is for inspiration, not imitation, for continuation, not repetition.
>
> ISRAEL ZANGWILL, *FORTNIGHTLY REVIEW*, APRIL, 1919

YOUR SHTETL OR TOWN DURING THE HOLOCAUST

Earlier in the book I discussed the International Tracing Service (ITS) in Germany. Another very important source of Holocaust information is Yad Vashem.

Yad Vashem in Israel is publishing a series of books called *Guide to Unpublished Materials of the Holocaust Period*. They offer a town-by-town listing of the towns represented in the Yad Vashem archives. Usually this material is taken from postwar testimony offered by survivors. You might find some moving and fascinating information about your towns here.

THE BLACKBOOK

In 1965, Yad Vashem published the *Blackbook of Localities Whose Jewish Population Was Exterminated by the Nazis*. This book contains a list of almost 34,000 localities in Europe with Jewish residents. Some of these localities contained thousands of Jews, and others contained just one or two Jews living among non-Jewish neighbors.

During the Holocaust, almost every town, city and village listed in the *Blackbook* was purged of its Jewish population.

The reader of the *Blackbook* will find listings of the most minute hamlets in Europe. If your ancestors came from small villages that have long disappeared from the face of the earth and that no contemporary maps indicate, the *Blackbook* will probably list them. Often you will be told the names of towns lived in by your family and you will be unable to find any reference to them. The *Blackbook* would be your best source to verify the existence of these towns—and the book will give you the number of Jewish residents in that town sometime before the war. The book will tell you the date of the census on which the population figures were based.

If your local Judaica library does not have this book, it should. Unfortunately, it is currently out of print and Yad Vashem seems to have no plans to reissue it. Perhaps you could arrange to see if your local Judaica library would be able to photocopy the book for its collection. It would be worth it.

I once gave a lecture in which I mentioned the *Blackbook*. I rather boldly stated that the book listed *every* Eastern European town. A young woman raised her hand and said, "The town my family was from, in Hungary, had only four people in it. They were all my family. That town will not be listed!" Well, the book, as we said, lists town names and their prewar population figures. We looked up the town which the woman had in mind—and we found it! And the population *was* four!

A skeptic was suddenly a believer.

> No individual can be constructed entire without a link with the past.
>
> AHAD HA'AM

HOW TO LOCATE YOUR SHTETL

It is not always easy to locate a shtetl, town, village or city. There are several possible problems.

1) The location might no longer exist, having been wiped off the map with its inhabitants during the Holocaust.
2) The name might have changed since your family last resided there.
3) You may know the location by a name in a different language from one currently used.
4) You may know the location by its Jewish name, but not by its more commonly used name.

5) Often a locality will be spelled the way it sounds, but this is not necessarily the way it is spelled on maps.
6) Since borders change throughout history, you may be looking for your town in the wrong country.
7) The town may have been hardly a town at all, and may simply not be found on most maps. Frequently, a town was no more than a few houses.

If you have tried, without success, to locate a particular town, do not give up. There are several possibilities, some of which might prove to be fascinating.

An extremely important volume has recently been published that makes the task of locating Jewish towns infinitely easier than before. *Where Once We Walked: A Guide to the Jewish Communities Destroyed in the Holocaust* documents over 21,000 towns in Central and Eastern Europe where Jews lived before the Holocaust. It pinpoints the latitude and longitude of each town, its direction and distance from the closest major city; includes population figures prior to the Holocaust; and indicates where other information about each town can be found. Also included are 15,000 alternative names for towns, including the many Yiddish names that some towns had. The authors use an ingenious system based on sound, not spelling, to help you to locate your towns. Gary Mokotoff and Sallyann Amdur Sack did a brilliant job in creating this most invaluable reference source.

Most libraries have an atlas collection and large public and university libraries often have extensive map departments. One of your first steps to locating your towns and shtetlach is to consult a gazetteer. A gazetteer is a geographical dictionary. You use it just like a dictionary by looking up the word by the various ways you think it would be spelled. A gazetteer will provide the "definition" of a location. It will tell you the country that it is in, its proximity to other well-known locations, the longitude and latitude and even a little about the current and historical situation.

Perhaps the finest gazetteer available is *The Columbia Lippincott Gazetteer of the World.* This book was published after World War II so it will often not be helpful for towns that were completely wiped off the map. In that case, you should check their earlier edition, known as *A Complete Pronouncing Gazetteer or Geographical Dictionary of the World*, published by the J. B. Lippincott Company in 1906.

A gazetteer in the German language that is also excellent is *Ritters Geographisch-Statistisches Lexikon.*

One problem that is difficult to solve is spelling. Often you will only know the pronunciation of a location and not the spelling. Your best bet would be to get a dictionary in the language of the name of the location and figure out how that pronunciation is spelled. Also, a good map librarian would be familiar enough with foreign pronunciations to be able to help you. A final suggestion is this: Whenever you learn the name of a town, try to find out where it was near. If you can locate a familiar spot on a map, then you can examine a detailed map of the area and try to locate the place by scanning the map. One of my ancestral towns is Przemysl. However, I was first introduced to the town by hearing its name—which is pronounced Pahshemishel. It took me a while to find it on a map, but after using some of the resources just mentioned, I was able to do it rather quickly. My one key was that I knew its general vicinity. From that point on, it was simple.

When you have exhausted the few sources pertaining to geographical locations mentioned here, as well as the many others discussed elsewhere in this book (a good example is the *Blackbook* on page 323), I would urge you to read an article published in *Toledot: The Journal of Jewish Genealogy,* Volume 2, Number 3 (winter 1978–79). Zachary M. Baker, currently head librarian at the YIVO Institute for Jewish Research, has written the finest study I have seen on the question of how to locate Eastern European towns. Titled "Eastern European 'Jewish Geography': Some Problems and Suggestions (Or, How to Get From Amshinov to Mszczonów Without Moving an Inch)," Baker's article is essential if you are having difficulty spelling, pronouncing, or locating your ancestral towns.

"Why are you crying, Mother? Because the house is burning?"

"Yes."

"We shall build another, I promise you."

"It's not the house, son. If I cry, it is because a precious document is being destroyed before our eyes."

"What document?"

"Our family tree; it is illustrious, you know."

"Don't cry. I'll give you another. I'll start anew, I promise you."

At the time, Dov-Ber was five.

ELIE WIESEL, TELLING OF THE MAGGID OF MEZERITCH,
A CHASSIDIC MASTER, IN *SOULS ON FIRE*

I never realized, when I was very young, how much I missed by never having met either of my grandfathers. Not having known a grandfather, I had to go out looking for him, and what I will try and set out here is simply the story of the search. The trouble is that, given my own type of mind, this is bound to take me further than a few nostalgic family tales. However, if it is a little grown up for the einiklach (grandchildren) at this stage, they'll get round to it one day. Above all, they will understand, I think, that I was not just looking for my grandfather but for myself.

CHAIM RAPHAEL, "ROOTS—JEWISH STYLE," MIDSTREAM

Tradition must be a springboard into the future, not an armchair for repose.

BEN-GURION

GENEALOGICAL SOURCES IN THE OLD COUNTRY: HOW TO DO RESEARCH LONG DISTANCE

Once you have determined where your family came from, you will want to figure out how to get information from those places. One way, of course, is to travel to your ancestral towns. One need not, however, travel to Europe or the former Soviet Union in order to get records from those places.

Having said that, it is important to make the point that the path is not easy, nor is it consistent. For years, genealogists thought that records behind the iron curtain would never be within reach. Today, things are different. We have more contact with archivists in Eastern Europe and the former Soviet Union than ever before. At the same time, it seems that things are changing in that part of the world quite rapidly: One day a Russian archives is answering genealogical requests for a low fee and rather quickly, and the next day the rates have jumped up and the service is slow. Or a records center asks for a certain fee before they do research for you and they find a lot of material, and then someone else sends money, gets a canceled check and never hears from them again.

I have been careful in this book to make sure that I send you in productive directions. I have seen many books on genealogy that fill their pages with names and addresses of overseas archives that hardly ever prove lucrative. The following are some pieces of general advice as well as some sources that some of us have found to be useful:

1) Don't underestimate the usefulness of comparing notes with other genealogists. Discoveries are being made every day. Wouldn't it be nice to hear of the successful experience a fellow genealogist has had writing to organizations in Poland before you do your own letter writing. Join a Jewish Genealogical Society; subscribe to genealogical publications; plug into the ever growing network of people who are doing Jewish genealogical research.
2) Subscribe to *Avotaynu* (see page 82) and purchase some of their back issues (see the index to *Avotaynu* on page 82). As you look through the index, notice that there are articles on just about every country in the world, written by people who have had firsthand experience with genealogical research.

   One thing you will notice when reading the articles is that the situation keeps changing. The clearest example of that is for locations in the former Soviet Union. There is no question that things have opened up considerably and that lots of people have received information that we only dreamed about just a few years ago. But it is also true that many of us have had radically different experiences, with great successes and great stumbling blocks.

   Nevertheless, a growing number of people are involved with contacting archives overseas, and with the increased experience has come some important sources.
3) The Mormon interest in genealogy is perhaps the most significant factor helping those of us who cannot travel to the countries of interest and don't want to rely on the often doubtful process of writing to local archives in Europe. The LDS Family History Library has the largest collection of Jewish records in the world. For example, I had no difficulty locating the birth, marriage and death records for my grandmother's family from Hungary because the Mormons have records for her little Hungarian town going back a few hundred years.

   The Mormon collections are remarkable and should not be underestimated. See the *Encyclopedia of Jewish Genealogy* (see page 112) for an extensive list of the holdings of the LDS Family History Library for Germany, Poland and Hungary. The Mormons have microfilmed records worldwide, and their collections grow daily. Simply put, anyone doing serious Jewish genealogical research must keep alert to the Mormon holdings.
4) An effective way to work with foreign countries is through the

aid of professional researchers who live in those countries. It is important to keep in mind that a hired researcher might spend lots of time without success. It may take many, many hours of research before something interesting is found. It can get expensive.

On the other hand, many of us have had great success when contacting reliable free-lance researchers in other places around the world. Once again, *Avotaynu* is a useful source. You will often see advertisements there placed by researchers looking for customers. In addition, there are articles written by free-lance researchers in *Avotaynu*.

5) Writing directly to the old country can be useful, but I confess that I am hesitant to offer specific names and addresses. Every book with genealogical sources is out of date by the time it is in print owing to the changes of names, addresses and so on. This becomes even more of a problem with sources in those countries where most of our families come from. Despite the vast changes over the past several years in Eastern Europe and the former Soviet Union, there just isn't enough consistent information at the moment for any country in that area of the world.

Having offered these words of caution, I can suggest a few sources to try based on some success that I've experiences and heard about:

POLAND

Civil records for any town might be available through local civil records offices:

Urzad Stanu Cywilnego
(town), Poland

The Polish State Archives in Warsaw has been helpful to some in either accessing records they have or sending the researcher in a productive direction:

Naczelna Dyrekcja Archiwow Panstowowych
ul. Dluga, 6
SKR Poczt 1005
00-950 Warszawa, Poland

LITHUANIA

Both the Central State Archives and the Central State Civil Records Archives in Lithuania have brought some success:

Centrinis Valstybinis Istorijos Archyvas
232015
Vilnius, Gerosios Vilties 10

Centrinis Valstybinis Ciuilinis Metrikacijos Archyvas
232600
Vilnius, Mindaugo, g. 8

BOHEMIA AND MORAVIA

Ministry of the Interior of the Czech Republic
Archivni Sprava
Trida dr. Milady Horakove 133
16621 Prague 6, Czech Republic

Ministry of the Interior of the Slovak Republic
Department of Archives
Krizkova 7
81104 Bratislava, Slovak Republic

6) One final note: Needless to say, there are other locations where our families are from. I cannot, in good conscience, offer names and addresses of archives that I have either no firsthand knowledge or reliable reports.

You also want to keep in mind that there are many people around the world who are involved with genealogical research, and most of them are not researching Jewish families. Therefore, although there is a vast literature available on genealogy, most of it is directed at non-Jewish research. I say this because you may be able to find literature on, for example, Polish genealogical research, that will provide you with general Polish sources that may come in handy. I'd urge you to go to your local public library to see what general genealogical sources are available. There are many "how-to" genealogy books of specialized interest. They can often be quite useful.

Visiting the Old Country

Sooner or later, every Jewish family historian considers planning a trip to the places in the Old Country whence they or their ancestors came. For years, I had the fantasy of walking the same streets in Poland that my great-grandfather walked as a child and as a young married man. I wanted to see the shops that were once ours; I wondered if the

Jewish cemetery still existed. Were there any Jewish records in the town? Were there any Jews still there? Did the citizens of the town remember my family? These questions and others ran through my mind hundreds of times.

I eventually made the trip to Poland and did visit my great-grandfather's town. Before I share that experience and discuss the things you ought to consider before making such a trip, it would be best to explore the "cons" of the argument as to whether or not to travel to the Old Country.

Several family members were upset with me for considering and planning such a trip. "How could you even step foot on the places where our people were murdered?" they asked. Other people said, "You have better things to do with your money than support those countries." Still others said, "If you want to go to find your roots, go to Israel!" People used all kinds of reasons to dissuade me from making the journey. "What do you expect to find there?" many asked. "Everything was destroyed." Or, "They won't let you see anything. You are wasting your time." Or, "I know someone who was there shortly after the war. Nothing is left."

I've heard all the arguments, and while I can appreciate them all, I nonetheless had my own private reasons for going. I had to see for myself.

Let me try to answer all of the above questions and objections as best as I can. Although I know that the decision of whether to travel to the Old Country is a personal one, I think it would be useful to share my own feelings on the subject.

I try to understand the bitterness felt by survivors toward the non-Jewish population in the countries where our people were murdered. I can understand them not wanting to have contact with people, many of whom just stood by watching while Jews were killed. Others, of course, did not just stand by, but participated. But I was born after the War, and as a new generation I feel I must have faith in humankind. I cannot harbor the same feelings as the generations before me. Although I am, for example, quite suspect of Germans who were adults in Germany during the war, I cannot declare them all guilty, and I surely can hold nothing against their children. The same is true for other countries in Europe.

As for the comment (which I have heard several times) that my "roots" are really in Israel so therefore I should go there instead, I have two responses. One is that I have visited Israel and feel that every Jew who has the opportunity should do the same. But my "roots" do not lie only in Israel. Maimonides was from Spain, Rashi from France, the Baal Shem Tov from Eastern Europe, and even the Babylonian Talmud was not written in Israel. Certainly my roots go *back* to Israel, but they travel far and wide outside of Israel as well. I want to discover *all* of my past.

I was quite influenced before my trip to Eastern Europe by those people who told me that everything was destroyed and that there was nothing left to see. If this was true, I thought to myself, then surely I would be wasting my time and money. I thought about it for a long time. What if the town was completely leveled and a new town built on top of it? What would be the point of seeing this? But finally I decided: I was going to Eastern Europe not only to see what was left but also what was no longer left! I had done enough research about the town, I had seen enough photographs of the places where my ancestors lived to know what it looked like when they were there. I wanted to see what had stayed the same and what had changed. Seeing *nothing* would also be important to me.

There was one additional factor in my decision to visit Eastern Europe: I have cousins who live there. My father's cousin, Josef Schlaf, lives in Warsaw, and my mother's first cousin, Gyorgy Barta, and his family live in Budapest. I wanted to visit them. This was the most important element in my decision. I finally decided to go.

While I was planning our trip, one book excited me the most. It was the *Traveler's Guide to Jewish Landmarks of Europe*, by Bernard Postal and Samuel H. Abramson (Fleet Press, New York, 1971). This volume is a country-by-country, town-by-town guide to Europe—and it includes Eastern Europe. Although far from complete (and now quite out of date), it can still be a gold mine of information for anyone planning a trip to Europe. When you are in the major cities of Eastern and Western Europe as well as smaller localities, the *Traveler's Guide* will inform you of many Jewish historical and current sights of interest.

When I checked the book, I was startled to find the name of my great-grandfather's town, Przemysl. To my surprise, I read that the Jewish cemetery still existed! How much I wanted to see that cemetery, to search for the graves of my family members, to walk through the paths and feel the Jewish history that took place there. I thought to myself that even if there were no Jews there, even if nobody remembered my family, even if everything else was destroyed—as tragic as it all would be—I would still be able to touch my past through the graves of the Jewish community. How many times my family must have stood in that cemetery to bury our dead.

Joseph Schlaf, cousin of the author. A Holocaust survivor who remained in Poland, he was discovered by the author through genealogical research.

The day finally came. I arrived in Warsaw. After spending a few days in that historic Jewish city with my cousin who lives there, I went to Przemysl. One of the first things I wanted to see was the Jewish cemetery. Everyone knew where it was. When I saw it, I was astounded for opposite reasons. I was shocked at how bad it looked and by how good it looked. It was interesting to learn that the major problem with Jewish cemeteries in Poland is *not* vandalism. It is neglect. The stones were not toppled over and crumbling from deliberate desecration. It was the seasons of bad winters, the overgrown trees and bushes, the tall growth of weeds and roots, and the total neglect of the whole area that caused the cemetery to look so bad. On the other hand, there it was, sitting there peacefully. Many of the stones could be read with ease. Others were quite worn but could still be made out. Still others were not visible at first, but after we pulled out giant weeds and pushed aside bushes and overgrowth, they too appeared! Some of the stones were 150 years old. Others were certainly older, but a good percentage of the old stones were totally illegible. Some were just slabs of rock with no inscription. Obviously, they once had words engraved on them, but time has worn them clean. I stayed in the town for five days. Three times I visited the cemetery, taking photos on each visit, recognizing names each time I uncovered new tombstones under the overgrowth. Visiting that cemetery was one of the most moving moments of my life. Each time I went, I prayed and somehow felt the presence of a Jewish community that once was so filled with life, and now is present only in the remains of the cemetery.

One of the many surprises in Przemysl was the number of people whom I found to speak English. English is taught in the schools and is apparently a popular subject. I had almost no problem communicating with people. The people who spoke English were happy to show me around and serve as my interpreters.

I was anxious to see where the synagogues were. I knew from my research that there were several synagogues before the war. Today, two of the buildings still exist. One is now the Przemysl Public Library. The other is a bus garage. This was obviously an upsetting discovery. I did not expect the buildings to still be synagogues (there are only a handful of Jews still in Przemysl); however, it was horrible to see this beautiful building turned into a bus garage. Somehow the library did not bother me as much. Actually, the reason is evident. Although I visited both buildings, I was most interested in the one that is now the library. This synagogue was a short distance from where my family in Przemysl lived, so I was fairly certain it was in this synagogue that my family prayed. Walking into the library, I was obviously a stranger. Only one member of the library staff spoke English and I was introduced to her. She was a young, pretty woman, very bright and warm. After an interesting conversation and a glass of tea, which I was served right in the middle of the library, the young librarian invited me to her home for that evening. I had a wonderful time, learned a lot about Przemysl from her and her husband, and I still write to them. They send me information about Przemysl and I send them magazines about tennis, their favorite pastime. They are, by the way, always on the lookout for Jewish items of interest to send me.

I could go on for pages about my trip to Eastern Europe. Suffice it to say that it was a deeply moving and profound experience for me. Again, both what I saw and what I knew I could never again see had a great impact on me. I visited concentration camps and former ghettos. I visited synagogues that were hundreds of years old and cemeteries that were even older. I met Jews who survived the Holocaust and stayed in

A former synagogue in Przemysl, Poland. It is now a bus garage.

Eastern Europe and I met some of their children. They are all eager to make contact with American Jews, and in this way I think my trip served a valuable purpose in showing a few lonely Jews that they are not totally alone.

Did I discover anything of specific genealogical value in Eastern Europe? I certainly did. When I was in Przemsyl, the city of my great-grandfather's birth, I went to the city hall and asked the man behind the counter (through the aid of a Jewish man who still lived in Przemysl and spoke some English) if he had my great-grandfather's birth record. He asked me when my great-grandfather was born. I said 1867. The man climbed up a tall ladder and reached up to grab a volume that was covered with dust. When he set the book down on the counter, I saw that it was a birth register of Jews from the 1800s! This particular volume was dated 1860–1870. Within a few minutes I found the name of my great-grandfather, along with his parents' names, their address in Przemysl and other information as well. It was the birth record from more than 100 years ago of my great-grandfather, Abusch Kurzweil.

I was told the myth so many times that all Jewish records were destroyed. The fact of the matter is quite different. There, in Przemysl,

Poland, was the birth record of the man after whom I was named. It was waiting for me all these years.

I have had the opportunity to do more genealogical traveling since my first trip. In addition to the wonderful time I had in Poland and Hungary visiting my relatives, I made other discoveries. One of my most extraordinary moments was locating the gravestone of one of my great-great-grandmothers in a tiny town in Hungary.

How to Plan Your Trip

Things have changed considerably since my first trip to Eastern Europe. They also changed drastically after my second trip. (When I entered the former Soviet Union, restrictions on travelers there were severe: Only a limited number of towns could be visited, the others were off limits. I waited for hours in Lvov, hoping for permission to travel to Dobromil, my father's birthplace. Permission was denied.) Today, in the former Soviet Union and in Eastern Europe generally, travel is much easier than it was only a few years ago.

Many travel agents specialize in trips to specific countries; I suggest you try to work with one of them.

More importantly, I strongly urge you to hook up with one of the Jewish genealogical societies (see page 217). Undoubtedly there are people in these groups who have recently made the kind of trip you are thinking about. There's nothing like good advice from recent travelers.

On the other hand, don't let the remarks of others about their experiences have too great an impact on you. For example, many people have had no success doing archival research when traveling to Poland. Others, myself included, have been able to walk into an archives, ask for information, and get almost instant results. So, keep an open mind, be daring, and stay optimistic. I believe that attitude is, possibly, the most important ingredient.

Of course, you should not travel to your ancestral hometown without having done your homework. You must learn about the general and Jewish history of the places you intend to visit. Otherwise you will not be able to appreciate fully your visit (see page 320). Try to locate as many photographs of the towns as possible so that you can recognize the places when you get there. Make copies of your family history notes and papers to bring with you. You might meet someone with whom you can have a rewarding family history conversation.

Often I am asked, "For how long should I visit my ancestors' town?" That depends upon how big the town was. If it is Warsaw or Prague,

The synagogue of Mateszalka, Hungary, birthplace of the author's maternal grandmother.

you can stay for days. If it is the average little village, one day is more than enough time (after which you will want to explore other places in the area, and so on). A small city might interest you for a few days. But do not think that your visit to a tiny old shtetl need take a week. Chances are you can walk every street and take every photograph and talk to every person within a few hours. Most of these places are rural and there is not much to see. On the other hand, your day or two might be among the most memorable moments of your life.

There are several sources that you will want to check for information about the locations to which you want to travel. One is the *Traveler's Guide to Jewish Landmarks of Europe* already described. Again, the book is out of date and far from complete. If you do not find your town, it does not necessarily mean that the town no longer exists. I visited many towns in Galicia that were not mentioned in the book but that had Jewish cemeteries still intact as well as other sites of Jewish interest. Of particular interest for me, in each town I visited, were three things: Where is the Jewish cemetery? Where are the buildings that used to be synagogues? Are there any Jews still in the town? Often I found cemeteries, buildings that were once synagogues and sometimes even Jews. None were listed in the *Traveler's Guide* or in any other source I could find, yet there they were.

Memorial Books (see page 133) are a must to check before your trip. If there is a Memorial Book for your town, it will provide you with pictures, names, history and sometimes even a map of the town! With a map, you can find sites of interest more easily. For example, since the synagogues have almost all since been converted into other kinds of buildings, an old map from a Memorial Book can serve as your guide to finding it. By the way, there are four things most synagogue buildings are now used for: libraries, warehouses, garages and movie theaters.

The *Encyclopedia Judaica,* mentioned often throughout this book, can be a good source of information about the current situation in the town of interest.

Landsmannschaften might also be a good source of information (see page 322) but I must make the following warning: I have found that members of the landsmannschaften I have encountered were both the first ones to discourage me from making the trip as well as the most interested in hearing about my experiences and seeing my photos when I returned.

Speaking of your return, when I returned from my trip, I did two things: I wrote an open letter to family and friends describing my trip. I could not write a separate note to each person, but I found it useful to write up a letter that I photocopied and sent around to interested people. The second thing I did was to make slides of my photographs (in some cases I took slides too) and invite the family to see them while I narrated. I did *not* put in all of my tourist shots—I did not want to bore my family with one more travelogue—but only the photos relating to the family history (along with a few general shots of Eastern Europe to put it into context). It was a very successful "party" when these slides were shown and it was appreciated by the family. Through my trip, they received a better sense of family history, and that was my whole purpose.

If you are planning a trip to Poland, you will want to first examine a book called *Scenes of Fighting and Martyrdom Guide; War Years in Poland, 1939–1945*. This book is a town-by-town guidebook describing Holocaust monuments throughout the country (not necessarily all Jewish) and how to find them. There is a description of the monument or location, a brief passage about what happened on that spot and directions on how to get there. YIVO (see page 224) has a copy of this book.

This house, still standing, was home to a branch of the Kurzweil family in Jaraslov, Poland.

A recently published travel guide might serve quite useful when planning your trips. It is called *The Jewish Traveler: Hadassah Magazine's Guide to the World's Jewish Communities and Sights*, by Alan M. Tigay (Jason Aronson, Northvale, New Jersey, 1994).

> Remove not the ancient landmark which the fathers have set.
>
> PROVERBS 22:28

ADVICE BEFORE TRAVELING TO EASTERN EUROPE AND THE FORMER SOVIET UNION

1) For many years people objected to my trips to Eastern Europe. "Don't go to those horrible places." "Poland is soaked with Jewish blood." "Don't bring them money." "There's nothing left to see. It was all destroyed." "Don't you have anything better to do with your time and money? Take a vacation!" First of all, there

are still Jews in Poland, Hungary, the former Soviet Union, etc. They want and need contact from us. Second, if there is something pulling you to those places, you must trust your own instincts and intuition. Despite the fact that many people told me that "there was nothing to see" I found that they were wrong. There is *plenty* to see—the way towns look; Holocaust memorials; relatives (There are 80,000 Jews in Hungary today. They have to be somebody's relatives!); historic sites; people who still recall people in the family; etc. Plan that trip!

2) You don't need to speak the language. English is probably the most popular language in the world. I found English speakers almost everywhere I went. As long as I was sincere and friendly, there was always someone to help. Young people in Eastern Europe and the former Soviet Union are looking for English-speaking friends.
3) Keep your expectations low. In some cases, you will find more than you ever dreamed you'd find. In other cases, you will not find what you are looking for. I'd suggest you don't have any specific expectations that will make or break the trip. If you have as your goal one small piece of information, and you don't find it, this is no reason to call the trip a failure. Keep your eyes open, make friends, be curious, take pictures, do your best.
4) Take single dollar bills with you. They make great gratuities. The American dollar is strong in Eastern Europe and the former Soviet Union. A small amount means a lot. A few dollars given to a local archivist is often the thing that opens doors.
5) Do your homework before you travel. Do some research about the town you plan to visit and the region it is in. Ask the country's tourist bureau for maps and other information. Don't just arrive in Warsaw one day, thinking you'll figure out the details of your travel plans once you are there.
6) Be in touch with people who are in Jewish genealogical societies. Many Jewish genealogists have already made trips to the places in which you are interested. They will have good advice. (Take *all* advice with a grain of salt: Just because someone went to your town and found nothing does not mean you will also find nothing.)
7) Government regulations in Eastern Europe and vicinity keep changing. Be flexible. And patient.
8) When you meet people who help you, try to stay in touch with them—or at least send a thank-you note. Not only is it a nice

habit, but it will also benefit the next person who travels through.

9) During my trips, I went from town to town looking for several things. First, I was looking for living Jews. In some towns I found one Jewish person, or two or just a few. These people are usually extremely grateful for the contact. I was also looking for the Jewish cemetery. Cemeteries in Eastern Europe suffer more from neglect than vandalism. Stones have toppled over, trees and whole forests have grown up around the stones. (I found one family cemetery in the middle of a cornfield; the farmer had simply planted around the stones.) Ask people where the old Jewish cemetery is; often the older people know. Sometimes you can locate old guidebooks in libraries that will indicate where things were. For example, I have a collection of old Baedeker's. These are travel guides that often date back to the turn of the century. These guidebooks have provided me with locations of Jewish cemeteries, synagogues, etc. Speaking of synagogues, I also look for them. Old Polish synagogues are often movie theaters, or warehouses, or garages. In my great grandfather's town of Przemysl, the public library was once a synagogue.

10) Don't expect local town archives to be either well staffed or well organized. Don't expect to walk into a Polish archives, tell them your great-grandfather's name and plan to receive a family tree. Sometimes you have to make a request one day and then return the next day (or week) for the results. This is obviously not always practical. I suggest you write for an appointment before you start traveling.

9

Jewish Cemeteries

THE HISTORY OF YOUR FAMILY IS CHISELED IN STONE

Apart from the personal significance that a cemetery has for the survivors of someone who has died, cemeteries also represent the history of people. There is something special, something strange yet basic, that you feel when walking among the graves in a cemetery. I have said this to people who have responded by calling me morbid. But a cemetery is not morbid. On the contrary, somehow a cemetery, on a quiet day, is filled with life. Scanning the stones, you can read: "Died at age 87," "Died at age 68," "Died at age 74" and you begin to have the sense that each of the stones that surround you represents lives that were filled with complexity, love, struggle, hardship, pleasure, celebration, faith, pain and exploration of life. Each stone is a lifetime, a family, a world.

In a cemetery, you cannot escape facing your own life. You are alive. This is what each stone says to you. You are alive. You are able to read the words engraved in the rock. You can read the names, the dates, the epitaphs. In fact, those words on the monument were put there for you, for that very moment when you wander over to it and wonder what this person's life was really like.

I would like you to go to a cemetery at a time other than when you must for a funeral because I want you to know what it is like to walk between the paths of graves in silence, with no one near you to distract your thoughts. I want you to know, as I have known, what it is like to read gravestone after gravestone, wondering about each person and the lives that they led.

But how can you know, from a few words chiseled on a stone, what the person was like? And what would it mean if you could? These people are strangers.

I cannot answer that in full; but in part, what a cemetery affords you the opportunity of doing is to see the world, for just a moment, frozen in time. Outside, in the busy streets and noisy rooms, the world seems to move too fast. It is difficult to see that this planet of ours is made of individual lives, each of whom has feelings, sensitivities, and his own concerns. But in a cemetery, the lives are still, and each grave stands there to be witnessed, each representing the end of time for an individual. Standing in front of the grave of a stranger—the same kind of stranger whom you pass on the street each day—the vivid sense has come over me that we are all so mortal, so unique, so special in our ways. Individual lives—this is what our world consists of.

But walking through a graveyard must be more than that, more than simply the ideas I have been trying to express. Otherwise, it would be enough to read this—and it surely is not.

Some people make sure to visit a cemetery when they go for a vacation. It is on the sightseeing list with the museums, parks and historic spots. How can a graveyard be a place to visit on a vacation? How can one visit it when sightseeing? Again, it has to be experienced to be known. But in part, a cemetery is a symbol (and the reality) of the history of a community and a people. When you stand on a piece of ground and read a stone that says "1803," you suddenly know, perhaps more than if you were told it or read it, that life went on at that very spot generations ago. And you know, as you stand before each grave and read the date of death, that it was just a day or two later that a group of people stood where you are standing, to bury a loved one. Each grave represents a life and the world left behind. A cemetery contains the monuments representing the people who made history; not just the famous individuals who make the history books and the headlines, but also each person who, in his or her way, brought time forward a few more years, to this very moment.

But this still is not all that a graveyard represents. There is more to this custom that we have of burying those who have died. The custom itself goes back to the earliest days of human history. The particulars have changed, but the custom and its importance have been a part of humankind and the Jewish people since the beginning. The Bible records burial customs as does the Talmud and other writings. Sometimes the burial was done in caves, other times in scattered graves, but always there was a great concern for this point in our lives.

Our cemeteries, as sacred as they are to us, have often been desecrated. History records the desecration of Jewish cemeteries as early as the Middle Ages, and today we still hear of Jewish graveyards attacked by vandals.

During the Middle Ages, when Jews were forced out of a community, the cemetery was frequently destroyed, the tombstones used for other purposes. Some old buildings in Europe can still be found with slabs of stone taken from Jewish cemeteries. In more recent times, such desecrations in Israel by Arabs have been witnessed on a large scale. Jewish tombstones have been stolen and used for a variety of calculated purposes.

We know that the desecration of Jewish cemeteries has always been widespread. It is important to note that there are no ancient Jewish burial grounds in existence, save for a few scant traces. Furthermore, an old Jewish cemetery such as the Prague Cemetery contains no graves earlier than the fourteenth century since the Jewish cemetery before that time was totally destroyed in April of 1389. In addition, it is tragic to note that popes Calixtus II, Eugenius III, Alexander III, Clement III, Celestine III and Innocent III had to specifically protect Jewish graveyards by means of Papal declarations. Also, Duke Frederick II of Austria declared in July of 1244, "If a Christian attempts to destroy a Jewish cemetery or to break into it, he shall be put to death after the manner of the law, and all his property, no matter what it may be, shall be confiscated by the Duke."

There were other rulers who also extended protection, for a time at least, to Jewish cemeteries, including Frederick the Great of Prussia (1786–1840) who put up a sign at the entrance of the Jewish burial grounds warning that anyone who harms the cemetery would have his head chopped off with an ax.

Unfortunately, these attempts at protection of the Jewish graves were few and far between. Desecration of Jewish cemeteries coincided throughout history with the persecution of living Jews as well. Neither the living nor the dead were left in peace.

After World War I, desecration of Jewish cemeteries was widespread in Germany, and continued until the Holocaust. During and after World War II, Jewish graveyards continued to be desecrated, and the destruction of Eastern European Jewry resulted in the absence of Jewish communities who could even maintain these sacred spots. Although many Jewish cemeteries in Europe have Holocaust memorials placed in them, the task of maintaining these sites becomes a greater and greater problem every day.

Cemeteries as Family Bonds

Often we will go to a cemetery on the sad occasion of a death and we will see members of our family and friends of the family whom we have not seen for a long time. We sometimes think to ourselves that it is odd to see these people at graveyards and nowhere else. But, in fact, a funeral is not just an occasion to bury the dead, but also to renew our ties with the living as well as to our past and tradition.

When we attend a funeral, we have the opportunity to reflect upon the past and upon the people in our families who were members of past generations and whose lives were the links between our own and history. A funeral is a time to go to a cemetery, to read the epitaphs of family members who have departed from this earth, and to remind ourselves of who we are and from where we have come.

Ironically, funerals and burial grounds often serve to renew our relationships with those people whom we perhaps have not seen since the last funeral. There may have been no contact since the last death in the family, but maybe this time there will be future contact "at happier occasions." A funeral is a time of sorrow, but it is not inappropriate or irreverent to think of the funeral or the presence at the cemetery as a deeply important opportunity from which to reap benefits. It is a time to think about one's childhood, to remember the last generations and their contributions to our lives, and to see the people whom we have not seen in a long time. Often those people remind us of happy times in our past and offer us a strong sense of who we are.

It is for these reasons, in part, that graveyards and funerals are so important in the Jewish Tradition. Cremation (forbidden by Jewish law) or other methods of treating the dead often prevent the coming together of people at a funeral, unveiling or cemetery. Even when there is a funeral, the absence of a grave means the absence of the opportunity for a visitor at a grave who can read the words on a tombstone.

Standing before the grave of an ancestor or a relative and reading the words on the stone is a unique and priceless experience. One has to stand in silence among the silent graves of a burial field to be in touch with a sense of one's own history in such a vivid way.

In my family, my father and his brother and sister come together to visit the graves of their parents at least once a year. Although the three of them see each other often during the year, there is something special about the annual visit they make. If they went separately it would be different. If there was no grave it would be different. If they got together and spoke about their deceased parents for hours it would be different. By coming together and in silence amidst the grave of their parents—and their grandfather, who is buried in the same family plot—they share moments that could never be replaced or equaled. Their silence at the graves says more than words could ever express. When the three children stand as grown adults at the grave of their parents, it is as if, in a sense, their family is together again. And, of course, it is not imagination, but reality, for their family *is* together for those moments at the graves. As they leave until the next time, they know that they come from the cemetery with much more than they arrived.

A Walk Through a Jewish Cemetery

A walk through a Jewish cemetery is a walk through Jewish history. Find the Jewish graveyard closest to your home or travel to one that has members of your family within its gates, and spend an hour or two wandering up and down the paths, comparing the monuments, reading the inscriptions, and absorbing the decades (or perhaps centuries) around you.

You will encounter, on your walk, the brief though often moving personal histories of many people. You will notice children who died before reaching their first birthday and great-grandparents who left this world after ninety-five years. Be on the lookout for unusual or instructive items. Perhaps you will wander over to a family plot and notice the more recent generations shortening the European last name. Speaking of names, a cemetery is an excellent place to observe the different naming customs from era to era. Names that were common sixty years ago will hardly be familiar today.

Do not think it bizarre to walk through a burial ground. The stones were engraved with words for people to read. The monuments were chosen to keep a memory alive. Certainly the family of the deceased would not mind if you stopped at a grave, read the inscription, and wondered about the person.

Notice the different shapes and sizes of the gravestones. Some will be tall and massive, others will be smaller and more modest. Some will be lavishly engraved with Jewish symbols and decorations and others will be simple, without any frills. The inscriptions, too, will be quite different. Some will be entirely in Hebrew, others totally in English. Some will include just the name of the person and the dates of birth and death, and others will include lengthy sayings and quite a bit of information about the person. Many Jewish gravestones even include photographs that are imbedded in the monument.

Read the inscriptions carefully. You will usually find the name of the deceased and then, in Hebrew, the name of the person's father. For the family tree researcher, this is, of course, an excellent source of genealogical information.

An inscription on a gravestone can offer more information about the life and the time of the people buried in the graves. You can discover the length of the person's life, for example. Often on a double gravestone, where there is room for a husband and a wife, one side is still empty, telling you that a spouse is still alive. Or both sides might be filled and you will know how long one person was alive while his or her spouse was deceased. You cannot help but wonder what the survivors of the family must be feeling when these graves are visited.

Family plots are a popular custom and you will surely find one that will tell a story about several generations of a family. You will find the graves of the great-grandparents, their children—the grandparents and their children. It is easy to pick out family plots, not only by the family name being repeated, but also by studying the inscriptions carefully. Since gravestones of Jews usually provide the name of the father of the deceased, it is a rather simple task to pick out the relationships, both by the names and by the positions of the stones. In this way, you can visualize entire families, imagine the lives of these people, study the names and see who was named for whom, who carried on the tradition in whose name, who lived to a ripe old age and who died tragically in his or her youth, who never married and who had many children.

A cemetery is rich in tradition and history. Jewish symbols abound on the stones that memorialize simple, common people. Their ancient names inscribed in stone stand as a tribute to lives of happiness, sadness, struggles and celebrations. You look at a stone and read a few words about a man; when he was born, when he died, what his name was, and what his father's name was. You glance to the right and see his wife's name and her father's name. You see how long they lived and wonder whether they were born here or were they born across the ocean in a Jewish community that no longer exists. You look to see where the graves are located and notice that this is not a family plot but the plot of a landsmannshaft, consisting of people from the same town who are now "resting in peace" among people from their community, their lifelong friends who journeyed to America too and established their families here. Suddenly, this is not the grave of one person at all, but it is, rather, a brief history. It is the history of a man, his family, his community, and his beliefs. He was born a Jew and he died a Jew. He was born within his community and he lies at rest in his community. He lived with his wife and now, as the inscription on the grave itself says, He is with his beloved forever.

As you walk through the narrow paths of the Jewish graveyard, the names and the lives of the people who a few moments ago were strangers are no longer foreign. By stopping by a grave and reading the few words on the stone, you touch the life of the person who is represented to you by the inscription. A moment ago you did not know her name; now you know her name. A moment ago you did not know her father's name; now you know this too. A brief moment ago you did not know her husband's name, or her age, or her English and Hebrew names, or the fact that she died a wife, mother, grandmother and great-grandmother. Now you know that too. Next to her grave you notice the grave of a child. The first name is the same as her father's, so you know that the child was named for a great-grandfather. Then you realize: the child is the grandson of the woman. She went to her grandson's funeral.

A walk through a Jewish cemetery is not an unusual or futile effort. It is an encounter with lives and generations. You will not learn about kings and battles, you will not encounter politicians and political upheavals, but you will meet the people who made Jewish history—by living and dying as Jews.

VISITING JEWISH CEMETERIES

Tombstones

Tombstones offer a variety of information. Some include lengthy epitaphs, others have photographs imbedded in the stone and still others include biographical information about the person.

Since the Jewish Tradition includes a father's name along with a person's name (and somctimes includes a mother's name, though not often), tombstones can help you to go back on your family tree an additional generation.

You may find that a tombstone offers differing information from what you have learned from other sources. Keep in mind that tombstones are often inaccurate. This is so for a few reasons: 1) Often there is no one available to give accurate information to the engraver; 2) when a mistake is made in the engraving, it is often not corrected; and 3) false information is sometimes given deliberately (to make a person seem younger, or older, at the time of death). Many people approach the question of age with peculiar biases. In any case, do not be surprised if you find a tombstone with conflicting information on it.

> No monument gives such glory as an unsullied name.
>
> ELEAZER B. JUDAH, *ROKEAH,* 13C

Cemetery Plots

There are several different types of cemetery plots.

1) Some plots are owned by entire families and contain the graves of family members. Often a large stone or archway can be found at a family plot with the name of the family on it. Family organizations such as cousins' clubs or Family Circles will own a plot. This would obviously be helpful to a family historian.
2) Synagogues often have plots for their members, or for those members who have purchased a plot.
3) Landsmannschaften and other fraternal organizations have cemetery plots. In fact, many of these organizations originally formed for the very purpose of buying a plot for its members.
4) Some people have individual plots with no affiliation or special location among other plots.

> Walk reverently in a cemetery, lest the deceased say, "Tomorrow they will join us, and today they mock us."
>
> HIYYA RABBAH
> TALMUD: BERAKOT, 18A

Tombstone Transcribing

When you visit a cemetery for family history purposes, make sure you transcribe all the information on the tombstone to your paper or notebook. Don't just jot down the names and dates, but rather record the inscription in its entirety. Although you should seriously consider photographing the stones as well, sketches of the tombstones are also worthwhile.

If you are visiting a family plot containing many tombstones of personal interest, you should draw a map of the entire plot and note the location of each stone with its inscription. Finally, do not forget to label your notes, indicating the exact location of the plots within the cemetery. Cemeteries are often quite large, and an exact record of the plot location may be helpful in the future.

How to Read a Jewish Tombstone

If a tombstone of interest is written in Hebrew (as most Jewish tombstones are—in part, if not completely), a few pointers will be helpful if you cannot read the language.

> After every funeral I used to stay on at the cemetery and copy tombstone inscriptions.
>
> JACOB SHATZKY, JEWISH HISTORIAN, IN MEMOIRS ABOUT HIS YOUTH

At the top of most Jewish tombstones is the abbreviation
פ״נ for a man and
פ״ט for a woman.
פ״נ stands for
פה נקבר meaning "here lies."
פ״ט signifies
פה טמונה, meaning "here is interred."

At the close of most Jewish tombstone inscriptions you will find the abbreviation

תנצב״ה, which stands for תהי נפשו צרורה בצרור החיים.

This is a verse from I Sam. 25:29, "May his soul be bound up in the bond of eternal life."

The tombstone may contain an epitaph in Hebrew, in which case you would simply have to copy the letters or take a clear photograph of the inscription and get it translated.

Calculating a date from the Hebrew on the tombstone will also be necessary. Actually, it would be useful for you to learn how to convert a Hebrew date into an English date for tombstones as well as any other Jewish document written in Hebrew. The system is quite simple.

The letters of the Hebrew alphabet each have a numerical value. They are:

א–1	ל–30
ב–2	מ–40
ג–3	נ–50
ד–4	ס–60
ה–5	ע–70
ו–6	פ–80
ז–7	צ–90
ח–8	ק–100
ט–9	ר–200
י–10	ש–300
כ–20	ת–400

When a Hebrew date is written, you must figure out the numerical value of each letter and then add them up. This is the date. But remember that this is the Hebrew date and not the date we use in daily life. In other words, each Rosh Hashanah, which appears on the calendar in September or October, we add a year to the Jewish date. In September, 1979, for example, the Jewish year was 5740. With this information you need only do a little arithmetic to change a Hebrew date to a secular date.

There is just one minor complication. Often a Hebrew date after the year 5000 on the Hebrew calendar will leave off the number 5 in the thousands column. In other words, taking the example of 1979 being 5740, you will usually see the Hebrew date written as 740 rather than 5740. To arrive at a Common Era date simply add 1240 to the shortened date. Therefore, 740 plus 1240 is 1980. Why 1980 rather than 1979? Because the Jewish date changes, as I have said, in September or October. Most of the year 5740 will be in 1980, not 1979.

Of course a tombstone as well as other documents will have the month too, probably the Hebrew months. Here is a list of them:

תשרי	*Tishre*		*September*
חשון	*Heshvan*		*October*
כסלו	*Kislev*		*November*
טבת	*Tevet*		*December*
שבט	*Shevat*		*January*
אדר	*Adar (Adar II in leap year)*	**אדר ב׳**	*February*
ניסן	*Nisan*		*March*
אייר	*Iyar*		*April*
סיון	*Sivan*		*May*
תמוז	*Tamuz*		*June*
אב	*Av*		*July*
אלול	*Elul*		*August*

Since the Hebrew calendar is not the same as the calendar that we use in secular life, the months indicated above do not correspond exactly. In a given year the corresponding months can be off by several days or even weeks.

Here is one example of how to convert a Hebrew date into an English date: If the year is

תרפ, the letter
ת is 400, the letter
ר is 200,
פ is 80. In total 680. As I pointed out, the 5000 is usually left off, so actually the date would be 5680. But using our formula, 680

plus 1240 is 1920. That is the date we are familiar with.

Tombstone Rubbings

Tombstone rubbing is the art of transferring the design and inscription of the surface of a tombstone to a piece of paper or fabric, using a special wax or crayon. The procedure is simple, does not harm the tombstone, and allows you to end up with an exact, life-size reproduction of the stone.

Although the art of rubbing is used to reproduce other images besides tombstones, old graveyards are probably the most popular sites for this ancient pastime. Rubbing tombstones is particularly effective for old stones with unusual shapes and lettering styles.

To obtain the supplies you need to practice this art, write to Oldstone Enterprises, 186 Lincoln Street, Boston, Massachusetts 02111. They are the largest suppliers of rubbing materials in the U.S.

> Perfect love, brotherhood and mutual assistance is only found among those near to each other by relationship. The members of a family united by common descent from the same grandfather, or even from some more distant ancestor, have toward each other a certain feeling of love, help each other, and sympathize with each other. To effect this is one of the chief purposes of the Law.
>
> MAIMONIDES, *GUIDE III,* 49

Photographing Tombstones

It is not in bad taste to photograph tombstones. A photograph of a tombstone or a cemetery can be meaningful and moving.

If you are visiting cemeteries for your family research, it would be a good idea to photograph the stones as well as to transcribe the engraved message. Pictures of your family's tombstones would be a significant addition to your family history collection.

Of course, taking photographs should not prevent you from visiting the graves again, for personal reasons as well as to make sure that the graves are in good condition.

> We always found out at a funeral whoever was great or distinguished in Jewish Warsaw. I used to attach myself to every funeral procession that seemed to me important—according to the number of mourners. Often I did not even know who the deceased was, but hearing the eulogies at the cemetery, I felt that it was a privilege to be there in such lifeless proximity to a living past. Instinctively I inherited that impersonal attitude toward one whose life had graced Warsaw's Jewish life, a life which first revealed itself to me at the cemetery.
>
> JACOB SHATZKY, JEWISH HISTORIAN

The grave of Rabbi Chaim Josef Gottlieb, the Stropkover Rav, great-great-great-grandfather of the author.

LOCATING CEMETERIES

If no one in your family knows where a burial plot is located, try to obtain a copy of the person's death certificate. A death certificate usually gives the location of the cemetery. When you arrive at the graveyard, inquire at the office for the exact location of the plot.

All burial offices will tell you the location of a specific plot, but they vary when it comes to giving you additional information about the individual and his or her family. They also have information in their files that might be helpful (such as the name of the spouse, address at time of death, etc.) but cooperation varies from office to office.

> A generation goes and a generation comes, but the earth stands forever.
>
> ECCLESIASTES 1:4

DEATH CERTIFICATES

The registration of deaths varies from place to place and year to year, but there is usually a death certificate on file for deaths that have occurred within the U.S. A death certificate can be helpful in your family history research because most of them include information such as full name, name of father, maiden name of mother, name of spouse, date of death, place of death, cause of death, place of burial, name of funeral home, place of birth, address at time of death and number of years in the U.S.

Any one of these pieces of information can lead you to more information. For example, if you know how many years a person was living in the U.S., you can narrow the field when searching for immigration papers and steamship passenger lists. If you know an ancestor's mother's maiden name, you can begin a new branch of your family tree. If you know the place of burial, you can locate the grave and obtain more information from the gravestone.

The best guide to help you locate death certificates is *Where to Write for Vital Records*, available from the U.S. Government Printing Office, Washington, D.C. 20402. It costs $2.25.

> Happy is he who grew up with a good name and departed this world with a good name.
>
> JOHANA, TALMUD: BERAKOT, 17A

CITY OF NEW YORK
DEPARTMENT OF HEALTH
BUREAU OF VITAL RECORDS

, New York, N.Y.

Below is a photostatic copy of a certificate on file in the Bureau of Vital Records of the Department of Health of the City of New York

Certificate of Death

Certificate No. 56-50-307449

1. NAME OF DECEASED: ABRAHAM (First Name) KURZWEIL (Last Name)

PERSONAL PARTICULARS

2. USUAL RESIDENCE: New York; Kings; Bklyn; 464 Columbia St.

3. SINGLE, MARRIED, WIDOWED, OR DIVORCED: Married

4. DATE OF BIRTH OF DECEDENT

5. AGE: 84

6. a. Usual Occupation: Pensioner

7. SOCIAL SECURITY NO.

8. BIRTHPLACE: Poland

9. OF WHAT COUNTRY WAS DECEASED A CITIZEN AT TIME OF DEATH? U.S.

10a. WAS DECEASED EVER IN UNITED STATES ARMED FORCES? No

11. NAME OF FATHER OF DECEDENT

12. MAIDEN NAME OF MOTHER OF DECEDENT

13. NAME OF INFORMANT — RELATIONSHIP TO DECEASED: Wife — ADDRESS: 464 Columbia St

14a. Name of Cemetery or Crematory — 14b. Location (City, Town or County and State): New Jersey — 14c. Date of Burial or Cremation: April 9 1950

21. FUNERAL DIRECTOR — ADDRESS — PERMIT NUMBER

MEDICAL CERTIFICATE OF DEATH

15. PLACE OF DEATH: (a) NEW YORK CITY: (b) Borough BKLYN; (c) Name of Hospital or Institution: 437 COLUMBIA ST. (synagogue)

16. DATE AND HOUR OF DEATH: APRIL 8 1950

17. SEX: M — 18. COLOR OR RACE: W — 19. Approximate Age: 84

20. I HEREBY CERTIFY that (I attended the deceased) from JAN 4 1948 to APRIL 6 1950, and last saw h[im] alive at 1P M. on April 6 1950.

I further certify that death was not caused, directly or indirectly, by accident, homicide, suicide, acute or chronic poisoning, or in any suspicious or unusual manner, and that it was due to NATURAL CAUSES more fully described in the confidential medical report filed with the Department of Health.

Witness my hand this 8 day of April 1950

Signature: Charles S. Hahn M.D.

Address: 781 Heeds St Bklyn

BUREAU OF RECORDS AND STATISTICS — DEPARTMENT OF HEALTH — CITY OF NEW YORK

This is to certify that the foregoing is a true copy of a record in my custody.

CITY REGISTRAR

WARNING: DO NOT ACCEPT THIS TRANSCRIPT UNLESS THE RAISED SEAL OF THE DEPARTMENT OF HEALTH IS AFFIXED THEREON. THE REPRODUCTION OR ALTERATION OF THIS TRANSCRIPT IS PROHIBITED BY SECTION 3.21 OF THE NEW YORK CITY HEALTH CODE.

NOTICE: In issuing this transcript of the Record, the Department of Health of the City of New York does not certify to the truth of the statements made thereon, as no inquiry as to the facts has been provided by law.

Death Certificate of the author's great-grandfather. It notes that he died in the synagogue on the holiday of Passover.

Wills

A last will and testament that is filed with the state is usually a public record and is often filled with family history data. In many cases, wills include names of children, grandchildren and other relatives. Also, you can learn a lot about a person by what he or she is giving to others in a will, as well as to whom the gift is being given. I have found wills indicating sums of money to go to yeshivas and other religious organizations, for example, which give me an insight into the religiosity or affiliations of the deceased.

Wills are located in a variety of places. Sometimes they are kept in Surrogate's Court, Probate Court or elsewhere. You should check the county clerk office for whatever location interests you and see where the wills are kept. Keep in mind that you are entitled to see these documents, except in specific cases for various legal reasons. I mention this because I have often gotten the feeling that wills are confidential. I have also met with resistance on the part of some clerks in a few places. Be insistent. You have a right to examine most wills.

> Cemeteries must not be treated disrespectfully. Cattle may not be fed there, nor a watercourse turned, nor grass plucked.
>
> Talmud: Megilla, 29a

Obituaries

Newspaper obituaries can often be key sources of family history information. The difficulty with them, however, is that there is no systematic way of finding an obituary for several reasons:

1) There are no indexes to obituaries that would be useful to the general population. (*The New York Times* issued an index but it is selective.)
2) There are two kinds of obituaries: the articles written by the newspaper, and the announcements provided by individuals. In order to find an obituary of a specific individual, you must first be able to locate the right newspaper. Then you must know the day or the approximate day of death. Then you must hope that either an article was written or that an announcement was published.
3) Back issues of newspapers are often available on microfilm in

the geographic area where the newspaper is published. This is true for defunct newspapers as well as those that are still publishing.

4) Do not forget to consider Yiddish papers. Again, this can present a problem since there were many Yiddish newspapers circulating at times, and you may not know which paper was read by the people who might have published a death announcement. Check with the YIVO Institute for Jewish Research regarding how to locate back issues of Yiddish newspapers.

The American Jewish Periodicals Center, Hebrew Union College, 3101 Clifton Ave., Cincinnati, Ohio 45220, also has an excellent collection of Jewish newspapers.

With all of the problems surrounding obituaries, they can still be of great use and should be considered when you are doing your research.

> Moses received the Torah at Sinai and handed it down to Joshua; Joshua to the elders; the elders to the Prophets; and the Prophets handed it down to the men of the Great Assembly.
>
> TALMUD: PIRKE AVOT, 1:1

European Jewish Cemeteries

Many Jewish cemeteries in Eastern Europe were partially or entirely destroyed during the Holocaust. Yet, a surprising number of them have survived and are intact. Some are quite old and are filled with family history.

Old Jewish cemeteries in Western Europe are also good sources of information, and a trip to ancestral locations should include such research.

If the town you are interested in has a landsmannschaft (see page 322), its members will usually know the fate of the town Jewish cemetery. A good, though incomplete listing of European Jewish burial grounds can be found in *Traveler's Guide to Jewish Landmarks of Europe* (described on page 332).

When I visited Poland, one of my main interests was locating old Jewish graveyards. Often as I entered a town we knew once had a Jewish population I asked people if they could direct me to the Jewish cemetery. Those whom I asked were always quite helpful and usually

Yahrzeit Calendar for the author's maternal great-grandfather.

knew where it was located. Sometimes it was difficult to find the cemeteries because they had been left alone for more than three decades and were now totally covered with weeds and overgrowth. Yet, as I pulled away and pushed aside the growth, I found well-preserved gravestones, some more than 150 years old (see "Visiting the Old Country," page 330).

My greatest success in searching for family tombstones came the second time I visited Hungary. I drove several hours from Budapest to a small town in the northeast corner of Hungary called Mateszalka. After locating the old Jewish cemetery in the typically overgrown, rundown condition I had come to expect, I searched the graveyard for a few hours. Finally, after almost giving up, I discovered the tombstone of my great-great-grandmother. Not only was it a moment of excitement, as I was able to look at and touch the tombstone, but it also gave me the name of her father, my great-great-great-grandfather. Suddenly I was back one more generation.

Appendix: A Family History Workbook

> Emperor Hadrian was walking one day when he saw an old man digging holes to plant trees. Hadrian asked the old man, "How old are you this day?" Said he, "I am one hundred years old." Said Hadrian, "You are a hundred years old and you stand there digging holes to plant trees! Do you expect to eat their fruit?" The old man replied, "I shall eat the fruits if my merits are sufficient. If not, I toil for my descendants, as my fathers toiled for me."
>
> MIDRASH, LEV. RABBAH 25

ORGANIZING YOUR RESEARCH

If any one of your ancestors took the time and energy to record information about his or her family, you would probably now be in possession of a more complete family tree than you would have been able to reconstruct by yourself. Many families own family trees that date back several centuries and that are filled with facts about brothers and sisters, aunts and uncles, cousins and children. How indebted you would be to that ancestor who had the insight to know that if not for his or her effort, so much would be lost to time.

At this very moment, you have the opportunity to *be* that ancestor for a future generation. You have the chance to be the driving force behind the sharing of information, names, dates, stories and photographs about your family. You can be the one who establishes the link between the present generation and history. You can uncover the names of towns that no longer exist but that were the ancestral homes of your family. You can discover the cemeteries where your relatives are buried, or stories about the immigration of your family to America. In short, you have the chance, at this moment, to preserve the history of a family.

Climbing a family tree is actually building one. The process is a step-by-step effort to collect the information that finally results in the story of your family and its history. On the pages that follow, you will find charts and forms to fill in, sometimes slowly and sometimes quickly. In doing this kind of research, you should start with yourself and build from there, adding the names of your parents, grandparents, and so on. Eventually, you will come to a point where you will not be able, with the information you have, to go farther. You will then have to begin to ask questions of relatives and friends of the family who will be able to give you the clues you need to continue.

This workbook will not be large enough for your family. You will need to add additional sheets to document generations farther back. Also, you might find that some branches within your family had more children than there are spaces on some of the forms. Again, you will have to add more sheets as you need them. But generally, if you can fill the forms on the following pages, you are well on your way to compiling your family history. As you examine each type of form, you will get an idea of the kinds of information you will be seeking. Keep in mind that this is merely the framework for a more extensive family history. You will want to collect photographs, stories, and documents. These pages do not provide much space for this, so you will have to keep those elsewhere.

You might want to use the workbook as a permanent record, or this might be just a place to record the information before putting it in a separate booklet that you can construct. Either way, the forms will be your first step to becoming a family historian and connecting yourself with Jewish history.

RELATIONSHIP CHART: HOW ARE WE RELATED?

How many times have you had conversations with relatives of yours when you tried to figure out how you were related? There is often confusion regarding the names of the relationships between people. For example, do you know the difference between a second cousin and a first cousin once removed? What does “once removed” mean? Is it possible for you to be your own cousin? The following chart will clear up any confusion you might have with the definitions of relationships. This is an easy system for you to use to answer the question: How are we related?

First we need to define some terms.

Common Progenitor. The closest ancestor two people have in common is their common progenitor. So, for example, you and your sister have your parents as your common progenitors. You also have your grandparents and great-grandparents in common, but for the purpose of this chart we are only concerned with your *closest* common ancestor. To give another example, the common progenitor of you and your first cousin is one of your grandparents. In other words, you and your first cousin do not have the same parents, but you have the same grandparents.

Removed. When we speak of a cousin being once removed, we are referring to generations. For example, if you know who your father's first cousin is, then you are that person's first cousin once removed. That is, you are one generation away (or removed) from that person. Subsequently, if you know your grandfather's first cousin, then you are that person's first cousin twice removed. You are two generations from that person.

Cousin. Your cousins are the children of your aunts and uncles, great-aunts and great-uncles, and so on.

With those terms understood, you will now be able to understand and determine your relationships with your relatives.

As you see on the chart following, there are numbers from 0 to 6 across the top and down the left side. These numbers represent the number of generations from a common progenitor. The square in the upper left corner that says "CP" stands for common progenitor.

The first thing you must do is to figure out who is the common progenitor between two people. For example, suppose you want to know the relationship between yourself and your first cousin's son. The first question to ask is: Who is the closest ancestor to both of us? The answer is your grandfather (or grandmother, but for simplicity, the chart shows only male descent, though it is the same for males and females).

On the left-hand column, notice that the square next to number 2 says GS, which stands for grandson. That is *you* (in our example). On the row across the top, you can see that the square below number 3 says GGS, which means great-grandson. That is your first cousin's son. Again, your grandfather and your first cousin's son's great-grandfather are the same person. On the chart, you are number 2 and he is number 3.

The square at which row 2 and row 3 meet tells you the relationship. That is, the square that says "1C1R" is the square where row 2 and row 3 meet. 1C1R means "first cousin once removed." That is your relationship to each other.

By the way, "once removed" works both ways. You are his first cousin once removed and he is your first cousin once removed.

Try the chart with a few examples from your family to get used to determining relationships.

Finally, to the question, "Can you be your own cousin?" the answer is yes. If, for example, your great-grandparents were first cousins when they married, then you are your own fourth cousin!

"HOW ARE WE RELATED?"

Relationship Chart

	0	1	2	3	4	5	6
0	CP	S	GS	GGS	2 GGS	3 GGS	4 GGS
1	S	B	N	GN	GGN	2 GGN	3 GGN
2	GS	N	1C	1C 1R	1C 2R	1C 3R	1C 4R
3	GGS	GN	1C 1R	2C	2C 1R	2C 2R	2C 3R
4	2 GGS	GGN	1C 2R	2C 1R	3C	3C 1R	3C 2R
5	3 GGS	2 GGN	1C 3R	2C 2R	3C 1R	4C	4C 1R
6	4 GGS	3 GGN	1C 4R	2C 3R	3C 2R	4C 1R	5C

CP =Common Progenitor
C =Cousin
V =Brother or Sister
R =Times Removed
S =Son or Daughter

N = Nephew or Niece
GS = Grandson or Granddaughter
GGS = Great-grandson or Great Granddaughter

YOUR WORKBOOK: SOME SUGGESTIONS

Direct Ancestor Chart. On the Direct Ancestor Chart, you can record the names of your direct ancestors: your parents, grandparents, great-grandparents and so on. The Direct Ancestor Chart does not have room for indirect or collateral ancestors such as aunts, uncles and cousins.

Two Direct Ancestor Charts have been provided for a family to use. One chart can be used by a wife and the other by a husband.

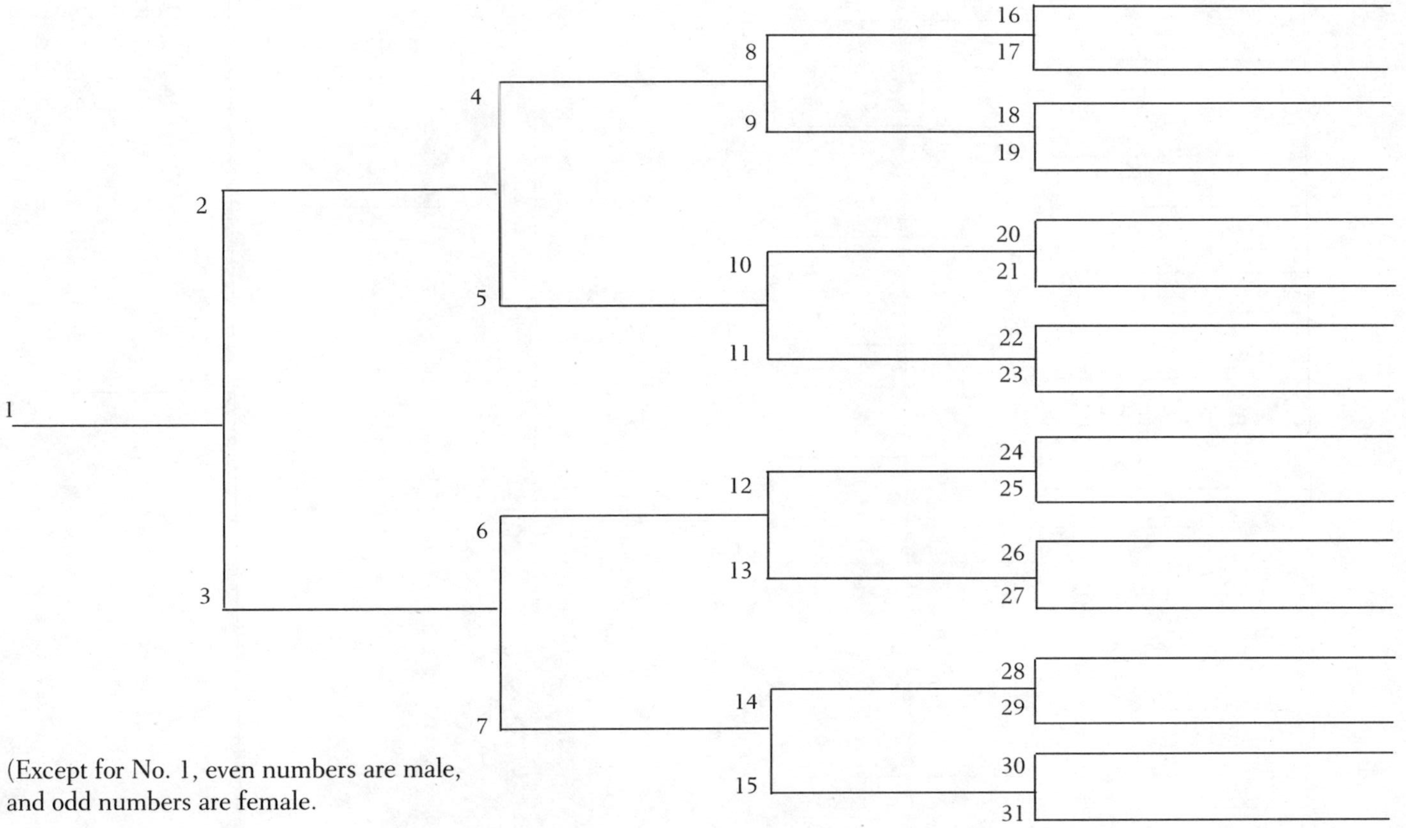

(Except for No. 1, even numbers are male, and odd numbers are female.)

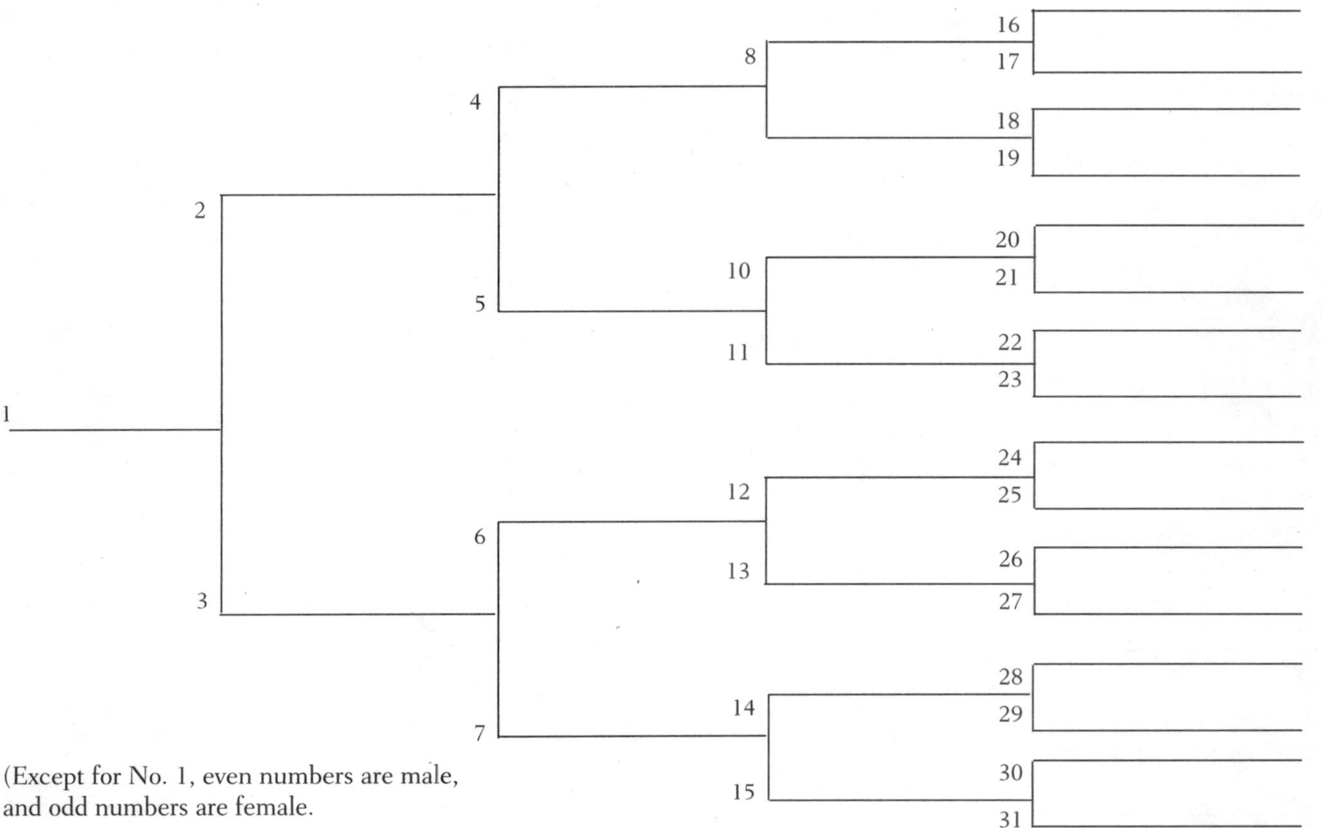

(Except for No. 1, even numbers are male, and odd numbers are female.

Family Group Work Sheets. Each Family Group Work Sheet will allow you to record information regarding individual branches of your family tree. It is on these sheets that indirect or collateral ancestors can be recorded.

The Family Group Work Sheets correspond to the Direct Ancestor Charts. As you can see on the Direct Ancestor Charts, each individual has a number and every two numbers represent a couple. Each couple should also have a Family Group Work Sheet. For example, on your Direct Ancestor Chart, numbers 4 and 5 are your father's parents. You should then have a Family Group Work Sheet (numbers 4 and 5) on which you can record some details about these people as well as information about their children, grandchildren and so on.

Cemetery Inscriptions and Notes. When you go to a cemetery, do not just record the information inscribed on the stones. As noted earlier, take down the entire inscription and if you have a family plot, draw a sketch of it, indicating the location of each stone and its inscription. Use the Cemetery Inscriptions and Notes page for this purpose.

Research Calendar. When you do library research on your family history, it is a good idea to keep track of your search. Use the Research Calendar to record your activities. You will be surprised at how useful your notes will be when keeping track of your searches. This is for your own sense of what you have done, as well as to aid you in the future. As you can see from the columns on the chart, there is room for the name of the library or institution, the call number of the item, the name of the source, the purpose of your search, the outcome of your search, and the date.

Correspondence Calendar. If you send for any of the documents suggested in this book, you will have to keep track of what you have sent for and what you are waiting for. Use the Correspondence Calendar for this purpose. Included on this Calendar is the date of your request, the amount of money sent (if any), a space for a followup letter if necessary, the date of the reply and refund (if any), the name and address of the place the inquiry was sent, the subject of the inquiry, the results of the inquiry and a file number—if you keep a file of your correspondence (which is a good idea!).

Direct Ancestors—Additional Generations. If you know information about any ancestors farther back than there is room provided on your Direct Ancestor Charts, record this information on the blank pages provided.

FAMILY GROUP WORK SHEET #'s____________________

HUSBAND, Name:
Birth: Place:
Death: Place:
Burial: Place:
Father: Mother:
Occupation:
Notes:

WIFE, Name:
Birth: Place:
Death: Place:
Burial: Place:
Father: Mother:
Occupation
Notes:

NAME	Date & Place of: Birth	Marriage	Death	Married to:	Date & Place of Birth Death
1.					
2.					
3.					
4.					
5.					
6.					
7.					
8.					
9.					
10.					

FAMILY GROUP WORK SHEET #'s________________

HUSBAND, Name:
Birth: Place:
Death: Place:
Burial: Place:
Father: Mother:
Occupation:
Notes:

WIFE, Name:
Birth: Place:
Death: Place:
Burial: Place:
Father: Mother:
Occupation
Notes:

NAME	Date & Place of: Birth	Marriage	Death	Married to:	Date & Place of Birth Death
1.					
2.					
3.					
4.					
5.					
6.					
7.					
8.					
9.					
10.					

Research Calendar

Library Call #	SOURCE	PURPOSE	RESULTS	DATE OF SEARCH

Correspondence Calendar

DATE SENT / $$$	FOLLOW UP	DATE OF ANSWER / REFUND	CORRESPONDENT AND ADDRESS	SUBJECT	RESULTS	FILED

ADVICE ON ORGANIZING YOUR RESEARCH FINDINGS

1) There is no "right way" to organize your research. Find a way that works for you.
2) Avoid trying to get all your information on one chart. No one sheet, however large, is practical. I know someone who thought a whole wall in a house would be perfect for the family tree. It too became too small after a while.
3) There are computer programs for a personal computer that work well, but all have pitfalls. The publication *Avotaynu* reports on this software from time to time.
4) Reproducing your findings is often extremely important. First, I assume you want to share what you've discovered with others. Second, the ability to share your findings will often produce more information. In other words, however you organize your material, do it so that it can be reproduced. And added to!
5) There are two kinds of genealogy: family histories and pedigrees. A family history considers all the descendants of a person (or a couple). A pedigree considers all the ancestors of one person. It is more useful to pursue family histories: everyone on a family history tree is related to everyone else. On a pedigree this is not the case. I'd suggest you pursue family histories, not pedigrees.
6) There are lots of books about genealogy that give great detail on organizing your findings. Look around for a system that fits for you. Or make up your own system; I did.
7) Go to a good Jewish library (like the library at YIVO) and ask to see samples of the genealogies they have received. These are the privately produced family histories that people have donated. They will give you good ideas. Some are stapled together. Others are bound in leather. Depending on your budget and taste, these will suggest possibilities.
8) Attend meetings of your local Jewish Genealogical Society. You'll get lots of good ideas from other people.

COMPUTERS AND GENEALOGY

I feel an obligation to remind myself, from time to time, that computers are only tools. The real work—the creativity behind the work process—

is a human function. No tool, no matter how dazzling, can replace the creative spark within the person using the tool.

Computers have entered the field of genealogy as they have just about every field. There are computer programs to help you organize your genealogical material; there are computers that store genealogical information at some museums and archives; there are programs that will print out elaborate family trees; and so on.

I have no recommendations for what to buy. I'd suggest that you subscribe to *Avotaynu*; check back issues for articles and reviews; and look for future evaluations. The pages of *Avotaynu* also advertise some of the software packages on the market.

The important point regarding genealogy and computers is that computers will not replace the hard work of tracking down relatives; interviewing relatives; writing to relatives; dealing with the libraries and goverment agencies; etc. And no archives or library has your family tree tracing back to King David, just waiting for you to ask for it, either. My advice is simple: Don't get distracted by the technology when there is so much hard work that you must do yourself.

Bibliography

Jewish genealogy is a doorway into Jewish history and tradition. As you discover your Jewish family history, you will learn more about events of the past, customs and practices of the Jewish people over the centuries and more. The Jewish family historian quickly discovers that the names and dates that appear on a family tree reflect much more than cold data. The lives of our ancestors represent a chain of history that is rich and complex.

The following books are just the tip of the iceberg when considering the vast literature reflecting the experience of the Jewish people. I recommend these books to you with the hope that they will provide the necessary backdrop to your own personal family history. Keep in mind, however, that these few suggestions should lead you to building your own Jewish library in order to enrich the understanding of your past and yourself.

GENERAL JUDAICA AND REFERENCE WORKS

Alcalay, Reuben. *Complete English-Hebrew, Hebrew-English Dictionary.*
Gilbert, Martin. *The Atlas of Jewish History.*
Gribetz, Judah. *The Timetables of Jewish History.*
Johnson, Paul. *A History of the Jews.*
Klagsbrun, Frances, ed. *Voices of Wisdom: Jewish Ideals and Ethics for Everyday Living.*
Strassfeld, Michael, et al. *The Jewish Catalog: A Do-It-Yourself Kit.*
Strassfeld, Sharon and Strassfeld, Michael. *The Second Jewish Catalog: Sources and Resources.*
———. *The Third Jewish Catalog: Creating Community.*

HISTORY OF THE JEWISH PEOPLE

Ben-Sasson, H. H. *A History of the Jewish People.*
Gilbert, Martin. *The Atlas of Jewish History.*
Gittleman, Zvi Y. *A Century of Ambivalence: The Jews of Russia and the Soviet Union, 1881 to the Present.*

Howe, Irving. *World of Our Fathers.*
Sanders, Ronald. *Shores of Refuge: A Hundred Years of Jewish Emigration.*
Seltzer, Robert M. *Jewish People, Jewish Thought: The Jewish Experience of History.*

HOLIDAYS, CUSTOMS AND LIFE CYCLE

Angel, Marc. *The Rhythms of Jewish Living: A Sephardic Approach.*
Donin, Hayim. *To Be a Jew: A Guide to Jewish Observance in Contemporary Life.*
Greenberg, Blu. *How to Run a Traditional Jewish Household.*
Greenberg, Irving. *The Jewish Way: Living the Holidays.*
Lamm, Maurice. *The Jewish Way in Death and Mourning.*
———. *The Jewish Way in Love and Marriage.*
Tellushkin, Joseph. *Jewish Literacy.*

THE HOLOCAUST

Berenbaum, Michael. *The World Must Know: A History of the Holocaust as Told in the United States Holocaust Memorial Museum.*
Dawidowicz, Lucy S. *The War Against the Jews, 1933–1945.*
Gilbert, Martin. *Atlas of the Holocaust.*
Hilberg, Raul. *The Destruction of the European Jews.*
Wiesel, Elie. *Night.*
Yahi, Leni. *The Holocaust: The Fate of European Jewry.*

JEWISH THOUGHT

Steinsaltz, Adin. *The Essential Talmud.*
———. *The Strife of the Spirit.*
———. *The Thirteen Petalled Rose.*

Index

Note: Numbers in italic refer to illustrations

Abbreviations, names from, 246–47
Abramson, Samuel H., 332
Abusch, Avrahum, 5, 6
Adoptees' Liberty Movement Association (ALMA), 72
Adoption, 67, 71–72
"Age Search Information," 67
Agnon, S. Y., 61
Ainicle, defined, 25
Alexander, Gad, 231
ALMA, 72
American Jewish Archives, 70
American Jewish Historical Society, 70
American Jewish Periodicals Center, 357
Americans of Jewish Descent, 113–14
Ancestral homes, tracing, 318–41
  Blackbook of Localities Whose Jewish Population was Exterminated by the Nazis, 323–24
  genealogical sources, researching long distance, 327–30
  Holocaust's effect on your shtetl or town, 323
  landsmannschaften, locating, 322–23
  locating your shtetl, 324–26
  Memorbuchs, 320–21
  visiting the old country, 330–36
    advice before travelling to Eastern Europe and the former Soviet Union, 339–41
    planning your trip, 336–39
Antin, Mary, 312
Approbations, 125–27
Arbeiter, Nancy, 231
Arbit, Norma, 231
Archives
  listed, 203–17
    American Jewish Archives, 203–4
    American Jewish Historical Society, 204–5
    Central Archives for the History of the Jewish People, 216–17
    Jewish historical societies, 205–15
  rules for dealing with, 74–75
Artifacts, interview questions regarding, 51–52

Ashkenazi Jews, names of, 240, 245
Association of Jewish Genealogical Societies, 281
Auslander, Jordan, 231
Avotaynu: The International Review of Jewish Genealogy, 82–111, 114, 328
  books available from, 107–9
  Family Finder section, 102–7
  index to first eight volumes, 82–102
  Jewish last names in, 258
  microfiche available from, 109–11

Baba Bathra, 77
Baeck, Leo, 226
Baeck, Leo, Institute, 77, 121, 225–26
Baker, Zachary M., 323, 326
Bathra, Baba, 77
Beer-Hofmann, Richard, 286
Beider, Alexander, 258
Benevolent organizations. *See* Landsmannschaften
Ben-Gurion, 327
Berg, Rebecca Himber, 255
Bernstein, Charles B., 231
Bialik, 312
Bibliographies
  Jewish and Hebrew Onomastics: A Bibliography, 257
  Rabbi Malcolm Stern's basic, 117–21
Bibliography of Jewish Genealogy, 117
Birth records. *See* Vital records
Birth rituals, importance of, 122
Blackbook of Localities Whose Jewish Population Was Exterminated by the Nazis, 323
Blatt, Warren, 231
Bloom, Philip, 232
Bohemia, records in, 330
Botwinick, Milton E., 232

Canadian research, 73–74
  historical societies, 213–15
  important resources, 74
Cassette tape recorder, for taping interviews, 43, 58
Cemeteries. *See* Jewish cemeteries
Census records
  city directories and, 69
  federal, 63–67
  indexes of, 64, 65
  state, 68
Central Archives for the History of the Jewish People, The, 216–17
Central Tracing Bureau, 268
Chain That Stretches from Sinai, The: Creating a Family Tree, 116
Chassidic dynasties, 127
Church of Jesus Christ of Latter Day Saints, Family History Library, 226–28, 328
Circumcision records (Mohel books), 121
Citizenship records, 67
City directories, 69
Clapsaddle, Carol, 232
Cohen, Sandra, 232
Collected genealogies, 120–21
Collecting stories, 43–44
Columbia Lippincott Gazetteer of the World, 325

Combined Displaced Persons Executive (CDPX), 268
Committee on Displaced Populations of the Allied Post-War Requirement Bureau, 267
Committee of Professional Jewish Genealogists, 229–36
Common last names, 61
Complete Pronouncing Gazetteer or Geographical Dictionary of theWorld, 325
Computers and genealogy, 372–73
Concentration camp, researching
  see also Holocaust/Holocaust research
  Hall of Names/Pages of Testimony Division of Yad Vashem, 272
  International Tracing Service, 269–70
  Mauthausen Death Books, 271–72

Daughters of the American Revolution, 67
Death books, 283
Death records, 354–55
  see also Vital records
Dennis, Daphne, 232
Dennis, Marsha Saron, 232
Deportations from France during Holocaust, 281–82
Descriptive names, 239, 245–46
Deutsch-Sinderbrand, Nancy J., 232
Dictionary of Jewish Names and Their History, 257
Dictionary of Jewish Surnames from the Russian Empire, 258
Displaced persons, tracing, 267–71
Divorce records. *See* Vital records
Dobromil, Poland, 1–11, *4*
Dobroszycki, Lucjan, 225

Eastern Europe, advice before traveling to, 339–41
"Eastern European 'Jewish Geography': Some Problems and Suggestions," 326
Einsidler, David, 131
Elisheba, 225
Encyclopedia of Jewish Genealogy, 112, 227, 230, 328
Encyclopedia Judaica, 112–13
  ancestral home research, 321
  index volume, 127
English names, 256–57
Ennis, Ruchel, 7
European roots, interview questions regarding, 49

Fackenheim, Emil L., 271, 284
Family Finder (*Avotaynu*), 102
Family history documents, 313
Family history workbook (appendix), 359–73
  direct ancestor chart, 362–64
  organizing your research, 359–60, 372
  relationship chart, 360–62
Family legends, 44–45
Family life, interview questions regarding, 49–50
Family photographs, 56
Federal census records, 63–67

First American Jewish Families, 1654–1988, 113–14
First names, 251–52
France, deportations from during Holocaust, 281–82
Franz Josef I of Hapsburg, 47–48
Freedom of Information Act, 68
Freedom of Information Privacy Act Request, 309
Freud, Sigmund, 274
Friedlander, Alex E., 233
Frucht, Philip, 8–11

Gazetteer, use of to locate shtetlach or town, 325
Genealogical societies. *See* Jewish genealogical societies
Genealogies, collected, 120–21
Genealogists, professional, 229–36
  listed, 231–36
  ten commandments for, 237
Generations, 313–17
Gottlieb, Asher Yeshaya, *23*
Gottlieb, Chaim Joseph, 26, 34, 126
Gottlieb, Maurice, 20, 25
Gottlieb, Pinchas, 30, *263*
Gottlieb, Zalman Leib, *19*, 30
Government agencies, dealing with, 68
Greenberg, Irving, 261
Grunberger, Hannah, 22
Gudis, Lucille, 233
Guggenheimer, Heinrich W. and Ave H., 258
Guide to Unpublished Materials of the Holocaust Period, 323
Guide to YIVO's Landsmannshaften Archive, A, 322

Halberstam, Rabbi Chaim, 27, 126
Hall of Names, 272
Handbook for the Search, 72
Hebrew names, 256–57
  see also Names
Hebrew subscription lists, 132–33
Heine, Heinrich, 317
Hertz, Dr. J. H., 216
Historical societies. *See* Jewish historical societies
History of the Jewish People museum (Jerusalem), 121
Holocaust Calendar of Polish Jewry, 284
Holocaust/Holocaust research, 260–86
  agencies founded to aid in search for missing persons, 277
  death books, 283
  deportations from France during Holocaust, 281–82
  discovering the victims, 264
  Gottlieb victims of Holocaust, 31
  Holocaust Calendar of Polish Jewry, 284
  International Tracing Service, The, 267–71
  Kurzweil victims of Holocaust, 17–18, 263, 265–66, *266*
  Mauthausen Death Books, 271–72
  memorial books, 275
  pre-Holocaust European phone books, 284–86
  Search Bureau for Missing Relatives, 280–81
  shtetl or town, finding Holo-

caust effect on, 323
survivors of Holocaust, 264
locating, 275–78
telling the story, 261–63
Yad Vashem, 268, 272–74
Horowitz, Rabbi Isaiah, 34, 35
House of David, 46

Image Before My Eyes: A Photographic History of Jewish Life in Poland, 225
Immigrant ancestors, 295–300
see also Immigration
landsmannschaften, 299–300
steamship travel, 298, 300–304
Immigration, 287–317
to Canada, 293
to Israel, 293–95
tracing your ancestors' journeys, 300–13
finding the ship that brought them, 300–302
finding steamship passenger lists, 302–4
naturalization records, 305–12
obtaining photo of steamship, 305
to United States, 288–92
1654–1825, 289
1825–1880, 289–91
1880–1929, 291–92
1929–1945, 292
1945–present, 292
Indexes
census, 64
Encyclopedia Judaica, 127
International Tracing Service, Master Index of, 268–69
name, 65, 134
Institute for Jewish Research, The, 25
International Military Tribunal (Nuremberg Trials), 270, 272
International Tracing Service, 267–71
concentration camp material, 269–70, 279
Historical Section, 270
Master Index of, 268–69
Post-War Documents collection, 270
Interviewing relatives, 40
questions to ask, 48–51
tape recording, 264–65
tips on, 51–52
Israel, Rabbi, 28–30

Jewish Agency for Israel, Search Bureau for Missing Relatives, 280–81
Jewish Agency for Palestine,277
Jewish cemeteries, 342–54
European, 357–58
as family bonds, 345–46
locating, 353–54
visiting, 348–58
cemetery plots, 349
tombstones, 348, 349–53
a walk through a Jewish cemetery, 346–48
Jewish Family Names and Their Origins: An Etymological Dictionary, 258
Jewish genealogical societies, 217–24

Jewish genealogical societies (*cont.*)
  outside of U. S., 223–24
  in United States, by state, 218–23
Jewish genealogy, basic sources
  see also Searching for family history
  Avotaynu, 82–111
    books available from, 107–9
    Family Finder section, 102–7
    index to first eight volumes, 82–102
    microfiche available from, 109–11
  basic bibliography (Rabbi Stern's), 117–21
    Bibliography of Jewish Genealogy, 117
    collected genealogies, 120–21
    manuals and sourcebooks, 117–18
    periodicals, 118–19
    research archives and libraries, 119–20
  Encyclopedia of Jewish Genealogy, 112
  Encyclopedia Judaica, 112–13
  first American Jewish families, 113–14
  Jewish genealogy and other genealogy compared, 78–81
  other Jewish genealogical publications, 114–15
  professional genealogical assistance, 229–36
  Talmud, on genealogy, 80–81
  textbooks, 115–16
  Toledot: The Journal of Jewish Genealogy, 111
  traditional sources, 121–33
    approbations, 125–27
    Hebrew subscription lists, 132–33
    ketubah, 121–23
    Mohel books, 121
    rabbinic descent, 123–25
    rabbinic dynasties, 127
    rabbinic sources, 128–31
    rabinnic texts, 131–32
  Yizkor books, 133–35
    bibliography of Eastern European, 136–200
Jewish and Hebrew Onomastics: A Bibliography, 257
Jewish historical societies, 205–15
  in Canada, 213–15
  in England, 215
  in Hong Kong, 215
  in Poland, 215
  in Scotland, 215
  in United States, by state, 205–12
Jewish Theological Seminary Library, 200
Judah the Pious, 251

Kagan, Berl, 132
Kaganoff, Ben-zion, 257
Kay, Dr. Alan A., 115
Ketubot, 121–23
Kirshenblatt-Gimblett, Barbara, 225
Klarsfeld, Serge, 281
Klein, Helen, *20*, 228
Klein, Laura Horowitz, 233
Klein, Morton, 22
Kurzweil, Amram, 15–16
Kurzweil, Arthur, family history of, 1–36

Holocaust victims, 17–18, 262
maternal history, 18–35
paternal history, 1–18
Kurzweil, Avraham Abusch, *116*, 308, 335
Kurzweil, Baruch, 15
Kurzweil, Dov, 16
Kurzweil, Joseph, 12–13
Kurzweil, Malya, *11*
Kurzweil, Saul, *44*
Kurzweil Family Circle, 12, 39

Landsmannschaften, 275, 299–300
defined, 8
locating, 322–23
publication of memorial books by, 202
"Landsmannschaften and the Jewish Genealogist," 323
Legends, family, 44–45
Leo Baeck Institute, The, 77, 121, 225–26
Letter writing, 57–58
importance of enclosing SASE, 75
Levanda, Lev, 203
Libraries, 203
American Jewish Periodicals Center, 357
Family History Library (Mormon Church), 226–28, 328
having collections of memorial books, 200–203
listing of, 119–20
New York Public Library
Jewish Division, 1, 200
Research Library, 61, 284–85
rules for dealing with, 74–76
Library of Congress, 67
Lifton, Betty Jean, 72
Lindenberger, Jesef, 283
Lithuania, records in, 329–30
Lost & Found: The Adoption Experience, 72
Lowe, Leopold, 312
Lowenthal, Hinda Ruchel, *116*
Lerner, Simon B., 233

Maimonides, 127
Manifests. *See* Passenger lists
Manuals and sourcebooks, 117–18
Marriage document (ketubah), 121–23
see also Vital records
Mauthausen Death Books, 271
Mautner, Herb, 233
Meltzer, Milton, 254, 304, 313
Memobuchs, 320–21
Memorial Book—Dobromil, 3
Memorial (Yizkor) books. *See* Yizkor books
Memorial Dates of the Martyred Jews of..., 283
Mémorial de la déportation des Juifs de France, 281
Migration patterns, 316
Milamed, Susan, 322
Military records, 67
Miller, Adele, 233
Mishnah, 74, 127
Missing persons, 67
see also Holocaust/Holocaust research
Mohel books, 121, 122
Mokotoff, Gary, 234, 325
Moravia, records in, 330

Mormon Church, 67
  Family History Library, 226–28, 328
  steamship passenger lists, 304
Morton Allen Directory of Passenger Steamship Arrivals, 301
My Generations: A Course in Jewish Family History, 115–16

Name indexes, 65, 134
Names, 238–59
  abbreviations and, 246–47
  change of, 253–54
  common last names, 61
  descriptive names, 239, 245–46
  determining dates with, 255–56
  Hebrew, Yiddish, and English, 256–57
  house signs as basis of, 241, 244
  importance of, 9–10
  "mann" added to wife's first name, 243
  meaning of, 257–58
  from mother's side, 256
  namesakes, 252–53
  nicknames, 246
  occupation names, 239, 245
  patronymics, 239, 243
  personal, 251–52
  in phone books, 61–62
  place names, 239, 244–45
  surnames, 10, 238–43, 313
    examples of, 247–50
    from mother's side, 256
  vocational names, 239, 245
Namesakes, 252–53
Nappaha, Johanan B., 128
National Archives, 70–71
  of Canada, 73
  federal census records and, 64
  genealogical information package available from, 67
  genealogical records branches of, by region, 65–67
  Mauthausen Death Books in, 271–72
  naturalization records for NY City area in, 311–12
  Regional Archives Branches of, 64, 65–67
  steamship passenger lists, 302, 304
National Tracing Bureau, 267
Naturalization records, 305–12
Nazi war criminals, 272
  see also Nuremberg trial records
New York City naturalization records, 311–12
New York Public Library
  Jewish Division, 1, 200
  Research Library, 61, 284–85
Nicknames, 246
Note-taking, 54–54
Nuremberg trial records, 270, 272

Obituaries, 356–57
Occupational names, 239, 245
Old country, tracing heritage in. *See* Ancestral homes, tracing
Oldest family member, identifying, 55, 58

Pages of Testimony, 272–74
Passenger lists, 253

see also Steamship travel
Canadian immigrants, 73
Patronymics, 239, 243
Pedat, Eleazer B., 253
Peretz, I.L., 55
Periodicals, 118–19
Persin, Judith, 234
Personal life, interview questions regarding, 49–50
Personal names, 251–52
Phone books, 61–62
Israeli, 61
pre-Holocaust European, 284–86
Photographs
family, 56
Polish collection of, 225
Place names, 244
Polakoff, Eileen, 234
Poland, records in, 329
Postal, Bernard, 332
Priever, David, 234
Przemysl, Poland, 332–36, 335
Public libraries
New York Public Library
Jewish Division, 1, 200
Research Library, 61, 284–85
phone books in, 61–62
Publishing a family history, 76–77

Questions to ask in interviews, regarding
artifacts, 51–52
European roots, 49
personal and family life, 49–50
religious life, 50

Rabbinic descent, 123–25
Rabbinic dynasties, 127
Rabbinic sources, 128–31
Rabbinic texts, 131–32
Raphael, Chaim, 217, 327
Rashi, 69
Rath, Blima, 23
Record checking, 60–77
adoption files, 71–72
Canadian research, 73–74
census records, federal, 63–67
census records, state, 68
city directories, 69
dealing with librarians, 75–76
dealing with libraries, archives, etc., 74–75
government agencies, dealing with, 68
National Archives, 70–71
phone books, 61–62
publishing your family history, 76–77
synagogue records, 69–70
vital records, 62–63, 67
Red Cross, 268, 278
Regional Archives of the National Archives, , 64, 65–67
Register of Jewish Survivors, 277
published lists of, 277, 279–80
Religious life, interview questions regarding, 50
Research archives/libraries, 119–20
Ritters Geographisch-Statistisches Lexikon, 325
Ritual objects, personalizing, 122
Rosenstein, Dr. Neil, 125–27, 130
Rosenvasser family, 21
Rosenzweig, Franz, 257
Roth, Pamela, 282
Rothschild family, 46
Russlier, Nicki, 234

Sack, Sallyann Amdur, 325
Sackheim, George, 234
Samuel, Maurice, 48, 57
Sandler, Michelle, 235
Schafler, Sara Edell, 235
Schepansky, Rabbi Israel, 284
Schlaf, Joseph, 333
Schwartz, Rosaline, 322
Search Bureau for Missing Relatives, 277, 280–81
Searching for family history
  see also Jewish genealogy, basic sources
  collecting stories, 43–44
  common family myths/truths, 46–48
  equipment needed for, 42
  family legends, 44–45
  family photographs, 56
  following leads, 53
  getting started, 38–43
  goals, determining, 42–43
  interviewing relatives, 40, 43–44, 48–51
    see also Questions to ask in inverviews, regarding
  keeping track of information, 54
  name changes/destruction of records, 41–42
  taking notes, 53–54
  tips on, 58–59
  visiting relatives and others, 55–56
  writing letters, 57–58
Selavan, Ida Cohen, 235
Self addressed stamped envelopes, importance of, 75
Sephardim Jews, names of, 244
Shtetl
  Holocaust effect on, 323
  locating your, 324–26
Singerman, Robert, 257
Skala Memorial Book, 276
Spelling, difficulties in location search with, 326
Spialter, Leonard, 235
Spiszman, Regina Wassercier, 235
Starkman, Betty Proviser, 235
State census records, 68
Steamship records
  finding the ship that brought your ancestors, 300–302
  Morton Allen Directory of European Passenger Steamship Arrivals, 301
  obtaining photos of steamships, 305
  passenger lists, finding, 302–4
Steinig, Renée Stern, 236
Steinsaltz, Adin, 52, 130
Stropkover Rebbe, 25
  see also Gottlieb, Chaim Joseph
Scholem, Gershom, 15
SHAEF, 267–68
Siegel, Stevcn W., 111, 114
Silberstein, Jacob, 283
Steamship travel, 298
  see also Passenger lists
Stern, Rabbi Malcolm H., 70, 113–14
  bibliography compiled by, 117–21
Stories, collecting, 43–44
Supreme Headquarters of the Allied Expeditionary Forces, 267–68
Surnames, 10, 238–43, 313
  abbreviations and, 246–47

change of, 253–54
descriptive, 239, 245–46
examples of, 247–50
house signs as basis of, 241, 244
"mann" added to wife's first name, 243
matronymics, 247
meaning of, 257–58
nicknames and, 246
occupational/vocational names, 239, 245
place names, 239, 244–45
Synagogue records, 69–70

Talmud, on genealogy, 80–81
Taping interviews, importance of, 42, 43–44
Teev Gitten v'Kiddushin, 26–27
Textbooks, 115–16
Toledot: The Journal of Jewish Genealogy, 111–12, 114, 226
Tracing Your Ancestors in Canada, 73
Traveler's Guide to Jewish Landmarks of Europe, 332, 357
Traveling to the old country, 330–36
advice before traveling to Eastern Europe and the former Soviet Union, 339
planning your trip, 336–39

UJA-Federation, 322–23
Unbroken Chain, The, 125–26, 130–31
United Nations Relief and Rehabilitation Administration (UNRRA), 268
Unterschatz, Batya, 280–81
Vital records, 62–63, 67
see also Synagogue records; *Where to Write for Vital Records*
Vocational names, 239, 245

Wallace, Irving, 254
Wallechinsky, David, 254
Wasserman, Eileen Joyce, 236
Weiner, Miriam, 236
Where Once We Walked: A Guide to the Jewish Communities Destroyed in the Holocaust, 325
Where to Write for Vital Records, 62, 354
Wiesel, Elie, 44–45, 261, 326
Wills, 356
Winerman, Geraldine Frey, 236
Wolfson, Harry, 216
World Jewish Congress, 277
Wynne, Suzan Fischer, 236

Yad Vashem, 268, 272–74, 323
Yarin, Jim, 236
Yichus, 124
Yiddish names, 256–57
YIVO Institute for Jewish Research, 25, 76, 200, 224–25
death books, 283
Guide to YIVO's Landsmannshaften Archive, 322
published lists of Holocaust survivors, 279

Yizkor books, 133–35, 338
  bibliography of Eastern European, 136–200
    countries and regions, 138–40
    general reference works, 137
    localities, 140–200
  Holocaust victims, researching, 275
  institutions that collect, 200–203
    obtaining copies, 202–3
Yohai, Simeon B., 72

Temple Israel